ARGENTINA'S PARALLEL CURRENCY:
THE ECONOMY OF THE POOR

FINANCIAL HISTORY

Series Editor: Robert E. Wright

TITLES IN THIS SERIES

1 Slave Agriculture and Financial Markets in Antebellum America: The Bank of the United States in Mississippi, 1831–1852
Richard Holcombe Kilbourne, Jr

2 The Political Economy of Sentiment: Paper Credit and the Scottish Enlightenment in Early Republic Boston, 1780–1820
Jose R. Torre

3 Baring Brothers and the Birth of Modern Finance
Peter E. Austin

4 Gambling on the American Dream: Atlantic City and the Casino Era
James R. Karmel

5 Government Debts and Financial Markets in Europe
Fausto Piola Caselli (ed.)

6 Virginia and the Panic of 1819: The First Great Depression and the Commonwealth
Clyde A. Haulman

7 Towards Modern Public Finance: The American War with Mexico, 1846–1848
James W. Cummings

8 The Revenue Imperative: The Union's Financial Policies during the American Civil War
Jane Flaherty

9 Guilty Money: The City of London in Victorian and Edwardian Culture, 1815–1914
Ranald C. Michie

10 Financial Markets and the Banking Sector: Roles and Responsibilities in a
Global World
Elisabeth Paulet (ed.)

FORTHCOMING TITLES

Convergence and Divergence of National Financial Systems: Evidence from the
Gold Standards, 1871–1971
Patrice Baubeau and Anders Ögren (eds)

The Rise and Fall of the American System: Nationalism and the Development
of the American Economy, 1800–1837
Songho Ha

ARGENTINA'S PARALLEL CURRENCY: THE ECONOMY OF THE POOR

BY

Georgina M. Gómez

LONDON AND NEW YORK

First published 2009 by Pickering & Chatto (Publishers) Limited

Published 2016 by Routledge
2 Park Square, Milton Park, Abingdon, Oxfordshire OX14 4RN
711 Third Avenue, New York, NY 10017, USA

First issued in paperback 2015

Routledge is an imprint of the Taylor & Francis Group, an informa business

BRITISH LIBRARY CATALOGUING IN PUBLICATION DATA
Gomez, Georgina M.
Argentina's parallel currency: the economy of the poor. – (Financial history)
1. Local exchange trading systems – Argentina. 2. Barter – Argentina. 3. Argentina – Economic conditions – 1983–
I. Title II. Series
332.4'982-dc22

ISBN-13: 978-1-138-66508-8 (pbk)
ISBN-13: 978-1-8519-6618-9 (hbk)

Typeset by Pickering & Chatto (Publishers) Limited

CONTENTS

List of Figures   ix

1 Economic Life as an Institutional Process   1
2 Perspectives on Complementary Currency Systems   21
3 The Political and Economic Context in Argentina   35
4 Launching the Club de Trueque   61
5 From Club de Trueque to Network   81
6 Governance of the Networks   107
7 Smaller Scale Trueque   133
8 Replacing Money for Economic Development   155
9 Conclusions   181

Notes   199
Works Cited   227
Index   247

LIST OF FIGURES AND TABLES

Figure 1.1: Size of *RT* in terms of participants and *Trueque* Clubs   5
Figure 1.2: Geographical distribution of *CT* in 2001   6
Figure 1.3: Relation between scale of *RT* and GDP growth rate, 1995–2006   11
Figure 1.4: Relation between scale of *RT* and unemployment, 1995–2006   11
Figure 1.5: Relation between scale of *RT* and poverty, 1995–2006   12
Figure 3.1: Three-year average of Argentine GDP as percentage of the average GDP of developed countries, 1885–2002   40
Figure 3.2: Argentina's real GDP, 1980–2006   42
Figure 3.3: Variations in main monetary variables, 1980–97, percentage   44
Figure 3.4: Activity, employment and unemployment rates (1980-2006)   49
Figure 3.5: Provincial currencies as percentage of monetary base, July 2001–October 2002   54
Figure 3.6: Relationships between policies, effects and institutions   60
Figure 4.1: The institutional action-information loop   67
Figure 4.2: Institutional action-information double loop   68
Figure 5.1: Factors driving institutional design   86
Figure 6.1: Number of participants by sub-network, beginning of 2002   114
Figure 7.1: Origin of products sold by respondents in the Trueque (n=386)   145
Figure 7.2: Labour status of respondents (n=386)   148
Figure 9.1: The process of institutional design   197

1 ECONOMIC LIFE AS AN INSTITUTIONAL PROCESS

In '*The Lottery in Babylon*', the Argentine writer Jorge Luis Borges describes a world in which nobody has a fixed position in society.[1]

> Like all men in Babylon, I have been proconsul; like all, a slave. I have also known omnipotence, opprobrium, imprisonment. I owe this almost atrocious variety to an institution which other republics do not know or which operates in them in an imperfect and secret manner: the Lottery. I have not looked into its history. I come from a dizzy land where the lottery is the basis of reality.

In the story, while the Lottery started out like any typical lottery, it evolved into one which not only gives prizes to the winners, but also inflicts consequences on the losers. Further evolution increased its complexity; the Lottery Company has total power and everyone participates. If fortune smiles on the player, he or she can win promotion into the councils of authority. On the other hand, if the player makes a bad choice, different kinds of infamy follow. The Lottery Company dictates all aspects of everyone's life. There are various conjectures on how it started:

> Some said the Company had not existed for centuries and that the sacred disorder of our lives is purely hereditary, traditional. Another judges it eternal and teaches that it will last until the last night. Babylon is nothing else than an infinite game of chance.

For most readers of 'The Lottery in Babylon', such an uncertain social life seems atrocious. While there is a structure and an order in that society, they are quite unbearable for the majority of people in the world. Still, in the 1990s life in Argentina was a microcosm of that in Borges' Babylon. Reforms inspired by the neoliberal policies of the government established the 'capitalist market' as the basis of reality. The state retreated, giving comprehensive powers to 'the Market', in the belief that it would create a powerful and efficient economy. The government had enough support at that point to impose the reforms. The goal was to unleash 'market forces', but no one questioned how the market started, who was behind it, and what its limits should be, even though it affected everyone's lives.

By the turn of the millennium, an economic meltdown thrust more than half of the population under the poverty line in a country where extreme poverty had been virtually unknown 25 years earlier. Owners of firms became homeless after their businesses went bankrupt. Doctors turned taxi drivers after clinics closed down or hospitals had to 'downsize' by slashing the number of their personnel. Retired teachers turned street vendors after they could no longer survive on their public pensions.

A difference is that Borges does not describe how individuals react and use their ingenuity to lift themselves out of disaster in Babylon. In the real world, however, Argentine civil society gradually built institutions to oppose the neo-liberal reforms and to reconstruct social life. As Robert Polanyi observes, the economy is an institutional process[2] and this implies that social groups can construct, reconstruct and change institutions, inspired by those gone or still present. In this way, agents can eventually recreate a social agreement that allows them to resume their economic activity, although under a different modality.

Agents in Argentina reacted indeed. They put together various economic schemes to partially restructure what they considered social or economic life 'as it used to be' and save whatever they could of their crumbled lifestyle. Among these schemes there was a set of complementary currency systems called *Redes de Trueque*, or Barter Networks. They were networks of local markets where the bankrupt entrepreneur, unemployed doctor and disenfranchised teacher met to exchange their self-produced goods and services. They were one of the new forms of income generation, with a stronger economic element and a weaker political resistance component than other alternative schemes. In a strict sense there was no barter involved in them but means of payment in the form of physical scrip called *créditos*. These were created by the organizers and voluntarily accepted by participants. Participants hence turned their backs on the regular economy and its currency, which was excluding them.

The creation of complementary currency systems is far from a novelty in the history of financial crisis. Irving Fisher described several experiments with 'stamp scrip' during the Great Depression in the USA and in Germany and Austria during the 1920s.[3] Most groups using stamp scrip were inspired by Sylvio Gesell and his ideas of monetary reform. In order to reduce hoarding, Gesell proposed to create a *schwundgeld*: depreciative money or money that disappears, because it loses its value as time goes by.[4]

The *Redes de Trueque*, however, were not created as *schwundgeld* but with stable face value. In fact, the Argentine organizers had no knowledge of either previous or current experiences with complementary currency systems like the one they had launched. They were also not acquainted with Gesell's ideas; they were much later.

There are further differences between the *Redes de Trueque* in Argentina, on the one hand, and past and present complementary currencies systems around the world, on the other. In comparison with other CCS operating in current times, the *Redes de Trueque* were much larger in amount of participants, number of local markets, variety of currencies used, territorial coverage, diversity of products and services traded, and social groups involved. The *RT* reached more than 2.5 million users in the beginning of 2002, which represented 20 per cent of the economically active population in twenty-two of Argentina's twenty-three provinces. Annual turnover was estimated at its peak in 1,000 million argentine pesos (until the devaluation in January 2003 this was equal to 1,000 million American dollars, and after that, to 300 million American dollars). Organizers claimed that individual members' consumption increased by 600 dollars a month, while the minimum wage was half that amount.[5]

In relation to the extended complementary currency systems in the USA and Europe in the 1920s and 1930s, the main difference was organizational: the *Redes de Trueque* were regional and national networks articulating local markets called *Clubes de Trueque* (*CT* or Barter Clubs). Each *Red de Trueque* (barter network) issued its own currency which was normally accepted in other networks too, so it was possible to pay for goods and services with the same scrip across the whole country. For some time there was an umbrella organization checking each others' monies; the rest of the time, scrip was accepted simply out of trust in the system. Similar integration has been attempted less successfully on a regional level in places such as Manchester, UK, where it led to loss of local identity.[6] Nowhere has an attempt been made to create a national, private, yet not-for-profit monetary system as was the *RT*.

How this parallel economy came to be needs to be explained. A common view is that it emerged out of the economic demise in Argentina and would disappear as the regular economy rebounds. Indeed, the health of the regular economy has a major impact on the fate of the *Trueque*, but it is not as straightforward as this common sense explanation indicates. First of all, the timeline does not correspond to the intuition: the *RT* plummeted during the economic crisis, when it would still take some months for economic recovery to gather steam. In turn, the *RT* grew together with the regular economy in several years (1996, 1997 and 1998). Most important, since 2004 the *RT* remains in a plateau, unaware of the vigorous growth of the Argentine economy. Far from disappearing, there are still thousands of participants keeping the *Redes de Trueque* alive and it is still the largest CCS in the world at present. Why do they keep participating in *Clubes de Trueque* that are still running?

There is also the issue that other countries experienced similar economic reforms and levels of unemployment but complementary currency systems did not emerge in them. If economic demise was all it takes for a massive community currency system to appear, then they should be more common.

The argument clearly needs to be refined. The rise and decline of the *Redes de Trueque* in Argentina call for closer scrutiny than simply explaining them as the 'offspring of a deep crisis'.

Within financial history, the *Redes de Trueque* were quite an exceptional phenomenon that challenges the conception of money as a creature of modern states or as emerging out of a commodity backing up scrip. The *créditos* were money issued and managed by communities and their leaders, somehow replacing the regulatory functions of the state. They are fully a social construction, as Ingham argues, an institution.[7] The *Redes de Trueque* emerged out of the reaction of social groups wanting to reconstruct their economies as 'institutional processes' and hence organized money, markets, and rules to regulate action.

Previous research on the *Redes de Trueque* has overlooked this process of institutional construction and design. The main reason for this is that most studies take one or a few *Clubes de Trueque* as the unit of analysis and cover specific aspects at certain points in time. The focus is mostly on the participants, their motivations and the impact on households. The data gathered are ethnographic and collected through interviews. This study attempts a wider coverage, looking at the *Redes de Trueque* as a large organizational form. The next section sums up the main findings of research on the *RT* so far. The following one explores the view of *Redes de Trueque* as an institutional construction.

This book attempts a wider coverage and focuses on explaining the *Redes de Trueque* at the organizational or meso level. Why did the *RT* emerge in Argentina and last for twelve years, during depression and recovery? Why did they achieve a scale and scope unpaired to other CCS in current times and with an organizational form that was never tried elsewhere before? Why did they collapse immediately after their peak and why was the slump unequal between networks? What are the rationales for their functioning, in comparison with the regular economy?

Introduction to the Argentine *Redes de Trueque*

There has been substantial analysis of the *Redes de Trueque* by Argentine researchers. There are also several unpublished theses by undergraduate and MA students around the world, only some of which are cited in this study because of the difficulty in accessing them. Most of the research was conducted around 2001 and 2002, at the peak of the *RT*. A book came out at that time out of a workshop organized in September 2002 by the Universidad Nacional de General Sarmiento with UNDP support. The main leaders of the sub-networks, practitioners, government representatives and academic experts took part in the workshop and the proceedings were compiled in an edited volume.[8]

Most research on the *Trueque* recounts the following history. The first CCS in Argentina was created in 1995 under the name *Club de Trueque* (henceforth *CT*). The idea was to make use of idle resources such as the time available to the unemployed, a variety of skills for which there was no demand in the regular market and unproductive plots of land in the neighbourhood. The scheme was almost too obvious: a small group of people met once a week to exchange goods they produced themselves, such as garden vegetables, handicrafts, home-made toiletries and foods, knitwear, and so forth.[9] By reconnecting production and consumption, participants became prosumers, a term coined by Alvin Toffler.[10] The initiative proved helpful for the impoverished middle class in the area of Bernal, a suburb in southern Buenos Aires. News of it spread by word of mouth and the number of participants multiplied quickly. The *CT* was replicated across the country at a pace that accelerated as the national crisis worsened and the scheme gained popularity. Most *CTs* were linked to each other and accepted each others' local currencies. Gradually the network became known as *Red de Trueque* because at that time it was one. When more appeared, the *Redes de Trueque* created an umbrella organization to control the issuance of currencies.

Figure 1.1: Size of RT in terms of participants and Trueque Clubs

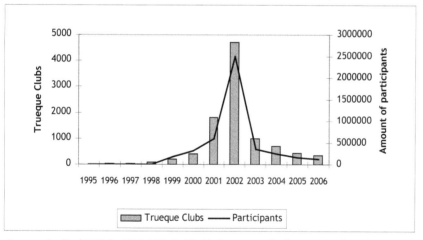

Sources: Ovalles (2002) for 1995–2002; La Nación for 2003; author's estimation for 2004–6 based on RT groups visited and information given by participants. Estimations refer to the beginning of each year.

The variation in terms of membership is marked. The first *Club de Trueque* (Barter Club) was launched in 1995 with twenty-five participants of the dis-enfranchised middle class. By 1996, just one year after it sprang up, there were already 1,000 participants involved in seventeen clubs operating in the metro-politan area of Buenos Aires. The numbers kept multiplying, particularly after

1999 when it jumped to 320,000 members in 2000, over half a million in 2001. It was by the beginning of 2002, with the regular economy melting down, that the *RT* reached a peak of at least 2.5 million participants in 4,700 centres across the country. With that scale, the *RT* ran into trouble and started to crumble around the middle of 2002. Soon afterwards the regular economy started to rebound and gradually entered a vigorous recovery. Within a year the *RT* slumped and by the end of 2003 it was reduced to about a tenth of its maximum size. Since then it has been stagnant and during fieldwork its size was estimated at 120,000 participants by the beginning of 2007. Figures 1.1 and 1.2 depict this evolution and geographical coverage.[11]

The data on membership require a note of caution. They are unofficial figures and rough estimations by *RT* leaders who normally did not keep accurate records. They include duplication when participants are associated with more than one CCS or drop out. Also, they only indicate registered individuals: for example, a one-time assistant counts as a daily participant of several years. There is no distinction between 'member' and 'household'; a single member may support several persons in a household while, instead, there may be several other participants from the same household. In short, the 'real' membership of the *Trueque* is quite unknowable and these data are just an acceptable indication of the dimensions of the phenomenon.

Figure 1.2: Geographical distribution of CT in 2001

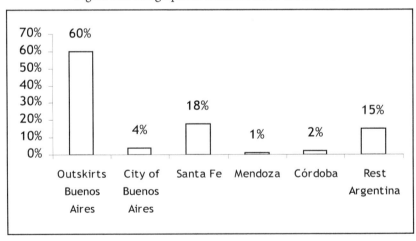

Source: Ovalles (2002)
Note: Ovalles (2002) calculated the percentages on a basis of 5.000 CT.

The profile of *RT* participants was the first aspect that drew the attention of scholars. Following path-breaking fieldwork in 2000, González Bombal emphasized the predominance of the disenfranchised middle class among the participants, unlike in other self-help income-generation schemes, where the structural poor are often in the majority. González Bombal found that the educational level of the participants was relatively high: 53 per cent had completed secondary school (twelve years of schooling) and 28 per cent had received some tertiary or university education, while only nineteen per cent had primary school education alone (seven years of schooling). Unable to maintain their consumption patterns, they were the right population segment for the early take-off period. In addition, the majority of members (56 per cent) were between forty and sixty years old, 44 per cent were unemployed and 24 per cent had vulnerable employment. González Bombal presented the *Red de Trueque* as a new form of sociability, reflecting the social capital of the middle class. The income-generation effects were beyond the scope of her work.[12]

These findings were later confirmed by other authors.[13] The socioeconomic background of the majority of participants – impoverished middle class – was a crucial determinant in the type of scheme that eventually resulted. The enthusiasm with which the disenfranchised middle class adopted the *RT* was crucial for its take-off because the system requires conditions not frequently found among the traditional poor (for example, initial capital, skills, tools and equipment, entrepreneurial capabilities). The relatively lower participation of the low-income groups may be explained by the fact that they had developed other ways of dealing with poverty which was already their everyday condition. In contrast to the middle class, the structural poor share an engrained habit of engaging in non-market forms of exchange, which is driven by the need they have for each other's support and their lack of material resources and entitlements.[14] Moreover, other survival strategies such as sifting through garbage for scraps and saleable items, street vending and employment as domestic servants were widespread among the structural poor and rather unthinkable for those with a middle-class background.

A second point that stood out in early research was the role of the *Redes de Trueque* in providing complementary employment. Already when the network was not too extended across the country, Morisio found that participants could cover a significant proportion of their needs through it in a context where 70 per cent of them earned less in the regular economy than half the value of an average household basket of products defined by the National Statistics Bureau INDEC.[15] The *RT* was a system in which the participants exchanged products (such as food and crafts linked to their middle class lifestyle) that they made on a small scale with equipment at home, using a different currency from the national one and different rules of trade. The system was not suitable for the traditional poor, who neither owned home equipment to make products for exchange nor had secure access to official money to pay for inputs and other goods not available in complementary currency. Morisio's view was confirmed by later research that found that every respondent had faced employment vulnerability in the previous two years.[16]

It was often the main breadwinner in the household who was unemployed and another household member who participated in the *Redes de Trueque* to earn a second income. This was typically a woman with no employment experience, attracted by the discovery that what she had until then regarded as a hobby could be transformed into an income-earning activity.[17] Up to two-thirds of the participants were women whose husbands were unemployed or did odd jobs.[18]

The link between gender and the *RT* has been emphasized in most research. Women were not only the majority of the participants but also the main drivers of the *RT*, the inaugurators and organizers of *CT*, which gave them the chance to build skills as managers and community leaders. Their prevalence is sometimes analysed in relation to class and some authors argue that the *Redes de Trueque* reflected the traditional household work and hobbies of middle-class women well.[19] The goods and services offered were typical of the consumption patterns of this stratum. Many of the middle-class women had never worked for money and their contacts in the public sphere were driven by gendered hobbies (for example, cooking and knitting) or through a social network of friends, fitness clubs, and so on, that they could no longer afford.[20] Other authors stressed that the *RT* enabled women to gain recognition because they were able to contribute to the household income.[21] Activities that used to be unpaid (taking care of children and the elderly, cooking and knitting) gained exchange value. The gender division of labour in the household reflected the type of money each breadwinner earned (pesos for men, complementary currency for women), but both were crucial for sustaining the household's consumption. Women would search for food and clothing in the *RT* while the pesos earned by men were used to pay for public services and meet other expenses such as taxes and rent that could not be paid in local money. In this sense, the *RT* was an instrument that made the unpaid work of women visible and valuable in the lifestyle of their household.[22]

The absence of state intervention even when the *RT* was at its peak is another aspect that made the Argentine experience unique. The *RT* appeared as a grassroots response that kept social peace in a context of institutional collapse.[23] Thus, it was in the state's interest to support it, unlike in most other countries where CCS are suppressed or barely tolerated.[24] The Argentine government promoted the *RT* actively to reduce social conflict as well as reintegrate people into the formal economy. Some local governments even accepted the use of its currency to pay municipal taxes. This expanded the realm and legitimate recognition of the *RT*.

A fifth issue that attracted researchers' attention was why the *Red de Trueque* had grown so much and so quickly in Argentina, in comparison with other similar schemes elsewhere in the world. As noted earlier, 5,200 CCS exist in fifty-eight countries, but none has achieved the durability, scale and scope of the Argentine one. Several authors attribute this to the unusual availability of idle resources following the crises of 1995 and 1998.[25] While the existence of a large middle class could explain why complementary currency systems started in Argentina, it is an incomplete explanation for why they achieved a scale that dwarfs that of other CCS around the world. Other authors combine this argument with the sociability aspects of the *RT*.[26] They contend that the *RT* supported the building of new social networks, which helped the participants breach the isolation caused by their diminished income and status. Powell adds another explanation: Argentines had unusually low barriers to the adoption of new forms of money since the state's capacity to regulate and influence behaviour had been eroded.[27]

The construction of a common identity in the *Redes de Trueque* led some researchers to approach it as a social economy initiative.[28] José Luis Coraggio questions whether the *RT* was an alternative economic space.[29] For example, the author points out the difference between trade in the *RT* and in the informal economy became marginal to many participants, as supported by later studies.[30] Participants slowly lost the awareness that they were part of a project that not only sought to improve household income but also created social cohesion and community bonds. They started seeing the *Redes de Trueque* as 'any job' or 'any other business'.[31] The only visible difference was the currency used. Deviation to the morality of an alternative development path became even more evident in the end.[32] The *RT* reproduced the pathologies of the global financial system and finally faced a catastrophic loss of confidence.[33] Participants were mainly driven to the *RT* out of need, while the project of a social or alternative economic space mainly represented the aspiration of the leaders.[34]

Still, the *RT* was not regarded as completely the same as the informal economy. The *RT* provided a replacement for lost jobs, both in terms of income and use of time and resources, expressed as 'feeling useful again' and 'there is still something you can do as a human being'.[35] Some participants said they preferred the *CT* to the 'degradation in the labour market' that followed the new hiring modalities and the informalization of employment in Argentina.[36] They had the capacities, resources and often equipment to produce goods and services and, in the words of a participant interviewed, found in the *RT* a 'friendlier atmosphere than outside, because outside, you're on your own'.[37]

While the *RT* cannot be assessed in equal terms as the informal economy, it does not exhibit the moral characteristics usually outlined in the literature on the social economy.[38] It combines traits of both, possibly because complementary currency systems change internally and in relation to the rest of the economy when they grow in scale and scope. They do not just become *bigger* versions of any standard CCS in the world but develop characteristics of their own, pushing it away from the assumptions of the social economy and closer to 'an economy within the economy', as the organizers of the *RT* described it. That is, the *RT* was a CCS regulated by institutions that structured the activities of large numbers of individuals and groups, with their interests and conflicts, different from those in the regular economy. It was a market regulated by institutions like any other market, but organized from the grassroots by specific social groups.

Other researchers have analysed the *RT* as a parallel economic system that bloomed with the collapse of the regular economy and disappeared when the national economy recovered. As said, this common sense explanation is not consistent with all the facts. Colacelli et al. (2005)[39] employed an econometric model that compared the use of stamp scrip during the Great Depression in the USA and in the *RT* in Argentina. They reason that the *RT* currencies supplemented regular money when it was in short supply, but once the relation between the amount of regular means of payment and goods was re-established, secondary means of payment disappeared. Their analysis is valid, though their final conclusion is tinted by the period when they did their fieldwork (2002 and 2003). It was the period when the *RT* fell apart and the regular economy was starting to rebound. The statistical significance of this anti-cyclical hypothesis decreases if the period of analysis is extended to 2006.

For the sake of an academic exercise, the hypothesis of an anti-cyclical dynamism in the *RT* was given closer scrutiny. Among macroeconomic variables, the data analysed were total GDP, its growth rate, and the unemployment and poverty rates. On the side of the RT, the number of *CT* and participants provided an indication of the *RT*'s scale.

Of all these, the closest relationship between the scale of the *RT* and the regular economy is observed in the GDP growth rate (Figure 1.3). It would seem that when the economy collapsed, the *RT* grew, but when the regular economy rebounded, the *RT* did not fall apart as could be expected. This suggests that participants sheltered themselves in the *RT* after the collapse of the regular economy but did not leave it once the GDP recovered. Other factors came into play once they were in the network; that is, the *Redes de Trueque* developed a life of their own.

The unemployment rate shows a weaker relationship to the growth of the *RT*, but again, the link is clearer during the economic collapse than during the recovery. This supports the finding that individuals enter the *RT* when the household is exposed to a difficult labour market but do not immediately or necessarily leave it once it improves.

The third variable looked at was the percentage of households under the poverty line (Figure 1.5). The relationship with the *RT* was stronger than with unemployment,[40] probably because unemployment does not automatically mean poverty (not all the unemployed are poor) and the most likely to join the *RT* are those who are poor *and* unemployed. Besides, a significant share of the participants were women who had never been employed and thus were not registered in the unemployment rate.

Figure 1.*3:* Relation between scale of RT and GDP growth rate, 1995–2006

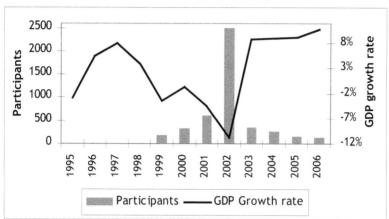

Sources: For the RT, as in Figure 1.1 but here expressed in thousands. GDP growth rates from <www.indec.gov.ar>.

Figure 1.4: Relation between scale of RT and unemployment, 1995–2006

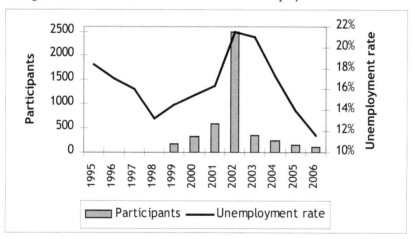

Note: Unemployment rates are for the second quarter (May) and include job-seekers receiving welfare subsidies.
Sources: For the RT, as in Figure 1.1 but expressed in thousands. Unemployment rates from <www.indec.gov.ar>.

Figure 1.5: Relation between scale of RT and poverty, 1995–2006

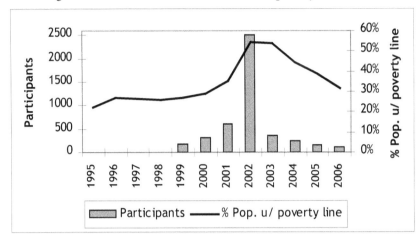

Note: Poverty rates correspond to total urban population (individuals) under the poverty line in
the third quarter.
Sources: For the RT, as in Figure 1.1 but expressed in thousands. Poverty rates from <www.indec.
gov.ar>.

The Redes de Trueque as Institutional Process

The *Redes de Trueque* were an exceptional case of institutions built from below
or by non-state actors. Without any state intervention, social groups organized currencies, markets, and rules to regulate their socio-economic action in
an effort to re-establish what they considered 'economic life as usual'. That is,
they ventured to recover the economy as an institutional process. In order to
understand the process of institutional reconstruction, this section revisits institutional economics and builds up an analytical framework.

The literature has approached comparable phenomena with a variety of
names. Some authors refer to bottom-up arrangements that organize economic
activity as 'spontaneous private orderings'[41] or 'spontaneous social order'.[42] In the
literature of the New Political Economy 'private interest governance' addresses
the organization of the economy by non-state actors, though usually in this framework the state retains a significant role.[43] Bottom-up arrangements in absence of
state intervention represent a puzzle for game theory scholars, who claim that
they are cases of 'Lawlessness in Economics'.[44] These are economies which are
not regulated by the rule of state law but are driven by common agreements of
voluntary compliance between private parties. The *RT* were of course somewhat
different. Common agreements and private orderings were not reached by firms
and governments, as most of the literature suggests, but by communities and
civil society actors. In this sense, they constitute a system of 'soft governance'.[45]

At this point it is necessary to define a few analytical categories in order to explain the emergence and construction of institutions within the *RT*. The rest of the section presents a brief conceptualization of institutions and elaborates three categories that will guide the analysis.

The fundamental point of departure of Institutional Economics is that the action of economic agents is ruled and coordinated by institutions, which raises relatively little disagreement in the social sciences. For example, prices, money, labour standards, laws and rules of exchange are institutions. Markets and monetary systems are clusters of institutions.

The key concept of institution admits quite a range of definitions. Institutions are defined as 'structured processes of interaction among individuals, relatively enduring and recognized as such'.[46] With more detail, they are also defined as 'formal organizations and informal rules, compliance procedures and standard operating practices that structure the relationship between individuals in various units of the polity and the economy'.[47] Institutions present possible paths of action for economic agents to decide about employment, production, exchange and the options between abiding by rules and shirking. They point out 'what has meaning and what actions are possible' in economic life.[48]

In spite of some variation in the definition, institutions are critical elements in the social structure which gives stability and meaning to human action.[49] Geoffrey Hodgson discusses institutions as 'the kind of structures that matter most in the social realm: they make up the stuff of social life'.[50] However, institutions and social structures are not, strictly speaking, synonyms. Institutions are a special type of social structure, those that are in principle codifiable and normative rules of behaviour and interpretation that have the potential to change agents, including their purposes or preferences. 'Potentially codifiable' means knowledge of them can be either tacit or explicit, but they are still the subject of discourse to facilitate their social and cultural transmission. 'Normative rules of behaviour and interpretation' implies that a breach can be detected and eventually sanctioned. The key term is 'rule' which is a 'normative injunction or immanently normative disposition that in circumstances X do Y'.[51] This means that rules, including laws, norms of behaviour and social conventions, are 'considered, acknowledged, or followed without much thought'.[52]

The fact that knowledge of rules can be tacit makes it problematic to determine whether behavioural regularities are due to instinct or genuine rule-following. The Old Institutional Economics, or Evolutionary Economics, distinguishes between instinct and habit, in the tradition of John Commons, Thorsten Veblen and Clarence Ayres, among others. Instinct is genetically inherited while habit is acquired culturally. Habits are dispositions to engage in previously adopted or acquired behaviour, triggered by specific stimuli or contexts.[53] Instinct explains just a small part of the variety of human actions and interactions. Habits, on the other hand, are ubiquitous and make institutions work because 'the rules involved are embedded in shared habits of thought and behaviour'.[54] A second crucial distinction is that habit is a disposition, a propensity, while behaviour is an actual effect.[55] In circumstances X, one is disposed to do or think Y.

Individual action is thus seen as being affected by institutions and networks. The assumption that individuals are rational, all-knowing, always calculating what actions to take in the name of self-interest is bluntly rejected. Individuals do have information and they are normally aware of their intentions and interests. However, whether they would chose to act in self-interest or not depends on their preferences, formed by learning in relation to other individuals. Agents are hence guided by 'rational learning', meaning that they are engaged in a rational process, but the very act of learning means that the learner does not have all information.[56] Since learning is ultimately an individual process, agents cannot be assumed to be uniform, equal or 'given'.

The conceptualization of institutions as elements of the social structure relates to their location between the extremes of agency and structure. Hodgson considers this a false dichotomy,[57] because agents' thoughts and behaviour create habit, which embeds the rules involved in institutions, which are in turn the constitutive elements of the social structure. In this way, actor and structure are connected in a circle of mutual interaction and interdependence.[58] This conceptualization is analogous to the 'theory of structuration' elaborated within sociology by Giddens and others.[59]

Repetitive action thus creates habit, which is how institutions emerge in an evolutionary manner. Habits (individual) and routines (social) are the most common type of institution guiding individual action.[60] They evolve out of repetition, practice, and regularity of action. They do not grow out of infallible design and can therefore be the outcome of mistake, speculation or coincidence, but once in place they acquire stability and resilience.[61] Habits and routines are durable, their resilience deriving from their creation of an immanent or unreasoned disposition to act in a certain way. Although the most common one, they are just one type of institutions.

At any given point in time, institutions are guiding behaviour before regularity of action generates new habits. These primary institutions constitute a basic platform on which others are based. For example, languages structure communication and the notion of individual property supports property rights. Max Weber pointed out in 1907 that 'some rules are followed without any subjective formulation in thought of the rule'.[62] Hodgson refers to them as 'prior institutions', though, rigorously speaking, they have also evolved at some point in the past (for example, languages may have emerged 50,000 years ago).[63] Discussing game theory, Alexander Field discusses the 'arena' in which the players define the rules of the game.[64] With reference to the prisoner's dilemma, for example, Field questions 'why escape or insurrection' are not even under consideration. It is because the 'arena' rules preclude them. In circumstances X there is only Y. These primary, prior or arena institutions constitute the second type of institutions guiding socioeconomic action. They are extremely resilient and, up to a certain point, 'self-sustaining'.[65]

Habits and prior institutions give stability to socioeconomic life by reducing uncertainty and complexity but situations rarely repeat themselves without variation. Sometimes they are completely or partially new, which may happen when changes in the environment make habits useless for achieving particular objectives. When there are no pre-reflexive tendencies indicating what path of action to follow, a response needs to be formulated. These situations pose higher complexity and risk of failure and are subsumed to intention and interest. Agents are pushed into reflection to assess the situation and this is where diverse intentions and interests come in play. The form is: when the intention is Z do Y in circumstances X. Several authors refer to the 'intentionality' of action as guiding conscious deliberation and self-reflexive reasoning.[66] Hans Joas defines intentionality as 'self-reflective control which we exercise over our current behaviour'.[67] Intentionality defines what course of action Y is acceptable for obtaining Z and will be repeated in circumstances X. As Friedrich Hayek argues, 'man is as much a rule-following animal as purpose-seeking'.[68]

Agents need to structure a response when novelty presents itself. That is, either X is unknown or has changed in such a way that Y is done but Z fails to happen. Agents are then forced into reflection and the networks of belonging shape experimentation for new solutions.[69] Networks are critical because they are sources of information and examples to imitate. They also shape intentions and interests, which affect the reasoning to search for new solutions. So while habit provides the cognitive means by which information is interpreted, the networks of belonging define what experimentation is possible and later imitate the chosen path. Eventually a new institution may originate if the response becomes a new rule of action.[70] These are the 'designed' institutions and they are the third category affecting an individual's behaviour.

The transition from a reflexive reaction to a designed institution may require negotiations between parties with diverse interests. Groups of agents then continue to explore possible courses of action until they reach an agreement that is acceptable in view of their diverse intentions and interests. Alternatively, one of the parties may impose a rule of action on the others against the intentions and interests of these, but then the imposing agents would have to be able to enforce the rule by the threat of punishment. This argument involves the simplification that abiding by both voluntarily agreed and effectively imposed institutions is in line with different intentions. Agents comply with rules out of conviction or at least lack of resistance, or out of their wish to avoid punishment. Hodgson[71] argues that agents' disposition to abide by the rules derives from both, the habit of doing so as well as the threat of punishment if they do not do so.

In conclusion, there are three categories of institutions guiding socioeconomic action: prior institutions, evolved institutions (habits and routines) and designed institutions. Hayek[72] formulates a similar distinction of 'layers of rules' in human society, placing at the top those that require conscious design and elaboration and at the bottom those that are mainly instinctive. Evolved institutions feed into the other two categories, acting as a hinge. Upstream, if habits and routines persist for a long time, they become arena institutions and sustain new evolved institutions. Downstream, habits and routines inform what experimentation and innovation is possible in order to design new institutions.

Characteristics of this Study

The possibility of researching how economies are organized bottom-up is quite uncommon in current times and the *Redes de Trueque* represent one such opportunity. As they grew in scale, so did the demand for organizations, institutions and rules to regulate internal behaviour. It is this scaling up into impersonal exchange that was unique to the *Redes de Trueque* in Argentina. Exchange no longer took place between a small group of neighbours, as was typical in social economy schemes, but became a socioeconomic activity involving thousands of people. Along with it came bureaucracies, coalitions and divergent interests. Eventually, the factions built different governance systems with varying degrees of sustainability. Each proposed distinct institutions for making decisions, distributing power and coordinating the socioeconomic activities of hundreds of centres and members. All in all, the story of the *RT* is one of institutional construction in which the various actors structured a socioeconomic system and then somewhat destroyed it. The *RT*, therefore, represents a clear opportunity to analyse the evolutionary nature of institutional construction and reflect on the rules of governance and sustainability of institutional systems. This study focuses mostly on the third category of institutions, those designed by agents.

Separate theoretical and analytical frameworks are created for each chapter. The study comprises nine chapters, including this introduction. Chapter 2 briefly reviews Complementary Currency Systems in the past and present and situates the *RT* among them. Chapter 3 presents the context in which the *Red de Trueque* was created. Chapter 4 analyses the launching of the first *Club de Trueque* and the emergence of new institutions by design. Chapter 5 focuses on the expansion of the first *Club de Trueque* into a national network, scrutinizing the intentions and interests in institutional design. Chapter 6 studies the rules of governance and sustainability of governance systems with minimal state regulation, like those that integrated the *RT*. Chapter 7 brings the analysis to the level of the participants after the decline of the *Trueque* and weighs its significance for them. Chapter 8 links the *RT* to the local institutional endowment and for local economic development. Chapter 9 summarizes the analysis, relates it to other experiences with complementary currency and outlines the main theoretical reflections of the book in relation to institutional theory.

Three periods of fieldwork were carried out to gather data. The first was from January to April 2003, the second from May to December 2004 and the third in November and December 2006. Ethnographic data on what happened between 1995 and 2003 is fragmented, so it is contingently included in chapters 4 to 6 but represents the bulk of the evidence presented in chapters 7 and 8.

The data collection was organized as follows. First, the initiators of the *RT* were interviewed extensively and repeatedly in order to reconstruct the evolution of the *RT* based on oral history. This first group included the three founders of the initiative (Horacio Covas, Carlos de Sanzo and Ruben Ravera), academic collaborators who joined the leadership of the *RT* later (Heloisa Primavera and Charli del Valle) and several participants in the early stages of the RT. Secondly, extensive and repeated interviews were conducted with leaders at the regional and local sub-networks. These were located in the city of Buenos Aires, the metropolitan area of Buenos Aires (western and southern suburbs), Mar del Plata and its outskirts (Buenos Aires province), La Plata (Buenos Aires province), Jujuy and Palpalá (Jujuy province), Venado Tuerto (Santa Fe province), Rosario (Santa Fe province), Capitán Bermúdez (Santa Fe province) and Bariloche (Rio Negro province).

The leaders provided lists establishing that a total of 1,000 groups were operating in the second quarter of 2004. Their lists were the basis for sampling, but attempts to contact the *CT* listed showed that about half had in fact closed down. In addition, the author found during the fieldwork that some *RT* participants were also members of *CT* that were missing from the 2004 lists. The number of *CT* operating in 2004 was thus estimated to be 700. The last follow-up period of fieldwork in 2006 found that this number was mostly unchanged: while a small number of *CT* had closed, others were starting again.

A total of forty-four operating *CT* were then visited and their coordinators interviewed. To ensure representation, two criteria were followed. Firstly, they were located in a variety of geographical areas across the country, in large and small cities, and in wealthy and poor locations. Secondly, they represented the different political factions within the *RT*. Semi-structured interviews were conducted with the coordinators of the selected *CT*. Another fifteen coordinators whose *CT* had closed were interviewed at their homes.

Between August and December 2004 a survey was conducted among the participants in eighteen of the forty-four *CT* visited, with a semi-structured questionnaire. These were chosen according to the same criteria as above, but also with a view to selecting representative numbers of small and large groups. The eighteen *CT* were located in the metropolitan area of Buenos Aires, Rosario, and Mar del Plata. Respondents for the survey were chosen at random while they queued to enter the markets or next to their stall while they were waiting for buyers. Sampling amounted to 15 per cent of those present in markets with fewer than fifty individuals and 8–10 per cent of those present in those with more than fifty. The survey obtained 386 effective responses. Two research assistants helped with the survey in Buenos Aires, one in Rosario and one in Mar del Plata. They were instructed to follow the closed questionnaire but to encourage respondents to justify or clarify their answers whenever they felt it necessary to do so. This tactic resulted in short interviews of twenty minutes each on average. A small number of them (fifty-six participants) were later asked to account their personal life history.

Focus groups of four to six participants were organized to discuss the contraction of the *RT* and its sustainability. These were in the following *CT*: Obelisco (Capital Federal), Las Dahlias (Mar del Plata), El Comedero (Bernal, Buenos Aires), Cuartel IX (Lomas de Zamora, Buenos Aires), Palpala (Jujuy) and ex San Cayetano (Rosario).

The fieldwork ended with a small canvass of official street markets functioning in the last months of 2004. Individuals selling goods (handicrafts, second-hand goods, antiques, prepared foods) were asked if they had participated in the *RT* between 1995 and 2004. Most had or were still going to the surviving *CT*. In semi-structured interviews, they were asked standard profile questions as well as their opinions on the main differences between the different *RT* systems and in what ways the learning experience in the *RT* was connected to their activities in the regular market at that time.

In addition, extensive interviews were conducted with experts and academic researchers, most of them from the Instituto del Conurbano of the Universidad Nacional de General Sarmiento, which is a leading centre on social economy research.

The first limitation of data collection had to do with the temporal span. The fieldwork was carried out after the strongest period of contraction of the *RT*. Whether this limited universe of members had different opinions from those who had left, and/or whether that has biased the findings of this research, is not known. However, judging by the canvassing referred to above as the seventh method of data collection, this seems unlikely. Secondly, people were interviewed in 2004 on events that had occurred during the previous decade. The answers are naturally tinted by their memories of the events, the changes over time in their points of view, and their own standing as participants or witnesses to the events. The problem of research on an extended period in time at a static moment is unavoidable and a well-known problem of oral history research. As many participants and witnesses as possible were interviewed in order to collect as many pieces of the puzzle as possible.

In addition, the accounts of conflicting witnesses made it difficult to assign responsibility for the contraction of the *RT*. The study assigns opinions to those expressing them and includes as many diverse views as possible. The author made every effort to interpolate accounts, but assigning responsibility was not considered to be within the scope of this research.

2 PERSPECTIVES ON COMPLEMENTARY CURRENCY SYSTEMS

The *Red de Trueque* in Argentina is one of the many cases of resurgence of non-state monetary systems.[1] Such systems are known with different names in different countries: community or complementary currency systems (CCS), *moneda sociale* in Italy, local exchange and trading systems in the UK, Canada and the USA, and *monnaies parallèles* in France. This section reviews the literature on community, complementary or local currency systems.

According to the broadly accepted definition of Ekins and Max-Neef CCS are a self-regulating economic network in which members issue and manage their own money in relation to the needs of a bounded community.[2] Lee[3] refines the concept to a local system of production, multilateral exchange and consumption articulated through single-purpose money independent of, but often related to, the prevailing national currency. The CCS is a complementary economy, fully not-for-profit and operates at the community or inter-household level.[4] In practical terms, it functions as a local association whose members offer and request goods and services priced in a local unit of exchange and then trade those commodities with other participants.

A CCS is created bottom-up by communities and it combines income and identity generation.[5] Other authors (for example, Blanc[6]) emphasize that they are an essentially local phenomenon and affect the local economy, in contrast to official money circulating in a whole country and abroad. The purpose is normally not to disconnect from the national monetary system, but to complement it, adjust it or adapt it. Although they have different names, such systems all share the characteristic of using an interest-free means of payment created by a non-state civil society actor.

As they spread across the world, community currencies adapt to local differences and legal frameworks in a variety of ways. Some communities issue notes or cheques to cancel payments which are accepted by another member. Others fix a unit of value, expressed in hours of work, notwithstanding the type of work offered. The British LETS functions mainly on the basis of an accountancy system: people who provide a good or service receive a 'credit' in their accounts which they later use to buy from other community members; everything is managed by a central administrator and a computer. In Argentina, the *RT* began with a credit accountancy system and later used vouchers of general circulation or scrip as means of payment.

Some sources have estimated that in July 2002 there were almost 5,200 communities using complementary currency systems in fifty-eight countries, approximately 3,000 of them in Argentina and the remaining 2,200 in the rest of the world: 425 in the United Kingdom, 405 in France, 322 in Italy, 297 in Germany and the rest in countries with less than 200 CCS each. Other sources reported that over 2,000 communities were active in the five continents and count the Argentine RT as one.[7] The online directory of the LETS-link organization informs that there are over 1,500 groups in thirty-nine countries using the LETS variety of CCS; none of the Argentine groups are registered in it.[8]

In terms of size, most CCS around the world are relatively small and gather up to a few members.[9] An Internet search performed in June 2007 has revealed that the largest CCS issuing scrip at present outside Argentina is the Ithaca Hours scheme in the state of New York with 5,000 members all over its network.

It has been suggested that these modern 'challenges' to national monies are not significantly different to historical forms of local currencies.[10] There is nothing 'natural' in having national currencies and before it was organized nationally, money was segmented by region, use and social class. Complementary monies have persisted through formation of national currencies up to the present.[11] They have been limited to a specific territory of community,[12] although in periods of monetary instability or inflation the use of other currencies proliferated rapidly.[13] Consumers then turned to more reliable or more abundant monies, whether foreign, privately issued or local.

The historical experience of the last century offers a broad variety of periods in which local or complementary currencies were used, normally in situations of economic collapse or financial scarcity.[14] These cases provide the closest precedents to a massive CCS as the *Red de Trueque*. The next section recounts some of the most salient examples of widespread use of complementary currency.

Historical Experiences of Extended CCS

The German speaking countries of Europe were perhaps the first to experiment with complementary currency systems. Irving Fisher referred to the first experiences as 'stamp scrip' because vouchers were stamped and lost value with its use, as time went by.

Reforming the monetary system to encompass complementary currencies that lost value with time was an idea conceived by Silvio Gesell.[15] A friend of his, Hans Timm, decided to implement the system in Erfurt in October 1929 and launched the Wära Exchange Society, a name that combines the German word for 'commodity' (ware) and 'unit of value' (währung). The Wära Exchange Society was extended across the country and after a while it had offices from Berlin to Bonn and from Hamburg to Cologne.

Timm issued vouchers to be used as means of payment among the members of the group. At the back, the vouchers had a table with twenty-four spaces where users were required to stick a stamp at the beginning of each fortnight. Stamps cost 0.5 per cent of the value of the voucher, so it would depreciate at a rate of 12 per cent a year. If members failed to pay the stamp, the vouchers were simply not accepted in exchange for goods and services.

Gesell conceived the depreciation of money as a means to discourage its storing outside the economic circuit.[16] He was convinced that one of the main causes of the economic crisis was the withdrawal of money from the economic circuit due to speculation or what John Maynard Keynes would later call the 'liquidity preference'.[17] He believed that people would be pressed to spend money as means of payment because they would otherwise have to pay for its depreciation.

The Wära vouchers were redeemable for Reichsmarks at any time, but with a charge of 2 per cent of the value. This implied that the group had to keep a permanent reserve fund of Reichsmarks to face claims which increased the stability of the vouchers.[18]

By 1931 the Wära were accepted in about a thousand shops and small businesses across the county. Still, the experiment only got significant public attention with the economic recovery of Schwanenkirchen, a small town in Bayern.[19] A mining engineer bought the local bankrupt coal mine in an auction and found it impossible to raise the working capital to set it to work again. He then contacted the Wära Society which lent him 50,000 units. He found and hired sixty workers willing to accept them as up to 90 per cent of their wages. Local shops accepted the stamp scrip because they were equally affected by the recession. Their suppliers and producers accepted them too, and eventually the vouchers circulated back to the coal mine owner in exchange for coal. Unemployment soon disappeared because everybody tried to buy goods with the Wära as quickly as possible and thus avoid paying the stamp of the scrip.[20] Werner Onken described Schwanenkirchen as an 'island of prosperity in the Bavarian woods'.[21]

Not everyone was so positive about the Wära and in October 1931 the Central Bank prohibited the issuance and circulation of any means of payment that were not the official ones. The Wära scrip stopped circulating immediately, the coal mine closed and Schwanenkirchen fell back into recession. The central bank referred to the Wära as *notgeld* (emergency money), the first but not the last time that complementary money was considered a creature of the economic crisis and gave the name with which they were known in the period after the Second World War.

The owner of the coal mine in Schwanenkirchen had a fluent correspondence with a friend in Austria, who became the mayor of the city of Wörgl and started a second experiment with complementary currency. In 1932 the city of Wörgl was affected by recession and unemployment, like the rest of the country, and the local government was heavily indebted with a bank in Innsbruck. With the support of his constituency and the local council, the mayor of Wörgl then launched a plan of public works that were financed with complementary currency issued by the local government.

It was again stamp scrip and a stamp of 1 per cent of the value of the voucher had to be paid at the beginning of each month. The aim of the stamp was to encourage users to spend them rapidly instead of storing them. The Wörgl money was also redeemable for the official schillings at a discount of 2 per cent. Public servants received half of their wages in complementary currency which was later increased to 75 per cent.[22] Shops and local firms accepted it without hesitation as the city government also received them as payment for local taxes. The economy of Wörgl recovered and unemployment fell while it was increasing in the rest of Austria.[23]

Small cities in the region around Wörgl imitated the experiment and others expressed their intentions to follow. There were some objections and pitfalls like the increase in risk for retailers accepting the stamp script for their sales while having to pay in regular currency for their supplies.[24] The main opposition came from the central bank of Austria which feared that it would lose its control over the monetary system and prohibited the issuance and circulation of stamp scrip.

Unconnected to the European experiences, in the USA several communities also resorted to complementary currency systems during the Great Depression as described by Irving Fisher (1933; 1934). Stamp scrip was first introduced in the USA by a Dutch follower of Gesell, Charles Zylstra, in the small town of Hawarden, Iowa.

In October of 1932 the city council, with the support of the local chamber of commerce, issued complementary currency to finance public works. Again, the version chosen was the stamp scrip with depreciation applied through a stamp per transaction. Each time a one-dollar-voucher was used, the buyer had to stick a stamp of three cents as a kind of 'sales tax'. The stamps were on sale in the city hall and the revenues of their sale constituted a reserve fund in official dollars with which the issuers guaranteed the convertibility of the local currency into regular dollars. Each voucher could be used up to thirty-six times after which the last user could claim one dollar in official money. The remaining eight cents financed the administrative costs of the scheme.

The Hawarden experiment was later copied by other cities across several states. The maximum amount of exchanges and the value of the stamps were variable, as was their taxation.[25] The issuers were not always the local governments but also local chambers of commence (as in Evanston, Illinois) and churches (as in Sioux City). A renowned case was the Larkin & Co. in Buffalo, New York, a retail store chain that issued 36,000 dollars of Larkin Merchandise bonds. It used the vouchers to partially pay the wages to its employees and accepted them in any of its stores. Other businesses and clients gradually started to accept them too. When the shortage of regular dollars eased, Larkin slowly withdrew the scrip from circulation. The original 36,000 dollars circulated back as payments worth 250,000 dollars of extra sales.[26]

Fisher[27] criticizes the Hawarden depreciation mechanism based on transactions instead of one based on the course of time on grounds that it misses the goal of disencouraging the storage of money: 'The use of the vouchers costs three cents, while storing them costs nothing'.[28] He also warned that using a stamp each time the note changed hands invited opportunistic behaviour because there was no way to check that the stamp was either bought or stuck as required.[29]

Whether these proved problematic in practice is unknown. Still, stamp scrip became widespread across the country. Some sources estimated that one million people, almost 1 per cent of the U.S. population at that time, depended on the 200 to 400 self-help and barter groups that existed in the United States from 1930 to 1936.[30] Initially, the U.S. government did not take measures to repress them, probably believing that stamp scrip was a creature of the crisis that would fade as employment recovered. However, in March 1933 president Franklin Roosevelt banned further scrip issue on grounds that the national government was losing control of the monetary system.[31] Other sources state that no fewer than half a million families were active in 600 organizations by the end of 1938, but as cooperatives settled among private individuals or companies that used accounts in 'points' or 'certificates' as means of payment.[32] They were seen as instruments of economic rehabilitation, creatures of an emergency situation with minimal chances of surviving into better times. In the short run they helped their members survive the Great Depression but did not constitute a durable solution: they were dependent on regular money to afford many supplies and faced the problems of low capacity in areas such as infrastructure and poor accountancy in the exchange systems.

Although unaware of the Wära and Wörgl experiments with complementary currency systems, the *Redes de Trueque* in Argentina show some similarities with the German and Austrian cases. Firstly, the Argentine *créditos* circulated as fiat money across the country among members (individuals, businesses and local governments) who had willingly agreed to accept them as means of payment. Secondly, the largest *RT* groups kept offices across the country to support the

expansion of the experience. Thirdly, the possibility of giving loans in complementary currency was discussed among some groups and happened to a small
local scale. Fourthly, the effects on the economy were similar to those described
by Fischer: households' consumption raised and the economy rebounded.

However, in contrast to the Wära, the *créditos* were not convertible to the
official pesos and most networks had no reserves of any kind to stabilize the
vouchers in circulation. Other aspects varied in time, for example the depreciation of the *créditos* at a rate of 12 per cent a year was established in 2004 after the
sharp contraction of the RT. Before that, the organizers simply advised members
not to accumulate them but they were not always heard. Another important
difference was the attitude of the state. At least officially, the central and provincial governments tolerated and for a brief period of time even encouraged
the *Redes de Trueque*. Municipal governments mostly encouraged the *RT* and in
many cases went further, participating in the network and providing venues for
the markets and transport for goods and members.

Recent Cases of Smaller CCS

The strong economic recovery after the Second World War pushed into history
the experiments with stamp scrip inspired by Sylvio Gesell. They were archived
as desperate emergency measures and were not repeated since then. Nevertheless, enterprises and retailers around the world have occasionally issued vouchers
as means of payment to boost their sales but this was far from organizing a
complementary currency system with multiple uses and actors. The countries
in transition in Eastern Europe suffered deep economic and institutional melt-
downs and they resorted to non-monetary exchanges, but these were mostly
direct barter to face temporary cash shortages rather than an organized complementary currency system.[33] As presented by Benjamin Cohen, the strength of
thinking in terms of a single sovereign currency within the territorial frontiers of
a country or monetary union seems to marginalize the fact that other currencies
can circulate as well.[34]

Since the Great Depression and the post-war periods until the 1990s the
organization of complementary currency systems has remained isolated and
anecdotal. In the last two decades, exchange networks with their own means
of payment have become recurrent as a consequence of economic need and the
desire to explore alternative economic systems. They appeal to some groups
because exchange networks enhance community ties, help members to discover
hidden talents and give them the pleasure of cooperation (Offe and Heinze,
1992). With counted exceptions, the modern experiments with CCS do not
apply a demurrage system. Most of them are based on accountancy systems,
rather than scrip, but there are experiments that combine both formats.

The most disseminated modality is the LETS system which made its appearance in Canada in the early 1990s. It functions as an exchange network based on an accountancy system instead of using physical vouchers. The first 'local exchange and trading system' (LETS, as named by its founder Michael Linton) was established on Vancouver Island in British Columbia, Canada, in 1984.[35] The economy of the small town of Courtenay (pop. 50,000 inhabitants) depended on two employers, a US Air Force base and a timber mill providing raw material for the paper industry. When the base was transferred and the mill closed, the town's population had no alternative employment possibilities. Unemployment rose dramatically and the amount of money in circulation within the local economy plummeted. Michael Linton then designed a mutual credit system he called LETS, by which his neighbours could buy and sell goods and services to each other without the use of regular money. A list of what is offered is published and distributed in the locality every month. Over the years the initiative grew, the number of participants rose to 1,000 and the system helped to offset some of the effects of the economic crisis.[36] There was no physical currency; only credits and debits in an accountancy system. In this sense, LETS represent a purely endogenous monetary system in which money is created at the point of transaction: when an exchange takes place, the members communicate it to the LETS 'bank'. The prices were denominated in 'Green Dollars', equivalent in value to regular money.

The idea behind the modern conception of the scheme was simple and it spread to other localities in need of economic rehabilitation. The model of LETS arrived in the UK in the late 1980s, starting in the city of Norwich.[37] There was a less well-known British forerunner called Link Opportunity which was introduced during the 1970s to encourage trading between retired people but had quite a limited scope.[38] The expansion of LETS in the UK took a while to gain momentum: there were barely five groups in 1992. By 1995 the number soared to 270[39] and at present there are about 300 (Letslink UK). The rise was partly due to the creation of LETSlink UK in 1991 and its coordination efforts as national LETS development agency.

LETS offers more security but less expansion prospects than issuing scrip. It is applicable only within small groups where members can get to know and trust each other and hence prevent abuses of the system. A critical risk is that a member can get goods or services from others without ever transferring anything in exchange. Social control mechanisms typical of small groups help to prevent that behaviour. Equally important are the provisions for sharing information on account balances.

Given those conditions, LETS are a quick and usually safe version of a complementary currency system. They do not require a large number of members to be sustainable. For that reason, they have expanded to a few dozen countries across Western Europe, the Americas, Australia, New Zealand, Japan and South East Asia.

There are other present forms of complementary currency systems that recreate schemes with scrip. A successful case is the SHARE (Self-Help Association for a Regional Economy) group in the Berkshire in Massachussetts, USA, and the Ithaca Hours in the state of New York. The SHARE group first developed a scheme to raise capital locally and self-finance their activities. As accounted by Pacione,[40] a member of the group was the owner of a local delicatessen restaurant. He printed 500 vouchers of ten 'deli dollars' to finance the relocation of his store. He sold each one of them to his clients for nine dollars, redeemable for ten dollars worth of goods in his new business. He successfully raised the capital he needed at a lower cost than banks would have asked and the debt was repaid in kind at a discount.

The Ithaca Hour is perhaps the largest CCS with scrip in the developed world. Paul Glover, the launcher of several LETS in the region, was inspired by the SHARE experience when he heard a radio interview in the summer of 1991.[41] He realized that the SHARE system with scrip offered some advantages in relation to the accountancy system of LETS: its scale would not be limited to the relatively small amount of users that know and trust each other. The circulation of vouchers as means of payment is easier for participants to understand than the method of informing a central actor of the transactions made. Trust is still a critical element but in a different way, as trust in the scrip takes precedence over trust in one another. In fact, both dimensions of trust are intimately connected because the currency represents the trust of participants in the system of which they are all part. The notes have special security features that make them almost impossible to forge. The exchange of professional services paid for in Ithaca Hours is subject to income taxes, making the notes a recognized financial instrument and, therefore, subject to state protection. This means their forgery can be prosecuted and penalized by imprisonment. However, the leaders of the scheme consider that social cohesion would prevent any participants from giving a forged voucher to another.[42]

Glover launched the Ithaca Hours scheme in November 1991. The average hourly wage in the locality was ten dollars, so it was decided that one unit of currency -the Ithaca hour- would represent ten dollars. Vouchers are issued in fractions of that unit (for example, half an Ithaca Hour is equivalent to five dollars). With its name the currency is meant to remind users that it represents labour. By 2008 there were over 900 participants publicly accepting it for goods and services. In turn, some local employers and employees have agreed to pay or receive partial wages in local currency. In terms of scale and scope it is one of the most successful examples of community currency systems and was reproduced in another twenty cities.[43]

Another modality of local exchange networks with unofficial means of payment are the Time Banks system in which people offer services to others in their community and can later claim back services from somebody else for the same amount of hours. It is different from simple bartering because services are not given and received between the same two persons but involve a relatively large number of members. The services provided are valued in terms of hours (one hour = one Time dollar), irrespective of the kind of service. The main goal of the system is to strengthen community ties. Since its design by Edward Cahn, it has extended to twenty-two countries in six continents.

There are a number of other modalities of complementary currency systems, depending on the context and the goals of the organizing community. CCS vary from using fiat scrip to accountancy systems or magnetic member cards, using internet payments or just mutual credit, bartering through an electronic platform, or combinations of these.[44]

One of the active non-governmental organizations in the field, the Strohalm foundation, lists the four methodologies most commonly used in CCS to promote local economic development.[45] The *controlled currency systems* start with a loan in complementary currency given to all members (informal local businesses) who subsequently use the currency to exchange with other members goods and services produced at a micro-scale. *Valuable local currency systems* start with the construction of public infrastructure paid with loans on which interests are paid in local currency and recirculated to local users and producers of the public good. *Circuits of consumers and commerce* are exchange networks of suppliers and buyers usually run by an electronic platform clearing mutual payments; there is no fiat currency but a clearing system of payments. *Commodity backed currency systems* are based on a central producer or seller of goods of general demand (e.g. basic consumer goods or fuel) who issues its currency to pay local suppliers and workers and commits the basic good as back-up to the currency.

The Argentine *Redes de Trueque* are difficult to compare to these current experiments with CCS across the world, mainly because of the differences in scale. Several authors[46] point out that the benefits of CCS in the developed world are difficult to assess as long as they are on too small a scale to happen. As a result, the CCS offer an insufficient range of goods and services, limited turnover, and small numbers of participants. Aldridge and Patterson[47] go even further after a broad evaluation of LETS in the UK and conclude that, at their present scale, the systems are far from offering an alternative to the poor or unemployed.

Beyond the scale, there are a number of organizational differences between the *RT* and other current CCS. These will be discussed throughout the book but will be briefly highlighted here. Like LETS, the *RT* began with a manual accountancy system. However, in the *RT* individual accounts were cleared back to zero at the end of each market meeting (once a week) and the accountancy system was abandoned in favour of fiat currency at a very early stage of its development. Physical scrip was considered more practical and the risks of forgery were underestimated. Another difference with the LETS system is that much of the *RT* formed a network of interconnected markets in which regional and local currencies were mutually accepted. The goal of promoting local economic development was considered a priority by many of the leaders but in practice the *RT* functioned as a parallel or complementary economy with a myriad of currencies rather than as a chain of alternative local economies like the LETS do. The *RT* are, therefore, roughly comparable with the Ithaca Hours that circulate across New York State, though the *RT* has several times the scale of the Ithaca scheme. What the *RT* shares with all the other systems mentioned are the social effects, namely the strengthening of community ties.

Motivations for Complementary Currency Systems

Launching a CCS can be quite difficult and time consuming, whatever the method chosen. Participants are often reluctant, especially in the beginning, to transfer their goods and services to others without the certainty that they will be able to obtain something else in the future. The application of legal norms as last resort is frequently unclear. There are also issues of quality involved – members are afraid that the goods and services offered would be defective or of poor quality.

Exchange networks need time to mature because trust in each other and in the system develops only gradually. This explains why CCS often die within the first year and why they are more successful in networks that had substantial social cohesion beforehand. That has been the experience in a number of cases, but there are still thousands of communities that have been able to run and expand their CCS. The sustainability of local exchange networks is related to their achieving one or more of the goals that motivated their construction.

The scheme links anti-poverty or income-generation goals with community social development. It helps in situations where the process of trading money for products is frustrated by a shortage of means of exchange and sections of the population are 'time-rich but money-poor'.[48] That is, where some households have economic needs to cover but are unable to do so through the regular market and lack the skills to fulfil their needs themselves, while others living nearby have the skills, time and will to satisfy them but cannot find a job at a reasonable wage. In this way, CCS provide an income-generation scheme for those excluded from the labour market, while integrating them in the local exchange network of their communities. They reconnect the unemployed by giving them the chance to transform their labour power and time into purchasing power, without the necessity of being employed by a firm, or of having capital, which is a sine qua non for earning a living by self-employment.[49] Gill Seyfang argues that CCS 'can be a vehicle for mitigating the problems resulting from unemployment and under-employment such as social exclusion, poverty, and an inability to participate in work'.[50] This was the central motivation for starting the *RT* in Argentina.

Those that sympathise with CCS[51] argue that the systems are more than simply a reaction to recession or a functional device for enhancing income. In principle, everybody with time or skills can participate, underwriting the exclusionary order of the formal economy.[52] They offer low-risk and fluent opportunities to develop skills or start micro- and small-scale enterprises to produce and trade in the community. In this sense, some research disclosed that the strength of CCS lies in improving employability: they provide a springboard into employment and self-employment for a small but significant proportion of member.[53] At first sight, the development of local entrepreneurial capabilities seems more likely than the bridge to formal employment, since one of the main advantages of CCS is to mobilise resources that, if community currencies did not exist, would remain idle. In Argentina, apparently there was a combination of both. Many went back to employment in similar areas where they used to be active. Others were not able to do so and launched their own small businesses.

A second motivation for starting a CCS is the regeneration of community ties, irrespective of its income generation effect. Community currency systems re-embed money in specific locales and social networks. Granovetter[54] argues that markets are embedded in social relations but the question is what *kind* of social relations. With fieldwork data, Thorne[55] elaborates on LETS as a socially re-embedded economy and finds that participants are indeed moved by their desire for social integration through trading. A space for social life alone can be enough to keep a CCS going.

In terms of re-embedding, organizers frequently believe that a CCS may be the first step towards creating a different moral community. Dodd[56] coins the concept of *monetary social networks* to explain why different monies are worth anything; money is explained as an expression of mutual trust, enabling the establishment of a private monetary network without central state backing. Others added that monetary social networks 'demonstrate that alternative moral stances are possible which can colour the practices of money'.[57] In Argentina, part of the leadership saw in the *Redes de Trueque* an opportunity to create an economy with an alternative morality and attracted participants along these lines, rather than just for its income generation effects.

Although CCS open a new set of possibilities, there is still insufficient evidence to support the view that they do underwrite the exclusionary order of the formal economy, for example in terms of gender and race. Seyfang[58] argues that the introduction of community currencies deconstructs the traditional concept of payment and reconstructs gender values. The author concludes that CCS can 'value and reward work, time and skills which are often neglected, redressing gender imbalances in terms of wages, skills valued and divisions of labour'. Instead, Lee[59] makes the counter-claim that 'LETS take on some of the class and gender characteristics of the wider economy'. The Argentine *Redes de Trueque* appears to offer evidence in both directions: some groups reproduced the class and gender imbalances of the regular economy and others tried to offset them.

For many communities launching a CCS, the main goal is to strengthen the local economy and its self-sufficiency. CCS appeal them as a response to the socio-spatial insensitivity of global financial systems. Globalization has had two important consequences in the economic use of space: it has led to uneven development of different societies and it has left an important part of the population excluded from the market system. Peter North[60] views CCS as social movements with a particular outlook of resistance.

The effects of the outflow of capital to areas of higher profit can be traumatic to local economies and CCS represent a possibility to re-localise social and economic relations and facilitate a certain degree of autonomy. An early advocate of CCS argued that CCS could partially delink the local economy from the global system.[61] From an economic point of view, complementary currencies cannot leave the network where they are accepted as means of payment, creating some kind of insulation for the local market from the swings of globalization.[62] A Keynesian 'multiplier effect' follows: increased circulation of the local money leads to increased production and economic growth. In the case of Argentina, the subgroups of the *Redes de Trueque* that operated at local and regional level seem to have achieved this goal, as will be discussed in chapter eight.

The link between complementary currency and locality indirectly questions the system of a single national money under the supervision of a central bank. Monopoly power over a national currency is relative recent news in the history of economic institutions.[63] In most states in the 19th century, currencies were divided by region and social class: 'the poor predominantly used low denomination tokens, often privately issued and not easily convertible into the official monies of the wealthy'.[64] Monies were tied to territory, a feudal estate or city, and were mostly worthless in other territories unless they were first converted into metallic means of exchange such as silver or gold. Later, once improved communications such as the post and railways enabled the central state to reach out to all the corners in the national territory, national monetary systems were established by rule of law, coercion and force. Since then money has become an important instrument of the state to demonstrate its sovereignty.

Complementary local currencies now contest this central power of the state, as they empower communities to decide what money they want to use and how it should be managed.[65] For this reason, governments do not always tolerate complementary currencies, as shown in Thailand[66] and after the First World War experiments in Wörgl.[67] In Argentina, the central and provincial governments were mostly tolerant with the *Redes de Trueque* and at the local level several municipalities joined the exchange networks as participants.

Since centralized monetary systems disregard regional disparities, a CCS is a mechanism to fine-tune local liquidity needs.[68] Jayaraman and Oak[69] developed a theoretical model showing that local currencies contribute to local economic efficiency by providing better signals about supply and demand than national currencies do. Local currencies partially insulate communities from an economic downturn.

The liberal economist Friedrich Hayek recommended giving people the right to use their preferred currency and letting the laws of supply and demand determine its fate.[70] By 'denationalizing money', as the Austrian School author called it, competition with other currencies would be created and it would spur the currency issuer to maintain its value, translating into a more efficient type of monetary system.[71] There are no current cases in which the benefits of that policy could be tested.

While there are various motivations for launching a CCS, there are also critics to the system. There is a risk that CCS may represent a return to the historical period when there was different money for the poor and for the wealthy and may deepen exclusion.[72] Community currencies are used by the poor and are difficult to convert into the national money used by the better-off. However, the lack of contact between the poor and the wealthy in their shopping practices is not explained solely by the use of different types of money.[73]

3 THE POLITICAL AND ECONOMIC CONTEXT IN ARGENTINA

A wave of structural reform or adjustment programmes (SAPs) was implemented throughout the developing world during the 1990s, inspired by the neoliberal view of how the economy should work. In the perception that institutions guiding economic agents' behaviour were counter-productive to the ways in which the neoliberal governments envisioned the economy should function, institutions became the target of SAPs. Institutions were earlier defined as rules of action, following Hodgson.[1] The objective of the reforms was to improve the overall efficiency of the economy by changing the rules of production and market exchange that organized it. The focus was on correcting the distortions caused by 'excessive' regulation, mainly the state's but also those resulting of social practice. Policies aimed at eliminating, reconfiguring or replacing the old institutions, seen as inefficient, by new ones. It was assumed agents would adapt their behaviour as the government advanced in the reforms.

However, the institutions subject to reform were part of the social structure, in the sense that they organized social life around rather stable patterns or behaviour. The adaptation of agents' actions was not as direct as initially believed. This chapter coins the term 'institutional gaps' to address the phenomenon that occurs in the institutional structure during the period of time until economic agents adapt their behaviour to the reformed or new institutions. Old habits, routines, stable patterns of behaviour and expectations no longer match the reality of an economic structure modified by policy makers. While agents struggle to understand the new institutions, their resources are redundant or underutilized. Although this is often regarded as a short-term problem, it can actually persist for some time and even become permanent.

The depth and speed of the reforms are critical dimensions affecting agents' adaptation to the reformed structure, as well as their agreement with or resistance to the policies. All in all, institutional change resembles a 'bricolage process',[2] the mixing of this and that, of the old and the new. The construction of the new concept of institutional gaps represents an effort to take a meso-level look at the effects of macroeconomic reform, which in turn feeds back on the macro level.

A situation in which institutions are missing constitutes the starting point for agents to pursue new solutions and formulate new patterns of behaviour. These, emanating out of purposeful elaboration, are termed 'designed institutions' in this study.

The case of Argentina is an example of how structural reform policies create institutional gaps. The country had a relatively dense institutional structure constructed through most of the twentieth century. Its per capita GDP placed it at a middle-income level in the world and its substantial middle class was a rarity among the developing countries. However, in the 1980s the state-promoted industrialization was running out of steam and inflation soared. The diagnosis that stabilization of the economy required reforming the economic and social structure gained consensus. In 1990, Argentina adopted a wide-ranging structural reform programme that was expected to tackle inflation and make the country more competitive in the world market. The programme followed the course of action proposed by the so-called Washington Consensus:[3] fiscal discipline, opening up of the economy, monetary restraint, privatization and deregulation. The structural reforms were initially successful and economic growth accelerated. However, by virtue of the swift reforms institutional gaps developed. Agents unable to adapt to the reformed institutional structure became disengaged from the regular economy. They had to seek solutions through individual and collective reflection in order to reformulate their economic activities. Among other schemes, they organized the *Redes de Trueque*.

This chapter discusses the emergence of institutional gaps as a consequence of the structural reform programme implemented by the Argentine government in the 1990s. The analysis is on three levels: a critique of the structural reform programmes from an Institutional Economics perspective; the elaboration of the concept of institutional gaps that allow agents to try new solutions; and a discussion of how the developments in Argentina affected large parts of society, creating a necessary condition for the emergence of new forms of economic organization. The chapter covers four areas that were the target of structural reforms: industry, labour, the welfare state and the monetary system.

Structural Reforms as Imposition

Structural reforms were first inspired by the Monetarist School and later included supply-side policies to correct imperfect markets.[4] They represent a specific conception of the economy, which claims that less state intervention leaves more ground for market coordination to take over.[5] The main aim, then, is to transform institutions in order to restructure the ways in which individuals relate to each other in the economy. The intention is to create designed institutions by policy which would be conducive to an increased economic efficiency.

The approach behind these programmes assumes that the laissez faire market is the most efficient or desirable mode of coordination.[6]

The rules of behaviour guiding economic activity should therefore be rearranged in line with this conception of the free market. Other forms of coordination –state regulation, private sector alliances, and often civil society networks– would push the economy into a suboptimal position, so they should be abolished.[7]

This view has been criticized by Institutional Economics scholars as a misunderstanding of the nature of institutions. They argue that, however deregulated markets are intended to be, they are still organized by institutions whose manipulation may cause more problems than they solve. For example, Bowles and Gintis[8] contend that markets cannot last without implicit rules of the game and explicit laws enforced by an authority or association. Public and private conventions discipline agents, strengthen contracts, reduce uncertainty and minimize risks in order to provide greater certainty and narrow the room for conflicts. As Chandler suggests, the visible hand of institutions must be added to the invisible hand of the market.[9]

The top-down design of rules of action may easily clash with the evolutionary emergence of institutions. Before they stick as stable patterns of social action, institutions evolve out of regularity in behaviour or are designed in line with agents' intentions and interests.[10] Policymakers proposing to create institutions top-down would need to generate compliance by promoting agents' participation or by enforcing the reforms through threats of punishment, which requires costly control infrastructure. In developing countries policymakers rarely have such state capacities at hand, so compliance with top-down rules becomes erratic and raises the overall uncertainty of the economy.[11]

When institutional reform happens bottom-up, in contrast, it takes place through a process of ongoing negotiation, resistance and adaptation in the political arena. It is not a once-and-for-all transformation in line with a blueprint but a series of gradual and partial adjustments. It starts when institutions become superfluous or undesired as a consequence of shifts in the balance of power or failures to resolve antagonisms, or when external or internal forces modify the strategies and interests in play.[12]

Institutional reform was described as bricolage.[13] Agents try to incorporate new elements to an existing structure, adapting, rearranging, permuting and reconfiguring the old ones. They do not operate on a tabula rasa but on already functioning economies and societies with the institutional legacies of protected economies, colonialism, populist welfare states and so on. Top-down structural reform programmes create discrepancies and inconsistencies by introducing new elements into a working structure and trying to adjust the old ones to match the new.

The bricolage of old and new rules of action has economic consequences. New and old institutions operate contingently and erratically while agents struggle to adapt their behaviour. The absence of clear rules of action Y for circumstances X cause confusion, inefficiency and increase the costs of the reforms. This situation is termed 'institutional gap'. It is a gap in the sense that agents do not know how to act, react or decide in situations for which they used to have understood responses, habits or prior institutions.

Before the reforms, in circumstances X, agents did Y and obtained Z. When policymakers implemented a top-down structural reform programme, they generated a Y' that they consider more efficient or desirable. They expect agents to adapt accordingly, but this may take some time. Y' may not be sufficiently specified, may be resisted or prove unfeasible in practice because, for example, the resources for action Y' may be missing. Due to the inertia of institutionalized life, agents may continue to do Y. So in reality circumstances X may provoke a reaction Y or Y', depending on the discretion of the agents. In turn, reactions to Y' may cause further uncertainties and lead to unexpected and unstable situations. The reform programmes have pushed agents into a world in which there are new situations for which there are no institutions guiding their behaviour.

Arguably, institutional gaps that arise from bricolage reforms will be resolved in the long run and agents will do Y' if policymakers are successful and Y" if they are not. The point is that it may take a long time to harmonize the organization of the economy again and it may happen only in a redefined structure. From a political economy perspective, the emergence of institutional gaps poses various questions. Institutional gaps do not affect all agents equally. While some agents face an increase in uncertainty and lose assets or power in society, others may be able to increase their income and power.

In fact, relative winners may induce institutional gaps on purpose, as a strategy to advance on others. Diaz[14] describes the restructuring process as having two effects. In the short run, it has a destructive face reflected in processes of social disarticulation, erosion of traditional forms of identity, anomie, and a declining capacity for collective action by the affected groups. In the long run, there is a less-visible process of re-articulation: new collective actors emerge, organizations are formed and institutions are reformulated While some groups of agents regain their capacity to react, re-articulate and re-organize, power and wealth may be captured by other groups.

All in all, top-down structural reforms tend to leave a chaotic picture of half-reformed (state) institutions, new markets that work imperfectly because of lack of adequate (new) institutional regulation and (new) segments of economic activity left entirely to the regulation of the invisible hand.[15] The concept of 'institutional gap' is useful to explain why in certain circumstances agents can take innovative actions that were not conceivable in the old structure. That is, it explains why they are motivated to seek alternatives to regain lost activities or benefits, reuse resources that become idle and reorganize the old institutions in such a way that they can restructure their actions again into new routines and practices.

A Quick Look at Argentina's History

The structural reforms in Latin America during the 1990s posed such a challenge that Smith and Korzeniewics[16] compare their outcomes to the Great Transformation in the nineteenth century analysed by Karl Polanyi.[17] The matrix of political dynamics and modes of organisation was redefined. On the destructive side, some of the most influential forces until then, like the trade unions and the military, experienced rapid erosion of their powers.[18] On the restructuring side, new actors emerged, new social movements and non-governmental organisations entered the arenas of national politics and the economy, representing the interests of segments of society that had until then been excluded and marginalized.[19]

In the beginning of the twentieth century Argentina was one of the ten most affluent nations in the world. The per capita income was higher than in other Latin American countries and in several Western European countries like Spain and Italy.[20]

Table 3.1: Argentina's GDP per capita as percentage of selected other countries' GDP per capita

	1890	1913	1929	1943	1963	1975	2001
UK	49	65	73	53	57	67	39
USA	58	64	57	34	42	48	29
France	85	96	83	141	61	59	36
Italy	125	132	128	133	73	72	42
Germany	79	91	89	64	55	59	34
Spain		148	132	158	117	86	51
Canada	90	80	79	56	55	55	34
Australia	45	69	84	60	64	70	52
Brazil	260	393	343	292	207	184	147
Chile		126	117	115	111	172	80
Peru		331	250	221	153	187	218
Avg Southern Europe		139	130	145	90	79	46
Avg South America	159	222	194	180	147	181	126

Source: Selected countries and years based on Llach.[21]
Notes: Figures are calculated in 1990 real $US, taking three-year averages of GDP per capita for all countries. Argentina equals one hundred.

This success owed much to the abundance of natural resources, export staples (meat and grain, which were also supplied to the domestic market), slow demographic growth, fast urbanization, large-scale migration from Europe, and the 'British connection' in trade and infrastructure investment.[22] The country promulgated a constitution as early as 1856, assimilated millions of migrants, had a stable society and integrated the international division of labour of that time.

The bonanza lasted until approximately 1930, when first the Great Depression and then the Second World War marked a turning point in Argentine history (see Table 3.1 and Figure 3.1). Growth then became more erratic, with alternating periods of progress and stagnation.[24] After 1950, Argentina changed its development strategy to a state-directed economy, protecting key sectors and implementing other usual ingredients of the import substitution industrialization model prevalent around the developing world at that time.

In the political arena, democratic governments alternated with military dictatorships, and between 1929 and 1989 no civilian president was able to complete the six-year-mandate period. One of the military governments introduced Juan Domingo Perón into politics in 1943. Perón consolidated his political power granting workers' rights and thus changed the face of Argentine politics.[25] He became a recognized political leader and started the *Partido Justicialista*,[26] better known as the Peronist Movement.

It is difficult to define the Peronist Movement it in political terms: a variant of Latin American nationalist populism, promoting a corporatist type of governance and blending authoritarianism in a pyramidal bureaucratic structure in which labour and trade unions provided the electoral base.[27] Perón and his

Figure 3.1: Three-year average of Argentine GDP as percentage of the average GDP of developed countries, 1885–2002

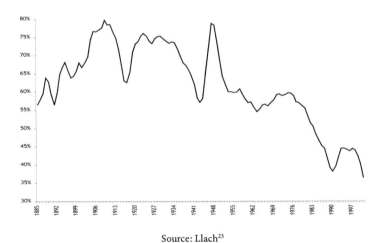

Source: Llach[23]

Notes: GDP three-year averages for Argentina and mean for OECD countries, at constant 1990 prices.

second wife, Eva, were immensely popular among many who praise their efforts to eliminate poverty and to dignify labor. Their detractors, however, considered them demagogues and dictators. The difference of opinion has divided the political arena between Peronists and anti-Peronists, the latter often associated to military coups, a division that still permeates today.[28] Perón ruled the country three times and died in 1974 and his wife, the then vice-president, without completing this last period.

In the economy, Perón consolidated an import-substitution industrialization strategy. Under it, the country experienced periods of growth and stagnation describing a stop-and-go growth model. By the 1970s, the economy was definitely running out of steam and creating permanently high inflation. In 1978 there was an attempt to implement a monetarist structural adjustment programme under military rule. It sought to control inflation through a tight monetary policy, deregulation of the financial system and a high exchange rate to favour imports. It failed totally to curb inflation but ended the developmental policies based on import-substitution industrialization. It pushed many firms, especially small ones, into bankruptcy and inaugurated unemployment rates above 5 per cent with an expanding black economy.[29]

In this complicated economic context, the government returned to democratically elected hands. President Raul Alfonsin was chosen to succeed a dictatorship that exacerbated political divisions and left 30,000 opponents 'missing'. In political terms the government made significant progress in consolidating democracy, but in economic terms it failed to pursue a clear development strategy. The national product shrank and GDP per capita fell by 21 per cent between 1980 and 1990.[30] The decade ended with hyperinflation and riot. A country that was among the wealthiest in the world at the beginning of the twentieth century witnessed at its end the looting of supermarkets by the poor.[31]

A second democratic president, Carlos Menem, took over in 1989, but there were still two periods of hyperinflation before he could define a macroeconomic policy. This was a programme of structural reforms in conformity with the prescriptions of the Washington Consensus. One of the most ambitious and swift privatisation programmes in Latin America was launched, involving almost all state-owned enterprises, public utilities, the pension system, much of the health care and the banking sector.[32] Additionally, to end inflation the peso was pegged to the dollar at parity in 1991. This was the Convertibility Plan, the cornerstone of the structural reforms' policy, which also transformed the Central Bank into a currency board and imposed a tight fiscal discipline. As Figure 3.2 shows, the structural reforms triggered a significant growth rate of 8 per cent a year from 1990 to 1994. GDP increased by 27 per cent between 1991 and 1994 but with

Figure 3.2: Argentina's real GDP, 1980–2006

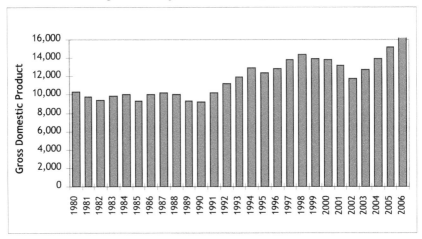

Source: <www.indec.gov.ar>.
Note: GDP in thousands of 1986 real pesos.

a marked heterogeneity between sectors: while the industrial GDP hardly grew, services bloomed and with it part of the middle class.[33]

In 1995 a major economic crisis hit the 'modernized' Argentine socioeconomic structure. It caused major disruptions in the balance of payments and the peg to the dollar almost collapsed. It was saved at the cost of a recession that skimmed 5 per cent off the national product in 1995. The unemployment rate, which had stayed around 5 per cent in the 1980s, soared to 18.4 per cent in 1995. The social costs of the structural reforms were beginning to be reported by the media, which revealed pools of poverty that had never been seen before. The *Red de Trueque* was launched in this context.

The crisis induced a moment of awareness. It was then that the public realized that the institutions regulating economic activity and the relationships between the private sector, the state and civil society had changed permanently. The rules of action were disrupted and destabilized by the top-down policies of structural reform. Other authors have accounted for the performance in the macroeconomic variables, the social fragmentation and the changes in the political economy of Argentina during the 1990s. The next section proposes a meso economic look at the reforms, following the disruptions and transitions in the institutions that organize the actions of individuals and groups of agents.

Continuity in Economic Practices

The structural reforms of the 1990 focused on transforming the organization of the economy once and for all. For decades policymakers in Argentina had struggled to control inflation and financial instability and it was finally achieved by formalizing bimonetarism in 1991. Monetary policy was based on assimilating the informal routines that economic agents had developed in practice to reduce uncertainty. It was not a top-down imposition but a creative bricolage of old and new institutions which eventually succeeded in curbing inflation.

In five decades, there was hardly any anti-inflationary policy that had not been tried and yet two-digit inflation rates had become normal. Given the regular fall in the value of money, it is no wonder that Argentines – including the government – had had a peculiar and flexible understanding of 'money' as a social construction that can be transformed and affected by policy. There was an engrained perception that money was basically a printed paper of variable and sometimes arbitrary value. This was related to the fact that the governments had written off a total of thirteen zeros and changed the currency four times between 1969 and 1991.[34]

What was socially accepted as money was equally a matter of social judgement and political decision. For instance, in the winter of 1962 the government paid civil servants their wages in bonds instead of official money. The fiscal accounts were then seriously distressed and the government wanted to avoid the inflationary effects of issuing money to cover its deficit.[35] These bonds were accepted by most shops and firms, and public servants spent them as soon as they could.[36] Later, in the 1980s, the issuance of surrogate money was repeated as measure of last resort by two small provinces that could not pay their employees' wages and printed small amounts of provincial bonds.[37] The bonds were accepted reluctantly as they circulated in the provinces, and once again the holders spent them as quickly as possible.[38] Shopkeepers referred to these quasi-money as 'hot bread', a reference to the desire to get rid of them quickly.

Monetary instability, therefore, involved both an inflationary problem and periodical changes in the currency. The search for a 'harder' currency then evolved as routine. At the institutional level, agents adopted the dollar as a de facto second currency: it became the rule of action Y to preserve the value of assets in circumstances of high inflation. Initially it was only a reserve of value but dollar-denominated prices gradually became institutionalized as unit of account and means of payment. Dollars were used to express the value of goods such as houses and cars and to stabilize the value of contracts. Later on, they also preferred to make payments in transactions for those goods and services. The origin of bimonetarism is explained as a failure of indexation to adjust quantities properly: price indexes tell a story of past price increases while the exchange rate reflects the increases currently going on.[39]

The substitution of a bad currency (peso) for a good currency (Dollar and Kraay), as in Argentina, was termed 'reverse Gresham's Law' by some specialists.[40] Uncertainty over the future purchasing values in pesos prevented agents from seeing the peso as the 'natural' unit of account. The 'natural' unit of account then became the currency that could effectively guarantee purchasing power in the future (the dollar). It became a practice, whenever inflation started rising, for agents to flee to 'good' currencies such as the dollar to protect the value of their payments, goods for sale and savings.

The inflationary problem worsened and there were three hyperinflations between May 1989 and the end of 1990, a period of less than two years. In July 1989, the monthly price index increase topped 200 per cent; the price index for the year as a whole increased by almost 5,000 per cent. The monetary aggregate M_3 (which includes banknotes in circulation, and current and savings account deposits in pesos and in dollars) fell to 6.8 per cent of GDP in 1990, from around 20 per cent a decade earlier.[42] It became common practice to pay all goods and services in pesos calculated at the exchange rate of the advertised value in dollars.

Although the actions to survive inflation were firmly institutionalized, the hyper-inflation around 1990 was a dramatic experience for Argentines. It became obvious that it was not part of a business cycle any more, but a failure in the structural organization of the economy, especially the public sector.[43] It

Figure 3.3: Variations in main monetary variables, 1980–1997, in per cent

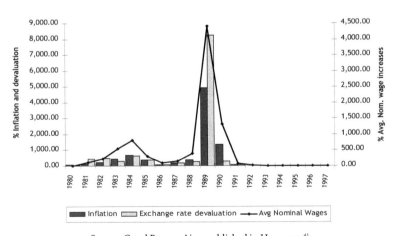

Source: Cepal Buenos Aires published in Heymann.[41]
Note: Monetary variables after 1997 stabilized. Inflation, devaluation and wage variations stayed nearly zero until the crisis of 2002.

created a strong social demand for stability at any cost: the public was ready for a full-fledged redesign of the institutions of the economy.[44] The top policy priority in 1990 was to reconstruct the institutions regulating the relationship between the population and money, the monetary system and monetary-defined property rights.[45]

The lack of trust in the national currency constrained policy options for the subsequent reform programme. Behind the steering wheel of the economy at that time was Domingo Cavallo as Economy Minister. He contested the monetarist view that the source of inflation was the quantity of money created in an economy and instead posited that it was the quality of money that determined agents' monetary preferences. He describes the monetarist theory of inflation as incomplete because it does not pay attention to the institutional aspects of money.[46]

Full dollarization at the macro level was discussed, but the idea did not gain ground.[47] Instead, the government opted for the Convertibility Plan. In March 1991 the Congress approved a law transforming the Central Bank into a currency board, pegging the peso to the US dollar at a rate of one to one and allowing all transactions to be performed in any currency of choice. The law forbade indexation in contracts but protected the option of denominating prices in dollars. This also applied to bank deposits over any term. It gave the Central Bank autonomy and specified the level of foreign currency reserves it would have to maintain.[48] In practice, this ensured that money would be issued in alignment with inflows of foreign currency. It was a short cut for the recovery of the institution of money, and the combined M_3 increased to 20 per cent of GDP by 1994.[49] Convertibility allowed agents to choose at any point in their economic activity what currency they wanted to use for what.

The Convertibility Plan constitutes an example of how governments can elaborate designed institutions assimilating those evolved as habits and hence regenerating the economic structure. The institution of money as a credible reserve of value, means of payment and unit of account was not a reality. Through social interaction and habit, agents filled the gap created by inflation. They introduced bimonetarism in their daily activities, thus regenerating a stable means of payment, unit of account and reserve of value. Instead of fighting it, the Convertibility Plan built upon it and achieved what no other stabilization plan could do in the past in Argentina: inflation disappeared for a decade and the credibility of the peso was restored. In contrast, most of the other structural reforms destroyed institutions and disrupted economic life. Three areas are analyzed below: industry, labour and social welfare.

Changes in economic practice

The Argentine industrial sector dates back more than a hundred years, and for half of that time it was ruled by the institutions of import-substitution industrialization with strong state intervention.[50] This policy orientation guided routines and expectations that organized the industrial sector around certain patterns. The actors were grouped in two poles. The first was a large number of small firms in the hands of local entrepreneurs and with relatively low technological needs, while the second group were the large public and foreign companies engaging in activities that required higher investment and technological complexity. The state was central to the process, imposing rules, choosing winners and losers, providing subsidies and tax exemptions.[51] On the downside, the inward-looking industrialization offered fertile ground for rent-seeking. On the upside, it achieved a significant accumulation of human and physical resources specialized in adapting imported technologies to the small size of the market and integrating links within the manufacturing process to reduce uncertainty in supplies.[52]

By the beginning of the 1990s, Argentine industry was not competitive internationally. The value of exports was low, while industry depended on imported inputs and technology. This type of industry was seen as the mother of all evils and the state then tried to correct this problem though an institutional reorganization. The policies chosen were the opening up of markets and the liberalization of trade. The assumption was that, faced with competition from cheaper imports, local industry would have to make the necessary investments and adjustments to improve its competitiveness. Average tariffs were reduced and industrial imports went up from 12.4 per cent of all imports in 1990 to 34.5 per cent in 1996.

This represented a huge change in the institutions that guided the economic actions of small entrepreneurs. Through the decades they had incorporated the routines of running a small firm in a protected economy with inflation, foreign currency shortages, periodical downturns and inadequate access to technology. Competing in an open economy was a novelty for which there were no rules of action to provide guidance. It was an unknown X' for which there were no developed Y' responses. Some firms left the market and others adapted to varying degrees. The 1994 industrial census registered 6,000 firms fewer than five years earlier. In the segment of firms with eleven to fifty workers, 21 per cent had to exit the market (FIEL, 1996). Another 20 per cent were sold to foreigners when their owners were unable to manage them.[53] Factories shed 37 per cent of their workforce in the first half of the 1990s due to bankruptcies as well as improvements in productivity.[54]

The majority of the entrepreneurs were not able to adapt to the open market as policymakers anticipated. In the framework of this study, the government expected a Y' of dynamic investment and innovation, strategic alliances, and exports. For this, it generated an open market economy X'. However, a large group of entrepreneurs were unable to adjust to Y' and instead stuck to their rules of action doing Y. That is, manufacturing an article of decent quality for an acceptable price at a small scale of production. This type of action had no place in the new economic structure. The results were numerous bankruptcies, generating de-industrialization and unemployment. Skilled and unskilled workers of failed companies, with technical and managerial skills accumulated over decades, were no longer needed. Many factory buildings, machinery, tools and other physical infrastructure were left idle.

In turn, privatizations and restructuring were set to reduce the state-owned enterprise sector. Some of them required substantial investment in technology. They were transferred to mostly local conglomerates with a transnational partner who dismissed workers, outsourced non-core functions, disintegrated vertically, incorporated state-of-the-art technology, and closed non-crucial sections.[55] All in all, privatized companies were able to do Y' in circumstances X'.

In the bricolage of structural reform, agents in the industrial sector found they were able to understand the full implications of the changes in the market circumstances. Institutional gaps appeared as a result of policies imposed top-down without consultation with the agents affected and without training, discussion or other preparation that would have allowed them to adjust.

The disruption of rules of action in the industrial sector had a deep impact in the labour market. Traditionally Agentina had near-full employment from the 1940s, mainly thanks to the labour-intensive industrialization, the low population growth and the domination of the Peronist movement. The economically active were under 40 per cent of the population of working age. Unemployment was mainly temporary, related to the stop-and-go business cycle, or specific by regions after a bad harvest. The tight labour market sustained high wages in the formal sector and the informal sector was small. Workers also enjoyed social benefits that enabled a family to live on one breadwinner's income. Younger generations could study longer than the preceding generations and at the other end of the scale, a pension system of universal coverage permitted retirement of workers at the age of sixty-five. Between 1940 and 1980, the urban middle class grew from 40.7 per cent to 47.8 per cent of the population, thanks to the upward movement of skilled workers in the manufacturing sector and blue-collar employees.[56]

Argentine workers, both those employed and self-employed, enjoyed the highest incomes in Latin America.[57] The Argentine labour market had been highly unionized and 40 per cent of all wage-earners were union members in 1950. Analysts point out that the main source of power of the trade union movement was the tightness of the labour market rather than its organizational capacities.[58] From 1960 to 1990, unemployment fluctuated between 4 and 6 per cent.[59]

Unlike most developing countries, informal workers in Argentina were far from the standard image of poor, marginal or dispossessed.[60] Many workers were unregistered but had considerable capital assets, an income similar to or higher than that of formal workers, stable business activity and social integration. Small entrepreneurs and freelance workers were called 'autonomous', rather than informal workers. They were considered part of the middle class, both for their income as their social behaviour. 'Autonomous' work was a particular mode of integration into the labour market rather than a subordinate sector.[61] In 1980 they represented 16 per cent of the urban labour market and were present across industrial and service branches. Nonetheless, a minority of short-term, unstable, poor and socially disintegrated informal workers existed.[62]

With the decline of the import substitution model in the late 1970s, the institutions that guided actions in the labour market started changing. As finding and keeping a well-paid job became more difficult, pensioners and women gradually entered or stayed longer in the labour market, pushing the active labour force above 40 per cent. Autonomous work also increased, absorbing most of those who did not find suitable formal employment.[63]

The government considered labour market deregulation critical for the structural reforms and started it in 1990. The goal was to create a flexible labour market in which wages would fall in order to create jobs without trade union interference. The government modified the mechanism of wage negotiation, rights to strike, and coverage of collective bargaining agreements. A series of new part-time and short-term hiring modalities became legal in 1991, undermining the institution of permanent employment.[64] Other statutory rights such as compensation for workplace accidents were changed.[65] Further labour market deregulation was attempted and resisted with partial success, but it remained a pending issue for the government. It tried repeatedly in the decade and gradually succeeded.

The financial crisis that started in Mexico hit Argentina around 1995 and introduced many Argentines to the traumatic novelty of not having a job. Labour demand was already feeble due to the changes in the industrial sector, the retreat of the state and the privatizations. The financial crisis exacerbated the situation and in 1995 Argentina had a record unemployment rate of 18.8 per cent (Figure 3.4). The term 'hyper-unemployment' was coined and replaced 'hyper-inflation' as the main socio-economic concern. The old institution of one wage per household being enough to guarantee a satisfactory standard of living was undermined. Real wages in 1995 were 68 per cent of their 1986 level and sixty-two per cent of their 1975 level. As they had done in previous economic downturns, households tried to place a second and then a third fam-

Figure 3.4: Activity, employment and unemployment rates (1980-2006)

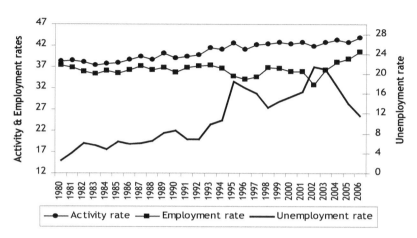

Source: <www.indec.gov.ar>

ily member in the labour market. In the Grand Buenos Aires area, the active labour force expanded from 40.9 per cent in 1990 to 45 per cent in 1995.[66][67] Among women, the percentage rose from 28.3 per cent to 35.1 per cent, while for men it went from 54.4 per cent to 57.8 per cent. Another rule of action guiding workers during recessions was to try 'autonomous' employment. They did that too, but the economic situation kept deteriorating and research found that autonomous work stopped offering a well-paid and safe alternative.[68] Another institution guiding the responses during recessions was to seek shelter in low-paid public employment. However, the structural reforms had closed off that option too; the state was reducing its workforce through privatization and rationalization of workers. The state released 200,000 workers between 1989 and 1994.[69]

The trade unions, which had been strong in Peronist times, were also hit by the structural reforms and unable to respond to the changes. They failed on two levels: unemployment undermined the main basis of their power (tightness of the labour market) and they were unable to launch effective resistance during the neoliberal reforms. The ruling party was Peronist and, in theory, supposed to be an ally of the unions. Labour leaders had supported the government, so their capacity to frame a credible resistance strategy was limited. They were mostly not consulted about most of the deregulation measures.[70]

It was not just the scale and scope of the unemployment and the distribution of power between workers and employers that had changed. It was a new type of unemployment. The old institutions signalled that in an economic downturn (circumstances X), the tested responses Y were to increase the paid work per household, seek public and autonomous employment, and support trade union resistance. However, in the new circumstances X' including privatization, de-industrialization, reduction of public employment and saturation of autonomous employment, the established rules of action were no longer valid or useful. Training or reconversion of workers parallel to the reforms may have supported responses consistent with the new institutions of the labour market, but the government considered it unnecessary to act in that respect.

In other countries that implemented structural reforms and had similar social problems – like Bolivia, Chile and Mexico – governments devised short-term safety nets to soften the pain of adjustment and win political support for their policies.[71] The Argentine government did not prepare anything of the sort. In the Peronist tradition, the country had a relatively well-developed welfare state that supported its citizens in times of need. The need for additional social policies was not perceived at that time. The buoyant growth rates between 1991 and 1994 and the initially strong social support for the reforms after the hyper-inflation experience made an extra safety net seem unnecessary, while the fiscal stringency imposed by the Convertibility Plan and the ultra-liberal approach of the government made it unfeasible.[72] The situation was paradoxical: support for the reforms relied on the existence of a safety net provided by the welfare state, but the welfare state was rapidly being dismantled.

Traditionally, the welfare state in Argentina was structured around 'protecting the worker and his family', in compatibility with an inward-looking development strategy and the incorporation of new consumers to expand markets and production.[73] It provided free universal coverage for health and education, subsidized public housing, pensions and labour protection, among other benefits. The corruption, 'inefficiencies' and 'high costs' of the state apparatus were blamed for the hyper-inflationary crisis of 1990.

The universal coverage principle was perceived as promoting 'negative incentives', so coverage started being focalized only on the poorest.[74] Wage earners were expected to pay for access to similar services in a parallel private system. Growing poverty and unemployment reinforced the view that resources were so scarce that it was best to use them only for the most needy.[75] Only in 1995 broader poverty alleviation measures were implemented, with funds from the World Bank and strictly targeted at the poorest children, handicapped and elderly.[76] The resources allocated to these programmes increased to 0.11 per cent of GDP by 1996. In 1997 a slightly more comprehensive programme of temporary employment for the poorest unemployed workers (Plan Trabajar) was implemented but altogether these policies reached only 7 per cent of the urban unemployed.[77] Additionally, local politicians quickly captured the decentralized social assistance for their clientelistic networks[78] and some authors argue that

Peronism then changed its power base from organized labour to peripheric clientelistic networks.[79]

An important component of state reform was decentralization, following the guidelines of the World Bank and other multilateral organizations. Several social and welfare services, such as education, health and aid to needy families, were transferred to the provinces, which in turn often transferred them to the municipal level. However, the funds that had to be transferred to finance them were insufficient. It was unclear which level of government should pay for what or how. Each province and municipality did what it could to keep hospitals and schools running, among other public services. The Argentine experience with decentralization was chaotic, leading to the increase in administrative fragmentation and reduced accountability.[80] Wealthier households preferred to pay for private schools and health insurances, while public services were de facto reserved for those unable to pay user fees.[81]

The distribution of funds remained a source of tension between the lean central government and provincial authorities that resisted change. The provinces needed more funds as they struggled to provide the decentralized social services and to increase public recruitment to limit unemployment. Bargaining over funds became an element in political horse-trading when the central government needed support to have controversial laws approved by the Senate. Provincial governors would instruct senators from their province to support a particular bill in exchange for a certain amount of funding from the central government. Transfers to the provinces increased when bills were brought before the Senate and in the run-up to elections.[82]

In addition, in 1993 the provinces were granted the right to increase taxes up to a certain limit (which they did) and to borrow from domestic and foreign private banks and capital markets. As collateral, the provinces could use the transfers from the central government[83] Loans did not need authorization by the central government, which meant that the capital market would determine the creditworthiness of each province. The majority of the provinces ran deficits, created by the extra expenses of decentralization as well as their refusal to reduce employment, which were initially financed by borrowing from their own provincial banks. In the crisis of 1995 provincial banks went bankrupt and the arrangement needed definite adjustment.[84]

Other lines of state reform were the privatization of services and deregulation to increase the participation of the private sector. A notable case was the privatization of the pension system. In 1990 the pension system was the single most expensive budget item in the welfare state, in spite of the meagreness of the payments. It was privatized in 1994, turning it into a mixed public-private system. Workers were entitled to choose whether they wanted to contribute to the fully private individual capitalization system or to the old public redistributive system. Those already retired would stay in the public pension system. As a result, a substantial share of the contributions of active workers went to the private pension funds while pensioners were still being paid through public funds. With the inflow of pension contributions drying up, this created a drain on the public treasury. It was thought to be a temporary problem that would solve itself as more workers retired in the private system, but it became unsustainable before that point was reached.

Argentina had been used to pockets of poverty for decades, but what was striking in the 1990s was that the poverty extended to a larger segment of the population and was much more visible. An early study of the social consequences of the structural reforms coined the term 'new poor' to describe households that had recently fallen under the poverty line in a country where about 70 per cent of the population had declared itself to be part of the middle class.[85] They were the shopkeepers, public servants, skilled workers, graduates, blue-collar workers, bank clerks, teachers and small-firm owners. Many of the sectors in which the middle class worked were targets of the reform policies and were thus overwhelmed by their disenfranchisement. Scholars define the new poor as those whose situation depends on their previous status, educational attainment, availability of savings and assets such as their house, personal capabilities and social network.[86] Their structural basic needs were covered, but with the drastic reduction in their income they could no longer afford their lifestyle. Their network of contacts was crucial in delaying the decline in their status but they no longer felt a sense of belonging with them. They understood the world differently from the structural poor and were demanding of society and the state. They were the poor with a voice.

The bricolage process of reform was slapdash in restructuring the welfare state. The old institutions regulating the relationship between state and society were restructured by top-down design that left incomplete or overlapping regulatory frameworks and various institutional gaps. In the circumstances X of being sick or old, the known Y of appealing to the welfare state was no longer valid. Under certain X' the provincial or municipal governments could assist, under other conditions X" new private actors were available and in some other X''' agents were left to their own devices. All in all, social action was unstructured and uncertain, and eventually depended on the own discretion of agents.

Revolt and the return from neoliberalism

A general balance of what happened in the first half of the 1990s is difficult to make. Unlike previous periods of economic downturn, the structural reforms of the decade led to an unprecedented redistribution of power and wealth. The rationalization and restructuring of the private and public sectors had two faces, the one of the winners and the other one of the losers. On the one hand, there was modernization and progress for the strata of the population that could then access better but more expensive goods and services. On the other hand, there was social deterioration and disenfranchisement for other social segments that were introduced to the novelties of economic failure, unemployment, and impoverishment. Unemployment replaced inflation as the most acute socio-economic problem and the definite fall into poverty affected many.

Under the new rules of action the economy was growing and inflation was under control. There was less state intervention, a more competitive private sector with a modern infrastructure, lower inflation rates and an open market in which technologies, inputs and credit were available. On the downside, many failed to understand the extent to which the organization of the economy had changed or how to adapt to it in order to resume their activities. In 1995 there was a recession again, but many of the practices that guided social action in those situations were no longer valid. A part of the toolkit of institutions stopped being useful.

The economic crisis of 1995 hence proved to be a first moment of awareness. New collective actors were formed within civil society and organized a series of initiatives combining income generation with a political project. The *Red de Trueque* was among them. It was the beginning of the attempts to reorganize socio-economic life, collective action and re-establish forms of representation. It would still take a while for them to be able to achieve widespread mobilization and demand a turn in political orientation.[87] In fact, president Carlos Menem was reelected for a second mandate that year, and was believed to be the only one that could steer the country in the crisis.

Argentina's recovery after 1995 was rapid but not enough to compensate for the fiscal deficit which was being financed with external debt. The currency board system left the Argentine government with no instruments through which to mediate the onset of crisis and the problem of capital flight. The economy was unable to withstand the effects of the global and regional turmoil that resulted from the Asian crisis of 1997, the Russian crisis of August 1998, and currency devaluation in Brazil soon afterwards.[88]

The moment of truth for Argentina's development model came then. In 1999 the country suffered a moderate recession (−3.4 per cent), which was met with more deregulation and structural reforms. A new government, formed by the opposition party, took office in December 1999 with its entire campaign based on reassuring the public that it would maintain the peso's peg to the dollar and continue implementing the Convertibility Plan. Unfortunately, it was able to do little to spur economic growth and one of its first measures was to raise taxes to correct the fiscal deficit. It was an unpopular measure at home though blessed by the IMF abroad. Tax increases delivered the Argentine economy directly into a recessionary trap with higher budget deficits and further cuts in government spending.[89] It was the beginning of the longest and deepest productive retraction in Argentine history. The economic demise of four years skimmed 20 per cent of the GDP between 1998 and 2002.[90]

At the turn of the millennium, the financial system was doing no better than the real economy. Banks were running out of cash and the Central Bank out of reserves. In March 2001 the Argentine financial system suffered its most intense outflow of deposits in the decade. The currency board was crumbling so the government limited bank withdrawals to a certain level, a policy known as *corralito* (fencing-off). This measure had a devastating effect on those who had moderate amounts of money in the bank and depended on cash to cover their needs, that is, the middle class, firm owners and shopkeepers. Those with larger savings had already sent them abroad. In September 2001, unemployment reached 20 per cent and 40 per cent of the population were below the poverty line.

The fiscal cuts applied to the provinces, too, some of which historically had high public employment and protests started there.[91] Instead of reducing costs and spending, several provinces decided to issue their own currency to pay wages. These were referred to as '*cuasi*-currencies' or surrogate money.[92] In September 2001, the provincial currencies represented 5 per cent of the national monetary base. Decreasing tax revenues pushed them up to 25 per cent in January 2002 and 33 per cent in October 2002, as shown in Figure 3.5.[93]

Figure 3.5: Provincial currencies as percentage of monetary base. July 2001–Oct. 2002

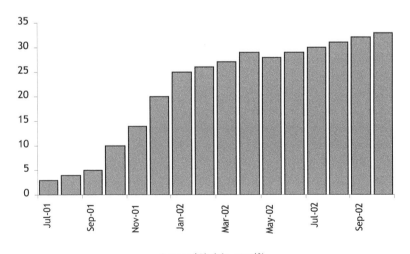

Source: (Chelala, 2002)[94]
Note: Total amount of provincial monies issued as percentage of the national monetary base

By then, well consolidated collective actors were reorganizing social life independently from the state, ensuring representation through new channels and promoting alternative income generation schemes. There were the *piqueteros* movement, groups of unemployed that organized roadblocks to press for political demands and economic support.[95] There were the *asambleas barriales*, neighbourhood assemblies with an initial massive participation, practising direct democracy behind the slogan 'out with all of them' in reference to cronies and traditional politicians.[96] There were regular *cacerolazos*, more or less spontaneous demonstrations of the middle class in which people went into the streets banging pots as a sign of protest and discontent.[97] Biased to income generation rather than advocacy, there were the Trueque and worker-run companies.[98] All in all, they were the expression of the break of representation between government and society, a frontal rejection to a self-serving and corrupt governing class and a loss of faith in neo-liberalism.[99]

The situation exploded in the last weeks of 2001 with popular upheaval, riots in supermarkets, and civil unrest. President De la Rua resigned on December 2001 and left the government's house on a helicopter. A few weeks of provisionary governments and panic succeeded until Peronist Eduardo Duhalde, head of the Low Chamber of Parliament, gained institutional command as president. He sought above all to restore traditional forms of governance and stability and called for a new alliance between state, markets and civil society. Appealing to the residual legitimacy of the national development project that had been overturned in the 1990s, Duhalde turned back to the old rules of action guiding socio-economic behaviour.[100]

In the weeks around the turn of 2002 the successive governments announced the default over the public debt, the end of Convertibility, the free floating of the exchange rate and the compulsory transformation of dollar-denominated debts and deposits to pesos. When the dollar was allowed to float freely, it reached a devaluation of 300 per cent in a few weeks. The year 2002 was written down in Argentine history as annus horribilis, with 56 per cent of the population under the poverty line. According to official figures, out of an economically active population of 12.5 million, 2.7 million were unemployed and another 2.9 million involuntarily under-employed. Around 5.5 million of those employed were in the informal sector. In May 2002 the government decided to implement a welfare policy by giving the equivalent of 150 pesos in the state's unofficial money to each unemployed head of household in exchange for community work. The plan was critical in re-establishing some rules of action in the relationship between the state and the society.

The 300 per cent devaluation proved extremely effective in boosting exports and there was a quick rebound. The default on the debt gave the fiscal accounts air to pursue other social policies to recover domestic consumption. There were also some price controls, crucial utility tariffs were frozen. Export taxes on popular consumption products were established to compensate for the higher real international prices and avoid inflation, while it was also a source of revenue for the government. Surprisingly, Argentina began to recover markedly and some started talking of an Argentine miracle. It entered an expansion period with GDP growth rates between eight and nine per cent a year (2003–6). The fast and consistent recovery began in 2002, accumulating a total increase of 34 per cent by the first semester of 2006. The population under the poverty line dropped to 31.4 per cent and unemployment, to 11.6 per cent by the same period. Inflation rates were under control.

In May 2003 Nestor Kirchner was elected president and continued reverting the Neoliberal model of the 1990s, with a strong commitment to employment creation and re-industrialization. The conditions regulating the operations of privatized companies were renegotiated and when that did not work as expected, some utilities were re-nationalized. The devaluation, the default on the public debt and record prices on exports explain much of the economic recovery miracle.

One of the main goals of the Kirchner administration has been to recover the developmental state institutions that organized economic life under the import substitution industrialization model. The efforts can also be read as the skilful manoeuvre of political elites to re-establish the legitimacy of the state and capital.[101] Key to that goal is to reincorporate the collective actors, protest social movements and unorthodox income generation schemes organized by civil society in the 1990s (*cacerolazos*, road-block groups, neighbourhood assemblies and *Redes de Trueque*) into the political and economic mainstream. At the beginning of 2007 it is still early to assess the blend of old and new rules of action that guide economic life after those last bricolage reforms.

Why did Argentina have Redes de Trueque?

The emergence and expansion of the *Redes de Trueque* in Argentina in 1995 is clearly related to an economic demise. If economic progress had continued and the majority of the labour force had maintained their jobs, the *RT* might never have existed. They are closely related to the economic crisis, but this analysis covers only part of the story.

Other countries have experienced comparable socio-economic downturns in the last decades.[102] Within Latin America, Venezuela saw its GDP shrink every year between 1998 and 2004, with the exceptions of 2000 and 2001. The worst years were 2002 and 2003, with declines of –8.9 per cent and –7.8 per cent per year respectively. In 1998 the Asian financial crisis skimmed 13.3 per cent of the Indonesian GDP and 10.5 per cent of the Thailandese GDP. In Africa, Angola lost 24 per cent of its GDP in 1993 to war and political instability. The contemporary extreme in economic demise is Zimbabwe where economic output has fallen every year since 1998 and accumulated a total decline of 35 per cent in real terms by 2006. All of these countries show severe and long-lasting economic downturns, which translate into unemployment and impoverishment, but none of them has hosted a complementary economic system like the *RT*.

The explanation of why only Argentina had a complementary currency system of the scale of the *RT* cannot be found in the fall of the GDP and unemployment alone. Deficient macroeconomic performance sets the background conditions for them but it is not enough to explain their emergence and expansion. This chapter proposes an institutional or mesoeconomic approach as additional element which entails an evolutionary look at the economy. This explanation accounts for the loss of faith of many Argentines in the regular economy and its capacity to solve their needs.

Argentina is exceptional among the economies of the world. From one of the richest countries in the world in 1900, it collapsed into a developing country a century later. By the turn of 1990, three hyper-inflationary periods clearly signalled that the import substitution industrialization model had to be reviewed. A structural reform programme was then launched to reorganize the economy in line with the Washington Consensus. There was barely any understanding that the structural reforms were not being applied on a tabula rasa but on an institutional legacy that allowed agents to make decisions and take actions in the economy.

The construction of a complementary economic system is explained as a reaction to the deep institutional reorganization experienced when Argentina changed developmental models. The country moved from an inward-looking import substitution industrialization to an outward-looking deregulated model. The Great Transformation, seconding Polanyi's expression, was done as a bricolage process. There was little consultation, preparation or full disclosure of the rules implied in the new development model. The conversion from one developmental model to the other required changes in socioeconomic action that took time to assimilate. In the transition, institutional gaps arose (unstructured segments of social action). Circumstances X had been replaced by X' and yet Y' was unclear and uncertain by virtue of the bricolage reforms. Therefore, many agents continued to follow the old rule doing Y in circumstances X' with the unsatisfying result that they did not obtain Z. For them, a period of economic disorganization followed. Resources then fell idle because many agents did not know how to put them to use profitably in the new reformed economic structure. Other groups adapted faster or took the institutional gaps as opportunities. The transition thus generated winners and losers, redistributing wealth and power.

An evolutionary analysis of the transition from one model to the other discloses a particular combination of old and new institutions that led to the emergence and expansion of the *Redes de Trueque*. Firstly, the rules of action regulating the monetary system were quite unique. Argentines had quite a flexible understanding of the meaning of money and of what means of payment were acceptable for the various social situations. The Convertibility Plan formalized the already engrained practice of bimonetarism into legislation. Ironically, it was the most effective solution tried in Argentina in five decades to curb inflation and it was implemented against the recommendation of the IMF. Its executor, the Economy Minister at that time, explains that its success was based on understanding money as one of the main institutions in the economy, one that cannot be simply structured by political decision and architectural design.

In contrast to what happened in the monetary system, in three of the four sectors analysed in this chapter there was a top-down imposition of new rules of action. Specifically, the effect was that many industrial firms were not run successfully and went bankrupt, workers became unemployed or underpaid, and the poor did not receive the education, health care and pensions they had grown to expect.

As a result, a new class appeared: the new poor. These were agents socialized in a middle-class identity, with the consumption patterns of a middle-class lifestyle and accumulated middle-class assets they could no longer afford. For the new poor the world had become unstructured and incomprehensible. They felt abandoned by the welfare state, which had made them poorer in terms of lost entitlements.[103] With their economic decline, the economy had also lost an important segment of consumers of goods and services that went beyond basic necessities. The myth of the large, dynamic and well-off Argentine middle class vanished along with them, as well as the belief in upward social mobility that went with a lifetime job.

The traditional organizations representing the voices of discontent were trade unions which had been co-opted into the government. They thus left an institutional gap in terms of representation, and new organizations had not yet been formed to fill the gap. The negative effects of the reforms were not evident until the economic crisis of 1995, so the motivation to organize resistance was not high enough until then. The middle class fell into poverty without being able to understand what was happening to them. As depicted in Figure 3.6, after 1997 there were people blocking roads, neighbourhood associations and workers in occupied factories.[104] The *RT* was not the only reaction.

So why did Argentina have the *Red de Trueque,* while other countries struggle through comparable economic downturns with other systems? In an attempt to resolve their economic life, agents relied on the institutions that had guided their behaviour until then. The *Red de Trueque* was hence launched in 1995 as a market to exchange goods and services, in an attempt to recreate segments of the market that had been destroyed by the structural reform policies. The idea of printing currency seemed a natural step in a country where central and provincial governments had done so in contexts of economic distress. In Argentina, money was far from an untouchable institution.

Certainly, other countries have undergone reforms with similar bricolage logic. Economic life there has been unstructured in institutional gaps as happened in Argentina. However, there were various important differences. The structural reforms in Argentina were implemented in a big bang, affecting all the important institutions severely and simultaneously. When reforms were implemented in developed countries, as in the United Kingdom in the 1980s, the welfare state was not dismantled to the point of leaving its citizens disenfranchised as happened in Argentina. All in all, the irresponsiveness and weakness of the welfare state system marked a difference. Developing countries that underwent similar disruptions of their economic life did not have a middle class comparable to the Argentine one, part of which was pushed into poverty. Self-help networks and survival strategies common among the structural poor were weak or insufficiently developed by the time the new poor needed them. This was a second key difference: the new poor were numerous enough, used to demanding solutions from the state and eventually capable of organizing civil society associations. Many of the unemployed also had technical skills and a small amount of capital from savings or a redundancy payment. They had never experienced unemployment and had perhaps tried self-employment with little success. This was a third relevant difference: unlike many developing countries, there was no vibrant informal economy of low-income work to resort to during economic downturns. The one Argentina had was not a counter-cyclical employment option but a well-paid personal choice.

There was yet another important factor that added to this explanation of why Argentina hosted a complementary economic system. Unlike other countries where CCS exist, the Argentine government did not repress it. At first it was indifferent and later found it useful to keep social peace. There are suspicions that some Peronist local cronies may have contributed to the decline of the *RT* around 2002.

The *RT* fully accommodates the old economic practices of the new poor. It is based on the idea of participants being self-employed and using their technical and entrepreneurial experience in a small protected market. It recreates an inward looking protected market and protects the work ethics of the middle class.

Figure 3.6: Relationships between policies, effects and institutions

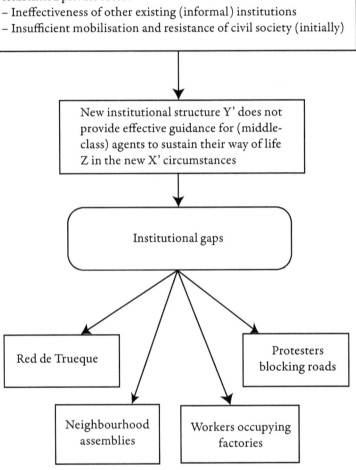

4 LAUNCHING THE CLUB DE TRUEQUE

The *Club de Trueque* appears as a pioneering complementary scheme to make an income in a period of economic hardship. The notion of a group of neighbours making their own money to exchange commodities in a suburb of Buenos Aires sounds extraordinary. However, the *CT* was the final outcome of a series of small innovations achieved by trial and error. The process included considerable hesitation and frustration on the part of the organizers.

This chapter looks at the *CT* as an example of a social network that made its own market institutions to exchange goods and services. The monetization of their system of payments with scrip was part of that construction. The *CT* is hence presented as a scheme that combined small innovations with overall continuity in the line of Argentine history.

All over the world market institutions are being organized as clubs to trade an endless variety of commodities, from new financial instruments in New York to maize and potatoes in the Andes to unwanted Christmas presents through Internet auction sites. Complementary currency systems, as presented in Chapter 2, are another example of these organizational efforts. The owners of the commodities search for an institutional infrastructure where their goods can change hands, and in circumstances when it does not exist, agents can elaborate it. Those fit in the category of designed institutions. Markets are defined as a mode of coordination under scarcity in which transactions are mediated by prices over which buyers and sellers compete and reach agreements.[1]

The Social Organization of Exchange

Modern societies are characterized as market societies, with monetarized exchange of goods and services dominating circulation and organizing the social order. Markets are a mode of coordination, in the sense that they present relatively stable relationships of otherwise disparate activities or events.[2] Coordination means that tasks and efforts are made compatible, while bottlenecks and other disjunctures are eliminated. Agencies are ordered, balanced, brought to equilibrium.

The 'market idea'[3] represents a central principle of social order, of integration and coordination that is both specific to modern societies and part of its most profound values. It permeates patterns of political, social and cultural organization.

Until the beginning of the Industrial Revolution, the majority of resources which were produced and consumed were related to a system of self-production and self-consumption (a non-monetarized system). The Industrial Revolution accelerated the process of specialization and exchange, either implicitly (non-monetized) or explicitly (monetized) with reference to the value of money.[4] Money enables a person to sell a product one day and 'store' the value in the form of currency till a purchase on another day, unlike with barter where one product is exchanged for another simultaneously.

Adam Smith wrote enthusiastically about the origins of this market society with monetized exchanges, the birth of many manufacturing activities and the flourishing of commerce in a nation that was still predominantly based on traditional agricultural activities.[5] Later, Polanyi was less enthusiastic when analysing 'the great transformation' of the nineteenth century, pinpointing the negative effects of the market capitalist society regulated by 'market prices and nothing but market prices'.[6] The individuals' sphere of action was circumscribed solely by their material means and the rationality with which they could deploy their market power. Such a transition could be understood as liberation of reason, freedom and progress from the irrational constraints of tradition, as Smith saw it, or as the erosion of communal life and decline of any social values that might stand above the merely economic measure of price, as Polanyi saw it.

The primacy of market exchange has increasingly marginalized and restructured other modes of exchange, though the real extent of this domination is disputable.[7] Different forms of exchange are appropriate for different social relationships: to lend money to a friend is different from a bank's logic when giving a loan. Modes of exchange are reflections of particular social settings, and on a more global level they reflect a certain social order. A simple overview of normal everyday allocations of all sorts of goods and services would be enough to illustrate the enormous diversity of the repertoire of exchanges a society has to offer.[8] By the end of the day agents have given food to their children, snatched a pen from the office, bought food in a supermarket, paid the electricity by direct debit, lent money to a friend, donated a few coins at church, exchanged fidelity card points for a gift, bought a lottery ticket (and won nothing), paid a toll for the use of a public highway, walked in a park maintained with tax money, sold a few second-hand books on eBay, and finally invited friends for dinner who had invited them the week before. The list of ways in which goods and services are passed along between social actors can be extended indefinitely, reflecting the complexity of overlapping social relations and networks, values and meanings, ethics and cultures.

What would induce agents to construct market institutions for monetized exchanges, rather than forms of coordination? The Austrian School tradition claims that markets are the superior form of coordination because they possess a unique capability to process the huge amounts of disparate information that is necessary to coordinate the plans of individual economic agents and achieve the maximum utility possible.[9] Their argument is that as long as individuals act in their own interest and make calculating decisions, the final result in social terms cannot be other than the optimum. Although the superiority of the system may be a consideration in persuading agents to create markets, there is evidence that in some circumstances markets are not the most efficient form of allocation. These are, for example, in the Prisoner's Dilemma situation and where there are distortions caused by asymmetric information, excessive market power, bounded rationality, externalities, restrictions on demand revelation, and public goods.[10] Hierarchies, networks and state regulations are then put in place to correct market imperfections. In addition, markets and the institutions regulating them are quite diverse. Price-mediated exchanges are affected by social considerations such as gender, ethnicity, proximity, so price coordination overlaps with a variety of relations of trust, law, shared values and so on.[11] These social considerations distinguish one type of market from another. The reasons behind creating market institutions for monetized exchanges are therefore not uniform either: they vary by the intentions and interests of the agents making them, the kind of market they had in mind and their social setting.

Club Markets as Designed Institutions

The idea that different market institutions are the outcome of the intentions and interests of the agents that created them and therefore guide actions divergently was already advanced by Fernand Braudel's concept of 'private' markets, as opposed to 'public' markets.[12] In public markets, participation is open to all and their institutions guide everyone's actions, while private markets are restricted to a closed network and their institutions apply only to its members. For Braudel, public markets are a gate through which local actors, actions and objects circulate in economic life, away from the non-market self-sufficiency of traditional domestic production. Private markets are exclusive to quite a different type of participant and operate above, behind and between the public markets. They are restricted to meetings and activities of those included in a particular network, in which participation is possible only through invitation or belonging to a certain group.[13] They function under the rules defined exclusively by and for the members. Braudel blames the decline of public fairs on private networks that he describes as 'anti-markets' that exclude non-members.[14]

More recently, other authors distinguished 'public markets' being subject to intensive state regulation from 'private markets' emerging in attempts to escape regulation.[15] However, they do have regulation but through market institutions that apply to a selective network of members. As said, such markets are the outcome of the values and intentionality of their members, who may also define restrictions to access. In that sense, it would be more precise to refer to them as 'club markets'. They are a variation of the 'private orderings'[16] and constitute 'private interest governance'.[17]

Club markets are markets that are built by strategic (collective) action and that, as associations that provide goods consumed jointly without rivalry but where exclusion of non-members is possible.[18] By non-rivalry they mean that a good can be consumed by one individual without reducing the consumption opportunities of others; of course, this is true only within a certain range. By excludability they mean the costless possibility of withholding access from others. When benefits are excludable but non-rival, the definition of club applies. In the case of markets, what is excludable and non-rival is the application of the market institutions and the access to buying and selling directly. Members choose not to allow non-members to buy and sell, but if the latter do become members they do not reduce the access of prior members, within limits, of course. At the same time, members refer to the rules of action prevalent in that club market and which are different to those in other markets. Cornes and Sandler[19] elaborate on the following characteristics of clubs.

Firstly, privately owned and operated clubs are voluntary, which means members choose to belong because they anticipate a benefit from membership and are willing to contribute a membership fee to support the club. In club markets, this means traders choose to exchange their goods in that setting because it offers them a benefit over trading in a public market, assuming that the latter exists. Members are willing to contribute to the club market's organization or finances.

Secondly, Cornes and Sandler[20] observe that clubs involve sharing, which leads to partial rivalry in consumption beyond a certain scale of crowding or congestion. As membership expands, there are benefits from sharing costs among more individuals but also losses in terms of deterred access, quantity or quality. The members may then decide to freeze membership at its current level. In the case of club markets, this would mean, for example, that beyond a certain scale trading would entail higher transaction costs. Therefore, the scale of the club market is finite because of its very nature, unlike that of public markets where size limitations may be caused by factors such as infrastructure (for example, by the physical size of the market).

Thirdly, Cornes and Sandler emphasize that when they face exclusion, non-members may decide to join or form another club. When the fragmentation is defined by geography, non-members may build their own club in their jurisdiction. In the case of club markets, non-members can trade in a club market ruled by their own institutions, in competition with one in another jurisdiction.

In short, strategic agents can create markets when they perceive that an appropriate setting for trade is missing. Thus, markets do not emerge out of acts of nature, but out of the purposeful action of agents who perceive an institutional gap. Markets constructed by strategic action are regulated by internal institutions and organization, including rules of excludability. It is in this sense that this study terms them club markets.

Markets 'Made to Order'

Club markets are regulated by the institutions designed for them. There are no markets 'in the beginning', as Williamson[21] claims, but 'after' economic agents brought them into existence.

In medieval Europe, chartered cities had the right to establish a market to support the population centre or build a new town around it with attached houses, workshops and shops.[22] Merchants were associated in guilds, which negotiated agreements with local rulers to create markets with guarantees of punishment for contract violations and later also monopoly rights.[23]

More recently, when physical commodities such as agricultural products lack a marketplace, one is constructed by agents. For example, Garcia[24] describes the case of a market for fresh strawberries in the south of France, established by sellers and the local government to fight power asymmetries that were biased against producers and make power relations more equal. A similar reaction is seen in the Netherlands and other European countries, where horticulture producers create their own auction markets in an attempt to counter the market power of large buyers playing sellers off against each other.[25]

Auction markets on the Internet, linking buyers and sellers among private individuals, have become a multimillion business in the last two decades. These have been constructed mostly by private corporations. A top concern is to generate trust between strangers.[26]

Financial instruments are traded in stock markets around the world, increasingly shifting to electronic market mechanisms to facilitate the meeting of sellers and buyers and the achievement of a clearing price. Insurance markets are in this category too.

The first *Club de Trueque* (*CT*) was created in a Buenos Aires suburb in 1995 after a local association began promoting recycling and vegetable-growing projects to help the disenfranchised middle class. Members did achieve a significant rise in their income, which enabled them to increase their consumption and replace some of their previous consumption in pesos with consumption in vouchers, thus saving pesos for other needs.

What do these examples of markets, in appearance so diverse, have in common? Above all, they are markets that have been elaborated by reflexive action following intentions and interests, either individual or collective. They belong to the category of designed institutions.

The examples also highlight the activity of the 'market-makers', a class of strategic agents responsible for organizing the designed market institutions. The market-makers design the 'playing field' for trade to take place, defining rules of entry, participation and exit, and ways to enforce them. Sbragia[27] uses the term 'market-builders' to refer to the state organizations that frame and regulate a market, as the Central Bank does, for example. However, market-makers are not limited to the public sector; they are often found in the private sector too (for example, industry associations) or in civil society (NGOs). Their motivation ranges from making profit as a business company (like the Internet auctions, financial stock markets and medieval merchants) to altruistic behaviour (like the *CT* and NGOs) or a redistribution of power (like the strawberry market in southern France).

The role of prior institutions is fundamental in the market-building process, which can only occur if there is already an institutional structure at work. Newly created institutions depend critically on the primary institutions. For example, new markets can only be constructed where private property and freedom are engrained, because if a central authority coercively appropriated surpluses there would be nothing to trade. Or if actors did not have minimal civil liberties to transport and exchange their produce they would not be able to engage in commerce.

Fourthly, the social networks where they originate play a key role. They are formed by the agents that initially engage in trade as producers, sellers, buyers, or referees. They are assumed to have acquired the habits and routines of market exchange, which is indeed the case for anybody living in a market society. In addition, engaging in trade means that the agents own or manage production surpluses to sell, and have skills, machinery, working time, capital or inputs. The interests and intentions of embedding social networks affect the actions of the market-makers.

These are all examples of club markets, as they are excludable and non-rival, at least for a finite scale. Participation in Internet auction markets is for registered members only and they can be expelled if they break the membership rules. Membership is free but sellers are charged a fee, and they are partitioned by country. The system is similar in the markets for physical commodities and financial instruments. In the early days of the *CT* in Argentina, only individuals referred by members could join and they were required to sign a document specifying their agreement with the principles of the organization. They highlight that the market-building process needs three fundamental elements: market-makers as a strategic group that bears the organizational costs; an initial network of members with market experience, available surpluses to trade and to participate in a club market; and working prior institutions that guarantee minimum stability to the functioning of markets.

Now that a typology of markets has been clarified in relation to excludability and rivalry, and the reasons for building club markets as well as the conditions for creating them have been discussed, the question arises as to how the process works for these elements to form a club market and link it to the existent institutions.

From Social Action to a Club Market

Social and economic action is informed by the three types of institutions discussed in the Introduction. Most routine or typical problems can be solved by the pre-reflexive tendencies and rules of appropriateness developed from experience.[28] These are the evolved and the prior institutions. However, there are new situations for which individuals have no pre-reflexive responses, so they require reasoning and intentionality. The institutions developed in these situations were termed designed institutions. This section picks up from there to frame a model of social action by which the three categories of institutions interrelate.

The relationship between institutions and individual behaviour describes an action-information loop going from one to the other (Figure 4.1).[29] As long as the routines lead to the expected results, agents do not need to change them.[30] In circumstances X, agents have a disposition to do Y and obtain Z. This regularity is precisely the strength of institutions. However, when a new situation appears or the results are not in line with the learnt expectations, this loop can no longer explain action because there are no pre-reflexive tendencies to guide it. What the agents have are intentions and interests to elaborate rules of action.

Figure 4.1: The institutional action-information loop

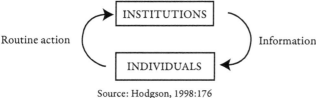

Source: Hodgson, 1998:176

In economic contexts of complexity, the loop is incomplete. According to Beckert, uncertainty makes it impossible not only to identify the best solution but also to link the causal relationship between means (strategies) and outcomes accurately.[31] Every situation has several readings judged as adequate responses by the actors. They resolve the crisis by experimentation, in which possible future states are considered along with the strategies to achieve them. Experimentation represents a creative achievement on the part of the actors that demands imagination and judgement, taking a reflexive distance from routine courses of action. Consequences are evaluated and tested until an acceptable solution is reached. The 'acceptable solution' need not be the 'optimal' one, but it resolves the problem.

The process is depicted in Figure 4.2. The information–action loop is now reconfigured into two loops. In the upper loop, agents in a standard situation X are inclined to do action Y, as in the model presented earlier. This will be termed the continuity loop. But the model now has a lower loop, in which agents face new, uncertain, complex situations. This will be termed the innovation loop. It is relevant when there is insufficient information in the continuity loop to find a response, no set course of action. Rational learning agents perceive an institutional gap in the form of a 'what is to be done next' question. Reflexive action takes over routine and the 'skilful actors' begin their innovation and learning.

The experimentation process is guided by pragmatism.[32] During experimentation, the prior and evolved institutions have a role as enablers and persuaders

Figure 4.2: Institutional action-information double loop

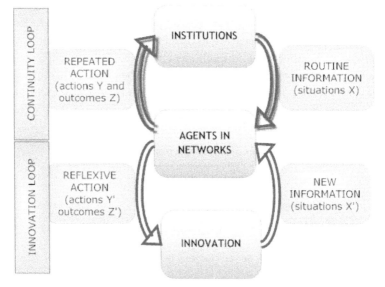

of action.[33] Experimentation is a social process in which diverse social networks define what is possible and what learning is achieved. Learning means the development of new representations of the environment in which they operate, new preferences, propensities and conceptual frameworks.

When actors succeed in framing a new rule of action and repeat it in similar situations, then 'something new enters the world'.[34] There is a new rule of action: in circumstances X' do Y'. It is a 'novelty',[35] although in rigorous terms it is only partially new because it is based and depend on pre-existent institutions. It does present an innovation in the sense that it is a new way of reducing complexity and asserting intentions and interests.

Designed institutions result of the transition from the elaboration to the repetition of action. It subsequently becomes locked in and social networks spread it. This is how the third category of institutions defined in this study (designed ones) relates to the second category (evolved ones). Agency restructures itself in what Hodgson terms 'reconstitutive upward causation'.[36] The author describes with this term the process by which elements of a lower ontological level affect those at a higher level. The process is compatible with Giddens's 'structuration theory' within sociology, which links structure and agency.[37] The inverse process is 'reconstitutive downward causation', when prior institutions inform and inspire the formation of designed ones.[38] The three categories are hence interrelated in the creation of market institutions.

Launching the Club de Trueque

The creation of the *Club de Trueque* (henceforth *CT*) in Argentina is discussed in this section in relation to the concept of club markets and from the perspective of the theoretical model of economic action developed. The macroeconomic context was characterized by profound and sudden changes in the organization of the economy. Especially for the middle class, the old routines and understanding of economic life were no longer valid. In addition, the national currency was a weak institution due to hyper-inflation which precipitated the creation of other socially accepted means of payment (national and provincial bonds).

In the *Club de Trueque*, the initiative to construct a market came from the market-makers themselves. It was the brainchild of two grassroots groups which were never formally registered as NGOs: *Programa de Autosuficiencia Regional* and *Red Profesional*. It was their first successful project after several failures. As with many other social processes, it is hard to determine the exact date of the *CT*'s creation, but the market-makers give the official foundation date as 1 May 1995. The choice of this date reflects the founders' wish to honour their personal history of defending workers' rights and socialist militancy. However, the process of creating the *CT* began much earlier and it framed the evolutionary path of what would become one of the main social phenomena in Argentine economic and social history of the 1990s.

The *Programa de Autosuficiencia Regional (PAR)*, founded in 1989 in the Bernal Quarter of Quilmes municipality, a southern suburb in the metropolitan area of Buenos Aires, was a publisher of environmentalist newsletters. It was led by psychologist and environmentalist, Carlos de Sanzo, and museum expert, Ruben Ravera. It was created to tackle both economic and ecological problems at the same time, restoring value to resources that had been labelled 'valueless waste' by others. It spread environmentalist practices through a newsletter called 'Hacemos Ecología Práctica' (We Practise Practical Ecology).

After the hyper-inflation and economic collapse of 1989, *PAR* launched an urban small-scale agricultural project using appropriate technology called Tecnohuerta. However, urban agriculture initiatives were not sustainable because hunger was not perceived as a serious social problem. While the project had little success it did help to build a motivated network in the course of many workshops and discussions. A routine also evolved among participants to give away or barter surplus vegetables, a routine that reinforced the feeling of belonging to the network. By the beginning of 1994 *PAR* was unable to summon enough participants to keep the project running.[39]

In terms of learning, the leaders realized during the Tecnohuertas project that people did not just need initial technical assistance that could be found in technical texts, but group interaction to provide support during the start-up of their micro-enterprises. They started *Emprendedores Anónimos* (Anonymous Entrepreneurs). This was a self-help group to help risk-averse individuals make economic decisions. As De Sanzo explained, 'As a psychologist, I tried to apply group therapy methodology to the problems of micro-enterprise creation. I had the idea that the method could help some people overcome their risk aversion'. The programme was implemented for most of 1993 and did provide some social interaction between participants, but it did not trigger any realistic productive initiatives. Perhaps the programme presented too much innovation and too little continuity of known practices.

By the beginning of 1994 *PAR* was once again unable to secure enough participants to justify any of its ongoing projects. It then came up with yet another innovation; the core members had been experimenting at their homes with breeding red Californian worms to transform rubbish into organic compost. During 1994 *PAR* distributed thousands of free boxes of red worms at different sites (40,000 in total). Everything was funded through the personal income of the leaders, but again the project did not catch on. By the end of the year, the organization was going bankrupt, unable to find sponsors to fund its initiatives or find a financially sustainable project. On the learning side, this failure taught

PAR that the formal market economy was not ripe for projects with a strong environmental goal.

A second group, completely independent of *PAR*, was involved in the creation of the *CT*. The *Red Profesional* (*RP*) was founded in 1992 by chemist Horacio Covas and a few friends, scientists, engineers and technicians related to the chemical, pharmaceutical and cosmetics industry. It facilitated information flows on labour opportunities and informal cooperation among members to provide assistance to small firms in developing cosmetic and pharmaceutical products. The members were self-employed consultants who obtained contracts from small and middle-scale enterprises and were paid fees for their services, as in the rest of the economy. By the end of 1993 many of their clients were badly affected by the opening up of the economy and several members of the *RP* then started accepting payment in kind as an alternative to not being paid at all. Covas recalls that he accumulated several thousand of dollars' worth of cosmetics and beauty products that he could hardly sell direct to consumers, not having the relevant marketing expertise and connections. Others accepted paper, wood, aluminium and hard plastic bottles, thinking they could resell or recycle them to earn money. Covas then sought advice from his old friend De Sanzo at *PAR*, whom he had first met at the age of seventeen when they were militants in the Socialist Party. They started exploring recycling as a possible source of income.

By the end of 1994 the two groups integrated their networks in a new project that combined the various stages of the economic cycle. They wanted production, trade and consumption to take place within a local exchange network where all the participants would contribute and benefit from each other's capabilities and resources. They were inspired by the evolved market institutions but recreated as a club market, with only those who supplied products being allowed to buy from each other. The new project was driven by a practical need: to improve the falling incomes of those who had been part of the Argentine middle class and were by then sinking into poverty.

The informal exchange of goods within a closed network of impoverished middle-class members was initially carried out in Carlos de Sanzo's garage. Participants offered and accepted home-made foods, handmade toiletries, organically grown vegetables, and handicrafts. The previous informal practice of exchanging surplus vegetables was extended to an array of environmentally friendly cosmetics, toiletries and cleaning and beauty products. In the beginning, members used nicknames to protect their identities, since all of them had friends and family who had suffered persecution during the military dictatorship and they were afraid of the scheme being interpreted as subversion. As socialist militants, they disliked the idea of recreating a capitalist market, but as Covas put it:

> Not all markets are capitalist, driven by profit. The market is a much older set of
> institutions; it is a social activity of giving and taking, of being creative, belonging
> to a network. What we recreated was this reciprocity system based on sharing own-
> work. Anyway, we had nothing against capitalism per se, but against what the crisis
> had done to us.

By around March 1995, after six months of experimentation with about twenty-
five participants meeting every Saturday, the group developed an exchange system
they found to be effective and practical. Participants came into the garage and
placed their products on a table. The value was calculated at the formal market
prices and was recorded on individual cards carried by the participants and on a
computer worksheet. When the value of everyone's products had been recorded,
all the participants went out and then returned as consumers to choose their
'purchases'. The value of these was deducted from the amount on their cards.
Thus, the higher the value of the products brought, the more that producer
could get of other people's products. Any producer who did not agree with the
price given to a product was free to withdraw it, but that hardly ever happened.
When people thought the price was low, they viewed it as a partial gift to others, which they would recover some other time when they obtained something
below the regular price. When they left, their 'purchase' was entered as a debit
on both the card and the computer worksheet. In this way, the balance roughly
returned to zero every week.

The system thus emulated a board game based on production and exchange
that Carlos de Sanzo and Ruben Ravera had used in the past for other projects.
They contend that it also contained elements 'combining environmentalism and
Trotskyist socialism', none of which were really priorities for the initial participants. From another angle, it was a recreation of evolved and prior institutions.
In the continuity loop, goods changed hands through a mechanism that resem-
bled the well-engrained practice of market exchange. It was multireciprocal, so
two individuals did not need to barter with each other directly. In the innovation loop, the payment system was a novelty. Transactions were recorded as
credits and debits in a computer system designed by Horacio Covas. It was an
ingenious transformation to standard market exchange, a club market with its
own rules. De Sanzo recalls:

> It was something everybody could follow. If you came in as a new member, it didn't
> take you more than a few minutes to understand how it worked and how much it
> could help you. It was self-evident. This was one of the main strengths of the scheme.
> It was something everyone had done before, but we were doing it in a different way.

In the early days of the *Trueque*, two goals were pursued: to create a socioeconomic system that would promote self-help among crisis-hit neighbours and to
recover the values and institutions that used to be the sociability model among

the middle class.[40] In other words, the *Trueque* was expected to support the participants not only economically but also socially. De Sanzo explains:

> We had little knowledge of the discourse of the social economy in which we got involved later. But we did know that we wanted the *Clubs de Trueque* to be a space where people could meet again. In our eyes, the Argentine middle class had had a lot of spaces to meet, to interact. The economic crisis first did away with a big segment of the middle class and then with these spaces. We wanted the *CT* also to help people get together again, to heal the social fabric.

When newcomers asked about the origins of the *CT*, the three founders used the story of one of the participants, Ana, to capture the experience vividly. Ana was a participant in the first *Club de Trueque*. Founder Carlos de Sanzo was harvesting too many pumpkins from his home garden and had a surplus that he termed 'idle pumpkins'. Ana, a pensioner, was going through an economic crisis, so De Sanzo gave her some of his pumpkins. Ana joined the *CT*, making pumpkin jams and sweets and over a year she 'earned' the equivalent of three times her pension. This true story was widely used for marketing later on.

The reality of the *CT*'s development, however, was less romantic and included mistakes and frustration. De Sanzo remembers that 'it was a social experiment under the sky, painful trial and error'. Covas says,

> For us it was an ideological turn. The armed struggle proposed by Trotskyism when we were younger got us nowhere. Now we were fighting in a different field, recreating a market that was not capitalist and not for profit. It was a market for and by neighbours, a new capitalism.

In the beginning, participants brought mainly goods that they produced at home. There were fruits and vegetables from the participants' gardens, various prepared foods and ready-to-eat meals, some artcrafts and home-made organic toiletries and cosmetics elaborated by Covas' group. Market-maker Ravera tested with making his own beer, which he described as a 'success' when the market meeting was finished.

The recreation of some old market elements in a new club market format is reflected in the name. The scheme needed a label to be introduced to the public, something easy to understand that would appeal to everyone. 'Multi-reciprocal exchange' was accurate, but long-winded and complicated jargon that would be understood by very few of the target group. Also, there was more of an element of innovation in it than the leaders wanted. Other alternatives such as 'Gift club' and 'Gift market' were considered, but they gave the impression of charity rather than reward for work. Finally, '*Club de Trueque*' was suggested and approved. The characteristic of being a closed group to which there was no automatic right of inclusion was captured by the word 'club' and the aspect of exchange was expressed by '*trueque*' (barter or exchange). Of course, it was not barter, since trade was mediated by prices expressed in the official unit of account, but exchange fitted.

Why Don't we Make Some Money?

In the first six months of its formal existence, the learning process in the *CT* continued as new problems appeared and situations changed. It was clear from the start that the *CT* had a strong gender bias, as it continued later. At least 70 per cent of the participants were women. As observed by other researchers[41] middle-class women were the most affected by the slide into poverty, as it deprived them of access to the public spaces they were used to visiting, and quickly accepted the proposal of the *CT*. Covas links it with the idea of institutional gaps:

> During troubled times people seek solutions where they are used to finding them. Men went to the labour market, women tried things at home and in the margins of the labour market. Women often told us they felt comfortable because their daily unpaid work suddenly had a value. They cooked food for the household and received affection. They cooked the same dish for the *CT*, naturally involving a little more effort, and received a payment with which they could buy food, clothes, or little luxuries.

Used to unpaid work, women were the first to understand that the *CT* offered satisfaction of needs without the mediation of money. The *CT* links directly to the reproduction of life: it 'fills the fridge, paints the home, gets a plumber to fix the pipes', Covas said. Esther, a middle-aged head of her household of three, explained:

> Women are not really interested in carrying money in our pockets but in getting things done. For example, I needed to have my watch fixed but I never had the five pesos for the batteries. I made some cherry pies in the cherry season and a young man in the Club fixed my watch. For someone like me, struggling to make ends meet, these little achievements are gifts.

It soon became clear that book-keeping on the basis of individual cards and computer records was a poor mechanism. As the membership reached sixty, De Sanzo and Covas felt that entering Saturday's transactions into the file the following day was too burdensome. Besides, Covas did not like the centralization inherent in the system:

> It was dangerous. I entered the data, so I knew who traded what and with whom. I was at the centre and we didn't like the idea of centres. As ecologists, we believed in autonomous self-regulation, like the environmental system is. The system of cards was blocking the potential of the scheme.

Updating records to allocate what belonged to each participant reflected the unquestioned belief in private property within the *CT*. As engraved in the name of the scheme, nothing was given, nothing was lost. People obtained benefits in relation to the work they put in. So the founders started thinking of an alternative without the use of expensive technology that would allow the *CT* to expand. The replication of the *CT* in other locations became an ambition of the market-makers as soon as they saw the system was working. According to De Sanzo, the initial success and potential of the scheme to alleviate the economic problems of the disenfranchised middle-class neighbours made them 'want to spread it everywhere'. Covas claims ideological reasons for its success:

> It was a modern or adapted version of what we struggled for. The nineties were no time for revolutions, it was the decade of neoliberalism. But a grassroots economic initiative that turned its back on the capitalist market, on waged labour and on exploitation had a much better chance of success.

At that point, the exchanges were made directly between buyers and sellers autonomously, like in most markets. The three leaders saw that the *CT* had tremendous potential because many people in the country had surplus goods, skills and production capacity. However, they felt the full impact could not be unfolded due to the small size of the group and because it was still new and uncertain. In the hope of finding partner groups, they re-established contacts with socialist and environmentalist militants, offering workshops on the scheme in Buenos Aires city. The goal was to 'infect others with our enthusiasm', says Covas. That goal was achieved at the beginning of 1996, when a second group was formed in the city and a third in a northern suburb.

The successful propagation of two more *CT* made the limitations of the individual card accountancy system more evident. It was time once again for reflexive action and innovation. Founder Ravera proposed printing vouchers for fixed amounts to be used in the *CT*. He recalls, 'One day I was walking by a print shop and saw their business cards. Then I thought, "Why don't we just make ourselves some money?". It was just about printing, right?'. The others liked the idea of using fiat money because of its practicality and because it removed *PAR* from the centre.

Time and again, small variations of old institutions won the preference of the *CT*. At first sight, it seems a major innovation for a civil society group to print its own money, but in Argentina it was not. It was an innovation on the practice of using several currencies at the same time. As explained in Chapter 3, there was already a second main currency circulating in the country as means of payment (the US dollar), plus smaller instruments of exchange such as provincial currencies. Additionally, the vouchers created by *PAR* were not called money but vouchers or *créditos*; simple pieces of paper that circulated among the members of a closed network. That is, one of the institutions of a club market.

They initially experimented with a means of payment that could only be used once. They called it 'unidirectional money'. Those who paid with that money as well as those who received it had to sign each note and at the end of the day all the vouchers were submitted for a sort of clearing-house operation. This was another experiment that did not work because it was too complicated and time-consuming. Covas recalls,

> Participants were already making promises to pay each other in the following meeting in order to avoid the paperwork of keeping records of every transaction. But how many promises of how many people can you actually remember? The vouchers made exchanges between persons more autonomous and removed us from the centre.

Surrogate currencies were instituted, one for each *CT*. In comparison with the card system, physical vouchers were easier to handle. 'Simple, it had to be simple or else we wouldn't be able to replicate it. It had to be cheap and convenient for users', observes Covas. Once again, the founders were able to recreate existing institutions, attract people's support and let them develop into disposition to action. Everyone understood how money worked but nobody saw the vouchers as a substitute for official money. The currency of the *Club de Trueque* was conceived as means of payment within a club market, very different to regular money supported by a state. Anyone in the network would accept it, but it was not convertible to pesos outside the club. The vouchers were simple photocopies cut by hand, with a red stamp and the signatures of the initiators. They were printed in denominations following those of the formal economy. They were generically known as 'exchange coupons' and depicted a tree as a reminder of the ecological orientation of the initiative. For pricing purposes, each unit was equal to one peso, or one US dollar under the exchange rate parity. The unit of account was called a *crédito* (credit) because 'we all give each other some credit'.

There was still further experimentation in those days. It was assumed that anyone who could produce for a certain value would have the right to print its own vouchers for that amount. This would have meant a complex system of as many different vouchers as there were producers that wanted to print them. Of course, such a system relied on reciprocal trust that the vouchers would be accepted by all users as payment for products. In reality, people only used the vouchers issued by the *CT* market-makers. Apparently, the leaders were the ones who were trusted most. This finding is consistent with Dodd's claim that 'maintenance of trust in the organizers of a monetary network is vital to trust in the currency itself'.[42] Besides, the network clearly did not have perfectly horizontal relations and the participants gave some authority over the *CT* to the market-markers, although they denied it.

The printing of vouchers to circulate as fiat currency among the participants of the various clubs unleashed the potential of the initiative. It transformed the *CT* from a curious experiment into an income option. In line with the club market characteristics described above, accepting *créditos* in exchange for goods was voluntary and committed members to sharing the costs and risks. The *CT* currency facilitated exchange and represented the main way in which the club market excluded non-members. Only those who sold goods for the vouchers were members and therefore able to buy other producers' goods.

Participation had clear benefits, but trading goods for a colourful piece of paper entailed clear risks. What led people to believe in the system was that, at least initially, there was no real awareness that the *créditos* were a kind of money. Covas says:

> Each member accepted vouchers, trusting that they would obtain something in exchange. It was a social contract people believed in. People were really convinced that the *crédito* was a piece of paper they could use to give and take things from each other. It was credit among participants. Nobody saw it as a reserve of value or at the same level as regular money.

For most participants in the *CT*, the scrip was not comparable to regular money. It was just an easier and cheaper way of transferring credits and debits to each other, eliminating the work of keeping records. They mostly saw it as an instrument that made Covas' life easier, rather than facilitate or speed trade within the network. An elderly participant recalls:

> Those days I made aubergines and other vegetables in oil. My son thought I was getting senile, because I spent half day cooking and exchanged the food for those funny little papers, as he called them. Then my grandson's birthday came and we didn't have money to celebrate it. So I said 'this old woman will pay for it'. I got sandwiches, a cake, a pullover to give him as gift, and even a clown to entertain the children, all paid in the *créditos*. Oh, then the little papers were not so funny any more. That day I laughed. I was so happy!

A Market and a Currency for Members Only

As a club market, the *CT* was a mode of coordination to exchange goods and services within a closed network. Excludability was ensured by the voluntary acceptance of a non-official type of money and the risks entailed in such decision. *PAR* had proof enough of the availability of idle resources (labour, land and technology) and the commitment of individuals to start organic agricultural micro-enterprises, but the infrastructure to trade – the *market institutions* – was not there. It had to be developed, which the market-makers did within their network. The *CT* was a creative arrangement to provide a small-scale market for a network of neighbours to use their idle resources.

The functioning of the *CT* depended on several working institutions of the regular economy. Among others, the recognition of personal property rights, functioning of courts or informal mediators for conflict resolution. Whether transactions were effected through a system of cards or complementary currency, the principles of market exchange were still present. Initially, regular market prices were translated into *créditos*, incorporating the relations of power implied in them. Private property and the right of the prosumers to trade goods freely were undisputed. Additionally, the *CT* was also linked to the Argentines' routine of bimonetarism by adding a third option – the *créditos* – to the list of possible means of payment. The creation of a currency parallel to the official one would have been illegal or bluntly rejected in other countries, but in the Argentine case it was within the acceptable responses. People were used to living with two currencies, so why not three?

However, participants did not perceive the first vouchers as money. Trade was already happening with verbal promises to pay each other. When scrip appeared, it monetized those promises, eliminated the work of keeping records and removed the market-makers from the centre. It highlights an issue in terms of the emergence of money: there was first a social network in which agents trusted each other and then it was possible to generate physical means of payment on this social relations. The point relates to Ingham's conception of money as a social relation, rather than a disembedded tool to reduce transaction costs.[43] In recreating a market as a club was a strength of the system in comparison with other alternative economic activities because it implied integration of the three phases of the economic cycle: production, exchange and consumption. By supplying the club market, participants demanded from it in an equal amount to that which they contributed, so consumption followed trade, which in turn followed production. De Sanzo argues:

> The strength of the *Club de Trueque* lay precisely in this integration of all the phases of the economic cycle for a certain group. In projects that don't integrate them, you cannot really be sure of the final result. That's what happened to us in previous projects, there were stages missing.

At an aggregate level, the card accountancy system used in the beginning was different from the use of a currency. Monetary creation would follow exactly at all times the rhythm of transactions and was not limited to an amount fixed a priori. In this sense it was an endogenous monetary system as described in the post-Keynesian literature.[44] It regulated itself autonomously to the amounts traded, so monetary inflation was not possible.[45] Later, the system with surrogate currency enabled saving for the next meeting, so production was equal to consumption only in the medium term. It was still an endogenous monetary system, but it regulated itself to the number of users of the currency, not the amounts traded.

A crucial factor that helped the *Club de Trueque* to take off was the social stratum to which most of the participants belonged. The fall of the middle class was a dramatic process for Argentina.[46] It was not a normal situation to which people could adapt, because adaptation implies that individuals are capable of making sense of their social environment and this was not so with the disenfranchised middle class.[47] On the other hand, the new poor participating in the *CT* could make sense of the market it emulated. It had innovative elements but was still based on familiar elements such as fixed prices, purchases equal to sales (which could be increased if they raised production), benefits based on own-work, payment in currency. It thus implied a partial recreation of their known world, while it added the social interaction of a network of equally disenfranchised middle-class members also trying to avoid the final fall into poverty. The new poor were gradually becoming excluded from the public market as they were affected by institutional gaps. They were learning that a wage was no longer sufficient for the entire household, that the welfare state was not going to help them and that they had to compete with cheaper imports if they wanted to maintain a small firm. While facing labour vulnerability or unemployment, they also had idle resources and capabilities to use. It was assumed in the club market that the participants had idle or discarded resources that could be used, reused or recycled, in the form of skills, machinery, tools, leftover inputs, or perhaps a small amount of financial capital. And, of course, free time to put to work.

The *CT* was not meant to reduce poverty in Argentina but to alleviate the effects of the decline into poverty of a particular sector of the population. It did not work as a desperate survival strategy, but as a patch on an institutional gap for people who had known better days. It was based on trading products and services, not on gifts or charity, not on promoting a short-term survival strategy, and it was not a social movement demanding a welfare policy from the government, all of which were more common characteristics of the structural poor. It promoted the creation of micro-enterprises and autonomous employment, which were traditionally seen in Argentina as middle-class activities. If the initiative had been embedded among the structural poor, its organization would probably have been different.

In many ways, the *CT* also represented a return to a closed, protected economy, where technical capacity to produce on a small scale was more important than competitiveness. As a club market, it excluded from the supply the products made by non-members, so it insulated prospective micro-entrepreneurs who could not bear the uncertainty and complexity of the regular economy. They faced lower start-up risks and had more time to learn. The small scale kept interactions personal, though it was large enough to provide demand and justify being called a market.

The construction of club markets with or without its own means of exchange comes to the fore as a tool for the regeneration of communities hit by unemployment and poverty during economic restructuring. The absence or instability of markets that work for the poor and unemployed hinders their income-generation efforts. This adds to other aspects of exclusion, like barriers to obtaining working capital, lack of information on how to locate demand, and aversion to taking the risk of not selling. Some of these barriers could be overcome in a market society by helping the poor and unemployed to build a club market in line with their needs. An obvious pre-condition is that a club market can only help those who have goods to offer or the capacity to produce them or to provide services (resources, skills, initial assets such as tools or working capital). This means it is not suitable for the poorest of the poor.

The relationship between the innovation and the continuity component is important in economic regeneration and development projects for low-income groups. The failure of the *PAR* to develop successful projects before the *CT* illustrates this point. While their first schemes proposed markedly new income-generation activities, with the high complexity and uncertainty that entailed, the *CT* only required a small move away from the old, well-known and understood market exchange principles. The combination between innovation and continuity was clearly more acceptable. These groups of agents would naturally be more averse to participating – investing their time and money – in projects of uncertain outcome. They would rather compromise resources and participate in projects that were consistent with the evolved and prior institutions, well-known and understood.

The case of the *CT* raises a final issue concerning the evolutionary theory of institutions. While *PAR*'s previous income-generation projects did not prosper into established institutions, they did leave 'footprints' or traces that were useful later for the creation of the *CT*. The practice of exchanging vegetables, the formation of a self-help network and the receipt of payment in kind were all elements derived from the earlier failures. Therefore, institutional evolution is based on both, the routines that graduate as institutions and the learning from failed experimental courses of action. Hence, every experience contributes to accumulating knowledge that may be useful for future institutional design.

5 FROM CLUB DE TRUEQUE TO NETWORK

While the first *Club de Trueque* was basically another case of social networks making market institutions, the second stage of the evolution of the *Redes de Trueque* in Argentina was undoubtedly unique. During the period between 1996 and 2002, the *RT* grew more than any other CCS in terms of scale, scope, regulation and geographical coverage. First dozens and then hundreds of *CT* emerged across the country, each one with their own rules and currencies but all integrated in a single network with a common regulatory body. This type of organization was unseen in the history of complementary currencies.

Increase in scale and scope of markets implies a transition from personal transactions to impersonal exchange.[1] Commerce becomes more complex, giving birth to uncertainty and rising costs of trade generically known as transaction costs.[2] The growth from personal to impersonal exchange demands more sophisticated institutions to reduce uncertainty and complexity. It implies a challenge on the efficiency of the system, its distribution of power and the inter-personal social relations on which it relies. Efficiency is defined as the minimization of waste, which includes costs of all types.

The analysis in this chapter starts from a small market, as the *Club de Trueque* was in the beginning. Transactions were embedded in a network where all traders knew and trusted each other and personal contact was enough to regulate economic action. However, as the amount of participants and the complexity of the exchanges increased, clearer and more transparent rules on an impersonal basis were needed. The making of those institutions demanded further innovations and intricate negotiations between the original organizers, the new leaders and the plain participants. How did this process take place? What drove the emergence of institutions of impersonal exchange? The word '*Trueque*' is used henceforth to denote an economic activity, whereas *RT* addresses an organizational structure.

Costs and Benefits of Expanding the Market

Specialization and division of labour have made possible improved productivity arising from technological change, better resource allocation and specialized production, the key underlying features of modern market economies. The evolution of impersonal market forces is critical in this process because it allows economic agents to interact across time and distance, fostering productivity growth. However, it also increases the costs of exchange. Neoclassical economists underscore the point and assume that trade is costless or barely costly, so it does not affect the economy. Other economic perspectives claim that the costs of exchange are important and exert a large impact on economic performance.

The definition of exchange costs and their relevance to economic performance are the departure point of the transaction cost literature.[3] The basic unit of analysis is the transaction rather than the commodity. What is assessed is the capacity of institutions and governance structures to minimize transaction costs. This view of the transaction as the basic unit of economic analysis was already advanced in 1934 by John Commons, a founding father of Old Institutional Economics, as credited by O. Williamson.[4] Commons advanced that governance structures mediate the exchange of goods and services between technologically separable entities. In Commons' analysis of different types of transactions, the capacity of different structures to harmonize relations between agents is central and leads to a process of institution building.

Picking up on Coase,[5] Williamson[6] elaborates the process as a comparative institutional undertaking. Alternative governance structures receive explicit attention. Williamson argues that with a well-working interface in the market, transfers occur smoothly. Otherwise, there are frictions between the parties, misunderstandings, conflicts, delays, breakdowns and other malfunctions or 'market failures' that add to uncertainty and increase the total cost of exchange. Provisions need to be made to reduce transaction costs, but this is also costly.[7] Transaction costs are defined at the micro level as costs other than price incurred in trading goods and services,[8] or, from a more macro view, as the costs of running the economic system.[9]

The two behavioural assumptions on which transaction cost analysis relies, and which distinguish it from neoclassical economics, are the recognition that human agents are subject to bounded rationality and the assumption that at least some agents are given to opportunism.[10] Bounded rationality is the generic term for limited competences of economic agents to process information (receiving, transmitting, storing and retrieving it) when formulating and solving complex problems[11] (Simon, 1979). Opportunism is described as seeking self-interest with guile, disguising attributes or preferences, distorting data and confusing transactions in different ways.[12] Bounded rationality and opportunism burden transactions between unknown partners, which North refers to as 'impersonal exchange'. By definition, when exchange is personal, transactions are embedded in a social setting of trust and common values that reduces these two problems.[13]

Douglas North explains disparities between developed and developing countries by the way they resolve transaction costs and uncertainties. He sees a direct link between economies of scale and specialization on the one hand, and transaction costs on the other. Development is a consequence of successfully achieving the transition from personal exchange to impersonal exchange. Small groups can transfer goods between members with 'simple personal exchanges'; that is, individuals engage in repeated dealings with each other or have a great deal of personal knowledge about each other's attributes, characteristics and features as well as each other's products. Norms of behaviour are seldom written down because trust is the crucial element in facilitating transactions. Formal contracting does not exist and formal specific rules are rare. Therefore, transaction costs are minimal where there are dense social networks. However, production costs in such societies are high because specialization and division of labour are limited to the extent and needs of the small group and its market.[14]

At the other extreme in North's analysis is a world of impersonal exchange, in which the wellbeing of individuals depends on a complex structure of specialization and interdependent ties extended in time and space. Transaction costs are higher among strangers because there are potential gains in cheating, shirking and opportunism. Measuring the attributes of what is being traded and enforcing terms of exchange becomes problematic and, even if viable, costly. For that reason, during their historical growth process, North elaborates, Western societies devised complex institutional structures to constrain agents' actions, reduce uncertainty of social interactions and prevent transaction costs from rising too high.[15] They have defined and effectively enforced property rights, formal contracts and guarantees, corporate hierarchies, bankruptcy laws, and so on, to enable gains from larger-scale production and improved technology to be realised. The presence of strong third parties – mainly the state – helps to resolve conflicts and enforce contracts. Informal institutions such as codes of conduct and beliefs are seen as efficiency-enhancing, too, but of a lower relevance given that they are only effective as long as the benefits of opportunism are not greater than the costs of compliance.

Developed countries seem to have succeeded in building a battery of more or less formal government institutions to provide an environment to deal with conflicts, regulating and stabilizing economic action on the basis of the exercise of authority. In contrast, in developing countries like Argentina imperfect markets predominate and government failure prevails.[16] States have constrained capacities and resources to set the rules of the system. Incomplete information results in incomplete markets and eventually in costly legal provisions. The 'costs of running the system' under this uncertainty are significant, caused by both market and government failures.[17]

In the case of club markets made by interest groups, expansion poses an organizational dilemma. In small economies, uncertainty and transaction costs are marginal, but they do not achieve the benefits of efficiency attributed to increased division of labour. To achieve specialization and efficiency in the realm of production, it is necessary to increase the market scale. However, more division of labour entails more trade between specialized units and these exchanges become more uncertain as the market expands. The problem, therefore, is how to maximise the benefits of specialization while at the same time minimizing transaction costs.

Club Markets: to Expand or Not to Expand?

Within the Institutional Economics perspective, the trade-off is resolved by building institutions as enablers and persuaders. Institutions organize individual and collective agents' actions in economies of impersonal exchange. Coase, and later Williamson, highlight the writing of contracts to protect transactions and building hierarchies as a complement to market exchange.[18] North argues that institutional devices are built to reduce scope for opportunistic behaviour.[19]

How are institutions built within a club market, in order to allow trade to expand to the scale of diversified economies and impersonal exchange? Although they are not elaborated in relation to the problem of scaling up from personal to impersonal exchange, Robert Boyer and J. Rogers Hollingsworth discuss 'three major interpretations' as different 'views of the world' that contribute to the explanation of how institutions emerge.[20] Each interpretation gives prevalence to one type of intention over the others and has its own strengths and weaknesses. These are approaches of New Institutional Economics, Economic Sociology and New Political Economy.

The New Institutional Economics centres on the idea that institutions are devices to increase economic efficiency, mainly in relation to solving transaction costs and uncertainties.[21] Self-interested agents with bounded rationality build institutions to govern their strategic interactions with the goal of achieving the optimal coordination in every market. From the Old Institutional Economics perspective, some authors note that explaining institutions as the end-product of the actions of individuals seeking to minimize transaction costs implies that individuals start acting in an institution-free environment.[22] This is hardly the case; agents build institutions starting from already existing structures, embedded in values and identities. A central question then is, what came first, transaction costs or institutions? In an evolutionary perspective, institutional design is at most the best achievable result within certain constraints but not necessarily the most efficient in terms of transaction cost minimization.[23] Other authors contend that the success of designed institutions depends on their effectiveness in enforcing claims, not on their allocative efficiency, so while institutions may be efficient in reducing uncertainty for some groups, they may raise it for others.[24]

The Economic Sociology approach follows in the footsteps of Karl Polanyi and has moral embeddedness of relations as its main concept. It argues that economic relations are socially embedded, constraining self-interest, allowing actors to circumvent the limits of pure rationality, and modifying the interactions typical of anonymous markets. Markets are supported by trust among actors, which lets them believe in the fulfilment of transactions.[25] Trust is the set of expectations about others' actions that could result in a negative response if not fulfilled.[26] It develops gradually after a learning process of trial and error, not as a conscious or rational choice but as the result of generalization of experience. It thus affects decisions to act in a certain manner, reducing exchange risk and uncertainty and diminishing the likelihood of having to enforce contracts. Among the benefits of trust are that agents exchange fine-grained information, solve problems together and can generally arrange the coordination of their economic actions in a more effective way than on the basis of the simple information contained in prices.[27] In a way, trust repersonalizes exchanges within networks that have built 'bonds and bridges'.[28] These networks grow by adding members with referral in a word-of-mouth system, in which trust is transferred to newly introduced actors.[29] In this way, transactions are less uncertain, not as a result of what the newcomers have done but because of the institutions existing before they joined the network. These have the capacity to limit self-interest and opportunistic behaviour. The main weakness of this approach is the vagueness of the explanation: how is trust developed and why do some individuals prefer to cooperate instead of behaving opportunistically? After all, the traditions so useful today for developing and sustaining economic activity are the outcome of past (collective) actions.[30] Perhaps also missing is the notion that negative social relations such as hatred, distrust and rivalry may play a part.[31]

The third approach corresponds to the New Political Economy perspective and centres on the concept of power as the main force driving the building of institutions. Individuals interact as economic agents through market competition, but at the same time they fight for political power, for example, to gain control over the rules of the game and to build asymmetries within the economy.[32] These asymmetries of power and conflicting situations often require corrections based on collective interventions[33] or coercive state action[34] to defend societal values. Political action pursuing divergent interests enhances the formation of economic institutions. Institutions are either points of compromise between actors with divergent interests or frozen points of power asymmetries in which powerful groups are able to cement their strength. Eventually, if the process of trial and error with the use of state power is sufficiently careful, a coherent regulation mode may emerge and deliver 'a superior configuration of institutions for almost any or all actors'.[35]

These three approaches were elaborated as general theories to explain what drives institutional building and design, and not specifically to explain what enables scaling up from personal to impersonal exchange in club markets. Each of them suggests different interests and intentions guiding institutional design: to improve efficiency, accumulate power and attend social relations. They are not mutually exclusive but act jointly, though one or another prevails at different points or with different actors. According to the first approach, in their quest to increase efficiency agents make institutions to reduce uncertainty, while power and personal bonds remain as contextual forces. In the second approach, agents make institutions to promote or protect their bonds and bridges and the traditional morality that embeds their interaction, while power and efficiency seeking are secondary motivations. And in the third approach, agents' main intentionality is to increase or resist power asymmetries in a political struggle, keeping the efficiency aim and social relations on a second plane. The interrelationship is depicted in Figure 5.1.

A final point on which the three approaches converge is on the problem of path dependency in institutional design, although each one considers it with a different emphasis. Path dependency clashes with the notion that existing arrangements are the most efficient in terms of transaction cost minimization. Institutions are resilient structures, so while agents may be perfectly capable of

Figure 5.1: Factors driving designed of institutions

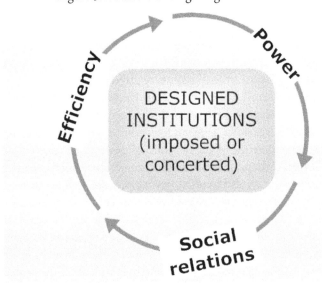

understanding institutional inefficiencies, they cannot do much about them because of the 'enormity of the collective action' to change them.[36] For example, institutions that resulted from the more powerful position of a group in the past may survive in spite of blatant inefficiency because other groups are unable to change them. In turn, organizations performing similar functions tend to be designed very similarly. They follow what the strong and powerful organizations in their environment do or the law of the large numbers, instead of searching what may be most efficient for their needs, scale and strength.[37]

In relation to club markets specifically, as agents perceive the increasing costs of running the system, they engage in institutional construction, juggling the need to increase efficiency, struggle for power and attend social relations. With this framework, the next section analyses the replication and expansion of the *Club de Trueque* into the *Redes de Trueque (RT)*.

Trespassing the Limits of Personal Exchange

The small group of agents that launched the *CT* as a club market followed common rules of action. Growth was initially gradual, mainly through participants spreading the news about the scheme to relatives, friends and neighbours. It relied entirely on word of mouth and thus was still embedded in personal exchange. Anastasio recalls:

> I don't remember what I thought the first day that my sister brought me to the Trueque. My wife had just died and I was very lonely and depressed at home. She told me to go with her. I asked what was I going to do there and she said I should just make some coffee. Why not, I thought. So I went with some thermos. And I learnt that day that just a warm cup of coffee in winter can make someone happy. A month later I invited two neighbours. One made croissants and the other one made hot chocolate. It was like that, each one was bringing someone else.

As membership grew, people travelled considerable distances to participate in the *CT* in Bernal. The market-makers, who were still the main decision-makers, decided distant participants would be better off if they had a *CT* nearer their homes. They perceived the growth of one *CT* alone as being contrary to the ideals of the scheme and were concerned about efficiency in terms of transport and time. De Sanzo explains:

> It made a lot more sense to motivate our participants to organise a *CT* in their locality than to let them travel two hours to come here. The organisational effort was certainly a lot less than crossing Buenos Aires. All they needed was a group of willing neighbours and a bit of know-how, which we could provide. Besides, we wanted to enhance self-reliance and a one-for-all *Club de Trueque* was against that idea.

The leaders perceived the advantages of growth and specialization with considerably clarity. Covas said they thought that 'the impact of the scheme on households would increase by incorporating more members and extending it to other locations'. They reasoned that the scheme had to go beyond the local level to expand its potential and broaden the supply, attracting resources and skills:

> More club markets meant the scheme as a whole got stronger and more accepted, nearer participants, more manageable, with more products and services. In a nutshell, it improved all the *CT*' chances of survival. In October of 1995 the nephew of a participant published an article on us in the Sunday magazine of the newspaper *La Nación*. We didn't look for it, but the days in which the expansion was done by word of mouth were over.

Searching for partner groups elsewhere, the *PAR* leaders renewed old contacts with socialist and environmental militants across Buenos Aires. According to Covas, their goal was to 'infect others with our enthusiasm. We saw it was a very good system, so it was important to transmit the experience. This opened a new phase in our development'. The choice of socialist and environmental militants reflected the existent bonds and bridges of the leaders and may not have been the 'most efficient' choice for expanding the scheme to include the unemployed. Perhaps an NGO focusing on the poor would have been a more obvious choice, but their own existent network was tested and reliable, so it served as platform for the initial expansion.

When there were five *CT*, all the market-makers decided to stay interconnected in order to allow participants of one jurisdiction to trade in another. There was no explicit discussion on the efficiency of the trade or what rules would be best to regulate it. Covas explained: 'It happened almost by inertia that participants moved to visit each other. But everybody got to the *Trueque* through somebody, so everybody was trusted. People were expected to behave responsibly'. Of course, this entailed each group accepting each others' scrip. So there were five different types of vouchers and participants in all five accepted them as means of payment. They thought trade across *CT* would be safe because they were still within the scope of personal exchange regulation. After all, all the groups shared a common past of political militancy and several individuals in each group –usually the new *CT* market-makers – had known and trusted the *PAR* leaders for several years, transferring their trust to the other members. Later research showed that trust was first in the leaders and only second in the *Trueque* as a system.[38] Covas described that trust:

> We saw the vouchers as only a means to facilitate trade, a means and not an end in itself. Why did people agree to hand over their products for just pieces of paper printed by strangers? At that point nobody asked. It was all new and easy. We said the *CT* worked in this way, using vouchers to pay and collect payments. I don't think

anybody thought of them as money. They were there to put in black and white what we owed each other. We all loved the atmosphere of the *CT*, without corruption and greed.

A number of terms came into being. The club markets were termed nodes, from computer science, highlighting the autonomy of units in a network. 'We were a human Internet', is how Covas puts it. The word coordinator denominated the individual that had contact with the leaders and organized the *CT*, the local market-maker. It was chosen over words like 'leader' to emphasize that there was no hierarchy. Coordinators were also in charge of managing the issuance of the scrip, called *créditos*. Participants were referred to as prosumers, linking their roles as producers and consumers in their club market.[39] The word *red* (network) denoted the group of *Clubes de Trueque*, articulated but in principle, autonomous. Covas explained:

> We believed in horizontality, which in our case meant that we were different nodes using a single 'operative system', the scheme invented in the first *CT*. It also meant that if any of the units was lost or the links were broken, the others could go on growing anyway. It was an idea coming from holographic forms of organisation and perhaps a spin-off from my education as a chemist and informatics specialist.

The double role of 'prosuming' fitted especially well with the traditional work of women in the household and strengthened the gender inclination. The *CT* required similar work as that in the household; that is, producing goods to satisfy basic needs (food, garden vegetables) and gendered hobbies (knitwear, handicrafts). The difference was that in the *CT* they would be consumed by other households, giving participants a sense that they were sharing and not just exchanging. As stressed by researchers later, the *CT* was paid housework outside the household, though paid in unofficial currency.[40] A participant recalled in an interview:

> Women are in daily contact with the real needs of the household. They are used to thinking what to cook in the evening and what ingredients they will need. Or how much wool you need for a knit, and so on. It was the same in the *CT*. The big difference, which we loved so much, was that in the *CT* we got paid. It made us feel good to be given scrip with which we could go to somebody else and get something in exchange. The attitude of men was totally different. In the best case scenario, when men saw the activity was helping the household, they carried bags to help their wives but stayed at the door [of the *CT*]. Others came inside but did not participate. They just looked at us with their arms crossed, as if they needed to make it clear that they were not part of the *Trueque*. Sure, the men were unemployed and the women working!

As new and unknown participants joined, the costs of running the system started to rise. It became more difficult to assess the intentions of the new members and their agreement with the principles of self-reliance and environmentally friendly production. Two new members were found using the *CT* as an outlet for expired food products that they could not sell anywhere else. The *PAR* leaders had considerably more clarity on the advantages of expansion than on its risks, as asserted by both Horacio Covas and Carlos De Sanzo interviewed for this study. They could have restricted the scale of the *CT* to the limits of personal exchange regulation, but it took them still a while longer to realise they needed to build impersonal exchange market institutions to prevent the clubs from collapsing.[41]

A pressing rule that the *CT* market-makers needed to establish was the transparency of the currency system to guarantee the value of the *créditos* and some price stability across the entire network. A rule of issuance was then decided, the organizers of the five *CT* agreeing that scrip would be issued at a rate of twenty *créditos* per new participant. They would receive them to be able to start trading when they joined and they were committed to give them back if they left, so circulation would adjust again. The rule of issuance became the first designed institution of impersonal exchange for the whole network. Its aim was to maintain trust in the vouchers as means of payment and to make the system clearer to newcomers. Besides keeping a stable relation between products and money, it worked as microcredit for new entrants to start producing and trading.

The media gave the *Trueque* a boost in August 1996, when the *PAR* leaders appeared in the show *Hora Clave*, a political programme with the highest audience in public TV. It introduced the *Clubes de Trueque* to a large audience across the country and was followed in November by another article in the Sunday magazine of the *La Nación* newspaper.[42] There were already eight *CT*, some of them already outside Buenos Aires. The publicity resulted in a flood of inquiries about how to participate in the scheme and how to start a new *CT*. Several groups appeared interested in replicating the scheme. Four new clubs were launched in the western suburbs of Buenos Aires, which later became the area with the largest number of members and clubs. The network was introduced to the public with the name of *Red Global de Trueque* (Global Exchange Network).

As a result of the media exposure, the scheme grew to the limits of personal exchange regulation. A trust relationship with the new coordinators had still to be built during the initial meetings, which meant a further step towards impersonal exchange. The *PAR* then started offering training courses to prospective coordinators, introducing them to the principles of the scheme and its environmentalist-communitarian ideology, and basically getting to know them. Subsequent meetings were dedicated to more practical matters like choosing the voucher to be used.

The know-how on 'how to create a *CT* in your locality' was becoming increasingly standardized: mobilizing a minimum number of participants, printing vouchers, electing a coordinator and finding a venue for the market. The standardization of the structure of the *Club de Trueque* resonates with isomorphism.[43] Maintaining the model designed by the *PAR* for all subsequent *CT* was faster, cheaper and more practical than framing a local variant. Maintaining a standard format was, if anything, an efficient choice.

Also as a result of the exposure in the media, another NGO, the *Red de Intercambio de Saberes y Cibernética Social*,[44] got in touch with *PAR* and added its efforts to the organization of the *Trueque*. It was led by Heloisa Primavera and Carlos del Valle, experienced activists in socioeconomic projects. They had tried several social and local development projects and Primavera thought the *Trueque* was a scheme with potential. They gave the *Trueque* an academic footing, since Primavera was a lecturer at the University of Buenos Aires. They put the Argentine network in the world map of community or complementary currency systems. They also gave the *Trueque* a slight turn of direction, pushing it into becoming 'spaces of permanent social and economic training on a new economy based on solidarity and reciprocity', as by Primavera and Del Valle put it. The network was renamed *Red Global de Trueque Solidario* (Global Network of Solidarity Exchange).

A final benefit from the media exposure was a new venue. Eduardo Valot, owner of a paper and toiletries company, liked the scheme and offered the abandoned building of what had once been *La Bernalesa*, a textile factory with 15,000 workers. He allowed *PAR* to use the building in exchange for its renovation, cleaning and maintenance. *PAR* inaugurated the venue for its *La Fábrica* (the factory) node, just metres from the cradle of the scheme. At this point (end of 1996), the total number of participants in the *Trueque* was 3,000 in seventeen *CT* spread across several areas of Buenos Aires, Córdoba, San Pedro, La Plata and Mar del Plata.

The scheme was taking on a life of its own and transaction costs grew with scale, as predicted by the theory. Most traders did not know each other and the monetary system was not clear enough. Newcomers were required to attend a couple of training sessions in which the system was explained to them. In the course of a few weeks of trading they became acquainted with the system and other participants. The *PAR* leaders assumed that all newcomers shared the values of the *Trueque* or would come to accept them as they traded their goods. Newcomers were asked to sign a letter of agreement with the main principles of the *Trueque*, which was little more than an informative sheet outlining the values the organization stood for. 'They signed the letter when they joined. This is a system of trust. Once in, we could assume they shared the values of the *Trueque*,' said Covas. The problem was that as more participants joined in, the 'common principles' were increasingly perceived as the principles of the *PAR* leaders.

My Network or our Network?

By 1997 transparent management of the *créditos* was becoming a pressing issue. Not all participants and nodes accepted the vouchers of all the others and it was broadly left to individual discretion. The *PAR* leaders then decided it would be better to reduce the variety of currencies to reduce confusion, make it more practical to move around the club markets and increase the impact on the household economy. To quote De Sanzo:

> We promoted localisation as a principle, but it is a fact that people tend to travel to trade. We saw a significant dissatisfaction with new vouchers because people could not go everywhere with them. So new groups gradually preferred to use our *PAR créditos* instead of one printed by themselves. [45]

The decision by some new *CT* to use the *PAR* vouchers depicting a tree instead of printing their own did not go down well with some coordinators and emerging new leaders, who regarded the practice as an attempt by *PAR* to accumulate power and keep the *Trueque* under their control. The issue came to a head when the network experienced its first case of forgery of scrip in the city of San Pedro.[46] Participants accepted the forged currency in good faith and then found they could not buy anything with it. Clearly, using a non-state currency beyond the realm of personal exchange was going to require regulation of impersonal exchange institutions. To resolve the problem as quickly as possible, *PAR* offered to replace the fake vouchers with their own. In the words of Horacio Covas:

> We were the only ones to propose this because the others perhaps did not have the means to do it. Pesos were required to print the vouchers and other groups did not have them or did not want to spend them. for whatever the reason, we set a precedent that the vouchers of one region could be used in another region with no additional risk. We showed this could be good for more transparent trading.

PAR underestimated or preferred to ignore the developing power struggle over the wider use of its currency. The problem was that while emerging leaders were not ready to accept the centralization of the currency in *PAR* hands, there were no institutional mechanisms in place that could regulate the *Trueque*. The expectation that there would be no shirking by participants was, to say the least, idealistic.

The government of Buenos Aires city then came into the picture, supporting the First Workshop of Multi-reciprocal Exchange. The event was attended by 1,300 and formally introduced the *Trueque* to Argentine society. It was also the first gathering of all *CT*, many of which did not know the others existed. The workshop participants recognized the advantages of functioning as an integrated network in terms of synergies, division of labour, and so forth, but many also resented that *PAR* was more powerful than the others and was trying to impose its rules.[47] 'What made them think this was their network? We were all spending our time organizing things and we were all risking our money in it', objected a *PAR* opponent. 'I saw *PAR* and an anti-*PAR* front, which didn't really propose anything different', recalls Heloisa Primavera. Others agree that the conflict was about leadership: 'There can't be more than one general in an army', observed an emerging leader.

The event represented a new step towards building institutions of impersonal exchange. It inaugurated the practice of meeting regularly, though in the beginning informally and without a structure. More importantly, the currency system of *créditos* was organized to improve transparency. Metropolitan Buenos Aires was divided into four areas (North, South, West and Capital), each with a regional committee to manage the *créditos* common to the region. These were breakthrough decisions apparently intended to improve efficiency and reduce the transaction costs of having so many different currencies. They also solved the asymmetry of power between the *PAR* leaders and their opponents, with the *PAR* voucher being effectively confined to the South region and being managed by the South committee. To what extent this indirect effect of limiting the power of *PAR* was not the main goal of the geographical organization of the network is a matter of discussion.

At the level of the *CT*, the increase in transaction costs was becoming evident in every day trading. Not all members were somebody's relatives who could be trusted by transfer of social relations.[48] Some new participants joined the *Trueque* attracted by the publicity and ignorant of the rules of action that regulate a club market. For them, the institutions expected in public markets still applied: atomistic behaviour, self-interested transactions, rational calculation and work for a profit. For example, a participant who offered hand-painted woodwork tells her story full of disappointment:

> Somebody joined a few weeks ago and he was buying many handicrafts from all of us, the artisans. He got painted woodworks from me, some dry flower decorations from my neighbour, and hand-made candles from someone else. He was selling sugar and cooking oil, things we all need but that you can just get from a supermarket, without putting any of your own work. Yesterday someone told me he saw my handicrafts in a shop. It seems this man was buying in the *Trueque*, selling in pesos and making a profit out of all of us. I will never sell to him again, but he should be expelled from the Club. I told the coordinator but she told me we should vote in the next meeting if everyone wants him expelled. There should be rules, I think, people should not be allowed to take advantage like that.

At the organizational level, meetings became more regular and formal, as well as more conflictive, over the course of 1998. At a second official workshop, the *Jornada de la Economía del No Dinero* (Workshop on the Non-money Economy) the structure of the network was designed.[49] It established committees to discuss specific issues (meaning of solidarity, identity as an alternative economic space, practical strategies to access to basic inputs, relations with other institutions and organizations). Some of the formal rules and regulations for the *Clubes de Trueque* were also defined. The institutions of impersonal exchange were finally formulated. Every *CT* was to hold regular general meetings to choose the coordinator, among other tasks. Nodes were integrated into regions, with a single voucher and common rules of issuance and control. Coordinators were representatives to regional committees, which were responsible for controlling the issuance and distribution of *créditos*.

The national Inter-zone Coordinators' Committee (IZ) was created. The IZ came the highest body in the network and met once a month with two representatives of each area committee across the country. It had a variety of functions (discussing problems, proposing strategies and projects, sharing experiences, and preparing training materials for new coordinators and prosumers). The crucial function was to control the *créditos* issued and distributed in each region, so all vouchers would be acceptable across the country. Each zone would present accounts on vouchers printed and distributed to nodes and prosumers. The Second National Workshop on Multi-reciprocal Exchange, in August 1998, confirmed this design. Primavera, who was a leading market-maker as well as a coordinator and later anti-PAR referent, points out:

> This bottom-up organisation was the most remarkable achievement of the *Red de Trueque*: Not the markets, not the fairs, but this political institutional construction. I admit it was somewhat confusing that the nodes jealously guarded their autonomy while at the same time imposing rules on one another. It was an extremely interesting social phenomenon. We were indeed reinventing the market institutions.

Far from being enthusiastic about the organizational design that came out of these meetings, the three *PAR* leaders regarded it as the politicization of the *Trueque*.[50] The IZ was for them an unnecessarily bureaucratic body that would delay expansion of the *RT* and block implementation of decisions in the network. They viewed the alleged democratization of the *Trueque* as a false pretence to pursue a project burdened by committees, detached from the real needs of prosumers, and very different from the original model.

Table 5.1: Organization of Red de Trueque

Types of agent	Organizations where they participate	Level of operation	Type of relation
Regional representatives	Inter-zone committees	National	Impersonal ties
Coordinators	Regional committees	Regional	Weak personal ties
Prosumers	*Club de Trueque*	Local	Strong personal ties

The original *PAR* leaders concentrated on combining environmental practises with income generation for the new poor, while the new leaders and organizers of the *RT* promoted it as an alternative and a radical transgression of the rules of capitalism. The *PAR* leaders conceived 'a self-help initiative', with club markets and generation of micro-enterprises placed in women's hands. According to Primavera, the IZ promoted 'constructing an alternative economic system in which the rules of competition and self-interested behaviour typical of neo-liberal markets would be curtailed'. It promoted a 'redesign of the rules of the market', to incorporate equality, solidarity and a dose of collective decision-making and sharing of each other's resources.[51] Nodes would no longer be just local markets where prosumers met as equals in trade – theoretically – but the income-generating tier of an alternative economic system where empowerment and democratization from below would start.[52] Thus, the *Trueque*'s new mission was to distance itself from the regular economy. The emerging leaders proposed that it should have neither 'waged labour nor exploitation', but self-reliance and collective autarchy. As described by Powell, 'there were those who see the establishment of an economy of solidarity necessitating an eventual break with capitalist modes of organization, and those who would like to see in capitalism a little more solidarity'.[53]

Coordinators were allocated the task of training participants 'permanently to re-socialise them in a different ideology to that of the capitalist economy'.[54] Embedded in ideological convictions, peer sanctions would keep opportunism and free-riding in check. The *RT* presented itself as a 'state within the state' in a political sense, and not just 'a market within the market' as the *PAR* conceived it. The *Trueque* was no longer seen as a purely economic system, but as a project of social and political transformation, 'taking off the clothes of capitalist socialisation', in the words of an anti-*PAR* coordinator. Many dreamt that, in the long run, it would compete with the established model of 'clientelistic democracy of old-guard politicians' and frame a 'legitimate bottom-up representative republic', explained an anti-*PAR* leader. The *RT* was also expressing the anger and discontent of the impoverished middle class with the government.

The institutional design of the *RT* was also oriented to reducing transaction costs, ensuring transparency and making the network sustainable. As long as all the zones printed the same amount in vouchers per member, the purchasing power of the *crédito* would be stable and more or less equal all over the country. The design also focused on limiting the power of the *PAR*. Some coordinators refer to personality conflicts. Over three years, the *PAR* leaders had made enemies among the coordinators, who supported 'any structure that would reduce their power'. Even coordinators that defined the IZ as 'a distraction from the needs of participants' said it was 'an effective way of limiting these three men in Bernal'. The main challenge of the IZ was, then, to maintain in one body two very different visions of the *Trueque*: the original one, an economic self-help project, and the reformulated one, a political alternative to capitalism.

Heterogeneity among nodes then became a prominent feature. For instance, some leaders believed prices should follow those in the regular economy while others promoted a different price system based on the needs of consumers, as is more frequent in personal exchange regulation. So there were in fact two systems of price-setting. Participants generally preferred to use a mark-up method: production costs plus a profit to reward the labour incorporated. When this calculation was impossible or too complicated, foodstuffs were equivalents, meaning people converted their products into kilos of sugar or flour.[55] In practice there was no unique stable relation between the peso and the *crédito* across the *Trueque*; it varied by product, locality, and trading partner. Gradually, double price-setting lead to differentiated monetary networks:[56] even using the same vouchers trade between regular customers had other prices than between strangers. In practice this translated into various monetary networks of different exchange rates between pesos and *créditos,* within and across *CT*. Ernesto, an unemployed middle aged cook, explains:

> I made pre-cooked pizzas and I had a customer who always bought from me. She used to sell croissants. We used to put our stands next to each other and we were always each other's first customer. When I walked around to buy other things, she would take care of my stand. I did the same for her. Sometimes she had a difficult time with money because she was a single mother with two kids. So I tried to help her and have her three pizzas when she paid for two. I didn't do that for anyone else, but she would have done the same for me, I think.

To sum up, while the institutional design of the *Trueque* responded at times to the intention of improving efficiency and scaling up from personal to impersonal exchange, this was not a constant over time or for all agents. It never ceased to be a factor driving institutional design, but power struggles and social relations between leaders were embedded in the organizational process and eventually explain much of the final outcome. In fact, efficiency was often invoked as an excuse rather than a real justification for decisions. The more agents interacted with each other, the more power struggles and antipathies were aggravated.

Somebody Must Give in

The organization of the *Trueque* around the IZ worked for some time. The nodes informed the regional committees how many vouchers they had distributed that month (the agreement was fifty *créditos* per new entrant) and the IZ scrutinised the accounts of the regions once a month.[57] The meetings also gave birth to a variety of ideas on empowerment and political participation. Both the *PAR* leaders and the anti-*PAR* front had reached a point of equilibrium, but it was an unstable one.

Tired of assemblies and discussions, the *PAR* leaders decided to reorganize the *Trueque* in line with their original project. In October 1999 they announced a method of distribution of vouchers and replication of *CT*, which they called 'social franchise'.[58] It was a practical starters' kit that made it easy to launch a new node. Prospective coordinators received a set of brochures, notices to hang in public places, a document containing the principles of the *Trueque* and instructions on how to get the new *CT* listed.[59] Prospective members were given the principles of the *Trueque* and fifty *créditos* each. Each kit cost two pesos and the money was used to support the organization of the *Trueque* and print vouchers. Launching a node was simplified to the point where it could be done by a determined coordinator in a few hours. The kits could be bought by mail, which saved time, effort and the cost of going to Bernal.

The social franchise had a few important implications. Firstly, it was no longer necessary to have lengthy discussions and meetings to mobilize prospective members for collective action and participation. The *CT* model had become a commodity and the language of 'prosumers', 'co-operation' and 'reciprocity' was replaced by 'customers', 'competition' and 'market acceptance'. Secondly, the *PAR* vouchers were available to anyone who bought the membership kit, anywhere in the country, in an existing or future *CT*. The zoning system of a voucher per region promoted by the IZ could be done away with. The *PAR* vouchers would be everywhere and its management was centralized in the hands of the *PAR* leaders. Thirdly, the IZ had no real function anymore because the transaction costs of using hundreds of local vouchers would disappear if the only voucher in use was the one of *PAR*. There would no longer be regional accounts to check either. Fourthly, the process to launch a *CT* was completely standardized; it was the reign of isomorphism. This did not imply that the *PAR* node model was the most efficient, but it was the one most used everywhere. It had become the institutionalized format for a *CT* and made it difficult for participants to see another model was possible, perhaps a more participative one or with a stronger political component.

For the anti-*PAR* front, the announcement of the social franchise was the final straw.[60] They said the *PAR* leaders were contravening the decisions of the majority as expressed in the IZ and that they had created an anti-participation monster. Even worse, the *PAR* leaders would collect official money for the kits (two pesos for fifty *créditos*), which provoked criticism in a group that radically opposed the use of national money in the *Trueque*.[61] The anti-*PAR* front saw this payment as promoting corruption among coordinators, who had been until then strictly unpaid volunteers. Primavera explained:[62]

> A group in the IZ insisted on banning national money from the *Trueque* entirely. A
> fundamentalist position, perhaps; they wanted to do away with all relations with the
> state, including its currency. If we were reinventing the economy, they said, why not
> reinvent it on our own terms? And then came the social franchise, selling fifty vouch-
> ers for two pesos and replicating a *CT* in every corner of the city. It was outrageous.

The *PAR* leaders found these criticisms absurd, as they explained in their official mailings and during the fieldwork interviews for this study.[63] They said the
social franchise was a 'practical and replicable model to preserve the essence of
the initial project'. It proposed 'common tools to achieve strategic coordination,
economic integration and sharing of resources'. A single national voucher was
more effective for income generation, in comparison to the 'bureaucracy of so
many committees'.[64] It was a 'social' franchise, reflecting that 'there is neither a
purpose to make profits nor to let a few become rich. We pursue the satisfaction
of human needs for all.' With the advantage of hindsight, in 2007 *PAR* leader
Covas continues to defend the franchise as a necessary strategic decision:

> We needed to get a contribution to finance the expansion. And we wanted to defend
> our original vision, which was being changed more and more. For example, coordina-
> tors were supposed to be social entrepreneurs and trade facilitators, but the design of
> the IZ made them political representatives. Of whom? Of what constituency? What
> was their legitimacy? Their mandate was to travel once a month across the country,
> paid by their nodes, that much I understood!

Together with the franchise, PAR started offering vouchers printed on special
paper to avoid possible forgery. However, they did not see this as a serious risk.
They regarded the *créditos* as 'papers to facilitate exchange with no real effect on
the activity in the nodes'.

Once again, the social franchise gave the appearance of being an efficiency-
enhancing institution that would minimize the transaction costs of using dozens
of local currencies. However, efficiency was only part of the intentionality of
the *PAR* leaders. There was a struggle for power to resolve, a struggle to control
the *Trueque*. With no function left for the IZ, the anti-*PAR* front would lose
its base. The design of institutions in the *Trueque* was driven by the search to
accumulate power and was embedded in the antagonistic relationships between
its leaders.

At the level of the *Clubes de Trueque*, the participants were also divided.
Some thought it a great idea to have a single voucher across the network.[65] They
felt comfortable with improving the efficiency of exchange and cutting the risks
of unknown vouchers. Improper behaviour of participants, if any, could be dealt
with through peer pressure and the coordinators' surveillance at the level of the
CT. They understood the need to make a contribution to maintain the nodes, as
long as they received something in return for their money.

> I changed from another *CT* to one in a Catholic school. They had heating, toilets, and the priest always keeps it tidy. He asks us for a contribution at the entrance, but I find it fair. Somebody has to be paid for the cleaning.

Beyond a small groups of agents who expressed their opinions, at the level of the *CT* participants kept on doing business as usual. They did not know what was going on at the organizational level or they did not find it relevant. They realized that certain vouchers were accepted at certain nodes while others were not. But they saw that the scheme was growing and that there were more *CT* nearer their homes. While the regular economy was still deteriorating, they could buy an increasing variety of goods and services with *créditos* paid with their own work. In fact, the *Trueque* was doing better than ever before. Sylvia recalls:

> We had more and more things and every week at the market meeting there was somebody new. Once I saw my hairdresser. She used to do to another *CT*, but in that one they had their own *créditos* so she couldn't go anywhere else with them. I was so happy that she changed to my *CT*, so I could pay my hair cut in *créditos*.

The *PAR* leaders thus pursued the social franchise and decided not to attend the subsequent IZ meetings to 'avoid useless arguments'.[66] The anti-*PAR* groups condemned the social franchise but could do nothing about it. Opposing the franchise, Primavera added:

> I would say that until 2000 the *PAR* scrip was just a regional voucher like any other, perhaps with some privileges because they invented the system. With the social franchise their nodes started growing faster than the rest, attracting members by the hundreds. It was clear that it wouldn't end well, but we couldn't foresee the loss of control that followed!

To the dismay of the anti-*PAR* front, the social franchise worked remarkably well in accelerating the replication of *CT*. Until its inauguration, the number of nodes using the *PAR* voucher was no more than those using others, but within a year more nodes were using the *PAR* voucher than all the others combined. Eventually, the *PAR* centres were the only ones the general public knew, increasing from 400 nodes in 2000 to 1,800 in 2001 and 3,500 in 2002.[67] Participants enjoyed the liberty of going to different nodes seven days a week, even travelling long distances to La Bernalesa, open twenty hours a day, where they could find most goods imaginable. A single voucher proved crucial in terms of expanding the scale of exchange and facilitated trade among participants. It was customary practice – away from the lengthy arguments in the meeting rooms – which eventually turned the power struggle decisively in favour of *PAR*. Primavera attributes this to the artificial dissemination of the voucher and argued:

PAR established this idea that the tree voucher was used everywhere, accepted across the country, convertible against all others. The 'dollar' of the *Trueque*, they said. But this was only half true because when I visited many of the *PAR* nodes I hardly found anything worth buying.

To meet the soaring national demand for the tree vouchers, the *PAR* leaders issued an unspecified amount of *créditos*. Rumours spread that it was way above the agreed fifty *créditos* per member. Refurbishment of La Bernalesa was paid for in vouchers printed and spent without strict relation to the value added in the nodes.[68] Additionally, the *PAR* leaders established regional offices across the country to manage the social franchise, creating their own hierarchical structure. They commissioned a group of assistants to promote the scheme across Argentina, explaining how to open a 'franchised node'. The assistants received a small commission per new member that bought the social franchise kit, in principle to 'cover their expenses' (travel, food, and so on). In practice, the assistants made an attractive profit.

The anti-*PAR* front found this hierarchy a further abuse and debated throughout 2000 how to react. The conflicts between *PAR* and its opponents escalated, though *PAR* rarely attended IZ meetings. The main argument was accountability for the issuance of vouchers, which, according to the anti-*PAR* front, was way out of control. Witnesses on both sides recall that at a meeting in September 2000, *PAR* presented a statement declaring it had printed 4.5 million *créditos*, 3 million of which had been printed under the social franchise. Roughly half were already in the hands of participants, but *PAR* did not specify to whom or where they had been distributed.

There are different accounts as to what happened next, depending on who is telling the story.[69] *PAR* promised to improve its accounts on issuance of vouchers but never did so. According to *PAR* leader Covas, 'given the conflicts with the IZ, it wouldn't have made a difference. The aggressive anti-*PAR* group would have rejected them anyway'. According to an anti-*PAR* leader, 'They couldn't come back to tell the truth, that they had printed vouchers non-stop'. A more neutral leader thinks that 'the IZ wouldn't have believed any accounts, but in my opinion the *PAR* didn't have any. They had lost track, they didn't know anymore how much they had printed'.

At the beginning of 2001, the *PAR* leaders changed the name of their nodes back to *Red Global de Trueque* and formally left the IZ. The very powerful West region decided to follow them and formed the *Red de Trueque Zona Oeste* (*ZO*). Led by Fernando Sampayo, it was second to *PAR* as a target of criticism because it also believed in a large-scale *Trueque* and found the social franchise an extremely practical method for achieving that.[70] However, Sampayo had a project of his own, far from merely following *PAR*. He explains why his network left the IZ:

The *Trueque* should be a catalyser of micro-enterprises like those that stimulated Italy's reconstruction after the [Second World] War. The IZ accused me of using official money – the famous two pesos for the *créditos* – and they wanted to know what I was doing with them. Getting the unemployed back to work, I said! In the IZ we were 600 people and there were 600 different ideas. I proposed we choose five and submit them to a vote, but then I got a list of arguments as to why we shouldn't vote. So I got fed up. There was so much to do to get people back to work, so many things we could accomplish ... Many in the IZ had wonderful ideas, but they didn't seem to implement any of them. They just discussed endlessly.

The *ZO* shared some of *PAR*'s ideas. Both believed in large-scale networks with crowded nodes, 'as many members as there are people willing to come'. They approved of the use of official money to support the nodes. And they preferred less variety in vouchers, so they agreed to accept each other's *créditos*, covering 4,500 nodes with just two vouchers. However, there were also some important differences between the *ZO* and *PAR*, especially in terms of leadership. The *ZO* had a uniquely strong sense of managerial effectiveness, using technology and accountancy systems, and was much less dependent on the goodwill of participants. It was also worried that the *PAR* leaders were issuing too many vouchers. 'I didn't think fighting the *PAR* was helpful. The anti-*PAR* front should have agreed to expand and outgrow the *PAR*, but it did not do so. It was a small tribe in which everybody wanted to be the big chief', said Sampayo. He, too, did not hesitate to make top-down decisions nor was he inclined to form representative bodies.

At this point, the efficiency goal of sustaining impersonal exchange seemed to be no longer part of the institutional design. According to Primavera, the *ZO* could have led the anti-*PAR* front to win the struggle against *PAR*:

> Sampayo was the one person who could have achieved that. He was an entrepreneur. The others were militants. He kept saying we needed to improve the logistics to support our nodes and make a collective fund in pesos. Instead, when *PAR* left the IZ with their ridiculous accounts, the hardliners took over and became inflexible on fundamental rules. Sampayo had no place there any more. We had lost the chance.

Power struggles, however 'inefficient' they could be considered to be in terms of reducing the cost of running the system, became the main driver of institutional design. Officially, the IZ broke up in April 2001, though *PAR* had not participated in its meetings since October 2000. The *Red de Trueque*, understood as one national network linking regional and interdependent *CT*, ceased to exist. There were too many opinions or visions about what the *Trueque* should be: a complement, an alternative or an improved capitalist economy; a new kind of informal economy, a desperate survival strategy, an economy of reciprocity and solidarity; a means to learn participation and democracy or a market by and for the poor abandoned by the state to fend for themselves; an environmentally friendly local initiative; a women-dominated economy. So when they broke up, each one was free to organize the institutions of the *Trueque* they thought best.

A Currency Network Like No Other

In the second phase of the *Trueque*, a handful of small *CT* grew to an articulated network of almost a million members across the country. This posed the challenge of designing institutions to resolve the uncertainties of exchange between strangers. The *CT* was at first a space of personal exchange, an environment of relatively transparent information flows and trust among participants, although it had limited possibilities to gain from diversification. When it grew and was replicated to a network of several dozen *CT*, it became a space of impersonal exchange. Division of labour and specialization became a reality, as did increased uncertainty and transaction costs. The risks of impersonal exchange became a reality.

In theory, the transition from personal to impersonal exchange is made viable by creating market institutions. This was the challenge for the market-makers in the second phase of the *Trueque*: to design institutions for a large-scale network typical of impersonal exchange, while at the same time sustaining the expansion that they believed would guarantee a significant economic impact.

When the group of market-makers split into pro-*PAR* and anti-*PAR* factions, attention was no longer centred on designing efficient institutions to regulate impersonal exchange but on how to deal with diversity, who was behind a proposal, what project it fit into, and which choices weakened rivals. The original market-makers appealed to efficiency-seeking arguments to persuade the new leaders to accept the *PAR* institutions of impersonal exchange. However, this was not enough. Power asymmetries and the embeddedness of personal relations had diverse degrees of priority for different actors at various points in time. While increasing efficiency was the main interest of a group of actors for some time, those still had to negotiate with actors that gave priority to other interests. For example, the efficiency aim justified the option of an articulated network to gain synergy and for structuring the IZ as a system to control each region's issuance of vouchers. At the same time, it allowed a consolidated anti-*PAR* front to face the *PAR* leaders together to balance their shares of power.

Personal rivalries and power asymmetries were central as intentions in the institutional design of the network at different times, relegating efficiency-seeking. Otherwise, the IZ would not have broken up into sub-networks competing for members and resources. Additionally, institutional design may be efficient even when efficiency-seeking does not explain the decisions behind its design. The 'social franchise' was the most efficient method of replication of nodes: simple to establish, fast, and with a single currency generally acceptable across the country. However, it was implemented mainly to win a power struggle and regain control over the *Trueque* and in the long-run it undermined the democratic organization of the project and its goal of enhancing participation. In turn, the infrastructure and capacities to manage a fast-expanding currency system were not in place when the decision was implemented.

There seems to be a weak relationship between the intention to improve efficiency and the outcome of institutional design. It may be the priority for some actors, but not for all. When improving efficiency is the priority, the path to follow does not seem stable and actors shift to other factors at different points in time. In the end, designed institutions may be efficient anyway, even if efficiency improvements were not sought. Efficiency is an outcome; it cannot be evaluated or taken as main motivation a priori. The cause-effect relationship between the aim of improving efficiency through designed institutions and the outcome is weak, if it exists at all.

In relation to the development of complementary currency systems, the institutions designed for the *RT* as an articulated network across the country made it a unique case. A first aspect that was unheard of was the articulation of regional complementary currency systems to trade across *CT*. Present CCS are almost exclusively independent and local or regional, and jealous of their autonomy.[71] Large CCS in the past mostly remained local and in those in which scrip circulated loosely across the country, it was printed by an issuer who backed the notes with commodities or promised to redeem them for regular money. The *RT* was a category of its own. It became an articulated network with a myriad of currencies backed by trust alone, in each other and in the *PAR* leaders. It took a while to improve this and the network built a system of checks and balances, the IZ, which also served as forum for discussion and decision-making. The IZ functioned as 'monetary authority' for the regional currency systems of all *CT* in the country. It added transparency to the complementary currency systems, making the regional networks accountable for the issuance of vouchers to each other. The IZ was a remarkable achievement but did not live for long. It was embedded in personal rivalries and hosted conflictive power struggles, while at the same time there was neither agreement nor enough commitment to its efficiency on behalf of all members.

The second unique institution that emerged in the *Trueque* was the social franchise. It proved an effective mechanism to multiply the *CT* of *PAR* across the country and justified the opening of a network of own offices to promote it. A monetary system emerged with one currency across the country, the 'dollar of the Trueque', as they called it. *PAR* functioned as 'central bank' for the complementary monetary system, deciding centrally on issuance, design of the notes, mode of distribution, and so on. The social franchise was also a way to obtain regular money and finance the organizational costs of the system. For its critics, it accumulated power excessively in one agent's hands, attacked the democratic principles under the scheme was founded and facilitated corruption. It was efficient to simplify the replication of *CT* and reduce the transaction costs of having too many currencies, but it was inefficient to the goals of empowerment, participation and self-reliance. Besides, it concentrated power on agents who were not accountable and did not have the control infrastructure to sustain the rapid expansion that followed.

Claiming that efficiency improvements are an outcome but not an intention implies that it hardly constitutes an argument to motivate agents to accept the solutions found by a group as a designed institution for all (that is, to adapt their behaviour in line with it). The weakness of the goal relates to structural reform programmes and development projects in general. Even if policymakers are capable of designing the most efficient solution for an economic problem, that does not in itself constitute a basis on which to persuade agents to adapt their economic action accordingly – unless, of course, it is accompanied by a battery of enforcement means. Instead, for a proposed solution to become a designed institution, two sets of conditions need to be met. The first is that the solutions of a group or network need to accommodate the intentions and interests of those making decisions on institutional design across groups or networks, those motivated enough to bear the costs of defining new rules for all. In the case of the *RT*, these were the market-makers gathered in the IZ to negotiate, divided into pro-*PAR* and anti-*PAR* groups. The second condition is that agents in general must accept and repeat it, internalizing it as a disposition to act in the same way in similar circumstances. In the case of the *RT*, the one currency model of the *PAR* became far more popular than the participatory model of the anti-*PAR* front and turned the struggle in favour of *PAR*. It was closest to pre-existent practice, in line with the evolutionary argument elaborated in Chapter 3 and it responded to the law of large numbers.

Naturally the definition of efficiency for different actors is also contested. In the *RT*, different groups responded differently to exactly the same conditions of uncertainty and transaction costs. While *PAR* regarded the social franchise as the most efficient method to make the *RT* grow rapidly, keep the currency under control and protect the original project, the anti-*PAR* front preferred a horizontal network based on participation and an alternative economic system of solidarity. The fact that there were at least two possible roads for achieving the 'most efficient' institutional arrangement suggests that there are different perceptions of efficiency. The ambiguity of what is the 'most' efficient solution further reduces the helpfulness of showing the efficiency of an institution to justify its emergence.

These reflections have implications for development projects. Showing stakeholders the ex-ante 'efficiency' of a project, rule or solution is insufficient to gain their support. Designed institutions need to accommodate power struggles and attend social relations as well. The failure to recognize this leads to much frustration on the part of donors and policymakers, who launch 'efficient' development plans and still get nowhere near the expected results. The stakeholders or local institution designers resist or boycott the 'efficient' design because it goes against their interests and intentions. However critical, designed institutions are in fact contingent points of compromise.

6 GOVERNANCE OF THE NETWORKS

The *Redes de Trueque* were sustained by civil society organizations that created institutions in a process of trial and error. They structured several rules and organizations, even complementary currency systems, in an effort to make impersonal exchange less uncertain and risky. But there was an underlying issue of governance throughout the process. One conflict was over who ruled the *Trueque,* already discussed in Chapter 5. There were equally important questions on the legitimacy, representativeness and accountability of the leaders. Why would people abide by the rules defined by and for the *RT*? Some of the *RT* leaders referred to principles like solidarity, common values and ideology, but these could neither be assumed nor checked. After 2001, when the once articulated *Trueque* network broke into several *Redes de Trueque,* each group sought to define its own institutions.

This chapter discusses the rules of governance and sustainability of the *Trueque* and their complementary currency systems. It covers the period of the bubble of the *Trueque* (2001 to 2003). It includes the worst economic crisis ever experienced in Argentine history, with a fall in GDP of 10.9 per cent in 2002 alone and a vigorous economic recovery with growth rates around 9 per cent for the years that followed (2003–6). It also covers the months when the *Trueque* achieved its maximum scale of 2.5 million participants (first half of 2002) and then plummeted to 250,000 members (second half of 2003). The chapter argues that the governance systems framed by the emerging networks were of various degrees of sustainability, which explains their differential resistance to the decline.

In the prologue to *States and Markets*, Susan Strange tells the story of a shipwreck and what happens to three groups of lucky people that survive in lifeboats.[1] The first of the three boats has an officer aboard who keeps a cool head and guides his group to safety on a deserted island. He then organizes the building of a shelter, collection of food and water, and a rough signal system to attract the attention of any passing ships. Gradually, the survivors get used to following his instructions and they do pretty well.

A second boat reaches another island, with a bunch of young students on board. They do not know what to do and talk endlessly about their predicament. They agree that it would be great to organize a commune, to each according to need and from each according to ability, but a few days later problems begin to appear. There are long arguments about who is to clean the latrines, a job nobody wants. Some of the castaways are apt to wander from their allotted jobs to enjoy the sunshine. Eventually, the food is not enough for everyone and the latrines begin to stink, but they all still think a commune is a good idea and so they keep trying.

The third boat lands on another island. It contains a diverse group including children and elderly. In this group, no one takes charge and everyone cracks open their own coconuts and catches their own fish. The elderly go hungry and mothers do not have time to build shelters and look after the children. They discuss their situation and somebody suggests trading, using nails found in the boat as means of payment, so each person can specialize in a task and they can exchange goods with each other. They divide the nails equally and decide to give a nail each week to a hefty person who will take care of security and sanitation and a nail to an elderly couple, who organize a sort of school for the children. The market starts well but then some problems arise. Growing crops is a good idea, but how is the growing period to be financed? If someone falls sick, who will take care of that person? Who should be entitled to use the boat for fishing, and for how long? In spite of the constant conflicts, most people in this market society are fed and sheltered and more or less manage.

Susan Strange tells this story in the context of international political economy, with her interest being in investigating what happens when the groups meet each other. The focus of this current study is different: in these systems, in which the rules have to be set and acceptance needs to be constructed, how is governance achieved and what makes it sustainable until rescue comes? Sustainability in the context of the shipwreck has a very literal meaning: whether each group and its socioeconomic organization survive until rescue comes. In real-life situations, sustainability refers to the durability or resilience of governance systems in which the rules of action and their compliance cannot be assumed a priori because none of the actors has the means to enforce them. Institutions have to be designed, legitimacy has to be constructed, compliance has to be obtained through voluntary decision and negotiation. Similar governance problems are observed in situations in which regulation by the state is not possible, desirable or cost-effective and it is done by business organizations or civil society groups.[2]

The Construction of Governance Systems

Governance refers to a particular kind of governing:[3] 'sustaining co-ordination and coherence among a wide variety of actors with different purposes and objectives such as political actors and institutions, corporate interests, civil society, and transnational governments'.[4] Governance is used in different contexts and disciplines with some divergence but it always implies giving up a top-down approach and including a multiplicity of actors in either the economy or the polity. It is conceived as a process combining negotiation, accommodation, cooperation and alliance formation rather than coercion, command and control.[5] Institutions help to reduce or resolve the conflicts and risks of the system.

A governance system is 'the totality of institutional arrangements – including rules and rule-making agents – that regulate transactions inside and across the boundaries of an economic system'.[6] That is, a cluster of mechanisms for co-ordination of economic activities, so that individual economic action may become predictable and stable.[7] Related concepts are 'mode of regulation',[8] coined by the French Regulation School,[9] and 'models of social order', preferred by some Political Economy scholars.[10] It is pre-eminently a meso-level analytical concept. A stimulating research agenda has developed around the study of economic governance systems and the viability – not so much efficiency – of these complex constitutional principles, institutions, incentive schemes and organizations.[11]

The *Redes de Trueque* were governance systems built bottom-up. How were institutions and organizations brought together in a governance system? Evolutionary economists claim that their configuration is achieved through a process of trial and error that reflects at a higher level what is feasible at each point in time.[12] Bob Jessop adds that the process is not continuous but happens in phases related to the economic cycle.[13] In periods of crisis and/or transition, actors seek to define new modes of regulation or governance systems through trial-and-error search processes that contain a considerable element of struggle and chaos. In periods of stability, the structural coherence of complex institutional forms prevails and confines economic action to the reproduction of the economic system. All in all, the evolution of institutions is pushed by factors such as political struggle, changes in social values and the search for improved efficiency, while stability is achieved when changes become consolidated in new institutions.

An early attempt to theorise on governance systems in which the state is not the central actor was made by Streeck and Schmitter,[14] using the concept of social orders in their path-breaking book *Private Interest Government*. They argued that governance systems are built around a 'central institution which embodies (and enforces) their respective and distinctive guiding principle' of coordination and conflict areas. Streeck and Schmitter[15] identify four social orders: community, market, bureaucracy and associations. They suggest that 'it might be more accurate to label them according to the principles that coordinate each: sponta-neous solidarity, dispersed competition, hierarchical control and organisational concordance'.[16]

In a community, actors are interdependent, their preferences and choices are based on shared norms and jointly produce satisfaction. Chiefs, notables, lead-ers, and so on desire the esteem of their followers, while the followers seek a sense of belonging and participation in the group. Sustainability is thus tied to the sat-isfaction of mutual needs and keeping a collective identity. Conflict often arises as a result of the relations between native members and non-members.

In an ideal market, actors are competitors and in principle independent. Entrepreneurs seek to maximize their profits, and by virtue of dispersed competi-tion they share with consumers the material benefits of technical progress. There is a basic conflict of interest between sellers and buyers (supply and demand) which is reflected in prices. Sustainability is tied to the capacity of markets to clear in spite of the uncertainty and risks inherent in compliance and incomplete information.

In a bureaucracy, actors are dependent upon hierarchical coordination and their choices are asymmetrically predictable according to the structure of legiti-mate authority. Allocation decisions are made by hierarchical centres and carried out by agents rewarded by career advancement and stability. Conflicts centre on disputes over privileges arrogated by rulers to impose obligations on the ruled. Sustainability is tied to the effective capacity to control action via hierarchy.

In an associational order, actors are contingently interdependent: the actions organized collectively can have a predictable effect on the satisfaction of others, which induces them to search for stable pacts. Collective actors are defined by a common purpose to defend and promote functionally-defined interests and mutually recognize the status of competitor organizations. Sustainability is tied to preventing fragmentation into rival communities, competing for resources and securing compliance from members.

This four-type taxonomy was based on ideal types of governance systems that are rarely present in reality. For example, a market regulated by a public or private regulator is still a market but it has elements of hierarchical control, so it is not driven by dispersed competition alone. A more flexible categorization of governance systems was later presented by Hollingsworth and Boyer.[17] Their framework categorizes governance systems while at the same time identifying two criteria to distinguish them: the action motive (what disposes individuals to behave in a certain way) and the coordination mode (how their economic actions are made compatible with each other). Coordination modes range from horizontal coordination, where many equal agents interact, to vertical coordi-nation, in which power relations are arranged in a hierarchy. The former is a 'non discrete organizational structure' and the latter a 'bureaucratic administrative control structure'. The authors argue that coordination in both markets and communities is by spontaneous self-organization; prices are the main coordinating mechanism in competitive markets while in communities mutual obligations grow spontaneously out of traditions and trust. The motives for economic action range from (the perception of) pure self-interest at one extreme to obligational action at the other, in which individuals are constrained and informed by social rules demanding compliance.

Though not explicitly elaborated by the authors, this framework allows identification of several subtypes of market systems, for example, according to their mix of institutions: competitive, cartelized, state-regulated and cooperative markets embedded in long-term relations. The market as a multilateral setting for exchange is still the core of these governance systems, but non-core institutions matter, too. Self-interested behaviour is more or less typical of all markets, but coordination at a social level is also achieved through civil society organizations voluntarily and state coercion. Hence, the strong dichotomy of hierarchies versus markets loses appeal, as markets are ensembles of institutions. The initial four ideal-type governance systems of Streeck and Schmitter[18] can be placed more flexibly along continuums regarding the action motive guiding behaviour and mode of coordination between agents.

What Makes Governance Systems Sustainable?

The categorization of governance system proposed by Hollingsworth and Boyer[19] offers an entry-point to analyse what factors make various governance systems sustainable. This question is critical in systems in which rules have to be created and enforced by actors without the monopoly over means of violence. Referring to regulation regimes, Jessop[20] claims that their life expectancy (sustainability) is given by the compatibility (coherence) of their mediation mechanisms (institutions). Boyer and Hollingsworth[21] follow a similar path and assert that they are 'viable' as long as the set of institutions that form it are coherent or compatible with each other. However, how is this coherence constructed and how can it be observed in research? The theorization is elaborated further here to set operational criteria.

A few issues, which are directly or indirectly related to non-state actors' setting of rules, stand out as critical to the durability of these governance systems. The first dimension is the acceptance or legitimacy of rules as basic institutions regulating the governance systems.[22] The concept of legitimacy is further categorized as input and output legitimacy.[23] By input legitimacy, the authors mean the process by which rules have come about and the setting of provisions to modify them in the future. It represents an ex-ante analysis; input legitimacy is created along the process of rule definition. It may involve shared values and idealism.

On the other hand, output legitimacy represents an ex-post generation of legitimacy based on the 'success' of the governance systems: the capacity to deliver results, solve problems and resolve conflicts.

The benefits delivered by governance systems are evaluated in relation to the costs for the actors involved. The capacity to deliver results, solve problems and resolve conflicts within the economy means achieving 'resource synergy'[24] building the ability to coordinate material interdependencies among internal and external agents, which is especially critical when resources are scarce.[25] On the other side of the ledger, there are the costs of running the system, generally referred to in Chapter 5 as transaction costs. In a system where the state is not available as a low-cost rule-maker, these are mainly of two types. First, the costs associated with uncertainties, risks and information asymmetries, normally defined as transaction costs.[26] Second, there are the costs of sustaining collective action, setting rules, making decisions, and redefining objectives when necessary; these are organizational costs.

Finally, policing functions are problematic because the ex-ante acceptance of rules does not mean ex-post compliance. The latter is an actual event, the real behaviour of agents, while the former is a disposition to act. Actual compliance is achieved by monitoring and enforcing rules even against resistance from agents.[27]

So, in principle there are four factors that make governance systems sustainable and which serve as analytical framework to study governance in complementary currencies systems like the *Redes de Trueque*.

1) Input legitimacy: to what extent does the process of rule definition help to win acceptance? The focus is on the process of rule-setting for non-state currency systems and the replication of nodes, besides factors like idealism and common values.

2) Enforcement: to what extent do institutional mechanisms of monitoring and enforcement operate? The focus is on ways to obtain effective compliance of rules, even against some resistance.

3) Benefits (in relation to output legitimacy): to what extent is resource synergy achieved to deliver results, solve problems and resolve conflicts? The focus is on management of scarce resources and activities in common to support the income-generation efforts of households.

4) Transaction and organizational costs (in relation to output legitimacy): to what extent are risks and uncertainties minimized? The focus is on the uncertainty of trading with means of payment accepted voluntarily – the *créditos* – with the risk of loss of value. To what extent are the costs of sustaining self-organization minimized? The attention is on the costs of decision-making in each governance system.

All these questions are framed in such a way that they could be graded along a high-low table or in numbers to assess the sustainability of empirical governance systems. The next section describes the governance problems of the *Red de Trueque* during the 2001–6 period.

The Bubble of the Trueque

October 2000 was the last time the articulated, all-encompassing *Red de Trueque* met through the IZ. The two largest sub-networks (*Red Global de Trueque*, which was the *PAR* network, and *Red de Trueque Zona Oeste*) stopped attending meetings, and some independent nodes followed suit. In April 2001 the break-up became official, the *Red Global de Trueque* and *Red de Trueque Zona Oeste* were formally declared outside the IZ and the remaining groups formed the umbrella organization *Red de Trueque Solidario* (Solidarity *Trueque* Network, or *RTS*). The name underlined their principles: solidarity and social transformation through the *Trueque*. They would keep holding monthly IZ meetings, with non-*RTS* nodes also being invited to attend.

The entrance of the government as a new actor rekindled the conflict. The Secretary for Small and Medium Enterprises in the Ministry of the Economy, Enrique Martinez, decided the *Trueque* had had a positive effect on the generation of micro-enterprises and provided aid and funds through a six-month cooperation agreement with the *PAR* leaders.[28] They became paid advisors to the government on how to expand the *Trueque*. The government provided assistance for the *PAR* website, infrastructure to facilitate its expansion, and supplies of food production inputs to sustain production.[29] The anti-*PAR* front were furious at being left out. Primavera complained: 'The agreement granted *PAR* a false pretence of legitimacy. They called their voucher the dollar of the *Trueque* and it was the only one issued without accountability!'. Primavera campaigned against the *PAR* and the agreement was not renewed.

Paradoxically, as the different factions of the *Trueque* were tearing each other apart, its scale, scope and public recognition were on the rise. It looked like a panacea for the unemployed and poor. It is impossible to know exactly how many people participated during its peak around the beginning of 2002. Its scale can be roughly estimated from the few data available (Figure 6.1). The *Red Global de Trueque* alone processed around 1.2 million applications[30] and the *Red de Trueque Zona Oeste* had a consolidated database of 486,267 members. The *Red de Trueque Solidario* did not maintain a unified database, but the sum of its main regions amounted to about 350,000 members. On the basis of the membership of these main sub-networks, the figure of 2.5 million estimated by Ovalles[31] for 2002 seems conservative. A national survey conducted by Gallup in May 2002 showed that 60 per cent of Argentines expected to make at least one transaction

Figure 6.1: Number of participants by sub-network, beginning of 2002

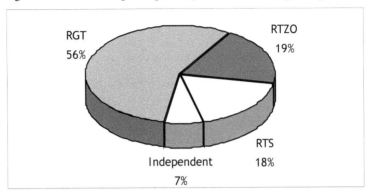

Note: Estimation by the author based on interviews with the leaders of the various Trueque
groups. Percentages are calculated on 2.5 Million participants

in the *Trueque* in the three months following the survey.[32] The average income
generated by full-time participants was well above the minimum statutory wage.
Norman[33] quotes the *PAR* leaders as stating that trade in the network in 2001
was equivalent to 600 million pesos, with membership of a million members,
who earned between 500 and 800 *créditos* or the value of a new small televi-
sion.[34]

Public opinion no longer treated the *Trueque* as an exotic creature of the
crisis. Scale and scope, as well as the media, had much to do with this change.
The coverage of the *Trueque* in the main newspapers, compiled in a database by
the Universidad Nacional de General Sarmiento, provides a rough overview.[35]
Between 1 May 2001 and the end of that year (245 days) the newspapers published forty articles on the *Trueque*. Between 1 January 2002 and 30 June 2002
(181 days) the number of articles rose to 168. The headlines reflected the same
point: the national economy in agony contrasted against the *RT* booming, giving answers to people, turning disaster into creativity. Men and women were then
participating in almost equal numbers, both affected by unemployment, unlike
during the initial years of the *Trueque* when it was dominated by women.

Local governments' intervention also became more common. The *Trueque*
spared them the financial burden of social policy and supported the local economy. Dozens of municipalities declared it 'of municipal interest', which did not
mean much in practice but gave the nodes freedom. A handful of municipalities
actively helped the scheme by providing buildings or vehicles to transport goods.
The relation with the central government was different, more of tolerance than
of acceptance. The *Trueque* did not exist in any law, so it was difficult to deal
with. The Congress started working on laws to regulate it but that came to nothing.[36]

In contrast to the treatment in the media,[37] there were serious practical problems and in many of the thousands of nodes across Argentina the situation looked like sheer anarchy. With some variations across regions and sub-networks, it was increasingly difficult to find suitable venues for the markets to meet. They used to be in community, cultural and sports centres, schools, union halls, churches, parking lots, abandoned factories, warehouses, even garages of large houses, if necessary. However, as participants satisfied more of their needs in the *Trueque* instead of just complementing their income, they started attending more than one market a week in different locations. The largest ones needed bigger venues, being visited by thousands.[38] For example, La Estación was a large node in the city of Buenos Aires and met in a four-storey railway building. The coordinator says:

> First we opened a second floor and for a second day a week. In the end we used four floors six days a week, the top one only for fruits and vegetables. We received a total of 4,000 participants on Saturday, our main day, who covered eighty per cent of their consumption needs in the *CT*. Participants queued for hours before the opening to be able to come in.

Visitors paid an admission fee in *créditos* that gave them the right simply to wander around or put up a stall and offer their products. This financed the rent or maintenance of the venue. Owners of the spaces normally charged nominal rent, but when the attendance rose to thousands they expected to make a profit and saw it as a business, so rents went up. Coordinators sometimes also regarded the entrance fee as their wage and raised it.

With the increasing scale of the nodes, diversity of supply expanded until there were few goods that could not be obtained in *créditos*. Members became incredibly creative in widening the scope of products offered: from vegetables and fruits to clothing and shoes, books and CDs, home-made toiletries, furniture, and electronics. Some services, such as haircuts, manicures, wedding parties and Tarot fortune-telling, were offered on the market premises. Others, such as legal counselling, car insurance, taxi and courier transport, holiday packages, and education and training, were advertised on bulletin boards. Even plots of land in the countryside and livestock were offered for sale in *créditos*.[39]

Squeezed by the economic crisis in 2001–2, the structural poor kept pouring into the nodes with barely anything to offer and desperate basic needs. The *Trueque* was not a solution to poverty, as Leoni[40] found. The author studied nodes dominated by the structural poor, which she described as the 'dictatorship of homogeneity'. The services most frequently offered were cleaning and gardening, for which there was no demand. Services such as electrical and plumbing work were in demand, but those skills were also of little help because none of the parties had pesos to buy wiring and spare parts. So if the majority of the participants in the node were structural poor, it became a battleground. The supply of basic food inputs was insufficient for all who wanted them.

An underlying class conflict then appeared in most nodes. The scheme was made popular by the disenfranchised middle class, for whom the *Trueque* was a good way of getting some value for goods made as hobbies (paintings, knits, hand-made dolls) or accumulated in better times (fur coats, toys, small furniture). Many had a small amount of working capital to buy inputs in pesos, which they either resold or processed into products for sale in the nodes. The resale of goods bought in supermarkets violated the principle of self-reliance and prosumption but was tolerated because there was dire need of basic food production inputs in the nodes. In contrast, the structural poor joined the *Trueque* later. They had no accumulated assets, no income in pesos and no working capital. What they could sell in the nodes was their own labour and second-hand goods such as clothes, shoes and toys that came from charities and donations. When they could get the ingredients in the *Trueque*, they were also able to produce food like bread, for example. Such ingredients were mainly provided by disenfranchised middle class participants. A critical balance had to be kept in the nodes between the disenfranchised middle class and structural poor in order to enable both groups to benefit.

The excess demand for food sometimes brought the node to the verge of anarchy. It became normal for nodes to be flooded with *créditos* and second-hand articles, but to run out of food and produced goods, pushing up the prices of the latter. People moved across nodes and sub-networks and municipalities, seeking a wider variety of goods or to sell high and buy cheap.[41] Repacking products into smaller bags to resell became a general practice. Large-scale *CT* were the site of many abuses, among them by the coordinators who were supposed to organize them, as was also found by P. North.[42] For example, coordinators charged a 'customs' duty, their self-attributed 'entitlement' to buy scarce goods before the other participants.

Excess demand for basic food production inputs gave rise to inflation in *créditos*. When prices were too high, coordinators advised members to refrain from buying. However, people needed the products desperately and the nodes became fertile ground for speculation and exploitation of those who had no pesos by those who did. That often meant exploiting the structural poor, who had less choice. Due to inflation in the prices of basic food production inputs, at the beginning of 2001 the *crédito* lost the one-to-one relation with the official money and its relative prices. For example, one hour of childcare was equivalent to two litres of cooking oil in the formal economy but 0.75 litres of cooking oil in the *CT*. Inequality centred on having or not having pesos.[43]

Excessive issuance of *PAR* vouchers was also a source of inflation. They were used to pay for all sorts of expenses: wages to the *Trueque* employees, gifts to friends and local politicians, self-awarded wages of coordinators, cleaning and maintenance of node market locations, and refurbishment of buildings. As with regular money, unlimited printing of means of payment gave rise to inflation. Ironically, the initiating group, which had been so innovative in finding solutions to the problems of participants, was unable to respond to its acute crisis. They were managing too many things at the same time, and how much the *PAR* leaders knew of the abuses in the network is a question that arouses much passion.

The final blow was large-scale forgery of the *Red Global de Trueque créditos* in the second quarter of 2002. The risk of forgery had existed to some extent almost from the beginning of the *RT*. As the network expanded and many goods and services could be obtained with complementary currency, it became profitable to print forged vouchers. It will perhaps never be known who was responsible for the forgery and the suspects range from normal criminal gangs to political brokers. Participants recall:

> You could see people selling packs of forged vouchers near the entrance of almost every large node. They were even available in the nearby kiosks. We wondered many times who has the capacity to do that. Printing costs money and these criminals must be making money. For me, the politicians were behind it because they didn't like the *Trueque*.

The *PAR* leaders tell a similar version. They emphasize that the forgery was on a large scale and meticulously organized, and that the police did nothing about it. The *Trueque*, they say, was no longer tolerable for Peronist leaders, who were unhappy that the clientele of their networks had an alternative source of income with elections coming up (P. North, 2005). Groups connected to the Peronist party also opened nodes specifically for their political clientele.[44] However, the anti-*PAR* front offer a completely different story. They viewed the forgery and excessive supply of means of payment as a result of mistakes and corruption in the *PAR* network itself.

Whatever the origin, members soon found out that it was easier to buy a pack of forged *créditos* than to produce goods to obtain them. Eventually, forgery became the main source of inflation and was clearly lethal for the *Trueque*. Coordinators across nodes were mostly unable to stop the inflows of forged vouchers, so they spread from one *CT* to another and then from one region to another. The sharp inflation that resulted can be seen in the price of a litre of cooking oil in a PAR network node, which rose from one *crédito* in December 2001 to 3,500 *créditos* in December 2002.

In October 2002, the *PAR* leaders estimated that 90 per cent of circulating coupons were counterfeit.[45] They then implemented a plan that ended in disaster. They collected all the *créditos* in circulation to weed out the fake ones. The real ones were partially replaced with a new voucher, on the basis of a progressive discount rate. The maximum given to any member, whatever amount they had before, was 60,000 *créditos*. The strategy caused heavy losses to participants who had lots of accumulated vouchers –against strong advice that vouchers were not a reserve of value. It was also too burdensome for coordinators, many of whom got fed up, split from the network or closed their *CT*. It seriously damaged the credibility of the system as a whole and was the death sentence of the *PAR*-led *Red Global de Trueque*.

Two additional factors contributed to the collapse. First, in May 2002 the government decided to implement a welfare policy giving 150 pesos to each unemployed head of household with children at school. Thus, for the first time in a decade, a welfare system offered an option, and precisely when the *Trueque* had lost its appeal. The government grant did not immediately cause a steep fall in the number of members but reduced membership over the medium term. Some beneficiaries, though, used the welfare money to buy food production inputs to resell in the *CT* or buy packs of forged *créditos*. The second factor was the vigorous growth of the regular economy after 2003. Since then, the GDP has been growing at an average of 8 per cent a year and many of the *Trueque* members gradually returned to regular employment.

Membership fell and the closure of *Red Global de Trueque* clubs accelerated towards the end of 2002. The *Trueque* in general became a corrupt and miserable ugly duckling nobody wanted to be involved with. A coordinator in the city of Mar del Plata tells:

> The sequence was as follows. In the beginning, you met your neighbour in the street and she asked you where you were going. 'To the node', you'd answer. And 'what is that?' she'd ask. Later she'd ask which one you attended and what that one was like. In the end she'd stare at you and would ask whether 'that' still existed.

Some coordinators would have liked to stay open, but the scandals left them without enough participants or without venues. Churches, schools and civic centres were denied to them. As de Sanzo put it, a tidal wave came in 2002 and by the end of the year it had swept away most of the *CT*. Of the 5,000 *Red Global de Trueque* nodes in April 2002, half were closed by December[46] and only 1,000 were still open by July 2003; around 300, barely 10 per cent of the number in its heyday, were operating in December 2005.[47] Of these, fewer than one hundred maintained contact with *PAR* and the rest operated independently.[48]

An Uneven Fall

Although the PAR-led *Red Global de Trueque* was the main one to be affected by the counterfeit *créditos* and the first to fall apart, there was a knock-on effect on other networks, too, because the majority of participants were unclear about the differences between sub-networks. However, not all collapsed in the same way. At the time of the fieldwork for this study in late 2004, a total of 700 nodes were estimated to be operating. Follow-up fieldwork at the end of 2006 found about half of them still surviving.

What was left of the IZ after 2002 was affected by further divisions and still unable to reach agreement on basic issues. The level of conflict reached a climax in September 2003, when the last IZ meeting was held. An assistant recalled: 'Unfortunately the groups left began to hate each other. The *Trueque* was in demise anyway, so the original raison d'être of the IZ had already vanished. It was the end of a fantastic cycle'.[49]

Some regional segments of the anti-*PAR* front's *Red de Trueque Solidario* fared well on their own and kept operating at a regional level. An example is Mar y Sierras, in the city of Mar del Plata and surroundings. 'Being smaller, we were always able to restrain opportunistic behaviour better, even if by expelling members', recalled its leader Carlos Perez Llora. So while the *Red de Trueque Solidario* ceased to exist, its member sub-networks kept operating as regional associative systems of governance. Much intellectual work on the idea of social money came out of that group, especially from Heloisa Primavera.

In 2003 the *PAR* leaders started again their *RGT* with their faithful coordinators in the southern suburbs, in spite of the loss of credibility both personally and of the scheme. They printed a safer voucher and once again opted for a regulated market governance system.[50] They formalized the coordinator position as a paid job financed from the entrance fee of two pesos per person. The new voucher included demurrage (a negative interest rate) to discourage accumulation, at a rate of 12 per cent a year.[51] Once a year, each voucher of twenty *créditos* was replaced with eighteen *créditos*, the remaining two getting 'lost'. Agreements on maximum prices were reached and abandoned due to lack of compliance; again, those with access to food production inputs in pesos raised prices. A list of rules was agreed on, but there was no supervision to check compliance.

The *Red de Trueque Zona Oeste* made some adjustments in its governance system to adapt to its new smaller scale, as will be discussed in Chapter 6. Fernando Sampayo still controls basic institutions like the distribution of vouchers, but the enforcement of rules lies almost entirely in the hands of the coordinators. *CT* are thus much more autonomous.

An undetermined number of *CT* became independent from the networks and were operating in isolation at the time of the fieldwork. They still believe that the *Trueque* is useful. In La Estación, for example, the largest node operating in the Capital of Buenos Aires in 2004, they see it as a meeting point of friends and an opportunity for women to generate an income. Very small nodes (with a few dozen members) continue because of the non-economic dimensions of the scheme. The members see them as social contact that enables them to earn an income, enjoy themselves, and feel useful. Women have become the majority (comprising 70–80 per cent of the members). The nodes are now dominated by the structural poor and the sections of the disenfranchised middle class that are unable to bounce back out of poverty. There are also *CT* that have become private businesses funded through entrance fees.

To some extent, the collapse of the *Trueque* could have been foreseen and needs little explanation. But the differences in the fates of the networks are considerably less obvious. They were all affected by similar problems, but did not suffer the shrinkage to the same extent. Some sub-networks disappeared or declined sharply. Others reached their nadir in 2004 and recovered in 2005–6. What is the reason for these differences? This study argues that the explanation lies in the governance systems that they had structured by 2002.

The *Red Global de Trueque* was the network of the *PAR* leaders. In the first quarter of 2001 the social franchise seemed to guarantee endless growth, more than anticipated by its leaders. It became by far the largest sub-network in Argentina, with the southern area of Buenos Aires as its stronghold. It also received the most media and public exposure. In the categorization above, it was a regulated market. It relied on spontaneous coordination and the nodes retained other decision-making powers, but central institutions such as printing of *créditos* and dealing with third parties were concentrated in *PAR*'s hands. Coordination at the level of *CT* and across nodes was spontaneous and mainly through price mechanisms. There was no discrete control structure across the network, only basic ground rules.

The *ZO* was a regional sub-network with its stronghold in the western suburbs of Greater Buenos Aires. Initially, it accepted vouchers issued by *PAR*, which in turn accepted those of the *ZO*. Its membership was almost a fifth of that of the *Trueque* and there was a collective fund in pesos to finance its costs and the development of enterprises organized as a supply chain. The *ZO* fits closer in the hierarchy type in which there was one centre for decision-making, rule-setting and enforcement for all nodes: its leader, Fernando Sampayo. Power relations were arranged vertically with bureaucratic administrative structures. Still, members exchanged goods and services guided by self-interest.

The anti-*PAR* front in the IZ decided to stay together and in April 2001 formed the *Red de Trueque Solidario*. It was organized regionally, each region having its own voucher but all being identified with a logo. Its strongholds were the Capital of Buenos Aires and its northern suburbs, which were the wealthiest areas. Altogether the *RTS* membership represented almost a fifth of that of the *Red de Trueque*. It was arranged as an associational model, with multiple centres converging into a negotiation and decision-making body, the IZ. Self-interest was constrained, at least in principle, by bonds of reciprocity that emerged in time and peer control was exercised. Coordination was achieved by mutual negotiation.

In addition to the sub-networks, there were an indeterminate number of isolated *CT* that traded using their own vouchers and had no contact with others. They typically operated as the club markets of closed groups such as schools, churches or small villages and comprised less than 10 per cent of the *RT*;[52] it is difficult to estimate their number and they have been researched very little so far. A few *CT* are described here as examples. They roughly correspond to the model of communities or clubs in the framework above. The action motive was obligation to abide by the rules arising from the community that gave birth to the *CT*. There was no discrete organizational structure for coordination. Some examples are:

1) *Comunidades Solidarias*, in Caseros, Buenos Aires, was started by a group of parents in a community school for mentally handicapped children. Close to the Catholic Church, the coordinator had spent some years in a seminary. Markets are held twice a week, being preceded by prayers. The groups use their own vouchers and participation is open to anyone who shares their values.

2) *Grupo Poriahju*, in Capitán Bermúdez (Santa Fe). The coordinators are teachers who, inspired by Paulo Freire, started a self-help group in a slum in the 1980s. They run a community library, various workshops and income-generating alternatives for the poor. They started a node linked to the *RTS* but later decided to become independent. This resulted in better group control over prices, quality and diversity of products. Decisions are taken by a committee of elected members. They use their own vouchers and membership is closed; new members are approved after a trial period.

3) *Barrio Belgrano* in the city of Rosario (Province of Santa Fe). The *CT* started as part of Rosario's *RTS*. It was located between public-housing blocks and a slum that suffers flooding during heavy rain. Markets were held in the open air, on a grassy plot belonging to the Catholic Church. The coordinator resigned years ago and officially closed the node, but members kept meeting spontaneously; 200 to 300 people participate in a market every day, trading with left-over vouchers, which are currently in bad shape. The products on sale include food production inputs given by the government and not consumed by the recipients, overproduction or scrap weeded out of rubbish, food from charities, fresh fruits and vegetables from the local

government community garden programme, and prepared foods from those who have access to pesos. There are no designated leaders; decisions such as the schedule are made by consensus by those who are present at the time. A participant explained: 'There are no real decisions to be made. Whoever wants to come can come and sell. If she sells at too high a price, nobody will buy. She will change or leave'.

Although it is an oversimplification, these were the four groups that emerged out of the break up of the *RT* around the turn of 2001. Each one of them organized their 'islands' with different governance systems, analysed in the next section.

Emergent Governance Systems

The regulated market of the RGT, the hierarchy of the ZO, the associational governance system of the RTS and the community-based model of the independent nodes all suffered the similar problems discussed above: excess demand for food inputs, opportunistic behaviour, forgery of the *créditos*, etc. The main question to be answered then is not why they fell apart but why the collapse affected them differently. This is done using the four criteria of sustainability defined above.

The first factor that makes governance systems sustainable is input legitimacy (willingness of actors to abide by the rules). The main institutions for which this factor was crucial were the currency system, mechanisms to replicate *CT*, handling of pesos, and negotiation with outside actors such as local governments. The *RGT* and *ZO* concentrated these in a centre in Buenos Aires and the *RTS* and local nodes decentralized it to each region and locality.

The *RGT* was a regulated market and its rules were mainly set by the *PAR* leaders. The willingness of members to comply with them was assumed by virtue of their membership, but was hardly asked explicitly. In fact, during the fieldwork the author established that most participants had not read the rules or did not know they existed. Nodes were replicated through the 'social franchise' at a rate of two pesos per member. To save on travel costs, this was often done by mail, so the coordinators did not know the *PAR* leaders personally. Coordinators were asked to stay in touch and to submit themselves for re-election by their nodes once a year, but during the fieldwork it was impossible to find any group within the *RGT* that had actually held such a re-election and very few coordinators stayed in touch. They only contacted the *PAR* leaders to buy kits of fifty *créditos* for their new members, also at two pesos each. With hundreds of new members a day, no up-to-date records were kept. The *RGT* relied on 'franchisers', intermediaries given the responsibility of extending the *Trueque* across the country. The rules were set by *PAR* with minimal, if any, involvement of the coordinators. The rules were poorly communicated and there was no provision to change them in ways that would generate legitimacy later. Acceptance of the rules was therefore very weak.

The *ZO* used a similar system to the social franchise but implemented it differently. Its leader, Fernando Sampayo, defined the rules for the *ZO* and exercised strong leadership, which others accepted because of his skills. 'He knows how to do it,' was repeatedly heard about him in several of the *CT* visited. From its early days the *ZO* invested in computerized databases and hired as many workers for data entry as were needed to keep up-to-date membership records. No new member received fifty new *créditos* before being registered. This bureaucratic structure was financed through the two pesos membership fee. Interested groups had to contact the *ZO* and the coordinators were required to take a four-week-course before being approved, so they met Sampayo at least once. Their autonomy was limited; they could only decide practical matters in the nodes, such as venues and schedules, and they were accountable to the *ZO*. Sampayo personally negotiated with other organizations or local governments on matters affecting the *CT*. Only Sampayo could print and distribute *créditos*. 'I printed 50 million *créditos* and we numbered them when needed. I hid them in my office. You could say I'm the central Bank of the *ZO*,' he told the author. In short, the rule-maker and centre of the *ZO* hierarchy was its leader. The process of rule-setting included only close collaborators, a practice which apparently went unquestioned. Input legitimacy was far from participative but fair thanks to the leader's skilfulness.

The acceptance of central institutions in the *RTS* resulted from the participatory process of rule definition. Rules resulted from lengthy discussions to build consensus in the IZ, after which they were transmitted downwards to the regions and nodes. Replication of *CT* was left to collective action by the grassroots. Nodes were kept as autonomous and local as possible. Exchange with others was seen as necessary to increase scale and scope. Each *CT* could use its own or its region's vouchers, but all *RTS* vouchers were accepted across the network. Issuance was checked once a month in the IZ. Primavera described them: 'The meetings of the IZ were something fantastic. Of course, you may wonder how much of what was decided was actually implemented in the *CT*. But a big gap between practice and theory is inevitable'. A rule under discussion for a long time was the use of, or ban on, pesos across the entire *RTS*; the prevalent opinion was in favour of their complete ban, but small amounts of formal money were needed to run the *CT*. The radical wing insisted that everything could be done without official money; coordinators just had to be creative. Negotiations with local governments were left to the regional sub-networks and nodes. The *RTS* not only included the wealthiest, but also the most ideologically minded and best-educated participants. As a result of the process of rule definition itself, the input legitimacy was high.

In the local or independent nodes, which were small closed communities, joining the *CT* amounted to agreement with the rules. Even so, they were often defined as being participatory, too, with opinions and interests of smaller groups in principle being accommodated. Of course, whether the interests of the majority eventually prevailed should be assessed case by case. All in all, acceptance of common rules was high and linked to the process through which they were formulated.

The second factor that supports sustainability of governance systems is the institutional mechanism of rule compliance and enforcement, even against resistance by some actors.

The PAR leaders assumed rule compliance would occur spontaneously by virtue of membership. If it became necessary, the coordinators would supervise and enforce rules. However, given the massive scale of the nodes, this was impossible. Some coordinators and franchisers instead took advantage of the situation. To speed up replication, the franchisers carried suitcases with *créditos* and returned with the fees paid in pesos. It became common practice to charge members more than the two pesos officially required and sometimes the suitcases of pesos would vanish. Of course, not all franchisers and coordinators took advantage, but that had nothing to do with the *PAR* leaders controlling them. Unable to handle 5,000 daily applications, *PAR*'s infrastructure and control mechanisms were overwhelmed. According to *PAR* leader De Sanzo, the franchisers were affected by 'common human weaknesses'. Critics blame the system itself; in the words of an anti-*PAR* leader: 'It was not only a way of stealing from the poor, giving them coloured paper for their money, but of teaching the poor how to steal from the even poorer.' *PAR* leader Covas assured the author he and his colleagues had tried different ways to improve control and enforcement of rules, but they had been ineffective or had engendered other abuses, so they left the monitoring to members. These did not have the capacity to carry out monitoring, either. In short, rule compliance was not monitored in the *RGT* and there were no institutional means of enforcement. It was not a franchise at all in the traditional sense.

Supervision and enforcement in the *ZO* was kept more or less under control in spite of the large scale of the nodes. Its leader Sampayo could not control over 400 coordinators, so he would show up unannounced in the *CT* and start trading incognito. That is, monitoring was random. If he found the rules of the franchise being violated, coordinators were asked to explain the lapse. Prosumers were also allowed to file complaints, though during the fieldwork it was impossible to find cases where that had happened. The *ZO* advised coordinators to have a team of assistants to police the nodes and enforce the rules, expelling trespassers if necessary. A few cases were found in which this had occurred. All in all, enforcement of rules in the *ZO* was fair and in line with the hierarchical rules of a franchise.

In the *RTS*, the autonomy of the clubs was jealously guarded and seen as a guarantee of rule enforcement. It was the most politically involved group of the *Trueque*. This was done through peer control or by the coordinators, who complained that rule enforcement relied excessively on them. Coordinators were seen as the guardians of the rules defined by the IZ and had the right to reject applicants if they doubted their commitment. The fieldwork identified a few cases where this had happened, though with limited success. A regional leader assured the author: 'The *Trueque* belongs to the people. That is how it works: local, democratic, and transparent'. There were discussions in the IZ on the importance of preserving solidarity and enhancing participation, transmitting the idea that the *Trueque* was a working alternative to capitalism.[53] Unfortunately, this was more in the discourse of the leaders than in reality of the participants. Enforcement of rules in the *RTS* nodes was variable but only fair; in some nodes, peer pressure worked well and enforcement was higher.

In the independent *CT*, rules were easier to enforce because of their smaller scale and pre-existent ties. Coordinators and members alike were part of a community beyond the node, to which they still belonged. So the rules of personal exchange applied and peer pressure kept members in check. Rule compliance was variable among groups but generally high. This was especially clear in the Barrio Belgrano node, which worked even without a coordinator and specific rules on prices or quality. Poverty and exclusion in common kept participants in line. A young man selling home-made detergents explained:

> I once burnt myself badly and could not work for months. My neighbours came to my room with a meal every day. I survived thanks to them. Sure, we all need to make the most of the *Trueque*, but when the market is done we go home together. And anyway, we are all poor, what can we squeeze out of each other?

The third factor supporting sustainability of governance systems is the benefits for agents based on achieving resource synergy, which in turn, raises output legitimacy. In the period analysed, basic food production inputs were the crucial scarce resource across all sub-networks through which to achieve synergy and secure the sustainability of the *Trueque*.[54]

In the *RGT*, the decision on how to obtain more basic food production inputs was mainly left to the nodes. At the central level, *PAR* used funds left over from the social franchise to buy food production inputs and sell them to those making food for sale in the nodes. Some nodes established an entrance fee in kind or in pesos, using the pesos for pool-purchasing of basic inputs. These responses met a small fraction of the needs of the participants. The *PAR* leaders pointed out to the author that the *Trueque* had never been intended to support over a million participants. To quote De Sanzo:

> We are not the state. The government asked us to let [people] in because there was no other solution for them. We did, we gave some a solution when the state had withdrawn. It was imperfect, we couldn't manage it, but there was nothing better in sight. Apparently, we made a mistake.

PAR tried to manage resources and gain synergies for the network, but achieved little success. The coordination of resources delivered minimal results to participants.

The hierarchical style of the *ZO* proved quite effective in achieving resource synergies, and in this respect the *ZO* is different from all the other networks. It structured a supply system of basic food production inputs by negotiating deals with firms in exchange for services such as transportation, cleaning or a share of the final production. The *ZO* also established collective factories and vegetable gardens with participants' labour. It managed a flour commodity chain: a mill would pay municipal tax arrears in flour, which the municipality would exchange with the *ZO* for maintenance of public spaces or bread for schools, which would be baked by *ZO* participants in collective *ZO* bakeries. For transportation, a team of *ZO* mechanics cannibalized several broken-down municipal trucks and assembled two trucks out of the parts. These were used to transport goods from one *CT* to another. The local government also received ten hours of transportation a week as payment. With similar agreements, *ZO* leader Sampayo obtained wood for furniture, land to plant fruits and vegetables, and warehouses to store goods. The resource synergies in the *ZO* proved to be the highest in the *Trueque*.

The importance of enhancing resource synergies was much discussed at the IZ but no decision was made to build supply chains. The official position was that coordinators should arrange for supplies with members. Some *CT* asked for a contribution in pesos so they could buy from wholesalers, later giving purchasing priority to those that made foods for the *Trueque*, but again the results varied. Where coordinators took up the task of pooling purchases, it worked fairly well. In other cases, it came to nothing. Some also tried to trade basic food production inputs with local governments or connect to their rural hinterlands. The achievement of resource synergies in the *RTS* was quite low, depending on specific coordinators and their strategies.

Local *CT* sometimes obtained donations from local governments. Pooling purchases was also tried, as were raffles. In *Comunidades Solidarias*, for example, members ran a grocery shop in the school and opened every afternoon to sell goods bought with a common pool of funds for pesos and *créditos*. Due to their small scale, local nodes had scarce resources for achievement of synergies. The relatively low economic benefits to participants, except where local governments support them, are the Achilles heel of local nodes.

The fourth factor supporting sustainability of governance systems has to do with the costs of running the system, which translate into output legitimacy. The costs studied here are transaction and organizational costs.

Transaction costs derive from trading with a non-state currency. The use of a single currency across a network of over a million participants reduced the risk of not finding goods to buy with *créditos*. The author found during the fieldwork that participants viewed their vouchers as a money parallel to that of the state, somewhat losing track of the risks it entailed. Some even stored the vouchers as a reserve of value. However, the large scale of the *RGT* made forgery attractive. So, while the system reduced transaction costs in the short term, it increased them in the long run. A similar description applies to organizational costs. In the short term, the effort in time and resources of setting up a *CT* was minimal. Making decisions was fast and easy, as the *PAR* leaders were the only ones in charge of regulation. However, in the long run this was impractical, since the three leaders by themselves lacked the capacity and the support infrastructure to make decisions over a network of thousands of nodes across the country or to respond quickly enough to forgery, conflicts and other threats. So in the end, organizational costs were high.

In the *ZO* the result was somewhat different. As it used a single currency across the network, uncertainty around the value of the *crédito* was low. The *ZO* voucher was also forged, but Sampayo's quick reaction replaced the counterfeit ones relatively soon after they had become a threat and that enabled the *ZO* to withstand the crisis better. However, while decision-making in the *ZO* was fast and costless, maintaining the system was not. The costs of the control infrastructure were paid through a collective fund financed through individual, very small, contributions. Moreover, reliance on only one person for strategic thinking raises the problem of his replacement in the future. The costs of making decisions were fair.

In the *RTS*, transaction costs around the variety of currencies used were the original basis for check-and-balance mechanisms in which all nodes inspected the currencies of the others. This required monthly meetings that made the means of payment reliable and their printing transparent. Thus, transaction costs were low. However, cross-checks entailed organizational costs that eventually proved burdensome in terms of time and money. The decision-making process became lengthy and rather inflexible. Therefore, the organizational costs in the *RTS* were high in the longer run.

In the local nodes, transaction costs of using non-state means of payment were not really a problem. The use of vouchers was mostly seen as an easier way to trade rather than bartering or reciprocity networks, so the transaction costs were generally low. Making decisions was relatively easy and costless, given the reduced scale of the groups and the fact that most members had known each other from before the node's formation.

To sum up, acceptance of rules in the *RGT* was very weak; it happened neither through the process of rule definition nor by explicit certification. In the *ZO* it was fair and elaborated through the training of the coordinators, among others. In the *RTS*, input legitimacy was strong and was obtained through concordance at the top. In the local nodes it was also strong and based on their small size or pre-existent relations. In relation to the second factor, rule supervision and enforcement was weak in the *RGT*. In the *ZO* it was fair and checked at random. In the RTS it was variable but only fair, and was left to the coordinators or peer pressure. In local nodes, rule enforcement was high thanks to their small scale. In terms of the third factor, resource synergy, the *RGT* achieved little of it, and the *RTS* and the local *CT* did not do much better. The main success was that of the *ZO*, which organized supply chains with private sector and state actors. The final factors analysed were transaction and organizational costs. In the *RGT* these were low in the short run but high in the long run. The concept of sustainability implies the long term, so the latter mattered most. In the *RTS*, transaction costs were low but organizational costs were the highest. The *ZO* had low transaction costs and fair organization costs, while the local nodes were less costly to manage.

Rules of Governance and Sustainability

What type of governance systems emerged in the second half of 2001, after the break-up of the *RT*? The *RGT* framed a regulated market system in which institutions promoted self-interest and coordination was achieved by a central regulator (the *PAR* leaders) that decided some basic rules and left others to be defined by each node and participant. The *ZO* structured a hierarchy in which participants were also guided by self-interest but coordination relied on an administrative bureaucratic structure managed by a strong leader. The *RTS* organized an associational network in which institutions enhanced compromise, first between the coordinators and then between participants, based on shared ideological convictions and recognition of mutual interdependency of interests. The local independent *CT* structured a community or club type of governance system, in which coordination was spontaneous and participants were guided by reciprocal obligation.

The fours main governance systems that emerged after the break-up of the *Redes de Trueque* in 2001 have been analysed in this chapter in terms of their sustainability, as summarized in Table 7.1. In the first three rows, the higher the rating, the more sustainable the system. In the last two rows, the low ratings indicate higher sustainability. At the risk of oversimplifying, the table shows that none of the networks scored highly in terms of the sustainability of their governance systems.

Table 7.1: Sustainability of governance systems in the Trueque, 2002

	RGT	ZO	RTS	LOCAL
Input legitimacy	Low	Fair	High	High
Rule enforcement	Low	Fair	Fair	High
Resource synergies	Low	High	Low	Low
Transaction costs	High	Low	Low	Low
Organizational costs	High	Fair	High	Low

Notes: RGT = Red Global de Trueque; ZO = Red de Trueque Zona Oeste; RTS = Red de Trueque Solidario.

The weak viability of the *RGT* regulated market was particularly problematic, as it was the largest group and the one by whose performance the general public judged the *Trueque*. It offered a mechanism in which people had to make little effort themselves; just find a venue, get the *créditos* and start trading. Rules were defined top-down, but the *PAR* leaders were unable to enforce them; they assumed that coordinators and prosumers would act 'responsibly' under peer pressure. The assumption of legitimacy without effective control capacities was a formula for disaster, which eventually happened. The social franchise system was in fact a strange aberration: franchises are based on hierarchical control capacities, which the *RGT* did not have. Controlling hundreds these nodes, with over a million participants, across the country and several dozens of franchise managers was impracticable. The only similarity between the 'social franchise' of the *RGT* and any private franchise was the name. The viability of the *RGT* regulated markets was minimal, with weak acceptance of rules, weak enforcement and weak resource synergies. In the long run, the transaction and organizational costs proved too high and, unsurprisingly, the governance system of the *RGT* fell apart. In doing so, it also dragged the rest of the *Trueque* down.

The strongest in ideological terms was the *RTS*, with its associational model. It was more sustainable than the *RGT* because it had high input legitimacy based on a participatory rule-setting process, fair enforcement and low transaction costs. However, it had minimal mechanisms to achieve resource synergies, and high organizational costs. It was particularly weak in its heavy reliance on the goodwill and commitment of coordinators and other organizers to enforce rules and achieve resource synergies. Primavera emphasized that the coordinators were the critical link. However, their capacities were not developed accordingly. The *RTS* failed to see this point early enough and it is conceivable that they may have corrected it in the long run. The weak spots became clear when inflation controls were needed. Much was discussed, but the associational network was distracted by political intrigues that blocked decisions. Inflation ran rampant. Discussion and consensus-building are, by definition, time consuming and the demise of the *Trueque* gave them no slack, but the political aspects of the *RTS* also prevented some solutions from even being considered. While ideological affinity acted as the glue that kept it together during its construction, it blocked the capacity to respond quickly to its change in fortunes. As theorized by Peter North[55] the limits of 'alternative' economies are set by the moral perceptions of those involved. The network eventually died, mired in negotiation and discussion, as the external circumstances of the demise of the *Trueque* affected it.

In contrast, local *CT* and the *ZO* appear to be the most viable systems and survived the collapse of the *Trueque* better, but this needs to be placed in context. The *ZO* had a fair legitimacy of institutions based on following a leader, fair enforcement of rules, excellent resource synergies, low transaction costs and fair organizational costs. It structured a hierarchy centred on the leadership of Sampayo, whose reputation and skill were well known. This created strong output legitimacy, but it is rather inconsistent with a scheme promoting participation and self-reliance of communities at a smaller scale. The *ZO* relied on bureaucratic structures to manage information and control the network, which were sustainable only on a large scale, for example on the regional level. In turn, it is at the expense of relying on a central leader and his managerial skills.

The fourth governance system was the local and independent node model. It was more sustainable than the other three and is how community currency systems around the world are typically organized. It scored high in rule legitimacy, high in enforcement and low in transaction and organizational costs. This was attributed to its reduced scale, at which the rules of personal exchange regulate a system. Its Achilles heel lay in the lack of resources with which to achieve synergies and create a significant income. This keeps them small and the gains of resource synergies are also small, though perhaps significant in terms of poverty alleviation. Some local nodes were able to ease shortages by involving local governments and donors to support the scheme. In that case, they were the most sustainable option to enhance participation and empowerment of its members.

Exactly How Small is Beautiful?

The problems of governance in the *Trueque* became evident as soon as the volume of trade, number of *CT* and number of participants demanded a system of governance that was comparable to a functional equivalent of the state; that is, an apparatus of rules and institutions to effectively regulate and coordinate economic action among 2.5 million participants as they were in the *Trueque* in the beginning of 2002. But it was virtually impossible; there was no functional equivalent of the state. A state accepts no substitutes, by definition. Was the scale of the *Trueque* the mother of its many evils? What does the experience of the Argentine *Trueque* indicate about scale and governance in community currency systems? Scale certainly matters, but bad institutional design is not necessarily corrected by reducing the scale.

The timing of the break-up of the *RT* (half of 2001) was also unfortunate. The economic crisis in Argentina around the turn of 2002 reached the proportions of a meltdown. The collapse of the regular economy strained the networks with 5,000 new members joining every day. Supply was insufficiently developed to satisfy needs on such a scale, creating scarcity and soon afterwards inflation. The *RGT*, benchmark of the *Trueque*, was incapable of controlling its vouchers which were later counterfeited, destroying the value of the currency. This was the ultimate blow for the *RGT* whose demise infected the other sub-networks, which were unable to face the challenges anyway, and the *Trueque* fell apart in a matter of months. However, the various networks collapsed differently and this chapter explained the variation as a result of the different types of governance systems framed by the networks.

The *PAR* leaders insist that the scheme was never meant to be the primary source of people's livelihood but to be a complement. Indeed, control was lost when the *CT* grew too much. The *PAR* leaders, who had shown extraordinary ingenuity in creating the *Trueque*, failed to keep pace with the changes in their masterwork. The nodes were out of control long before they became 'too big'. The question still remains as to whether remedial steps could have been taken.

The associational model of the *RTS* could solve some deficiencies but was also overwhelmed by the hordes entering the nodes. In the relatively quiet period of growth, its coordinators carefully enforced the rules, promoted commitment and enhanced participation, and responded to members' needs. During its best period, the *RTS* created the most democratic governance system in the *Trueque*, although some considered it too politicized. However, in the turbulent period that followed, the associational model was ineffective in structuring a response and incapable of sticking to dialogue. The *RTS* eventually fell apart but its associational model survived in the regional networks that comprised it. At that intermediate level, associational governance gets the best of both, growth in scale and scope and the legitimacy of participatory rule-setting.

The *ZO* proved to be better equipped to resist the challenges posed by the multiplication of membership and expanded its bureaucratic structures accordingly. Moreover, it made the most of its scale by developing supply chains. In this way it could ease scarcity and enter the sphere of enterprise production, achieving resource synergies that had been unheard of before in the world of community currency systems. The conclusion that hierarchies are effective and sustainable at large scales is not new.[56] Satori[57] claims that hierarchies can integrate the activities of very large groups of people as long as planning and communication are effective. These two conditions were met in the *ZO* through the skills and hierarchical style of its leader. All in all, a hierarchy seems the most sustainable governance system for large-scale operations such as the *ZO* had in Argentina. But it still has two limitations. First, leaders like Sampayo are relatively uncommon; a less-able one could have driven the *ZO* to disaster. And second, it creates the problem of succession if the community currency system is to survive its first generation of prosumers.

Finally, local independent nodes show great heterogeneity but relatively little is known about them. The participants were typically members of closed communities (schools, churches, neighbourhoods and slums) and the node was appended onto these, like most community currency systems worldwide. Their main problem was the lack of a pool of resources with which to create synergies. Independent *CT* that could resolve this problem through support of local governments and donors survived the demise of the *Trueque* remarkably well. In the extreme case of Barrio Belgrano, there is now even no need for a coordinator; the members are all poor, excluded from the regular economy, and need each other. They get minimal support from the city government and the Church. Barrio Belgrano represents an ideal case of a self-organized market, what Hayek[58] called a 'spontaneous private ordering', although a slum populated by structural poor participants is probably not where Hayek would have expected to find it. The fundamental condition that allows this market to work without the regulation of any authority is an undisputed mutual recognition of poverty and the engrained acceptance of prior market institutions. All in all, when assisted by local governments or donors, local nodes present the most sustainable model of the four studied here.

In conclusion, CCS governance systems need to respect a certain match between organization and scale. On a national, large scale, there seems to be no sustainable governance system for a CCS. After all, that is what the state is, not just the actor that has monopoly over means of violence but also the bureaucracy that spreads all over a territory to regulate the economy with an acceptable level of legitimacy. The analysis showed that a hierarchy worked best at the level of a region but it needed a skilful leader at the top capable of building infrastructure. On an intermediate scale, an associational governance system was sustainable as long as the number of actors involved was limited and the commonalities were clear enough to avoid tearing the network apart through internal politics. On a small scale, independent local groups appeared to be a sustainable option but they need to increase their resource base from other sources. When that was achieved, they constituted the leading case for CCS.

7 SMALLER SCALE TRUEQUE

The collapse of the R*edes de Trueque* in the second half of 2002 and the first half of 2003 was like a big-bang, to the point that some observers announced the *Trueque* was dead.[1] However, it was far from dead. The *CT* just became much smaller, of a scale comparable to other experiences of CCS around the world. They also changed in various ways.

In the years of exponential growth, *CT* had mostly lost the connection to their local communities and participants could come from quite far. After its decline in 2002–3, the coordinators and the most committed participants in each *CT* got to make critical choices again. The most pressing decision was whether to keep the node open and, in that case, under what conditions. That is, whether to operate independently or articulate to a network with other nearby *CT*. In 2004 the surviving nodes inaugurated a new stage in their development, one of empowerment of the coordinator and reconnection to the local level. With a smaller scale, the local context and the non-economic motivations for continuing with the *Trueque* regained significance.

CCS are an institution that localizes economic activity, while at the same transforming the quality of the exchanges.[2] In the last two decades, a few hundred regions, localities and communities in both the developed and the developing world have created community currency systems in an attempt to increase the control over their resources.[3] Their purpose is not to disconnect from the national economy, but to complement and adjust to it.

This chapter discusses four rationales for the creation of CCS to study the motivations of *CT* to continue after 2004. The first discussion is to what extent seigniorage constitutes an attractive income for the leaders of the *Trueque*. The second one is that *Trueque* changed the qualitative characteristics of exchange, embedding transactions in social relations which go beyond income generation. The third one is that it protects the local economy and stabilizes it through the national business cycle. The last one is that it provides households an extra opportunity to diversify their sources of income. Monetary networks and complementary currency systems are used as synonyms in this chapter.

These hypotheses will be tested by delving into the micro-world of the *Trueque* at the level of the participants. The data on which this analysis will be based were collected during a survey in the second half of 2004 and follow-up fieldwork in the last quarter of 2006 (details in Chapter 1). The survey got 386 effective responses from participants in eighteen nodes in the metropolitan area of Buenos Aires, Mar del Plata and Rosario.

As discussed in Chapter 2, national monetary systems with a single currency regulated by a central bank became normal only in the 1900s, and so are younger than many other economic institutions.[4] Yet, after two centuries of monetary sovereignty, at a time when global financial flows are blurring national boundaries and countries are regrouping around single currencies, localities and communities are again trying to establish their own currencies.[5] CCS seem an illogical curiosity, seeking to root exchange transactions in a specific area by means of a local transformation of the monetary system.

There are many types of community currency systems. On the basis of whether they are tied to geographical boundaries or not, Blanc[6] distinguishes two types: territorial and community. A territorial CCS is created for exchange transactions in a certain space, respecting no other restrictions than the boundaries of the area or authority of the issuing institution. It can be guided by an official authority with some sovereignty over a sub-national territory like a province or municipality. Though normally articulated with a monetary authority of higher rank and a hierarchical banking structure, it nevertheless represents a break from national monetary systems. Some examples of a territorial CCS are Estonia establishing its own currency out of the rouble area in 1992, the province of Buenos Aires in Argentina issuing the *patacón* in 2001 to pay off debts, and the French chambers of commerce printing 'currencies of need' (*monnaies de nécessité*) between 1914 and 1923.[7]

Community monetary networks have different boundaries. They restrict the use of monetary instruments exclusively to voluntary participants of a community, so the space of application is not necessarily bounded geographically but restricted to individuals who wish to take part. They include most local monetary networks that have emerged in the last two decades, like the *moneda sociale* in Italy, local exchange and trading systems (LETS) in Anglophone countries, *monnaies parallèles* in France, and *Red de Trueque* in Argentina and other Latin American countries.[8] In most of the *Trueque*, currencies circulated in more than one *CT* and even in a national network, so they are technically community or complementary currency systems, rather than local.

According to Blanc,[9] monetary theory offers a very partial explanation for processes of local monetary networks. The theory of optimum currency areas pioneered by Robert Mundell poses that the creation of secondary currencies turns an improvement in economic efficiency in regards to labour and capital mobility, wage flexibility, and fiscal redistribution of tax inflows in a region.[10] Fisher later suggested that the creation of a local currency is motivated by the search of an income from seigniorage and the freedom to manage monetary policy away from the Central Banks.[11] Indeed, these two perspectives help to understand the rationale for local monetary networks but do not analyse it in its complexity or in relation to the objective of developing the local economy.

A recent elaboration on local monetary networks distinguishes four main rationales for them, which often combine with each other.[12] The first relates to income collection through seigniorage, as advanced by Stanley Fisher.[13] Seigniorage is the revenue earned by organizations that issue money, calculated as the net difference between the total nominal value of scrip and the costs of printing it. For community monetary networks, the seigniorage argument was given little relevance. Many local monetary systems are accountancy systems with no physical scrip; there are no reserves and even when bills are printed, they are given free to participants. In turn, the funds were normally used to fund the nodes' activities and were not kept by the issuing institution, as Central Banks do.

The second rationale is a qualitative transformation of exchange. That is a change in the nature or conception of exchange transactions and their context. This idea draws on Polanyi[14] description of exchange transactions as atomistic and disembedded, meaning that social contact begins and ends with each transaction, independently of the social relations that nest it.[15] In contrast, the creation of a local currency entails a bond of trust between buyer and seller initiating a mutual credit, a 'bond of customers'.[16] In the Argentine *Trueque*, transforming the qualitative nature of exchange transactions was a goal in the early days of the *CT*, when *PAR* actively promoted environmentalism. It continued to be a priority for groups that viewed the *Trueque* as a means for participation and empowerment.[17] Several authors[18] analyse whether the *Trueque* represented a new type of sociability that brought the impoverished middle class together to reconstruct the social fabric. Other researchers on the *Trueque* refer to political emancipation and see it as a social movement with an economic angle.[19]

The third rationale for CCS identified by Blanc is protection of the local economic space against external monetary disruptions; that is, when means of payment are scarce (a recession) or excessive (inflation). Since local currencies are not compensated for outflows by inflows that would preserve the local monetary balance, CCS reduce the amount of cash flowing in or out of the region. When the national or global economy collapses, currency shortages constrain the circulation of goods in the locality, generating unsatisfied needs. These could be covered without central money by producers in the area. The mismatch between supply and demand could be solved by local means of payment, with the additional advantage that they would continue to circulate there Pacione.[20]

The fourth rationale is to promote local economic development. Improved dynamism of the local economy results from either locally locking in activities previously carried out elsewhere (repatriation of exchange transactions) or accelerating regional transactions. The regional economy is a 'very small open economy with limited tools to control the entrance and exit of physical resources, human and financial'.[21] Several authors[22] argue that CCS enhance the local economy's independence in line with Agenda 21 of the 1992 Rio Summit.[23] Like any currency, local money coordinates a productive system, tying together producers and consumers. It helps create new jobs, put local resources to economic use, and improve the general standard of living in the area. Developing the local economy thus represents a more ambitious goal than simply protecting it. In this sense, CCS could foster local economic development because income generated in local money is geographically restricted to being spent there. The role of the Trueque in promoting local economic development is the main focus of chapter 8.

There is a fifth rationale in addition to those given by Blanc:[24] diversification of income sources. The poverty alleviation effects of CCS have received less attention because most research on them has been conducted in the developed countries, where aiding the poor is not really a priority and CCS are more related to an alternative lifestyle.[25] The Argentine *RT* was fundamentally about generating an income during an economic crisis. However, the poor in developing countries live permanently in situations of economic emergency and need to diversify their income sources. CCS thus connect to another strand of theory. The livelihood approach, or asset vulnerability framework, approaches poverty by looking at what poor households have in relation to five types of assets: human (skills, health), physical (infrastructure, equipment), social (networks, connections), natural (land, water) and financial (money, credit).[26] Local institutions mediate how agents have access and manage these assets, so they affect the lives of the poor. In Argentina, the functioning of a *CT* meant there was an extra local opportunity to generate an income.

These five rationales motivate the creation of CCS around the world. They will be used as guidance to study why 10 per cent of the *CT* in Argentina decided to stay open in spite of the collapse of the *Trueque*. The next section accounts for the fall of the *RT* and how the networks reacted.

Reconstructing the Trueque Locally

Although the *PAR* network *RGT* was the main one to be affected by the forgery of *créditos* and the first one to fall apart, the demise spread to the other networks because the majority of participants were unclear about the differences between sub-networks. The demise in the other networks started towards the end of 2002, triggered by contagion. When the *RGT* fell apart, members spread to the nodes of the other networks. These did not have the resources to absorb the ex-members of the *RGT* and were also suffering from the shortages of food. Some of other networks had their vouchers forged as well, although not to the extent seen in the *RGT*. At the time of the first fieldwork (late 2004) a total of 500 nodes were estimated to be still in operation. A follow-up fieldwork by the end of 2006 found about a third of these still operating.

By the turn of 2004, the *PAR* leaders finally framed a response with a handful of coordinators in the South suburbs of Buenos Aires. They printed a safer voucher and once again opted for a loosely regulated market governance system. They formalized the income of the coordinators as a paid job (from the entrance fees). The new voucher included a demurrage of 12 per cent, so once a year each voucher of twenty *créditos* would be replaced by eighteen and the remaining two would be 'lost'. After two years, the demurrage scheme was abandoned in most of the new *PAR* nodes, mainly because participants did not understand how it worked and it was too complicated to implement it in practice.[27] A few dozen *PAR* nodes stayed afloat with 200 to 800 participants in each market. Agreements on maximum prices were made in some of them but were abandoned because they could not be enforced. This smaller scale and more committed coordinators achieved a minimum compliance with the rules which made the *CT* slightly more livable. An unstable balance between supply and demand was re-established and after a while the expansion of *créditos* in circulation could be controlled.

In the *ZO* the 1,300 nodes and 400,000 members in the beginning of 2002 dropped to thirty-nine *CT* and 30,000 members by the end of 2004. All their collective enterprises closed because the scale was no longer enough to sustain them. Vouchers were forged too but Sampayo saw it coming and was ready to change them as early as the beginning of 2003. The new safer voucher was ruled to expire by the end of 2004 with the intention that each note could be recalled and replaced by a new one. Sampayo says that the forgery of the créditos was bound to happen sooner or later:

> To supply means of payment to a system adding 4,000 new members a day, we needed a lot more *créditos* and they had to be better, durable and safer. The *Trueque* grew to become a state within the state, so it had to be managed as a state. While this is easy in a town of 100 inhabitants, it is different with 400,000. That was the amount of participants the *ZO* once had and of course not all of them were as honest and idealistic as you would like. But as a good state, you need to plan ahead also for them.

The *ZO* tried to re-register members at three point five pesos per person to re-create a collective fund and reorganize itself but not all participants cooperated. The *ZO* faces, after that, the problem of re-calculating the 'right' amount of vouchers for a rather unknown scale (many members trade in the nodes without re-registering, so there are more effective users than the vouchers circulating allow). The *ZO* is perhaps the only sub-network that allows trade across nodes and the only one that started adding members and nodes again after 2006. The nodes became more autonomous and most decisions lay in the hands of the coordinators. Sampayo is confident:

> The *Trueque* will rebound and I expect to be at the start line when that happens. Even if the economy is flourishing in 2020 with three per cent unemployment, many of those that are poor today will remain poor then and will remember they once had a better life with the Trueque. Besides, its strength lies in the fact that it can be combined with work in the formal economy, selling candies in a square, or raising children at home.

The demise of the *Trueque* spread to the *RTS* too which could not frame an organic response. What was left of the *IZ* was affected by further divisions and still unable to reach an agreement on basic issues. The level of conflict reached a height in September 2003 to the point of requiring police presence to prevent fights in the monthly meeting. Charlie del Valle recalls:

> The last meeting took place in Concordia where the *Trueque* was still working decently. Those of us from Buenos Aires were gladly surprised. Unfortunately, the differences of opinion became too large and with the system in decline, people became overly aggressive. The groups hated each other. The *Trueque* was in demise anyway so the original raison d'etre of the *IZ* had already vanished. It was the end of a fantastic cycle.

There were no more *IZ* meetings after that but several member sub-networks fared well on their own and kept operating at a regional level. They could enforce their rules of behaviour better than in the large networks and the crowded nodes. An example is *Mar y Sierras*, in the city of Mar del Plata and surroundings, which operated as a network until 2006. 'Being smaller, we were always able to restrain opportunistic behaviour better, even if by expelling members', recalls its leader. So while the *RTS* ceased to exist, its member sub-networks kept operating still as regional associative systems of governance. A great deal of intellectual work on the idea of social money came out of the group, especially from Heloisa Primavera.

Finally, an undetermined number of *CT* continued to operate but became independent. It was possible to locate thirty-five ex-*RGT* nodes in the suburbs of Buenos Aires and La Plata. Four of them were visited in the fieldwork. Their coordinators think the articulation of a network after the fall of the *Trueque* makes no sense any more. They stick to the belief that the *Trueque* is beneficial for most people, both because of its economic impact and for the social contact. Some nodes have become a private business run by a self-employed coordinator charging an entrance fee. Others operate at the local level, independent, insulated in their own communities, like *Comunidades Solidarias, Centro Poriahyu* or Bar*rio Belgrano*, described in chapter 6.

In *La Estación*, the largest ex-RGT node still operating in the Capital of Buenos Aires by 2006, they see the node as a meeting point of friends and especially as an excuse for women to leave their homes and generate some income. It meets twice a week with 300 to 400 visitors. They use the old *PAR* voucher (both real and forged ones) stamped at the back so they could stop the expansion of means of payment. New members, who have *PAR créditos* left, are accepted after their vouchers have been stamped. This has led to a rapid expansion of means of payment and caused inflation, but the coordinator is confident that it is only a temporary process until the amount of circulation adjusts. The node left prices float freely until the parity reached a peso for around 1.000 *créditos* by 2006. She explains:

> We have no communication whatsoever with the *PAR*. Why would we? All participants had their *créditos*, so we have enough vouchers in the node. We also know how to run it, we know the advantages and the problems. We have a venue of our own and our own assistants to check members who think they are smarter. So what could the *PAR* offer us?

In the surviving nodes, women have become the majority again (70–80 per cent). They speak of the *CT* as a 'meeting place', a space for social inclusion. The nodes are also dominated by the structural poor and the disenfranchised middle class that will not rebound off poverty any more.

All the *CT* visited, whether independent or part of a network, share a salient characteristic; they are considerably more autonomous than ever before. Most coordinators know the *Trueque* for several years. They have accumulated much expertise on how to run a node and have developed the capacities to set rules, if necessary, and get them enforced to a minimum level of compliance. The coordinator of a *ZO* node assures:

> The coordinator is the one here. What participants see is us. When they have a problem they come to us. The ones that decided to open a node again were us. The network is a label that you hang at the door to show that you are serious and that your *créditos* are safe to use.

Of the 386 respondents to the survey, 86 per cent were women, and 46 per cent were between forty-six and sixty years old and had a relatively low level of education (only half of them had complete secondary school education). The respondents cannot be regarded as being typical of the structural poor: 67 per cent of their households owned a home (half through public housing plans), 63 per cent had been on holiday at least once in their lives (two-thirds through unions or with the help of the welfare state) and 60 per cent had a family member who could use the Internet.[28] Half the respondents were heads of households (main breadwinners).

Regarding their participation in the *Trueque*, half of the respondents (52 per cent) started participating in the years when it reached massive proportions (2000–2), a third were already members before that and the rest joined after the *Trueque* fell apart (2003–4). More than half (55 per cent) did not stop participating during the *Trueque*'s collapse; they just found other nodes that were still open. The respondents were mostly regular visitors to the nodes: 45 per cent went twice a week, 31 per cent more often, 15 per cent once a week and only 10 per cent had no fixed routine or were new.

Seigniorage in the *Trueque*

Seigniorage was defined as the revenue earned by organizations that issue money, calculated as the net difference between the total nominal value of scrip and the costs of printing it. When the *Trueque* was adding 5,000 members a day, the income for those networks that charged pesos for the vouchers, namely the *RGT* and the *ZO* must have been significant. In the rest of the RT, the vouchers were given free to participants so there was no seigniorage.

The *RGT* and the *ZO* collected two pesos in regular money for every fifty *créditos* lent to newcomers, while the cost of printing the vouchers was about twenty cents. That means that the each time a new participant joined, the networks earned one point eight pesos in seigniorage. For the *ZO*, the use of the funds is precisely recorded in public accounts. They were spent to finance a number of social enterprises discussed in detail in chapter 8.

For the *RGT*, the allocation of the seigniorage earnings has not been recorded in written. De Sanzo says that the network then had many costs and these were paid mainly with the seigniorage income. He recalls:

> Vouchers had to be printed and that was expensive and paid in pesos. Besides, there were all sorts of organizational costs like rent, telephones, transport, and so on. When there was money left, we used it to buy food input products like flour and sugar that were then sold in our main nodes.

The *créditos* proceeding from those sales were used for the security, cleaning and maintenance of the *CT*. Other services contracted from participants were also paid with *créditos* that came out of the prints and were an injection of complementary currency. The coordinator of the main surviving node of *RGT*, *El Comedero*, explains:

> We had as expert that checked the condition of the food. We considered it important to have someone check the hygiene, the expiry dates, the freshness of the food, and

so on. We paid him in *créditos* and it was a service of the node to its participants. We used *créditos* also for the people that did the cleaning and the rent of the venue where we held the markets.

Assuming the seigniorage earnings were actually spent as told by the *PAR* leaders, this allocation represents an important difference with what Central Banks do as issuers of official money. In the *Trueque*, the income was mostly spent in goods and services for the nodes or for the network. It benefited those who were in fact paying for the use of the vouchers and for the right to join the *CT*. So while complementary currency produces seigniorage earnings like regular money, this is mostly distributed among participants in goods and services.

However, there were doubts among participants and observers of the *Trueque* in general on the extent to which the seigniorage earnings were effectively used for the benefit of all. Many suspected that what was left after covering the operational costs of the network was hijacked by the *PAR* as their own income. It really cannot be ascertained. The *PAR* leaders were then working full time in the organization of the *RGT* and had no other income from employment. After 2004 there were no new vouchers printed, so the seigniorage income was reduced to nil.

Qualitative Transformation of Exchange

The second rationale for complementary currency systems is the goal of changing the quality of the exchanges.[29] The hypothesis is that CCS transform the relationship that agents establish with each other as consumers and producers in the market. It relates to Polanyi's concept of embeddedness, which means that exchanges are situated within social relations.[30] This factor would allow the analysis of economic phenomena with attention to power, gender, values, intentions and motivation, trust, traditions, and so on.

Thorne researched whether LETS in Great Britain represent a 're-embedded economy' and the complementary currency is a 'moral money'.[31] The author looked at the motivations of participants for involvement in the CCS, to what extent they shared a political project of emancipation and the importance of a local dimension in their activities. The study was used as guidance for this research on the *Trueque*.

During fieldwork in the second half of 2004 participants were enquired on why they continued to visit the *Trueque* after the system had collapsed. They were asked to mention their main reason to participate and a second reason. The main reason quoted was clearly economic and 78.2 per cent of the respondents said their households could not go by without the income they made in the *CT*. The social contact enabled by the *Trueque* was mentioned as main motivation by 18 per cent of the respondents. Social contact achieved the highest score as secondary reason: 47.4 per cent said that the *Trueque* offered a chance to socialize with others in similar conditions. A female member explains:

> While you buy and sell in the node, you talk, you laugh, you make jokes with others. You gossip about the children and the neighbours. You just forget all the things outside. I go back home and I am already looking forward to the next meeting. I used to be depressed, but now I use the *Trueque* as a therapy.

The exact phrase 'It is like a therapy' was heard repeatedly when respondents were asked to detail what they liked about the social aspects of the *Trueque*. In their meaning making process, participants associate the *CT* to healing. Other phrases in the same course were: 'It gives me a good feeling about myself'; 'It boosts me out of depression'; 'I meet people like me'; 'I am not lonely at home any more'; 'I've found I can do many things I never thought I could'; 'It strengthens my self-esteem'.

However, not all share a positive opinion of the social aspects of the *CT* and 22 per cent of the respondents said there was no second reason to participate other than making a living. These members usually expressed what their occupation and their position was or used to be 'outside' in the regular economy. A middle aged man complained:

> I come because I am unemployed and my family needs to eat. The *Trueque* is better than other ways of making a living. I am a carpenter, but I only have work occasionally. I think that when people say they like the *Trueque*, they lie. Coming here is like admitting you're a loser in the real economy. However, I must say, at least the *Trueque* is honest, you don't beg and you don't steal.

Table 7.1:Reasons for participating in the Trueque after its collapse

Motivations for participating	Main reason (360 cases)	Secondary reason (360 cases)
I need the income / economic	78.2	17.6
I come for the social contact	18.0	47.4
Others	3.8	12.8
No reason other than income		22.2
Total	100.0	100.0

In comparison to Thorne's study in the UK, only 1 per cent of the respondents mentioned as their main reason that they participate because they shared the political project of emancipation and solidarity behind it.[32] 3 per cent mentioned it as secondary reason. The proportion was similar across nodes, including those previously articulated with the *RTS*, in which leaders promoted the *Trueque* as a radical transgression to the capitalist system.

The survey also enquired about the level of trust between participants. The question was phrased: 'Considering your experience in the *Trueque*, would you risk selling on credit for about seventy five *créditos* today and get paid next week?' The amount in the question was changed in the different nodes, so it would always represent a bottle of cooking oil or two kilos of sugar at the local prices. For most of the participants in the *Trueque*, that amount would not threaten their survival but would prevent them from buying other commodities they needed.

Table 7.2: Would you sell on credit and get paid next week?

Level of Trust	Main reason (360 cases)
Yes, to most people	42.2
Only to those I know well	45.0
No, or only exceptionally	12.8
Total	100.0

The percentage of members that would only sell on credit to those they know well was, unsurprisingly, the highest. For small shops in the regular market economy, selling on credit to trusted neighbours is common practice. This is a well-researched advantage of proximity.[33] The existence of inter-personal networks of trust within the *CT* was already discussed in Chapter 5.

It is the proportion of those who would sell on credit 'to most people' that is unusually high. The strong expectation that participants would pay back without directly knowing them indicates that the level of trust in the *CT* was generally high. This is not related to relationships of kin or friendship; only 8 per cent of the respondents celebrated holidays like New Year together and only in the space of their *CT*. Participants were asked to provide further details to explain their trust. A minority thought the coordinator would act upon it and exert pressure on the non-compliant participant but most did not find that necessary. While some members related to a 'specific morality' of the node, others added peer pressure and reputation as factors to control rogue behaviour:

> I know that there are good and bad people in the *Trueque*, like everywhere else but after a while coming, you understand it works different here. We all have families to feed and children and things we can't afford but this is like a safety boat after the ship's wreckage, so you need to be extra careful. You don't ruin it, because you don't want to fall deeper than here.
>
> I can't think I won't get paid. It is more or less the same people that come here each week. If they don't pay me, how can they come back? Nobody will sell on credit to them. No one wants to risk living without the *Trueque*.
>
> You don't behave in the *Trueque* like you do outside because here we're all in a difficult situation and we all need what the others bring every week. So it would have to be someone really very desperate not to pay. Yes, I know some people only eat a

warm meal when the *CT* is open. Maybe if I sell on credit to someone in that situation, she might not be able to pay. But if I ever get to that situation myself, I hope
someone will give me rice too! The *Trueque* is like this, we all need to help each other
out a little bit.

The answers explain the relatively high level of trust in the *Trueque* in terms of
trading repeatedly within the same network. In turn, they refer to similar unsatisfied needs as a commonality between participants as a basis to induce reciprocity
or at least restrain rogue behaviour. Could these characteristics also develop in
the regular economy with official money? There is no reason why they would
not. However, a CCS guarantees that trade takes place within a closed social
network; those that have decided to accept the means of payment. Since it is perceived as a second-class currency (less appreciated than regular money) the use
of the *crédito* is related to curtailed opportunities to make a living. The *Trueque*
thus transmits the perception of exclusion which contributes to the 'morality'
of a node. This is a morality prevalent in their economic activities among the
poor.[34]

There is no evidence that after 2004 the *Trueque* re-embeds economic life
in a political project of emancipation or is an anti-capitalist movement. Most
participants join it to generate an income which is in line with what some previous researchers have argued.[35] Nevertheless, through participation in the node
it appears that a large proportion of them develops bonds that go beyond the
exchange itself. Trust and reciprocity result from trading repeatedly with the
same group and sharing exclusion, as a common perception. The *Trueque* thus
re-embedded economic life in a particular morality, different to the one prevalent in the regular money with official money, but still incipient and not of a
'political' nature (challenging structures of power).

Protection of Local Economic Activity

The third question to explore is the role of the *Trueque* in protecting the local
economy. The original project was to provide economic help to a segment of the
population that in 1995 was suffering the effects of the structural reforms and
unemployment. With the economic collapse, it became a full fledged survival
activity.

Typically, participation in the *Trueque* was the equivalent to employment of
own account on small scale and at low productivity. Households where the main
breadwinner lost the job in the regular economy or earned too little to make a
living resorted to the *CT* to offer goods and services. For them, it was like setting
up a micro-enterprise for which the cost of entry was low, measured against the
minimal opportunity cost of staying at home without the income. They served

a complementary market with local products and local consumption and they generated an income in surrogate money until they could re-enter employment.

As postulated in the literature, the participants thus established a variety of links to the regular economy that protected local economic activity. They were asked about the origin of their products on sale (see Figure 7.1). A quarter of the supply comprised second-hand articles that people had at home and could spare. The sale of these had no macroeconomic impact beyond providing income to the sellers. Another 9.5 per cent of the products originated from the government's social welfare schemes or charities. To keep figures conservative, it is assumed that these were bought directly elsewhere and had no impact on the local economy. The remaining 65.4 per cent of the goods sold by the respondents had an impact on the local economy. Participants themselves produced 28 per cent of the products on offer; this was normally done at home and therefore represents extra local production.[36] Another 18 per cent of the goods were bought in nearby shops and resold in the *CT* without processing. This added local demand, which might not have existed otherwise, to the regular economy. Goods discarded by third parties comprised 10.5 per cent of the supply, which did not stimulate production in itself but reduced the amount of waste requiring disposal. Finally, shops and local businesses participated in the *CT*, selling idle stocks and overproduction; this constituted around 9 per cent of the goods on offer.

The breakdown of the supply thus shows that the *Trueque* protected economic activity in the region in several ways: by increasing production, adding demand when the regular market collapsed, reducing waste for disposal (a positive environmental effect) and providing local businesses with a secondary or outlet market. In general, the *Trueque* satisfied more needs with the same income

Figure 7.1: Origin of products sold by respondents in the Trueque (n=386)

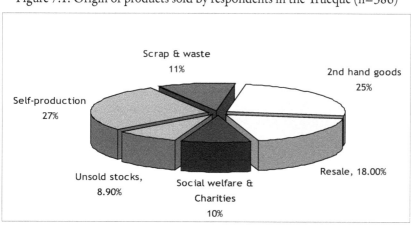

in pesos, restoring some value to second-hand goods, reusing waste, and exchanging unwanted goods received as gifts for those needed by the participants.

Local factories and shops participating in the *CT* compensated for part of the sales lost in the regular economy by directing overproduction or excess stocks to the *Trueque*. Out of the forty-four *CT* visited during the fieldwork, sales in pesos and complementary money were observed in twenty-nine; this has also been reported by other researchers.[37] Shops typically go on with business in both the regular market and the *CT*. A woman trader said:

> I've had a shop for twenty five years but things have not been going well for some time. So I come to the *CT* twice a week. It sells a lot easier than in the shop because people want to take goods home instead of these little pieces of paper. Of course I prefer pesos, but I fill the fridge with vegetables and other home-made foods from here. It helps me a lot. That is why I do it.

In two of the eleven *CT* where no shop owners were found, they were banned for ideological reasons; another three were located in slum areas inaccessible to shop owners and six were too small to attract shops. The percentage of shop owners among participants was invariably small (7.8–10.3 per cent), with more presence in *CT* in relatively more affluent areas. When asked to estimate the relevance of their sales in complementary currency, 62 per cent considered them 'crucial' or 'very important' for enabling them stay in business. A third had closed, but even so, all but one of owners of the closed shops indicated they had liquidated their machines, tools and stocks in the *CT* and that had enabled them to satisfy basic household needs for some time. The *Trueque* did not necessarily save shops and businesses, but it supported them in the crisis.

The participation of local businesses was considerably more marked during the peak of the crisis (2001/02) than when the fieldwork was carried out. Once the regular economy rebounded, the shop owners left the *Trueque* to continue business as usual. The owner of a bakery said: 'Clearly we all prefer pesos because we must pay our suppliers in pesos and not in pieces of coloured paper. But when there are no pesos you need to stay afloat. All things considered, this is a good alternative'.

The *Trueque* thus represented a useful 'emergency market' for shops and small producers affected by the collapse of the regular economy. The rebound of the regular economy did not make the *Trueque* disappear completely. According to *ZO* leader Fernando Sampayo, the *Trueque* continued to exist even when the regular economy was booming because people had adopted it as one of their habits. In addition, a factory can nearly always compensate for insufficient sales in pesos with sales in *créditos* at any time in the business cycle in order to improve efficiency and stock rotation. Sampayo explained:

The *Trueque* stabilises the scale of production and sales because the retailers and small local manufacturers can sell their overproduction, what the market in pesos does not buy from them. Unit costs go down when the scale of production is increased. If there is a crisis, that prevents it from worsening. It gives companies a greater chance to recover after a bad period or gain competitiveness if they are in a good period. It always helps.

In short, the protection of economic activity in the locality occurred as described in the literature; some small firms and shops badly hit by the economic downturn used the *Trueque* as an alternative channel to sell the products that the market in official money was not able to buy from them. They dealt with the overproduction in several ways: discarding the products, giving them to employees, using them for part-payment of wages, or selling them in the *CT* as a complement to their sales.

Diversification of Household Income

A fifth rationale for creating CCS was suggested in this chapter, in addition to the four theorized by Blanc[38] and others.[39] Complementary currency systems support households in diversifying their sources of income. They present an addition to the institutional endowment of localities with a specific focus on the excluded: the poor, the unemployed, the low-waged workers and the individuals engaged in unpaid work (typically women). At least in developing countries, this motivation should be regarded as a fifth rationale for CCS.

The orientation of the *Trueque* towards households stricken by poverty, unemployment and vulnerability is presented in Figure 7.2 and Table 7.3. In relation to the labour market, the largest group of participants were the unemployed. The second-largest group were unpaid home-workers who had never had an income. Waged employees and retired participants explained that they had joined because their wages or pensions in the regular economy were too low to maintain their livelihood. Therefore, they needed a secondary source of income and the *Trueque* was at hand.

Participants were asked how their economic situation had changed after they joined the *Trueque*. Their responses provide clear evidence that it protected their lifestyle: all but two of the 386 respondents said their households' economic situation had improved (42.5 per cent) or stayed the same (57 per cent).

The large majority of the participants (360 out of 386 respondents) indicated that their household had an income in pesos and 154 declared two other sources of income in pesos. These were normally insufficient to cover the expenses of the household. Official currency typically came from another member of the household in regular employment (37.5 per cent) or in temporary/irregular

Figure 7.2: Labour status of respondents (n=386)

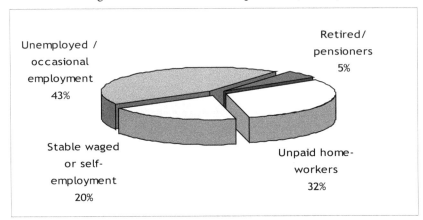

Notes: The category 'Self-employed' implies a regular occupation requiring specific skills and equipment but no wage relation. Workers alternating irregular informal work and unemployment are considered unemployed. Unpaid home-workers are typically women not participating in the paid labour market.

employment of the same member (34.2 per cent). The rest of the participants (about a third) received a pension, a welfare subsidy from the government or financial aid from relatives and friends. In addition, about 40 per cent of the households had a third source of income, typically in irregular and own-account employment.

Table 7.3: Percentage of respondents with household sources of income in addition to the Trueque (n=386)

Other income sources	Respondents with one other income (360 cases)	Respondents with two or more other incomes (154 cases)
Regular employment	37.5	0.6
Irregular, own-account employment	34.2	58.4
Pension	15.3	9.7
Welfare system	7.8	16.2
Help from family, relatives, friends	5.3	14.9
Total	100.0	100.0

The typical situation in such cases was to use the two currencies (pesos and *créditos*) for different expenses. Pesos were insufficient to cover all the needs of the household, so some needs (mainly food, clothes, shoes and toiletries) were satisfied in the node. Expenses like medicines, transport, rent and utilities required pesos. These were kept for the strictly necessary, or, where possible, were only incurred when pesos were available.[40] Participants then got from the *Trueque* as much as they could of their other needs. The earmarking of currencies for different expenses corroborates the perception that the *Trueque* does not resolve poverty. It is complementary to some employment in pesos.

The *Trueque* was an option in the menu to diversify income and cover the needs and wants of the household. Respondents overwhelmingly indicated that their households would not get by without the *Trueque*. Most were unable to detail what share of their expenses was paid in each currency, but 303 respondents did roughly assess the share of their basic needs that was met through the *CT*.[41] The *Trueque* appeared to be a critical source of income for some; a small group of 7 per cent had no other income at all and another 18 per cent covered 75 per cent of their basic needs through the *Trueque*. They said some members of their household did not eat on the days the *CT* was closed.

Table 7.4: Share of household expenses covered through CT in 2004 (n=363)

Less than a quarter	33
About half	42
Up to three-quarters	18
All (no other income)	7
Total	100

This extremely poor group, like all the others, could participate in the *Trueque* only if they were first able to get something to sell. The variety of what they obtained from various sources was quite broad, including food donations given but not consumed for health or taste reasons;[42] scrap and leftovers from factories and shops (pieces of fabric, defective items, slightly deteriorated food in damaged cans and boxes, and produce such as fruits, vegetables, bread or dairy products coming to the end of their shelf life); second-hand goods (clothes, shoes and toys) received from charities; scrap weeded out of rubbish in wealthier areas; donations from churches and NGOs; and goods from their kin. They also used state welfare payments and donations to buy goods they could sell in the *CT*. As long as they obtained something to sell, the structural poor could survive on the *Trueque*. 'Survive' means that they remained in poverty or even extreme poverty, but could at least satisfy the most basic needs.

The situation was easier for less-poor participants among the respondents. About 42 per cent covered half their basic needs in the *Trueque* and 33 per cent about a quarter. These two segments of participants represented 75 per cent of the respondents and they had assets accumulated in the past by themselves or kin, or an income in pesos with which they bought goods for the node. Some sold them directly, while others preferred to process food production inputs because they could then charge a mark-up for their value added, but this depended on the extent to which they were able to find inputs in the node.[43] Many respondents emphasized that the *Trueque* works best when a few pesos are available to buy supplies and process food production inputs.

Some participants said that in the past it had been possible to live entirely on the *Trueque*. In 2000–2 its scale and scope were much larger, as was also the need of participants to survive the crisis. The fieldwork was carried out when the impact of the *Trueque* had diminished and poverty in the country had fallen markedly. When asked to assess the share of household expenses covered through the *Trueque* during the economic collapse of 2000–2, only 248 respondents were able to answer (the rest were not participants then or could not remember). From those who did answer, it became clear that the *CT* was crucial: 63 per cent covered 75 per cent of their basic needs or more and 25 per cent met half their basic needs in the *Trueque*. It was the basis of their survival during the crisis. These responses are naturally tinted by the positive memories of a past that is gone and which some participants refer to as the 'magic' of the *RT*. 'I was able to buy so much at that time that the bus driver didn't want to let me in to go home', a participant added to her answer. In reality, the impact of the *CT* was probably less than they remember, but that still does not invalidate its importance.

In spite of the considerable reduction in its size, the *Trueque* was not too small to stop being useful after its decline. By 2004 the nodes became much smaller but 96 per cent of the respondents said they were satisfied with the scale and scope of the goods on offer. Most said it just required a different buying style (40 per cent bought what they found that day that could be useful). They added that coordinators had been able to regain control of the situation, so the return of regulation somehow compensated for lost scale. However, after 2004 the participants are more likely to be older than fifty years, less qualified, structural poor and with less entrepreneurial capacity than those who have left the *Trueque*.

What reinforces the satisfaction of participants is perhaps the realization that the alternatives are not better. Participants were asked where they had received help. Out of 305 respondents, 35 per cent received assistance from friends and family, 17 per cent from the state, 15 per cent from neighbours, 12 per cent from churches and 4 per cent from politicians outside the official channels. However, participants often added that they did not seek help from anyone other than friends and family.

The *Trueque* thus appears to be a critical option in the income diversification menu of households, consistent with the view that a CCS in developing countries is an institution designed for the excluded. It improves access to a market network and management of the assets of the vulnerable. However, the diversification of income by the participants of the *Trueque* shows that it does not constitute an instrument to raise people out of poverty. Only a minority of the poorest, those who were able to obtain something to sell, participated in the *Trueque* and comprised no more than 30 per cent of the *CT* participants. It offered them the opportunity to eat and clothe themselves. Less-poor participants neatly incorporated the *Trueque* as a source of household income, earmarking currencies for different expenses, finding ways to obtain food production inputs, calculating mark-ups, alternating production and resale as was convenient. The disenfranchised middle class and the not-so-poor have some access to pesos, skills, tools, or contacts to access such resources. Nodes mixed participants from different social backgrounds and were meeting places for the excluded in general: the unemployed, the disenfranchised middle class, the structural poor, the low-paid and the unpaid workers.

Rationales and Types of CCS

Previous research highlighted four rationales for CCS: generate revenues of seigniorage, change the qualitative nature of exchange, protect economic activity, and promote local economic development. The latter is discussed in Chapter 8.

Complementary currency systems can generate seigniorage income when the use of the vouchers is charged for in official money or spent in contracting goods and services. Most CCS around the world distribute free the vouchers, but the *Trueque* shows that complementary currency is like any other money and can generate seigniorage earnings. The difference is that those earnings are spent on benefits to all participants.

The second rationale discussed was the qualitative change of the exchanges. At least in the *Trueque* after 2004, no evidence was found of an interest in a political project of emancipation or an anti-capitalist social movement. Most participants join it to generate an income. The rationale behind the *Trueque* differs from the findings of research in USA and UK; where the political motive was stronger than the economic one.[44] However, the difference may be the result of the limitations of CCS in the North to generate sufficient economic impact, which is the main strength of the *Trueque*. Evidence was found of the 're-embeddedness'[45] of trade in the nodes in a morality of trust and reciprocity, but this is probably too weak to be a transformative force in the regular economy.

The third rationale was the protection of local economic activity during the crisis. It was the main reason why the Argentine *Trueque* expanded to 5,000 centres across the country and it occurred in line with the effects predicted by CCS theory: it added to local production with local inputs, raised local demand, reduced waste and offered a market for businesses to sell overproduction and stay afloat. Some observers believed that protecting local economic activity in the crisis was the core rationale for the *Trueque,* so it would disappear with the recovery of the regular economy. While the enthusiasm for the *Trueque* cooled down, it still exists after fifty months of uninterrupted economic recovery. The paradox reflects that after 2004 the nodes achieved higher levels of institutionalization than a temporary survival mechanism. Participants see them as a legitimate way of making a living parallel to their income in regular money.

A fifth rationale was discussed along that line: at the institutional level the *Trueque* offers an extra option to diversify income sources. It enables the poor and unemployed to interact with other social actors, and participate in or form networks that were previously unavailable to them. This finding corresponds to the idea expressed by Williams and Windebank[46] that community exchange schemes – of which the *Trueque* is a case – could be a valuable complementary approach to creating additional jobs in deprived areas, given the increasing shift away of economies from full employment. Although it cannot raise them out of poverty, the *Trueque* was a vital source of income for households to go by.

Why is the *Trueque* Not Dead?

At the beginning of 2007, after fifty months of uninterrupted growth in the regular economy, the *Red de Trueque* is starting to look like an inessential leftover of the economic collapse of 2002. Some observers[47] argued that the *RT* was bound to disappear. Still, a few hundred nodes are alive, much against the anti-cyclical hypothesis and a few new ones opened in 2006. There are several reasons for this.

To start with, as this study has emphasized, the background conditions for the emergence of the *RT* were not simply the meltdown of macroeconomic variables but the institutional gaps that resulted from reforming the economy. Agents whose lives had become unstructured and uncertain found that the *Trueque* restructured their socioeconomic activity in line with the institutions they had been used to. Agents were able to reintegrate into the regular economy when it rebounded, as happened after 2003. However, many could not return and the *Trueque* still contributes to their livelihoods. They can understand it and make meaning of it, at least more than the modernized economy.

The profile of individuals most likely to participate in the *Trueque* is consistent with the groups that labour market experts term 'unemployable'. They are unlikely to find a job again and will probably stay under the poverty line and hence in need of complementary income-generation schemes.[48] The *Trueque* is one such option and it has already become part of the new Argentine economy as a secondary or tertiary labour market.

Another reason why the *Trueque* has not died in spite of the thriving regular economy is related to gender. At least three-quarters of the participants are women, normally middle-aged and doing unpaid work. The characteristics of their continuous participation differ according to whether they are new or structural poor. The disenfranchised middle-class women were most affected by the loss of access to the public space as a result of the decreased income of their households, as has also been found by other researchers.[49] Those women discovered in the *Trueque* a new space of sociability. Their participation in a node was frequently based on hobbies, which became the basis for producing valuable goods for sale. Alternatively, women that had employment experience but were no longer active in the regular economy were able to use their skills again in the space of the nodes. When the regular economy rebounded, many were able to reinsert themselves into it, sometimes remaking their *Trueque* activity into a micro-enterprise in the regular economy.

The *Trueque*'s effect on women among the structural poor was different. Leonie and Luzzi[50] found that the *RT* enabled them to obtain recognition for their work because they were able to contribute to household expenses. The women's activities that used to be unpaid within the household (taking care of the children and elderly, cooking and knitting) became a source of income in the *Trueque*. For this reason, women often saw it as an extension of their daily housework and attended the node markets with their children and other family members. These women are today the majority in the nodes that survive and they express pride at being able to contribute to the daily needs of the household with their work at the *Trueque*, even if their husbands are again employed in the regular economy. The *Trueque* has also enabled them to learn skills or to enhance entrepreneurial capabilities they did not know they had.

While the *Trueque* after 2004 has become more inclusive of the structural poor than in its early days, the scheme is not really designed for the poorest of the poor. In the beginning the *Trueque* was populated by the disenfranchised middle class. Participation was driven not only by survival needs but also by the desire to protect or recover a middle-class lifestyle. On the social level, the *Trueque* enabled them to fashion a new social fabric to replace the one lost when they fell into poverty.[51] Though they had sunk under the poverty line during the national crisis, their infrastructural needs were covered and perhaps allowed them to view their poverty as temporary.

As far as the structural poor are concerned, the *Trueque* included them into networks that are better endowed with resources but they could benefit from the scheme only when they could meet two conditions. First, they need to stay being a minority of the membership of the nodes, in order to preserve its diversity in the supply of goods. As increasing numbers of the structural and extreme poor started participating in the *Trueque*, the markets became saturated with second-hand goods obtained from charities or by sifting through waste, as well as services such as cleaning for which there was limited demand. The survey carried out for this study gave a rough indication that extremely poor participants who can only offer these kinds of goods and services should not comprise more than

25–30 per cent of a node in order to obtain substantial benefits from it. When the proportion increases beyond this threshold, the nodes become anarchic battlegrounds of individuals struggling for food production inputs and other basic needs. This point also helps to answer the question of why the *Trueque* expanded so massively in Argentina: there was a large not-so-poor population comprising up to 70 per cent of the membership in thousands of *CT*s across the country. In nodes in which the majority were the structural poor, the *Trueque* represented 'an illusion' because there were not enough goods to trade.[52]

There was a second condition that needs to be fulfilled for the structural and extremely poor to reap benefits from participating in the *CT*s. They first need to obtain goods to sell, from social security, charities, donations, kin, gifts, or by sifting through waste. This condition may lead to an apparent paradox: the structural poor first need to obtain assets that raise them above their poverty. But it need not be a contradiction. It can constitute a useful guideline for donors, charities and social policy decision-makers. Even if the poor cannot themselves use the products given to them out of charity, by exchanging them in a club market they can obtain something else that they do need. A CCS can thus concentrate the large pool of resources that the poor are able to tap into, and through exchange it can redistribute them to satisfy needs. It combines the resource allocation efficiency of market exchange with the material and social benefits of donations.

8 REPLACING MONEY FOR ECONOMIC DEVELOPMENT

The circulation of complementary means of payment is usually restricted to a locality or region. The attempts to extend the *crédito* massively across Argentina, as *PAR* did, did not work out in the long run. The restriction of the *créditos* to the boundaries of a locality or region achieved better results and in the cases in which the complementary currency mediated a significant proportion of the local exchange, the *Trueque* became a key institution to reduce poverty and promote local economic development. This chapter discusses in detail the rationale of CCS as a tool to support the local economy.

The role of the *Trueque* as an instrument to promote local economic development will be studied by delving again into the micro-world of the nodes after 2004. The data on which it is based was collected during the second quarter of 2004. The survey received 386 effective responses, but only the 140 responses of the participants in the 4 *CT* of the ZO visited during fieldwork will be reported. The ZO was chosen because its explicit emphasis on promoting local economic development. The cases of ZO and of Gente Linda are also reported here because of their exceptional concern for promoting the regional economy. In no way do these two networks constitute average cases, but they are examples of ways in which CCS can have an active role in promoting the local economy.

There has been a 'rediscovery' in the last decade that in regions where there are strong institutions, proximity is a crucial factor in improving economic performance.[1] This is the central argument of the Institutional Regionalism perspective[2] according to which economic performance depends not only on positive macroeconomic conditions but also on local institutions that channel and promote selective cooperation between agglomerated actors.[3] It claims that ties of proximity enhance cooperation and learning, integration of local public goods and other assets that have a direct impact on a region's competitive potential. To quote MacLeod & Goodwin,[4] 'the capacity to territorially *embed* global processes in place is now conditional upon a plethora of social, cultural and institutional forms and supports' (original emphasis).

The economic success of regions is related to 'relational assets' or 'un-traded interdependencies' among local actors.[5] These include rules, practices, networks and institutions that 'generate region-specific material and non-material assets in production'. By banding together, agents develop social networks and common identities that enable future cooperation.[6] Voluntary associations are a prelude to local networks of producers that create synergies[7]

With this institutional perspective on territory, Amin and Thrift[8] develop the concept of 'institutional thickness' to explain why some regions are successful in embedding or locking in economic activity. Four factors are critical to strengthening institutional thickness in a locality.[9] The first is the presence of institutions that provide a basis for social, economic and political practices; they are the building blocks of the local economy. The second factor is networks among actors, including the local government, firms, financial institutions, training organizations, unions and other civil society associations. The third is the structures of power that give voice to divergent collective interests, socialize costs and control rogue behaviour. The fourth is the mutual awareness of the actors involved that they share a common enterprise, loosely defined as an 'agenda'; that is, the social identification with cultural traditions, region, ethnicity, and so on.

There is some scepticism about the usefulness of this concept of institutional thickness because it focuses on the number of institutions instead of their quality.[10] There are cases of strong institutions locked in laggard economic sectors that prevent development instead of promoting it[11] as well as weak local economies with well-developed institutional capacities and strong economies without them.[12] Therefore, the concept needs to be refined to make it more operational.

The proposal is to link the concept of institutional thickness to particular agents or groups of actors. Institutions are not equally relevant to all actors; they are part of the social structure and affect the process of differentiation among agents. As a result, they guide the behaviour of particular segments or groups of agents differently. On the other hand, development is unequal by groups of actors. Local economic development does not include everyone in the same manner. The economic success of regions should not be judged by the wealth produced in one area of the private sector alone. So any discussion on institutional thickness needs to be referred to the specific agents affected by the thickness of institutions.

In the UK, O'Doherty, et.al.,[13] found that local monetary networks reinforced civil society in a locality and enhanced the benefits of a web of personal networks deriving from the social and economic areas. The next section focuses on the excluded (mainly poor and unemployed) who participated in the *Trueque* and for whom it represented an addition to the local institutional endowment that affected their livelihoods.

The four factors that need to be looked at from an exclusion-focused institutional thickness perspective need rephrasing. Thus, the first factor becomes the presence of institutions in the area guiding the action of the poor and unemployed and affecting their inclusion in the social, economic and political processes of the locality. The second factor is the networks where the excluded are included, where they may be able to interact with the local government, firms, financial and training organizations, and civil society organizations. The third factor is the possibility of the excluded forming coalitions or structures of power to voice their claims on income diversification options. And the final factor is awareness among the excluded of their situation, leading to elaboration of an agenda to improve their condition. In this way, institutional thickness is not just a static endowment of institutions but a dynamic process of designing institutions that affect the excluded.[14]

In response to the restrictions and opportunities posed by globalization, new regional policies promote a bottom-up endogenous development in which the centre moves to network forms of governance. They include new agents and institutions and seek to extend coordination to sectors of the economy and levels of government previously neglected. Helmsing (2002; 2003) characterizes them as multi-actor, multi-sector and multi-level local economic development policies.

The local economic development (LED) approach is defined as 'a process in which partnerships between local governments, community- based groups and the private sector are established to manage existing resources, to create jobs and stimulate the economy of a well-defined territory'.[15] It involves designing institutions that facilitate diversification of income sources; that is, improving access of the poor and unemployed to, and their inclusion in, networks and organizations that can strengthen their capacity to influence economic structures and processes. Setting up a local monetary system, for example, represents an institutional construction to promote community economic development, since it offers a possibility of income diversification. The configuration of a club market for small-scale exchange transactions, referred to in Chapter 3, presents another institutional design for the poor.

There are three categories of LED policies, as elaborated by Helmsing.[16] The first is business development, consisting of initiatives that target enterprises or clusters of firms, such as deepening specialization and improving access to markets. The second category is locality development, defined as management of economic and physical resources, especially infrastructure-building and service provision. The third is community economic development, focused on facilitating diversification of the economic activities of the poor by intervening at the meso-level. Examples of this are support for home micro-enterprises and other survival strategies in the informal sector. CCS are mainly involved in this category, as they present an additional income option for households experiencing unemployment, poverty or vulnerability. However, the Argentine *Trueque* also had an impact on the first category (business development) because it promoted creation of enterprises in the local market.

Trueque's Effects on Local Economy

In its ten years of existence the *Trueque* enhanced the creation of micro- and small enterprises. Participants formed home-enterprises to sell in *créditos* but later many managed to 'graduate' into the regular economy, launching a business operating in pesos. This was especially relevant for groups normally unlikely to show such entrepreneurial behaviour, like the structural poor or women doing unpaid work. The *Trueque* was an entrepreneurial experience; it operated as a space where members built a network of potential buyers and learnt through practice how to develop a marketable product. In this way, the nodes supported the thickening of institutions and promoted economic activity in the locality.

The effect was felt across the entire *RT*, but the explicit commitment of the *Zona Oeste* network to enterprise development made the results more obvious there. For that reason, this section reports only on the 140 responses gathered in the four nodes of the *ZO* visited in the survey.

The graduation process into the regular economy normally started when participants dared to test whether their activity in the *Trueque* was viable in regular money. According to respondents, a successful graduation depended on two factors: the marketability of the product developed in the *CT* and the network of buyers to whom the product could be offered. After 2004, buyers were often ex-participants who still wanted to consume the goods and services of the node but paid in pesos. These ex-participants were the disenfranchised middle class who bounced back with the recovery of the regular economy and left the *CT*.

In terms of products, the favourites were handicrafts and a variety of home-produced foods that could be sold at weekend street markets. Those products were already in high demand in the *Trueque*. Exactly how many individuals have made the transition from the *Trueque* to the regular economy is not known; however, during the fieldwork it was possible to research the transition dynamics by identifying participants in the *CT* who were selling the same good or service in regular money.

Considering that most participants had none or minimal experience in commercial activities and had received no support, it is remarkable that eighty-three out of the 140 respondents (59 per cent) had dared to test their product or service in the regular economy, typically in weekend street markets. The motivation for trying to sell in the regular economy that was mentioned most frequently was that they just needed pesos to live on or to buy inputs for processing or resale in the node (forty out of eighty-three respondents). This answer was closely followed by one that indicates that the *Trueque* developed entrepreneurial attitudes: thirty-five out of eighty-three respondents said they wanted to try something they had never done before, they believed their product to be marketable, and/or they had received encouragement from other participants in that direction.

The motivation of the participants indicated a 'learning by doing' process that promoted economic development in the locality. Respondents often said they had never thought their hobby or daily work at home (for example, cooking or knitting) could become a source of income. It was a 'discovery' when they started selling their goods in the *Trueque*. In fact, 64 per cent of the eighty three entrepreneurs said they would never have tried to sell their products in official money if it had not been for the *Trueque*, 21 per cent said the experience in the nodes had been valuable and 16 per cent did not see it relevant. Most learning took place at the *CT*. Though learning was mostly by doing, 18 per cent of those who sold in pesos had received their training in the node, too. The tools and equipment for their activity were sometimes bought there (18 per cent) as were inputs (62 per cent).

The achievement in creating micro-enterprises needs to be put in perspective. In macroeconomic terms, the contribution of these micro-enterprises to the regional economy is probably small, but it provides an economic opportunity to a segment of the population that normally lacks options. In this sense, the gender impact makes it most valuable: thirty-six of the eighty-three micro-entrepreneurs were women who had never engaged in paid work before and another twenty-four were women with employment experience but who had lost their jobs. Therefore, for thirty-six women, the *Trueque* was their first and only experience in paid work and was the platform from which they launched a micro-enterprise.

The women entrepreneurs felt that their position in the household had changed since they started contributing to the family income. Maria says:

> My husband started taking my activity seriously after seeing that food and other basic necessities came out of the *CT*. The day I come here the fridge is full. He is now finding employment again as an electrician, but then we can save the pesos and live a little better. And now my opinion counts too in the decisions that need to be made at home, we became equals.

The *Trueque* clearly pulled women out of the private domain and created confidence, which enabled them to set up an economically profitable activity. Some of the respondents indicated that the main value of the node was that they could leave their homes for a while 'as if they had a job'. Others saw it more as a pleasurable activity or 'a therapy'. However, this does not necessarily indicate empowerment. Although women participants feel more confident, more independent and more respected in and out of their households, the *Trueque* did not affect the perception that the main breadwinner should be the husband. The men are paid in pesos, generally accepted money, while the women earn *créditos*, a local currency that can buy only some goods. Even when women provide the basic necessities of the household and did so when there was no other income, they continue to view their work as complementary to that of men. 'I can now help my husband at home' was a frequent response, placing the participant's work in a subordinate position to her husband's. The *Trueque* thus imparted value to a part of women's work which had been unpaid until then, but paid for that work in a secondary currency and so did not change the perception of women's labour as being secondary to that of men. A woman around sixty years old explains:

> I used to work as an assistant cook at a school's cafeteria until got married. My husband didn't want me to work and I was busy enough at home with the children. I would like to have a job again now but at my age nobody is going to hire me. So I learnt here in the node how to make hamburgers with soja beans. And I work on that five days a week, making them and then delivering in the node and outside. I have clients in *créditos* and clients in pesos. I never thought I'd be earning my own money again.

The *Trueque* functioned in practice as an incubator to the extent that forty-two of the eighty-three participants who tried selling in pesos are still active after one year or more. It offers a relatively high survival rate for micro-enterprises born in its realm. *CT* thus help the poor and unemployed to establish a micro-enterprise and generate extra income for their households, at least for some time. This enhances the institutional thickness of the local economy, as it offers an option to make a living. Whether these new businesses grow to the point of offering a secure and reasonable income to households could not be determined. In principle, once the business in pesos takes off, the entrepreneurs should abandon the node; however, this was not the case.

The forty-one participants who had tried a business in the regular economy and abandoned it were asked the reasons for their failure. It was an open question and the three reasons given most often were: sales in weekend street markets are lower than in the node (39 per cent), entry costs there are too high (16 per cent) and conditions are inconvenient (13 per cent mentioned they had to stay in the market all day long, could not be accompanied by their children, and had to be outdoors when it was cold or raining). Official weekend street markets require payment of a fee in official money, which is rent for the stand and payment for security and cleaning. Participants indicated that their sales hardly covered those costs, so they stayed in the node where they received relatively higher revenue in kind, did not have to pay a fee, and could be accompanied by their children.

The difficulty of selling enough in pesos to make the effort worthwhile was confirmed by the answers given by the eighty-three participants who sell in pesos as well as *créditos*. Asked why they did not leave the Trueque completely, they typically replied that they needed both incomes to cover different expenses, while agreeing that the revenue in *créditos* (valued in goods) was higher than in the regular economy. A participant explained:

> When I sell my handicrafts in a street market, I see people passing and looking. They all say my knitwear is nice but they don't buy because they don't have the money. When you have *créditos*, you want to spend them right away. If you find soap, you buy soap. It's better than going back home with coloured paper!

That participants combine sales in both markets suggests that their businesses are incapable of generating enough income to make a living, so they still require the *Trueque* for a complementary income. This needs to be tested in future research. However, the decision to keep a foot in each market also casts doubt on whether graduation into the regular economy really indicates success or failure of the *Trueque*. The goal of community economic development is to manage resources, create income and stimulate the local economy. The idea behind it is to improve households' standards of living and reduce their vulnerability. The *Trueque* seems to be doing that, even if not in official money.

The *Trueque* operated as a practical school where individuals could experiment with running their own business. A good product was not enough, they found; they also had to 'learn by doing' to calculate costs, control stocks, manage inputs and outputs, and so on. Then, either pushed by necessity or self-confidence, they ventured into the regular economy. Seyfeng[17] found a similar process occurring in the UK, where the scheme was successful in creating new informal employment opportunities for socially excluded groups.

Promoting Local Development: Two Case Studies

The evidence linking the Trueque to the promotion of local economic development will be complemented in this section with two case studies of in which the concern with promoting LED was exceptional.

In the *Redes de Trueque* in general, promoting the local economy was not an explicit priority and there is in fact little evidence to suggest that it happened. Only a small number of *RT* groups, two of which are discussed in this section, took it up as their goal. They organized local networks and built local institutions in which the excluded were included. Both of them enhanced the institutional thickness of their localities in the expectation that that would support the excluded and would also strengthen the local economy in the longer run. They are in no way representative of the whole *Red de Trueque*. One is an independent node, *Gente Linda* in Venado Tuerto (Santa Fe province) and the other is a regional network, the *Red de Trueque Zona Oeste (ZO)* in the western suburbs of Buenos Aires.

Enabling Development: Venado Tuerto

Gente Linda in the small city of Venado Tuerto assisted members to articulate their own projects or integrate new networks, linking them with actors normally out of reach of the poor and unemployed. Launched in 1999, when the collapse of the regular economy was only beginning, it operated in isolation from the rest of the *Trueque* and used its own local currency called '*puntos*' (points).

Gente Linda was the initiative of an agricultural engineer, Daniel Ilari, and his group of friends, who were sensitive to the deterioration of the social situation. Ilari comes from a traditional local family and is considered a 'notable' in the area. He envisioned three aims for *Gente Linda*: to introduce a self-help alternative for the poor and unemployed, to foster solidarity among neighbours and to establish a relatively autonomous local economic system. The first two are more or less in line with the goals of most Argentine *CT*s; the third aim was a novelty. Ilari explains:

> Those who have money spend a lot of it in the bigger cities. We need it to stay here, where our unemployed live, so they can stop being unemployed. A *CT* is a great way to help them, but also to help our local economy in general.

Although Ilari insisted there are no leaders in *Gente Linda*, he is undoubtedly the leader of the group. He manages the monetary system, makes changes to resolve problems and is responsible for maintaining relations with the municipality, the church, the shops and other businesses. To pursue a local economic development vision, his strategy was to incorporate more and more actors in the locality with a wide range of offers so that the system would strengthen and sustain itself. From the outset, he sought creative ways to spread the *puntos* across the city and did not hesitate to start with his own personal network of contacts.

The *CT* recruited one hundred participants in 1999, and when it reached its peak in 2001 it had almost 2.000 members, including middle-class residents experiencing unemployment. In 2004 it had 562 registered members, in line with the general sharp decrease of *Trueque* membership across the country after the regular economy rebounded and the middle class mostly regained their jobs and lifestyle. The poor stayed in the node. It was still operating in the beginning of 2007 with a stable scale.

Although *Gente Linda* followed the model of *CT*s elsewhere, it is different in several ways.[18] Illari's commitment and strong leadership already marks a difference. Besides, the node has always operated autonomously from the *RT* across Argentina, in consistency with the goal of creating an independent local economic system. Another peculiarity of *Gente Linda* is in its monetary regulation – inspired by radical economist Sylvio Gesell – which includes demurrage. It is implemented by having vouchers that expire every four months. The amount left in participants' pockets is then exchanged for the same amount minus 5 per cent in new vouchers. The revenue from this negative interest rate is used to pay the *CT* assistants. If total liquidity is perceived as being too low to permit regular exchange transactions, members can vote in an assembly to inject currency.

New members fill in a form specifying the products or services they will offer and attend a few meetings to be introduced to the principles of the group. They pay one peso for their badge and as a contribution towards printing the vouchers. They are then listed in a public directory of participants, classified by branch of goods offered. This is atypical within the *Trueque* in Argentina. For this exercise, *Gente Linda* relies on a support infrastructure that, once again, is Ilari's contribution.[19] He maintains the computer database, which improves the overall efficiency of the group, and manages the collective fund to pay for expenses.

Another difference between *Gente Linda* and the rest of the *Trueque* is the integration into the regular economy beyond weekly markets. It is a direct way of increasing institutional thickness and linking the poor and unemployed to consumption they would not be able to afford otherwise. Ilari persuaded neighbours and friends who own regular businesses to accept *puntos* in part-payment. There are eight of these businesses, mostly in the city centre (a bakery, a butcher, a pasta shop, a greengrocer, a place for renting films, a cleaning products shop, a furniture shop and a computer shop). A veterinarian also accepts *puntos*. The bakers, who accept *puntos* for 30 per cent of the sales amount, explain that they started accepting *puntos* mainly out of solidarity with the poor as well as because 'we are friends of Daniel'.[20] They have used *puntos* to pay a painter and a mason and for English lessons for their son. The butcher accepts *puntos* for 20 per cent of sales and uses them to pay municipal taxes and buy detergents. He is happy with the arrangement, observing that the participants are 'extremely loyal customers. My business has certainly improved'. Customers who pay partly in *puntos* in these shops receive the same service as those paying fully in pesos; sales in *puntos* are seen as an additional demand that would not be there otherwise.

The local monetary network in Venado Tuerto has also been responsible for the promotion of new organizations in the city. It has fostered a new type of business taking advantage of the lower barriers to entry that go with a complementary currency: less-burdensome state regulations, no taxation, reduced risk in case of failure, an extended learning period and a loyal market of buyers. The idea of these businesses, the *proveedurías*, was presented as a way to expand trade beyond the weekly markets. *Proveedurías* are grocers that only trade in *puntos* and are open six hours a day, six days a week. They are set up by regular participants in locations that are well apart from one another to balance competition. The venues are rented in *puntos* or are spaces that are not being used by the owners (for example, a garage at the home of someone who does not own a car). People bring their goods there to sell. The *proveedurías* buy them in *puntos*, sell them on consignment, or exchange them for other groceries in the shop. Ilari explained:

> The *proveedurías* were not well-accepted in the beginning because others feared they would reduce trade in the weekly market. It didn't happen. People appreciate being able to buy in *puntos* near their homes six days a week. Nobody can survive buying food only once a week, right? The *proveedurías* make life easier.

What Ilari also understood early on in his local economic development strategy was that no local economic network would really stand much chance of success without the integration of the local government into *Gente Linda*. Therefore, the Venado Tuerto municipality is involved much more in *Gente Linda* than most other municipalities in the country are in *CTs*. One indication of this involvement is that in August 2002 the local council voted to accept up to 30 per cent of local taxes in *puntos*. Ilari used his reputation in the city to persuade the council to take this step, contending, 'We are not talking of great amounts of money here. A simple calculation shows that it is less than 5 per cent of the local revenues and still can help a great deal. It also legitimates the node'. In the first nine months of 2004, the local government received an average of 12,500 *puntos* a month from 450 of Ilari's neighbours listed as members of *Gente Linda*, which was negligible in comparison with the total revenue of the municipality but of great strategic significance. Ilari told the author of this study:

> The possibility of paying taxes in *puntos* is a major argument in getting shops and other middle-class participants involved. It integrates us with the local economy. People can help others without really losing anything.

The acceptance of taxes in *puntos* was a novelty for a small city in Argentina. The municipality created a Social Welfare Area to distribute the *puntos*. Each of six boroughs in the Area is served by two to four social assistants, who allocate them to extremely poor households; 140 households receive eighty to one hundred *puntos* a month to spend in the *proveedurías* and markets. The *puntos* keep most households from going hungry. *Gente Linda* has thus helped to add organizations to the region, which in turn have improved social inclusion and stimulated other sectors of the local economy.

Beneficiaries of the social welfare scheme are encouraged to use *Gente Linda*, motivating them to start offering goods and services as well. According to Ilari, 'less than half of them do, in fact, because they lack production resources: skills, tools, inputs, even the will'. It is one of the weaknesses of the scheme: as these households buy goods –especially food – without contributing to the supply in *Gente Linda*, they often create food shortages. In response to this situation, the households are offered a special contribution in *puntos* for investments that would transform them from welfare beneficiaries to producers. Ilari explains:

> About fifty people have started a business at home in this way. It is usually small equipment, such as a sewing machine or an oven. Some stop after some time and sell the machine, I know, but at least some are still selling in the node and a few also in the regular economy.

Finally, the *Gente Linda* network has integrated into itself small villages in the rural hinterland of Venado Tuerto that have never been part of any integrated local economic system. Small farmers and poor rural workers take their produce (mainly vegetables, fruits, eggs, and small animals like poultry and rabbits) to sell in the node. According to the owner of one of the *proveedurías:*:

> We never thought about this before. We have always bought milk from the largest milk company in Argentina, which is now French. So we have people producing milk a few minutes away from here, they sell it to these companies that in turn bring it back to Venado Tuerto at ten times the cost. Well, the node finally gave us the chance to buy milk produced here directly from the people that live here. We sell it cheaper than in the supermarket, but with an interesting mark-up on the local producer's cost.

Rural sellers are perennially short of clothes, toys, shoes and school supplies, but they have plenty of food, while cities have shortages of food and a surplus of non-food products. What was missing was institutional channels to connect supply and demand. Nobody had organized it before within the regular economy because it was unnoticed or unnecessary, or because of the efficiency differentials between large-scale production and small-scale production at the local level. The existence of local money as a central institution brought supply and demand together.

With regard to the hypothesis posed for this section, *Gente Linda* enhanced institutional thickness focused on the poor and unemployed. The *puntos* fostered self-employment and connections to better-endowed participants. It allowed them to diversify their income sources and included them in a network from which they would otherwise have been excluded, integrated by regular shops, middle-class participants, the local government and the rural poor. Their consumption added to local demand.

A crucial factor in the whole process was the favourable departure point; it started as the initiative of a strong leader with a wide network of social connections, who had the promotion of local economic development in mind. A coalition of supporters and organizational infrastructure formed at an early stage, which was also a precondition for further development. The first addition to the institutional endowment of the city was a local monetary system, which led to the creation of a public database of members with idle goods, skills and resources. In order to improve the effectiveness of the scheme, *Gente Linda* articulated with the local economy by using *puntos* for part-payment in shops and payment of municipal taxes. This led to new institutions and organizations: a local social welfare policy, the *proveedurías* run by unemployed participants, and a small credit policy in *puntos* to buy tools and start micro-enterprises. The integration of the rural hinterland was an unexpected side-effect that improved the standard of life of the rural poor in the vicinity. All the initiatives are still operating.

Managing Development the Zona Oeste

The second case displays a more interventionist or managerial approach on the part of the sub-network's leadership. It was one of the earliest organizations in the *Trueque*, the *Red de Trueque Zona Oeste* (*ZO*) or regional network of the western metropolitan suburbs of Buenos Aires.

A few *CT*s were already using their own currencies in 1996, and around the end of 1997 a group of them decided to print a single currency for the area. According to Fernando Sampayo, who later became the main leader of the *ZO*:

> In 1997 several *CT*s in this area got together. Three were already using their own scrip and the others were using the vouchers of the *RGT*. We then decided to use one local *crédito* in the four nodes. It started circulating at the beginning of 1998.

Other *CT*s in the western suburbs joined later and by the end of 1999 there were seventeen nodes. The *ZO* became dominant in an area with approximately 5.5 million inhabitants. It grew quickly, as the western metropolitan suburbs were fertile ground for a self-help scheme for the disenfranchised middle class left behind by the structural reforms.

In sharp contrast to the geographical isolation of Venado Tuerto, the western suburbs are part of the metropolitan area of Buenos Aires (population 13 million). Their economy is fully integrated with that of the city in terms of supply and demand. There is no obvious differentiation between articles produced there and in other municipalities. However, *ZO* members were required to have a current address in the western suburbs and the organization did not involve businesses outside that area. In this sense, its activities are seen as locally rooted.

In its most glorious period (at the beginning of 2002) the *ZO* had 1,350 *CTs* with a total of 400,000 participants. It was affected by the demise of the *Trueque* after the middle of 2002, but much less than the rest of the network. By the end of 2004 it was the largest *RT*, with forty centres and 30,000 participants. After 2006 five new *CTs* were opened.

In 2000 the *ZO* achieved enough critical mass within the *Trueque* and Sampayo launched a series of more ambitions projects for local economic development. New participants then began contributing a two peso fee to join the *ZO*, in exchange for which they received a badge and a pack of fifty currency units to start trading.

The contribution financed administrative expenses, printing of vouchers and updating of the database. The plan was also to use it in the future to provide initial capital for the organization of a local micro-enterprise-based production system around the *ZO*. With this in mind, members were asked to fill in a form giving information about their skills and previous labour experience, which was entered in a computer file. The idea was that they could be summoned when the need arose for their skills in the future. For Sampayo, the *Trueque* is a pillar to complement and improve the regular economy:

> After the Second World War, there were no big industries left in Italy but each household became a small factory. Italy then progressed. The *Trueque* is similar; impoverished middle-class households can turn into micro-enterprises with their many idle skills and resources. They are workers earning a decent living with vouchers.

The *ZO* prepared itself for local economic development promotion with a collective fund and a database of the available resources and skills of the participants. Additionally, it prepared its basic support infrastructure to organize a local production system. The *ZO*'s infrastructure was a rarity in the *RT* due to its costs and risks. It derived from Sampayo's past as an entrepreneur and his insistence on transparency and control to optimize the scarce resources of the organization. The central database of participants was one of the administrative tools that made the *ZO* atypical among local monetary networks in Argentina. From 2001 onwards it used six computers, with twelve people working in two shifts to update the data; they were paid wages in vouchers and transport costs in regular money. The *ZO* had another six computers for accountancy, organization of agendas and meetings, logistics and training. It kept detailed accounts of all transactions and movements of money and resources. It had centralized logistics, publicity on local radio, and additional infrastructure such as a press to print its own publications.

The *ZO* was also of great importance in widening and deepening the network around its currency. It established institutional links with traditional organizations of the third sector like the Catholic Church, local government representatives and small industries. These were seen as potential partners in joint projects to promote local economic development, although the final strategy matured and was put into practice later. Sampayo strongly believes that the *Trueque* played an important part in enabling small industries to survive the economic crisis:

> The *Trueque* stabilises the scale of production and sales because retailers and small manufacturers can sell their overproduction, what the market in pesos does not buy from them due to the crisis. By maintaining large-scale production, a company has a greater chance of recovering or becoming more competitive than those that simply hope for the end of the crisis.

The crucial aspect that differentiated the *ZO* from other networks was the long-term strategy implemented in 2000 to promote local economic development. It organized several collective enterprises in the area to produce articles that were in high demand in the *CTs* as well as strategic inputs. These included products like pizza bases, breads and other bakery products; spaghetti and other dry pastas; and cakes. The *Trueque* in general lacked a supply chain to secure access to basic food production inputs such as flour, cooking oil and sugar and so they had high value.[21] Members who could obtain them in the formal economy could make a handsome profit by selling them for *créditos*. These few were feeding the many that only had their labour to offer, which appealed to some members' solidarity and to others' speculative spirit.

The circuit combined local and official currencies. After a while, two plots of land totaling twenty hectares were bought for participants to grow fruits and vegetables. A 2,000m^2 warehouse of was rented for storage. A carpentry workshop provided tables for a mega-fair and later for the *CTs*. At its peak, the daily output of the network's enterprises amounted to 300 kilos of dry pastas, 1,300 pizza bases, fifty tables and twenty benches, and 150 baskets of fresh vegetables, in addition to breads, biscuits, pies and pastries. With the funds from its fairs, it bought a light truck to transport the goods from the collective enterprises to the *CTs* or to the warehouse.

Participants paid for everything in vouchers. The *ZO* retained part of the funds to finance other productive projects and the rest were distributed among the workers. All transactions were registered and the records were publicly available. However, pesos were needed for some purposes. An assistant to Sampayo explains:

> The *ZO* contributed a travel allowance in pesos from the collective fund because people need to travel to go to work and the cost could not be paid in vouchers. Pesos came from the membership fee and from the revenues of special events like the fairs. But pesos were always scarce and placed a limit on everything we wanted to do.

A partner organization then suggested that they sell part of the production of the enterprises in the regular market in order to get more pesos. This suggestion was rejected because the *ZO* feared that sales in pesos would reduce the supply of products in the *CT*s. The collective enterprises were the main organizations formed by the *ZO*, adding a production volume equivalent to 140,000 dollars to the local economy every month. They generated seventy jobs paid in a mix of *créditos* and pesos, plus jobs for an undetermined number of apprentices. In the context of the institutional thickness of the western suburbs, the *ZO* became the dynamic centre of a network of collective enterprises exchanging goods and knowledge with each other and with the *CT*s, increasing the connectedness of poor and unemployed participants and providing their households with a source of income.

In terms of integrating the *Trueque* with the local economy, the *ZO* also tried to get local businesses involved, but was mainly driven by the need to obtain critical basic inputs that could only be bought in pesos. It tried various schemes that typically involved direct barter with local firms, with different degrees of success. For example, it secured several months' supply of flour – the critical input of several collective enterprises – by providing manpower and pesos to small wheat producers in exchange for the crop, which was taken for grinding to a flour mill on the verge of bankruptcy. The mill received part of the flour as payment and the rest was supplied to the enterprises.

Like *Gente Linda*, the *ZO* sought to integrate local governments in its network, but it received a cold response. Its requests ranged from access to goods in disuse to payment of arrears in raw materials, venues to hold the markets and tax payments in vouchers. According to Sampayo:

> The idea was to take our database of 100,000 members, a third of whom were owners of local homes. We proposed that those who had tax arrears be allowed to pay them off in vouchers. The municipality could then buy goods and services from our participants with those *créditos*. They said the accountancy was too complicated and there were legal restrictions. So then we asked them to give us access to whatever was idle, like trucks. They have hundreds of trucks out of order and we have a hundred unemployed mechanics ready to start working tomorrow. If we got ten trucks going, we would keep two or three and they could have the rest. The idea was to provide services to the municipality: repairing, gardening, collection, maintenance. We had countless participants whose capital was just their hands and their will to work. To be candid, we only convinced a few.

The few municipalities that cooperated with the *ZO* network preferred payment in kind: arrears of third parties paid in food and raw materials were given to the *ZO* in exchange for finished products. The municipality of Moreno, for example, provided flour in exchange for 10,000 kilos of dry spaghetti, which it used to feed children of extremely poor families in its soup kitchens. In another scheme, it gave the *ZO* wood left over from a bankrupt sawmill that had tax arrears and the *ZO* made desks and benches that partly went to municipal schools. Most often, municipalities lent community centres, clubs, schools and other spaces to hold the markets in exchange for maintenance work. Thus, municipalities chose involvement with minimum risk. The building of awareness and a common agenda failed to appeal the local governments, which were afraid of being part of a scheme they had not launched and did not control. The network-building of the *ZO* was clearly less successful than that of *Gente Linda*, partly because of its location within a large metropolis and partly because Sampayo lacked the personal contacts and reputation that Ilari had in Venado Tuerto.

After the collapse of the *Trueque* across Argentina, these *ZO* schemes to promote local economic development crumbled. 'They lacked time, perhaps another six months were needed to formalize the cooperatives and make them sustainable. It worked great within the *Trueque* but they could not make it into the regular economy', Sampayo laments, though he is thinking of trying again if the *RT* rebound. Still, the fact that the *ZO* shrank less than any other network perhaps reflects the degree of institutional thickness and interconnectedness it achieved. The core of the vision was to regenerate economic activity of the actors in the region, by creating collective and individual enterprises, while Ilari in Venado Tuerto had a stronger commitment to the locality.

The failure of the collective enterprises to achieve the transition to the regular economy makes it hard to evaluate the long-term local economic development effects of the *ZO*. However, the *ZO* also used the *CT*s to increase confidence among participants that the local monetary system provided them with a sheltered market and a relatively loyal demand to test their own productive projects. Although Sampayo believes that collective enterprises have greater chance of success than individual ones – the former achieve a larger scale and are stronger – he accepts the creation of individual micro-enterprises as a second-best solution. The *ZO*'s success in generating micro-enterprises is evaluated in the next section.

Local Economic Development with Local Money

Banding together around the use of local money as a central institution created synergies between groups of the population frequently excluded from networks with sufficient assets and resources. The nodes aided the launching of micro-enterprises through learning-by-doing and transformed previously unpaid work into paid work. They paved the way to paid economic activity for groups of agents who normally do not show high entrepreneurial capacities, like women with no employment experience. They were inclusive of a multiplicity of agents, acted at multiple levels and moved resources across multiple sectors. These are the core aspects of the new generation of local economic development policies.

In the local development literature, the formation of a CCS is hardly considered a viable or significant policy tool. Most CCS worldwide did not achieve enough scale to reach that status. The *Trueque* allows to investigate this new link, whether CCS are a local economic development instrument. The *Trueque* was generally not conceived as a tool for local economic development, but a small number of networks were ambitious enough to go along that path and produce long-term effects. Two of them were studied here as examples of the process.

A series of conditions were highlighted as necessary to pursue a local economic development strategy. First, *Gente Linda* in Venado Tuerto and *Zona Oeste* in Buenos Aires formed a collective fund in regular money to enable them to launch more complex projects in their locality. Second, they used part of those funds to create a computerized database. Both invested labour, time and resources to generate information on workers, skills, assets, and so on. Third, they both revolved around strong leaders who contributed time, personal contacts, organizational skills and physical infrastructure. In the case of Ilari, personal reputation was crucial, while Sampayo contributed his managerial experience. Finally, in both cases they designed new institutions to pursue a bottom-up local economic development strategy.

The contrasts between the two cases were as marked as the similarities. An obvious difference was due to geography. Venado Tuerto lies in the countryside, three hours from any large modern city, while the *ZO* is part of a metropolis of 13.5 million inhabitants. So *Gente Linda* was clearly better positioned to gain autonomy and set clear boundaries on local economic development projects. In addition, while both worked on the institutional thickness of their regions, they reflected divergent visions of how to develop a local economic system. While local monetary networks in Venado Tuerto were conceived as creating synergies and strengthening participants' autonomy, the *ZO* viewed itself as the central organizer of idle resources in the area. *Gente Linda* thus worked on widening and deepening the network, enhancing interrelationships and alliances, integrating the hinterland, obtaining the participation of the local government and eventually pushing for a welfare and micro-credit policy for the poor. The *ZO*, in contrast, constructed a logistics system that made it the brain of a growing and dynamic organization that included collective enterprises, funds in pesos and vouchers, a system for distribution of goods and capital, and a wide range of weak agreements with small industries, local civil society groups, and local governments.

In view of these differences, this chapter considered *Gente Linda* to be a case of enabling development, while the *ZO* was seen as a case of managerial development. *Gente Linda* supports the activities of others, while the *ZO* made itself the

management centre of all the activities. Eventually, the local economic development results of *Gente Linda* were sustainable and that network's growth now
comes from attracting new users. The *ZO* did not reach such a level of sustainability because its activities require a larger scale and crumbled with the collapse
of the *Trueque*, although, admittedly, the web of relations and practices it built
did protect it from shrinking to the extent that the rest of the *Trueque* did.

All in all, the diversity between the *Trueque* and other CCS in the world
and between the groups of the *Trueque* suggests some lines to advance their classification. The scope of strategy needs to be considered. While some networks
start and end with the defence of economic activity, others propose a long-term
plan of action to integrate a local economic system. In both cases, the idea is to
strengthen the local economy so that it can survive future crises better. However,
defence of economic activity represents a bridge to a post-crisis economy, while
integration of a local economic system seeks to reform the economy. It engages
economic and non-economic factors alike to diversify the local institutional
endowment and raise the general level of development. Their long-term vision
thus represents a larger scope of action, including the offer of business support
services like micro-credits in local money, the search for partnerships with other
actors –principally local governments and small industries – and the organization of a governance system. As underlined, *RT*s with a wide local economic
development vision were rare in the *Trueque*.

Another criterion for classification is related to openness. One option is
to allow anyone to participate freely, combining sales in local vouchers and in
official money and moving resources in and out of the local monetary system
from and into the regular economy. Another possibility is to restrict CCS to
the poor and unemployed (no businesses or shops), ban the use of all other currencies except the local one, and impose sanctions for transition in and out of
the CCS. In the *Trueque*, the fear that openness between the regular economy
and the local monetary system would undermine the *CT* was widespread. After
all, micro-enterprises graduating into the regular economy implied the loss of
participants and resources for the *CT*. And the sale in the *CT* of products from
mechanized industries would create unequal competition for goods produced
by hand at home. So while open local CCS reflect a complementary position in
the economy, closed ones pose an alternative, a sharp qualitative change in the
nature of the exchange. The effects of openness to and disconnection from the
regular economy are yet to be researched.

A third possibility concerns the active and passive roles of organizers of
CCS. Active organizations place a well-informed and well-intentioned social
entrepreneur at the centre, coordinating resources, workers and skills. Active
organizations can increase awareness among participants of the options of own-
account employment, offer a stable sheltered market to 'learn by doing', and

provide tools to evaluate the risks and advantages of making a transition to the regular economy. Evidence was presented to support the view that active organizations such as the *ZO* achieve a high rate of survival of micro-enterprises, at least as a secondary source of income in households and especially empowering women. In contrast, the organizations of the *Trueque* typically played passive roles and expected participants to define individually how far they wanted to go with the *CT*. The disappearance of most of the *RT* suggests that the participants did not want to go too far.

A final reflection relates to institutionalism and the Regionalism perspective. Critics of the concept of institutional thickness point out that there is more emphasis on quantity of institutions than on their quality. This study suggests an avenue to elaborate the concept further by identifying the actors whom institutions involve or whose behaviour is affected by institutions. The cases analysed here indicate that not all local institutions are of the same relevance to everybody. Indeed, any level of the economy presents institutions of diverse quality and relevance to different actors. Money is clearly a fundamental institution in any market economy, supporting and regulating transactions, enabling accumulation and stimulating activity in general. Local money is more relevant to the poor and unemployed, though in certain cases it becomes fundamental to developing a local or regional economic system.

It is not the existence of a CCS per se that provided protection to local economic activity or promoted its development. The process by which the *RT* was organized was perhaps more relevant in achieving these results; that is, the ways in which the aims of the *Trueque* organizations were defined, the leadership they pushed forward, the networks they brought together, the connections they maintained among actors. In the successful cases of local economic development, a CCS seems to have acted as a means more than as an end. 'The complementary money per se cannot get you anything. It is what you do with it that makes a difference in people's lives and the local economy', Daniel Ilari summarized. Perhaps the same could be said of the other rules of action contributing to the institutional thickness of a region, that it is a means to foster development rather than an end in itself.

Trials and Errors of the *Trueque*

A number of lessons can be drawn from the *Trueque* that could be useful when reviving it in the future or organizing a CCS elsewhere. A question to be discussed is the scale desired, because this choice will determine others. If the goal is to expand the network in order to benefit from economies of scale and scope, division of labour and specialization, the point of reference is the *Red de Trueque*.

Growth presents a tension. As they grow, nodes became more autonomous economic systems inclusive of low-income groups, but they also attracted participants who were less ideologically minded. The problem is how to balance both aspects. On the one hand, CCS need to preserve social cohesion, for which growth needs to be restricted to the scale made possible by sustainable collective action. On the other, they need to expand and diversify the supply of goods and services in order to offer an attractive income-generation option and meet the organizational costs. So they need to be 'large enough' to reap the benefits of a market (for example, through diversity of supply) while at the same time being 'small enough' to sustain social cohesion. The question is how to offer participants the maximum income-generation possibilities with the minimum damage to governance and the minimum organizational and transaction costs. This trade-off applies to club markets in general.

The problem of scale is common to social economy or third-sector schemes, which tend to remain too small and marginal to offer an attractive income to participants or become too big, depersonalized and too oriented to profit maximization.[22] There are a myriad of possibilities between the two extremes. CCS may achieve low economic impact but still be valuable to the structural poor. For example, in an independent node visited during the fieldwork, participation by the poor made only a small difference in terms of obtaining food but it enabled them to access the services of a local doctor who used the *créditos* to pay for house maintenance.

The *RT* experience produced two intermediate solutions that worked reasonably well. One option was to restrict the scale to the limits at which ideological cohesion could be sustained, as the *RTS* regions did. There is enough experience showing that the social cohesion typical of personal exchange can be sustained when there is a strong ideological motivation.[23] This path is difficult because collective action is just as costly among those who share an ideology[24] and also because as groups get larger they breed factions of political opinion that endanger schemes.[25] The second solution was to abandon idealism and to build bureaucratic control structures with a reliable leader at the top, like the *ZO* did. Motivated coordinators did unpaid work to sustain their networks on the basis of their ideals; otherwise the costs would have been prohibitive.

In principle, it thus seems possible to increase the scale and impact of CCS without damaging their sustainability, provided certain rules of governance are respected. Local *CT*s, the *ZO* and the regional components of the *RTS* were sustainable and yet very different in their scales and their approach to CCS. A hierarchical model seems to be best suited for larger scales of operation. The advantage of size lies in the capacity to develop complex projects and management institutions (bureaucratic structures, value chain agreements, collective enterprises and alliances with local governments). The model does have disadvantages, though, one of which is that a rather large scale is the minimum threshold for the sustainability of projects and a leader to organize the network is critical. A major drawback of the hierarchical model is that it could be seen as contradicting the principles of self-reliance pursued by CCS.

At an intermediate level, a regional sub-network with an associational model also proved sustainable and capable of correcting the problems of the national associational model. A region represents a larger scale than a locality and so the resources available are also richer in scale and scope. This enables complex projects of local economic development, integration of rural and urban areas, and financing of necessary administrative structures. Additionally, the divergence of interests and political conflicts of the associational model are more manageable at regional level than at national level. A basis of ideological motivation is more likely to endure at an intermediate level. The risks of this model are linked to the system of representation, that the CCS could be co-opted by elites or self-elected leaders with their own agendas.

Finally, community-based or local CCS appear to be a suitable option for combining economic and extra-economic impacts. These are ruled by the considerations of the social economy or personal exchange, so in terms of governance they do not present major weaknesses. The direct relationship between their limited scale and restricted resources can be worked out as part of the collective efforts of the group. Two possibilities emerge from the experience of the *Trueque* in Argentina in this respect: seeking participation of local governments or external donors, or expanding the network to local businesses and shops.

In terms of the size of the individual nodes, the experience of the *Trueque* indicates that at least fifty members are needed to start with, and no more than 200. Although a rule of thumb, these are the numbers that come up over and again from *Trueque* leaders and coordinators. With larger numbers supervision becomes necessary to avoid the problems of impersonal exchange. With fewer members than the minimum threshold, the pool of resources is often too small. If the resources of the network are too scarce, there are two possibilities: finding a donor to obtain basic food production inputs or setting up a micro-credit programme in the complementary currency.

A practical and effective way to increase the pool of resources available to the nodes is to integrate the rural hinterlands of small cities into the nodes. They would thus be able to reach agents who normally do not find ways to participate in low-income urban schemes. In this way, rural households would gain access to goods that are scarcer in rural than urban locations (clothes, toys and household gadgets) while the urban poor would benefit by gaining fundamental access to products that are scarcer in urban than rural areas (for example, fresh vegetables, eggs and small animals). Overall, rural-urban integration improves the supply chain.

A drawback of the *Trueque* as it was organized was that it was costly in terms of organizational and collective efforts. To sustain these costs, commonalities among participants, such as ethnicity, religious beliefs, gender, disabilities, or a pre-existent shared space like a school, club or church, are helpful. The participation of an NGO or local government to cover the organizational costs would be an asset and would be possible within the social policy efforts of local governments.

The inclusion of local governments as actors in the *Trueque* brought a number of advantages and it is a recommendable course of action. It can expand the scope of the initiative and it proved effective for extending the membership of the *Trueque* to other social strata. The appeal of a complementary currency is, by definition, related to what can be paid with it. By allowing local taxes to be paid partially or fully in complementary currency, local governments aroused the interest of a wider circle of the middle class, businesses and shops in the *Trueque*. Where local taxes could be paid in *créditos*, participation in the node offered taxpayers an implicit discount in relation to the regular payments. Businesses and shops then supplied the nodes with food production inputs and other necessities, which were crucial for the structural poor. In short, participation by the local government increases the social mix in the CCS, generally broadening its horizons.

In some districts, the legal framework forbade local governments from accepting means of payment other than those issued by higher levels of authority, that is, the central government. A way of getting around this in the *Trueque* was to accept payment in kind instead of community currency. Either way, the local government had to decide how to use the community currency or the payment in kind. In Argentina, a handful of local governments viewed the scheme as a welfare policy that demanded very few resources from them and kept the poor out of protest demonstrations. They gave the goods received as payment in kind to the structural poor and in that way supported the nodes. In the exceptional case of Venado Tuerto, the municipality accepted the community currency directly and framed a local social policy, including micro-credits, in complementary currency.

It is in the interest of local governments to support CCS, but in a new scheme the material benefits may not be obvious in the beginning. CCS have positive effects on the local economy, protecting the level of activity and promoting development. They support income diversification and community networks. However, local leaders in the *Trueque* had to work out creative ways of showing local governments the material benefits for them. For example, nodes would take over tasks that local authorities normally carry out, like maintenance and cleaning of community centres, schools, sport halls or open spaces in exchange for the use of the venues to hold markets. Another service that can be obtained from local governments, as the experience of the *Trueque* showed, is the use of municipal vehicles to improve logistics or integrate rural areas. A more ambitious possibility is to engage the local government in more complex supply chains, as the *ZO* did, using idle municipal resources or persuading the local government to accept goods as payment for taxes in arrears.

A model of replication to consider is a social franchise, but then with appropriate control mechanisms. The model of franchised local nodes with centralized management of the currency system relies heavily on management capacities at the central level and means to ensure that the franchisees abide by the rules. A system based on social franchise offers the advantage of fast and easy replication but its effectiveness comes at a cost (that is, control infrastructure). Its implementation makes sense only on a large scale, when participants can contribute a fee. An incidental issue is that, to some degree, such control is contrary to the participation and democratic principles that most CCS stand for.

As mentioned above, at a large scale the *Trueque* emulated the regular economy without the state's control capacities. A possible avenue for solving the problem of enforcement is to go one step further in emulating the regular economy and bring the state back on the stage. Where partnerships with local governments are possible, these could have a role in providing supervisors to perform policing functions at markets or as a last resort in conflict resolution. The local governments could perform these functions with the same personnel that supervise the markets of the regular economy, but adapting the rules to those decided by the CCS members. This was not tried in Argentina but could be an inexpensive and effective solution to the problem of enforcement.

Achievements of the *Trueque*

The *Trueque* was a valuable learning experience that achieved several points. It made the unpaid work of women visible and valuable in accessing services and goods that made a difference to the lifestyle of their households, as was also found by other researchers.[26] The gender division of labour in the households was restructured by the kind of money each breadwinner earned, which was a pattern in common in both new and structural poor households.[27] Women would search for food and clothing in the *Trueque* nodes while the regular money earned by men – often from odd jobs or in the informal economy – would be used for the rent, public services, taxes and other expenses that could not be paid in *créditos*. By 2007, many husbands found employment in the regular economy again, but many women do not want to retreat back into the home. They value the social contact and income, which may empower them to try other ventures in the future.

The motivation is different for women-headed households; they must have a job earning regular money due to the constraints of the *crédito* as a secondary currency, and they participate in the *Trueque* more out of need than because of the social life it offers. For them, participation is critical to their survival. The valuable access of women to the public sphere can be regarded as proof of their empowerment and an achievement of the *Trueque* in the long run, though it needs to be explored specifically in future research.

What else was achieved? Most obviously, around 2001 and 2002 the *Trueque* increased the income of households by an average of 600 pesos, which at that time was equivalent to twice the minimum wage or barely below the poverty line for a family of four.[28] So a *Trueque* participant visiting markets daily could roughly support a household.[29] It should be noted, however, that the increase in household income is an average and needs to be analysed further. The structural poor did not achieve the same increase because they had fewer resources and less capital, tangible and intangible, to use in the *Trueque*. They barely covered their basic food and clothing needs, and with considerably less choice than if they had had regular money. The disenfranchised middle class, and especially those who could 'risk' a few pesos in an enterprise, made more. So the average income increase from node market activity hides class inequalities, which is a common feature of all markets.

As observed earlier, the *Trueque* also offered a new space of sociability to the new poor and unemployed during a difficult period in their lives. For the disenfranchised middle class, the *Trueque* was an opportunity to share a social life with other individuals suffering a similar experience of impoverishment and confusion. It was part of their search for a new identity and probably enabled them to maintain their self-confidence so that they were able to return later to the regular economy.[30] The structural poor could interact with the disenfranchised middle class in conditions of less inequality than in the regular economy.

Another result of the *Trueque*, which was barely discussed in this study and could be a subject for future research, is that it offered an alternative to clientelistic networks. The poor, most likely the structural poor, tend to fall prey to politicians at the local level, who trade food and favours for political support.[31] This problem has been researched by several authors[32] who explain how the structural poor were coopted during the neoliberal reform programme in exchange for access to a network of favours. During election periods, they were picked up in buses to swell political demonstrations in exchange for a box of food termed a *bolsón* (literally, big bag), but in more recent times, the *bolsón* has been replaced by the promise of a social welfare subsidy (allocated at the local level but financed by the central government). The disenfranchised middle class, as newcomers to poverty, were not part of this circuit and felt better contained in the nodes.[33]

Another topic for future research is the environmental aspect of the *Trueque*.[34] About one-third of the supply to the nodes came from recycling, recovering and reusing second-hand goods that were idle in the households of the new poor, had been discarded by others and given to participants as charity, or was waste from either other households or factories. The structural poor often sifted through rubbish in wealthy areas and factories and found clothes, toys, bags, or raw materials for handicrafts such as fabrics and wood. They also visited supermarkets, where food was discarded around the day of expiry or because it was not saleable (for example, crushed cans or a product missing a component). The recovery of goods that have lost exchange value seems to form an area of economic activity that generates an income for the poor and could contribute substantially to their livelihood.[35] It needs to be researched for its aggregate impact on the environment and on the efficiency of the economy. Waste means different things to different agents; in the *Trueque* it means something different than in the regular market.

Finally, the *Trueque* locked in activity geographically and sometimes contributed to local economic development. When the national economy collapsed, it helped regions to maintain some level of economic activity to see them through the crisis. And it provided a longer-term option for diversification of income to the poor, especially the new poor, who made the most of the nodes as protected markets to start a micro-enterprise. The *Trueque* also integrated the rural hinterland and connected the poor and unemployed with networks from which they are normally excluded. CCS thus have potential as tools for promotion of local economic development. This is specially so when they are able to make investments in bureaucracy, raise a collective fund to finance projects and have managerial structures.[36]

The *Trueque* proved to be a particularly effective tool for micro-enterprise creation and self-employment, judging by the survival rates. The nodes enabled participants to 'learn by doing' with lower risks and lower entry barriers. This is the positive side of a club market; it restricts buyers to the supply offered in the nodes and thus sustains a regular level of demand to spend the *créditos*. Micro-enterprises in the *Trueque* thus needed a low threshold of competitiveness to be viable businesses. The incubator effects were clear: more time to learn, leniency over mistakes, low risk of failure, and low barriers to entry or to making changes. Participants who had no experience at all in self-employment discovered that they were capable producers and traders. The possible role of club markets as an alternative in micro-enterprise creation programmes, not necessarily through non-state currencies, needs to be explored further.

9 CONCLUSIONS

This study showed that the *Trueque* had a strong anti-cyclical component but other factors are necessary to explain its emergence and growth. In macroeconomic terms, there was no reason why the economic activity in the *Trueque* could not have taken place in the regular economy. In theory, there was no need for a special currency, since the resources (physical and intangible) were there.

So why did the production of the *Trueque* not occur in the regular economy? The difference lay in the institutions that governed the 'active' and the 'idle' (unemployed or not economically active) parts of the economy. The *Trueque* coordinated actors and resources into production and exchange in ways that the regular economy could not. It filled the institutional gaps left by the missing mediating mechanisms in the regular economy. Therefore it was not lack of resources that deepened the crisis in the Argentine economy and kept its agents unemployed, but the lack of institutions by which they could be coordinated. There was no impediment in the static conditions (that is, the resources available) but in the dynamic ones (coordination mechanisms). In short, lack of critical resources and downturns of the business cycle are not the only causes of unemployment. The lack of appropriate institutions to coordinate the use of resources also needs to be examined.

Following this reasoning, the participation of the disenfranchised middle class emerges as critical to the take-off of the *Trueque*. Participation in the regular market was not available to the new poor, who had no jobs and no other income. On the other hand, transferring goods and services as gifts or charity or within a reciprocity network, as often observed among the structural poor, was not an acceptable solution in a middle-class context. The *Trueque* took elements of both and adapted them in the club market: it mixed the institutions of the market with the social cohesion of a closed network. What would have been a gift became a commodity to exchange, though for community money, not regular money. Transfers were facilitated by the non-state money of those who accepted it by becoming traders in the club market.

A key element in this regeneration of economic coordination was the printing of a non-state currency to complement the regular monetary system, filling the gaps in that system. The *Trueque* did not start with bartering but with a note-book in which credits and debits were written down. When membership grew, the system evolved into scrip to be used as means to facilitate payments. Initially, the *créditos* were not exactly a new unit of account (the *CT* copied the prices and denominations of the regular monetary system) and they were certainly not a reserve of value (they were only meant to facilitate transactions). Scrip was printed only after participants trusted each other enough to receive printed vouchers in return for their goods. The very name '*créditos*' reflects the principle claimed by one of its initiators, that 'in the *Club de Trueque* we give and receive credit. We believe in each other'. The creation of money that serves only as means of payment (not as reserve of value) constitutes an interesting policy option to explore during a crisis, as suggested already by some authors.[1] It regenerates the coordination of exchange.

A monetary system implemented in the absence of an authority that decides the amount of money to circulate *a priori* has been theorized as an endogenous monetary system by the post-Keynesian monetary school.[2] John Maynard Keynes[3] conceived a 'credit theory of money'. Post-Keynesians argue that credit money develops an endogenous or autonomous monetary system in which promises to pay are created with each transaction. Means of payment develop along with exchange, in contrast to being a policy instrument of the state, which decides the amount of money in circulation.

In the *RT*, the rule for adding currency was to inject a certain amount of *créditos* per person after they joined and increased the total value added. Unlike the official monetary system of the Central Bank, the *Trueque* had an endogenous monetary system in which means of payment were increased at the same rate as its scale and aggregated production. At least that was the idea until the vouchers were overprinted and forged. As a result, the amount of money grew with the goods and services to be exchanged. Prices stayed stable and there was no monetary scarcity. The right amount of currency in circulation was relatively simple to calculate at the micro-level when small-scale production predominated and the needs for means of payment were similar for each trader. The *RT* corresponded to the credit theory of money. An equivalent calculation in a regular economy with heterogeneous producers and traders, each with diverse needs for money, would be considerably more complex.

The *Trueque* leads to a reflection on the history of fiat money in Western Europe, when issuers were a relatively small number of agents with a reputation to safeguard. Money then relied also on social networks in which there was either a minimum trust that credits would be honoured or that the untrustworthy issuer could be punished.[4] Some authors conceive money as a medium of communicating anonymous promises to pay[5] and for communication to take place effectively, both parts need to speak a 'common language' (money). Agents constructed 'money' as a promise to pay and the rules of action associated to it. At some point money was an institution designed by a network of agents to achieve a common goal. In circumstances X, do Y and obtain Z. Money was one of the possible solutions they could have found. This view is at odds with the approach that allocates intrinsic value to a specific commodity, which would serve as general means of payment for all other commodities.

There is a second parallel with the origins of fiat money. Historically, depersonalized and transferable promises of payment were woven into deep and complex layers of debt in which the most trustworthy promises to pay were kept as base-money and the others were used to make daily payments. In a similar fashion, in Argentina regular money was used for general purposes or as reserve of value, while the *créditos* were spent the same day they were received to buy the basic needs for which households did not have enough official money. The fact that the monies were used for different purposes does not suggest that either one of them was replacing or displacing the other. They circulated in separate places or areas of the economy and they met in the households, where they were converted into commodities to satisfy needs and wants.

The combination of currencies in Argentina suggests that a monetary system works only when means of payment are attached to a monetary network that trusts the issuer (for example, the citizens of a country where the issuer can impose sovereignty) or are linked to a more reliable means of payment (for example, a currency board or monetary union). Though following a completely different theoretical approach, this finding is consistent with Cavallo's theorization on the quality of money. If the quality of money is very low (for example, when inflation has undermined the monetary sovereignty and trustworthiness of the issuer), agents resort to the next accessible and more reliable currency.[6] The currency that is no longer viable will not be acceptable, whatever the quantity in circulation set by the Central Bank. So policies that control the quantity of money to prevent inflation could gain from looking also at the quality of their money. This relates to the point made in the beginning of this chapter on the lack of institutions to coordinate the use of resources for production and exchange in Argentina. Regular money that creates a profit (interest) may not serve as means of payment in an economic crisis. Money of a different quality may be needed, like a complementary currency that only serves as means of payment.[7]

Like the regular monetary system, the complementary or local currency of the *Trueque* eventually generated a qualitative transformation in the social relations of production. Historically, money became dematerialized and depersonalized, third-party debts were cancelled by other third-party debts and those were not tied to specific goods or services.[8] Money became disembedded of the social setting that gave it its original value, and became an abstract means of payment, store of value and unit of account. Subsequently, printing and managing money created two classes of social actors: those who created it, or the issuers, and those who used it, or traders.[9] The *Red de Trueque* followed a similar path: the *créditos* became disembedded as the number of users grew. Community or complementary currencies then became depersonalized, dematerialized, abstract and transferable promises to pay that initially emerged from a social network with some degree of trust to give certainty to claims. The network gradually incorporated a large number of participants and hence became anonymous and disembedded and communicated the promises to pay of other anonymous users of the same currency. However, there were a few substantial differences between regular money and the *créditos*. The latter was constrained to some goods and services. It created a club identity of 'us and them' between those who participated and those who did not. The system still relied on social relations. The absence of state authorities to regulate it – including the power to punish those who forged currency – made it rather unstable when used on a national scale.

While restricted to an effectively manageable scale and scope, complementary currency systems can still achieve a larger scale than other social economy schemes (for example, cooperatives, collective resource management or mutual funds). They are an emulation of the regular economic system in which some aspects are changed by the down-scaling while others, namely the use of an impersonal and abstract means of payment, stay the same. Social economy schemes are ruled by trust, reciprocity, and the institutions of personal exchange, at least in theory. A local exchange and trading system based purely on these rules would not really need any physical means of payment. Goods and services would change hands all the time between parties and gifts would be reciprocated at some time in the future. In contrast, a CCS uses an abstract means of payment to embody transactions, so it is just one step ahead into an impersonal exchange system.

In sum, a complementary or community currency is the central institution of a hybrid economic system which lies between personal and depersonalized exchange, as extremes in a continuum. CCS have in common with personal exchange systems the social cohesion crucial to sustain them. At the same time, CCS share with impersonal exchange systems the use of depersonalized means of payment that add certainty to a larger scale system and enable it to grow beyond the very small scale of personal exchange systems.

A Last Review: *RT* as Institutional Construction

Explanations for the evolution of the *Trueque* need to go beyond the anti-cyclical mechanism hypothesis and focus on the national context in which the *RT* constructed institutions regulating an area of the economy where low-income groups achieved a livelihood. This section summarizes the institutional explanation of the *RT* presented in this study.

Argentina had relatively well-developed institutions and organizations to coordinate the economy in comparison with other developing countries. People's behaviour was structured around them. Their swift and rather reckless transformation during the 1990s resulted in institutional gaps, areas of uncertainty and unstructured behaviour that left individuals without guidance on how to proceed with their economic activities. New microeconomic uncertainties created by the reforms came to the fore, complementing old macroeconomic imbalances. The crisis around the end of the 1990s was not simply a downturn in the macroeconomy but a general loss of faith that the regular economy could, on a daily basis, resolve the problems besetting production, trade, and income generation.

The institutional gaps that resulted were not unique to the Argentine structural reform programme; other countries had experienced them, too. What was different was the context in which they sprang up and the reaction they evoked. The institutional gaps in Argentina resulted in the shedding of a vast pool of resources – material and intangible – that are not typical of the developing world in either quantity or quality. Yet the Argentine situation also cannot be equated with that in countries with a similar endowment of resources, because in those countries there are alternatives and safety nets (for example, the welfare state) while Argentines were left to their own devices to develop new livelihoods and devise new collective solutions that could restructure their economic activities. Self-help networks were insufficiently developed to support survival efforts or even emigration. At the risk of oversimplifying, Argentina was facing a Third World type of crisis with First World types of resources and institutions.

The quality of the resources left idle was more similar to those in developed countries: a substantial middle class, rich in skills, accumulated assets and social connections, but in many cases unable to put them to use in the restructured economy. For example, many had technical skills and a small amount of capital from savings, adequate to produce a technically correct product but not competitively in the new open economy. A large number of workers were experiencing unemployment and labour vulnerability for the first time in their lives, with wages well below the level needed to support their normal lifestyle. The crisis affected the structural poor, as always, but in the 1990s in Argentina it affected part of the middle class as well. They became the voiced poor, a group in a two-pronged search for institutions to give meaning again to their lost middle-class identity and the means to recover some of the consumption that was typical of it. What was also specific to Argentina was the instituted practice of using various means of payment, most obviously the dollar along with the peso but also various provincial currencies. Printing non-state scrip to enable transactions for a closed social network was almost an obvious step. Agents needing to resolve the problems in their daily socioeconomic life responded with attempts to patch the institutional gaps in ways that were unthinkable elsewhere. The confluence of these factors made a social phenomenon such as the *Red de Trueque* possible.

The establishment of a club market for small-scale trading of goods produced by the new poor and unemployed became a solution as soon as the market-makers capable of setting it up emerged. In the first *Club de Trueque*, participants used their own scrip to enable exchanges and generate income outside the regular economy. Testing turned the innovation into a new solution and eventually a new rule of action for the first participants. The *CT* was described as an extreme case of market-building, in which the set of new institutions designed included money (although initially it was not perceived as such). Participation was voluntary and entailed acceptance of the club's currency.

Rebuilding a market with agents excluded from the regular economy, regulated by the primary and evolved institutions of any market economy, combined continuity with innovation. The club market solution was spread and imitated by a pre-existent network, embedded by trust and social relations that justified the belief that the rules of the group would be complied with and that actions would be stable. This was a world regulated by personal exchange, for which the *CT* was a new designed institution.

The scheme proved effective for participants and quite simple to replicate in other locations where similar conditions existed. The market-makers set growth as one of their main objectives, aware of the gains from division of labour and the strength of larger numbers. The number of participants grew rapidly, and with the expansion came the uncertainties and transaction costs of impersonal exchange. These had to be resolved with minimal or no state intervention. The designed institutions of the first *Club de Trueque* had to be adjusted to be applicable across social groups and localities.

At this point, the Argentine *RT* experience became different from those of other complementary currency systems around the world. It was not only larger but also the only one formed by independent *CTs* articulated in a single network with rules in common, as was observed also by Peter North.[10] They had an umbrella organization, which allowed participants to visit any node in the country using any of the various currencies, even if people hardly knew each other.

The organizers of the *Red de Trueque* sought solutions to control the costs of exchange. They started by setting rules of replication, formalized in black and white the principles to guide participants' behaviour and eventually came up with a structure of representation in which the groups in the *RT* would control each other. But then the strength of seeking to improve efficiency as the driving force of institutional building was subordinated to other factors. The organizers entangled themselves in coalitions with divergent interests and intentions, conflicts of power and personal tensions. While the initiating group of the *Trueque* promoted a vision that concentrated power and allowed them to control the rest of the network, opposing groups formed a front to resist their authority.

An outcome of the power struggles was to devise the social franchise mechanism. It served to replicate *CT*s quickly and simply but also as a means to bring the control of the network back to the initiators' group. It promoted the use of their currency well into the regions of their opponents. Thus, it pushed the conflict to a climax that resulted in the definite break-up of the network. This was the achievable solution in the standing circumstances, not the most efficient one.

With all its problems and conflicts, the *Red de Trueque* achieved a larger scale than any other complementary currency system around the world. It was also able to enhance growth and division of labour by allowing participants to move around, trade different goods across nodes and complement regional production. This was done, clearly, at the expense of relaxing the controls typical of the rules of personal exchange. Opportunism was quick to thrive, which is hardly a problem in other CCS around the world organized as personal exchange.

The groups that emerged from the break-up of the *RT* as an integrated network formed various governance systems in combination with other institutions in the economy. They were free to organize regulation according to their own vision of what the *Trueque* should be like. The problem of governance is typical of economic schemes in which there is no default organization in charge of regulation, like a state, so compliance needs to be constructed. None of the actors in the *Trueque* had power to force others to comply. The governance systems in the *Trueque* were a regulated market (the *RGT* of the *PAR* leaders), a hierarchy (*ZO*), an association of regional sub-networks (*RTS*), and the community or club model of local independent nodes. In the regulated market system of the initiators' *RGT*, institutions promoted self-interest and coordination was done by a central regulator (the *PAR* leaders) who decided basic rules, leaving others to be determined by the coordinators, and assumed spontaneous compliance in the nodes. In the *ZO* hierarchy, participants were also guided by self-interest, but coordination relied on an administrative bureaucracy managed by a leader at the top. In the associational network of the *RTS*, institutions enhanced compromise, first among the coordinators and then among participants, based on shared ideological convictions and recognition of each other's interests and opinions. Coordination was achieved through bottom-up negotiation in the search for consensus, and once agreement had been reached at the *IZ* level, the rules were expected to be complied with at lower levels. The independent nodes structured a community or club type of governance system, in which participants were guided by the rules of personal exchange and reciprocal obligation to their neighbours. Coordination was achieved rather spontaneously.

After the *RT* as an integrated network of these groups broke up, the *Trueque* reached its maximum scale and soon afterwards collapsed. The fall was explained by exogenous factors such as large-scale forgery of *créditos*, interference by political clientelistic networks, implementation of a welfare policy and the rebound of the regular economy. However, the *Trueque* had already been crumbling due to its own shortfalls. The endogenous factors responsible for its demise were opportunistic behaviour, lack of basic food production inputs, rampant speculation, price inflation, and mismanagement, mainly by the *PAR*.

The analytical framework for analyzing the sustainability of governance systems considers four factors: input legitimacy or acceptance of basic institutions resulting from the process of their definition and intentions, mechanisms of enforcement, resource synergies that derive from benefits for participants, and transaction and organizational costs. On the basis of the criteria, none of the governance systems of the *Trueque* showed a high degree of sustainability, though some fared better than others. After the *Trueque* plummeted, the coordinators and the core of most committed participants were left to decide whether to keep the node open or not. An estimation of 700 of them opted for maintaining the *CT* running, but they became more autonomous and did more of the rule-setting of the nodes. There were some exceptions of *CTs* that still integrated regional networks, like the ZO.

Theory on local monetary networks identifies four rationales for the construction of CCS; this study added a fifth. Seigniorage income is typically not an issue among CCS, but in the case of the large-scale *Trueque* the revenue was substantial. The qualitative transformation of the exchanges was also observed, but not at a political level that would transform the prevalent structures of power in society. The maintenance of economic activity during a crisis was the typical impact on the local economy. The *Trueque* added to local production with local inputs, raised local demand, reduced waste and offered a secondary market for businesses to stay afloat.

The rationale for the organization of CCS added in this study was the construction of meso-level institutions to diversify sources of income and enhance the livelihoods of low-income groups. This is the essential side of community economic development. The *Trueque* brought together the resources of the poor and unemployed, and integrated them in a network where they interacted with other actors, better endowed with resources. It was an inclusive market of the low-income groups excluded from the regular economy.

Finally, two specific cases were analyzed for their commitment to promoting local economic development. A series of conditions were highlighted as necessary for achieving this goal: a collective fund in regular money to finance projects, bureaucratic infrastructure such as a database of participants and resources, and strong leaders well-endowed with local contacts and managerial capacities. The two cases were classified as enabling and managerial. The former supported the creation of synergies and strengthened participants' autonomy, while the latter organized idle resources in the area and collective enterprises around central leadership. In both cases, there was heavy dependence on a central organizer and on having a minimum scale – rather high in the case of the ZO – to sustain their activities.

The *Trueque*, as the largest experiment with complementary currencies in the world in current times, offered a broad scope of adaptations to localities and communities. It was thus possible to build a typology useful for future experimentation with CCS worldwide. An aspect to consider is the temporal scope, a short-term survival strategy or a long-term local development horizon in which social and identity aspects are also strengthened. A second facet is the degree of openness to or disconnection from the regular economy, related to the political ideal of posing a complementary or an alternative economic scheme. A third feature is the style of the organizers, an active or a passive role.

Triggers to Institutional Construction

The evolution of the *Red de Trueque* in Argentina illustrates the problems of creating a market and eventually an economic system within the regular economy. It is now time to take a step back and analyze in detail the stages of the process of institutionalization performed by agents through a reconstitutive upward causation.[11]

Why do agents engage in designing new institutions? Institutional design and change is, essentially, a reaction to the state of the socioeconomic structure. This is composed of the primary institutions that sustain all others, the habits and routines that evolve out of regularity or practice and the designed institutions that result from previous reflective action.

Agents react to institutional gaps; they perceive that the rules of action they follow are unintelligible, incomplete, or unsatisfactory. Rules of action are meaningless when the conditions in the environment have changed and the actions that used to apply in those conditions no longer result in the expected outcome. Following Hodgson,[12] a rule of the type 'in circumstances X do Y' and expect a Z outcome has become invalid because circumstances have become X'. Since there is no rule of action to follow in these other circumstances, if agents continue to do Y the outcome is not Z. The pre-reflexive disposition to take an action becomes reflexive by virtue of the failure of Z to happen. It may not be immediately obvious that the unexpected outcome is the result of responding with old actions to new circumstances, so this reflexive process may take a while to be set in motion. When it does, agents individually or collectively attempt to find a suitable Y' for the new X'.

The second type of institutional gap is when pre-reflexive tendencies are incomplete. This is the case when a new situation appears and new rules of action need to be developed. Agents are then pushed to seek the Y that will resolve the situation X.

The third type of institutional gap is when pre-reflexive tendencies of action are unsatisfactory to agents. Although the rule of action indicates doing Y in circumstances X, this does not mean full acceptance on a reflexive level. It means that Y has been imposed by a more powerful agent with the means to enforce the rule or by the practice of previous generations. Z is then perceived to be detrimental by a group of agents. This is the conflict type of institutional gap that triggers collective action, because in fact there is a rule of action but it is resisted. Finding a new Y' involves changing the socioeconomic structure, which is costly, difficult and normally involves significant collective action. Therefore, agents will engage replacing the institution only if they react strongly against it.

In this framework, structural reform programmes represent attempts of a certain group of agents (policymakers) to change the rules of action of an economy and obtain a different outcome; that is, organise the economy differently. Since policymakers can only operate on X, they create X' conditions in order to lead agents to do Y' and obtain Z'. Unfortunately, agents may fail to perceive what the expected response is, may find other reactions more suitable, may find no acceptable response at all and exhibit inertia or may find the new outcome unacceptable and therefore resist implementing it. These are all examples of institutional gaps that may – and in reality do – result from policy-induced institutional reforms.

The theorization on structural reform programmes therefore needs to incorporate an evolutionary perspective on institutions. Neglecting this perspective creates a high probability of failure when policymakers are designing institutions (failure means that the expected new rule of action does not stick in practice). That is, of course, unless the policymakers have sufficient means to enforce rules, which is rather difficult and costly. Institutions can only be adjusted by policy if the process is accompanied by agents' reflexive action, an element of lower ontological level[13] or Giddens' structuration theory.[14] In that case, conscious elaboration results in designed institutions, so pre-reflexive dispositions to act are replaced by reflexive dispositions to act.[15] When policymakers attempt to change the organization of the economy, agents first need to understand and accept that in circumstances X' they are required to do Y' for the result to be Z'. Again, that depends on whether Y' is resisted, agreed or imposed, and in the last case, whether it can be enforced.

Although agents can change old institutions with new designed ones, there are limits to what can be changed. Institutions act on agents' enabling and constraining behaviour.[16] There is no tabula rasa; institutions designed by policymakers are bound to the prior and evolved rules of action prevalent in the relevant space, time and circumstances. The consequence is that designed institutions cannot be transferred from one context to another with the expectation of the same results.

There is a second implication concerning the relationship between designed institutions and what policymakers can effectively impose. Institutional design is related to intentions and interests, as elaborated by several authors.[17] If the new rules of action elaborated by policymakers clash with the intentions and interests of the agents who are expected to behave accordingly, then policymakers will need a battery of means of enforcement. This is not always viable, especially in developing countries. The alternative is to generate consensus around the designed institutions. So a distinction is drawn among designed institutions, between those imposed top-down by policymakers and groups with power and those formulated bottom-up by agents, individually or collectively, through negotiation or agreement. Institutions designed and imposed top-down may generate resistance and require means of enforcement to elicit the required behaviour. Institutions built bottom-up would generate less resistance, but compliance with them is not assured either.

To sum up, elements of a lower ontological level (agents) can bring about changes in elements of higher ontological levels (institutions). Designed institutions can change other ones by repeatedly forcing reasoning at the moment of action. They become habits and routines, too, when repetition makes them pre-reflexive tendencies to act. Similarly, evolved institutions become primary ones when they are ingrained to the point that another course of action is unthinkable.

Institutional Innovation

The second step in the process of institutional construction or reconstruction is experimentation to reach a solution. That is, defining an acceptable response that could later become a new rule of action. Economic action flows between an innovation and a continuity loop. In the continuity loop, agents behave according to the existent rules of action (prior, evolved and designed institutions). In the innovation loop, agents are immersed into reflexive action, testing possible solutions. Networks embed trial-and-error experimentation, inform what kind of testing is possible, support new paths of action and discuss outcomes until a solution is found. Inter-subjectivity, therefore, embeds experimentation.[18] Imitation, repetition and refining of the response may later establish it as a new designed institution across groups and networks. A 'novelty' has entered the world: a new rule of action Y' for that network to do in circumstances X' and obtain Z'.

Three conditions were identified as necessary for the design of institutions, and were discussed in the context of constructing a club market. First, the presence of 'market-makers', who are generically the collective action entrepreneurs who build networks, launch a scheme and bear the initial organizational costs. The second condition is the involvement in the initial phases of a network of agents with interests and intentions aligned to the search for a new rule of action. The third condition regards the presence in the continuity loop of pre-existent institutions that set the limits to experimentation and enable the search for new solutions.

The implication is that no new institution is entirely new or a complete innovation but contains recreated elements of the pre-existing ones.[19] Institutional construction is evolutionary, in the sense that present options are restricted by choices made before and by structures prevalent at each moment. Every new solution is a priori path-dependent.

Institutional evolution shares with technical progress the essential characteristics of being accumulative processes in which error leaves traces, so part of the theorization on technical progress could be applied to institutional evolution as well. In turn, institutional evolution combines not only solutions that flourish into institutions but a portion of the learning from failed courses of action or that had no significant effect. Learning takes place both with success and with failure. Failure leaves 'footprints' that may be vital later on. Individuals accumulate social memories that they or other agents can retrieve in subsequent learning processes at the same time as they add their own, creative elements. An interesting theoretical cross-fertilization could be explored in future research. How do social innovations compare with technical innovation? What triggers them and how can they be enhanced through policy? Is there a life-cycle in the durability of institutions?

Institutional evolution is also different to biological evolution. Richard Nelson[20] observed that biology is the main source of inspiration of economists and yet many of its categories and concepts need to be adapted or reinvented before they can be used to explain the economy. This is one adaptation: institutions are evolutionary but they do not follow a unidirectional evolutionary path. There are partial and total failures, retrogressions, second attempts, and continuous adaptation. Besides, a good share of these are remembered, recorded and registered by individuals or groups, sometimes in written form.

The conceptualization of new institutions as a combination of new and old structures has practical consequences in the field of development and poverty alleviation. The actions of the poor are shaped by their need to survive, which limits their inclination to innovate. Transiting to the innovation loop (that is, trying something new) can be expensive and a risk the poor cannot afford without endangering the livelihood of the household. The scope for innovation is thus restricted to the affordable solutions of the continuity loop, where risks can be assessed easily. The implication is that the poor are conservative, in spite of being perhaps the group that has more to gain from change. Hence, the poor often persist in using old solutions that have been tested and shown to work, at least partially. They may reject more beneficial options if those are untested and thus riskier. Consequently, known solutions are most likely to be adopted when the targeted groups can relate them to their continuity loop.

This reflection goes beyond emphasizing that context matters. It is not just context, but the institutional legacy that matters. The question is the 'distance' between the continuity loop and the innovation loop. An intuitive notion emerges of the 'distance' between the continuity loop and innovations. This idea is not alien to evolutionary economic theory. Nelson and Winter[21] suggested that diversity of agents was a condition for creating novelty. Later Bart Nooteboom postulated that diversity in knowledge matters, calling it 'cognitive distance'.[22] Evolutionary economic theory contends that 'people perceive, interpret, understand, and evaluate the world according to mental categories' that differ from those of others because they have developed them 'in interaction with their physical and social environment'.[23] The concept of 'cognitive distance' is applied to differences between mental categories, while this study focuses on differences between an innovation and the continuity of rules of action. There are some differences, but both concepts suggest that if the distance is too large, the innovation will not flourish.

From Experimentation to Design

Experimentation processes finish when a solution is tested and found acceptable. However, different networks and groups experiment simultaneously and arrive at diverse solutions. The one that eventually institutionalizes across groups in society first needs scrutiny in relation to different intentions and interests. This is the third stage of the process of institutional construction that was investigated: the transfer of solutions across groups to construct common institutions.

New solutions are accepted within networks operating as sources of information, limiting what experimentation is possible, sharing the costs of testing and eventually deciding on rules of action. This represents an intermediate level of institutionalization, in which the rule of action is valid only within a certain network,[24] appeals to Elias' concept of 'figuration' to describe how new solutions are first adopted by specific networks and later become part of the social structure. Figurations are intermediate interaction orders between agents and institutions.

Transferring or sharing new solutions with other groups across society is not automatic. It is conceivable that reduction of transaction costs is at some point the main goal behind institutional design but institutional construction entails a complex process along which actions may or may not be calculated in that way.

But ex-ante there are other factors driving institutional design. Once agents start interacting with each other, efficiency-seeking goals get mingled with pre-existent bonds, asymmetries of power, interpersonal relations, divergent interests and intentions. These other factors constrain social interaction and compete with the aim of enhancing efficiency. The institutions and organizations that eventually emerge from the process nest the tensions between improving efficiency, considering social relations and resisting or promoting power asymmetries. So even if agents perceive the superior efficiency of one solution over others, they may relegate it to promote the solution developed by their own network.

In turn, the concept of efficiency means different things to different people, so it is difficult to assess how strongly it guides institutional construction. It is formally defined as the minimization of waste, that is, the achievement of wellbeing with minimal use of resources.[25] New Institutional Economics conceptualizes it as minimizing the uncertainty of exchange, a situation where the system creates the minimum waste possible. So the 'efficiency' of the institutions eventually achieved can only be evaluated ex-post and in line with the conception of efficiency of the agents involved.[26]

The claim that efficiency is an outcome and not a determinant intention driving institutional design implies that it cannot be relied on as an argument to persuade agents to accept a solution as a rule of action across groups and networks. Even if it were possible to design the 'most efficient' institutional solution for a certain situation, its efficiency would hardly be a basis for making it succeed at an institutional level – unless, of course, it were to be imposed and backed by a battery of means of enforcement. In relation to policy, it is not enough to show that a certain project formulates efficient solutions for a certain situation. Power struggles and social relations need to be taken into account to make the proposed project acceptable to decision-makers and agents in general. It needs to satisfy intentions and interests across groups.

In development cooperation and poverty alleviation, divergences in this area explain the frustration of donors, who sometimes feel local groups in developing counties fail to understand and adapt their behaviour to the designed institutions proposed, which are more efficient than those accepted locally. The alleged superiority of their designed institutions in terms of efficiency does not strike the right note. Donors promoting development projects need to contemplate the intentions and interests of the target populations, in addition to the institutional legacy that guides their behaviour.

Agents in different groups share varied interests and intentions, carry out experimentation separately and define their own solutions to problems. Some are indeed shared, imposed or negotiated later, but various groups or networks regularly apply different rules of action. So the format of an institution could be presented more complex: if you are A, in circumstances X do Y to obtain Z. The analysis applies when the grouping criteria are categories such as class, gender or ethnicity. So there are institutions that create a tendency to act in a certain way for one category and in another way for another category. That means, for example, that in circumstances X men have disposition to do Y_1 and women, to do Y_2. The prevalence of distinctive institutions for different (target) groups should guide the choice of development projects and the assumptions behind that choice.

Governance of Institutions

The final stage in institutional construction is the coming together of institutions. That is, the rules of governance and sustainability of an economic system. Designed, evolved and prior institutions form clusters or governance systems.[27] Governance systems in an economy are a coherent group of institutional arrangements that organize, coordinate and manage the interdependencies of actors inside and across the boundaries of an economic system. The concept of governance systems is a useful tool for understanding regulation of economic action in situations where none of the agents has means to enforce compliance of rules by the others. Jessop[28] and Holingsworth and Boyer[29] identify the critical factor for the sustainability of a governance system as coherence or compatibility among the institutions that form it.

Four main criteria for assessing the sustainability of governance systems were advanced. The first is the input legitimacy of the institutions, which focuses on the process by which they were designed. Participation and consultation during the experimentation phase, for example, increases input legitimacy. The second criterion is the construction of mechanisms to control enforcement of rules and eventually obtain obedience even against some resistance on the part of agents. In situations where none of the agents has the means to impose rules on others, control can be achieved through peer pressure, by checking compliance at random, or by establishing an accepted police body. The third criterion is achievement of resource synergies by which the material benefits of abiding by rules of action are shared. These are familiarly known as the 'carrots' of the system. They create output legitimacy for the rules by appealing to the rational calculation capacity of agents. In a system in which no agent has the means to enforce rules, material benefits for those who abide by them generates incentives to comply. The final criterion relates to the transaction and organizational costs of the system. These are the counterpart of the previous criterion, the benefits from resource synergies. A distinction is made between the costs of running the system (associated with uncertainties, risks and information asymmetries) and the costs of decision-making (starting and sustaining collective action, making decisions, and redefining objectives).

Governance systems constructed beyond state regulation are sustainable when agents consider the rules legitimate by virtue of how they were defined or because they represent a shared ideology or values; when their failure to comply will be socially exposed or penalized; when it is materially beneficial to abide by the rules; and when the shared costs of running the system are affordable. Clearly, some of these factors may be more relevant than others at different points in time. So there are a variety of reasons why these non-state governance systems are sustainable, why agents may support them and why the state, to the extent that it has a say, admits them.

There is considerable romanticism over the self-regulation of the informal and social economy, as transmitted by the label 'solidarity economy' which some authors apply[30] and others criticize.[31] The analytical framework developed here suggests that shared values and trust can generate considerable legitimacy for the governance system, but there are still three other factors that need attention. However strongly agents may cling to their ideals, there are still the problems of enforcement, production and distribution of material benefits, and keeping transaction and organizational costs low. The assumption that idealism will automatically compensate for failures in these areas is the source of considerable frustration, at least in the long run. These challenges confront many cooperatives and collective enterprises in the social economy, which rely on participation, checking compliance of rules, delivering material benefits and the other critical aspects discussed above. When they fail in one or more of these areas, they become unsustainable and collapse.

Similarly, development programmes sometimes build governance systems focused on generating resource synergies and distributing their material benefits but neglect to generate ideological support for the rules that agents are asked to comply with or placing enforcement structures to control them. The governance systems that emerge from such development projects become unsustainable as soon as the resource synergies diminish, unless a battery of enforcement mechanisms are in place, which is often costlier than the resource synergies achieved.

A Stylization of Institutional Emergence

Having analysed the different stages of institution-building in detail, it is possible now to put the whole process together. Figure 9.1 shows different categories of institutions and their relationships with agents and events in the environment. It represents a summary of what has been presented in the previous section. This kind of layering follows the work of several authors.[32] This stylized analysis can help to make policymakers aware of the decisions they can effectively implement to reorganise the socioeconomic structure of society, both through reform programmes and development projects.

Figure 9.1

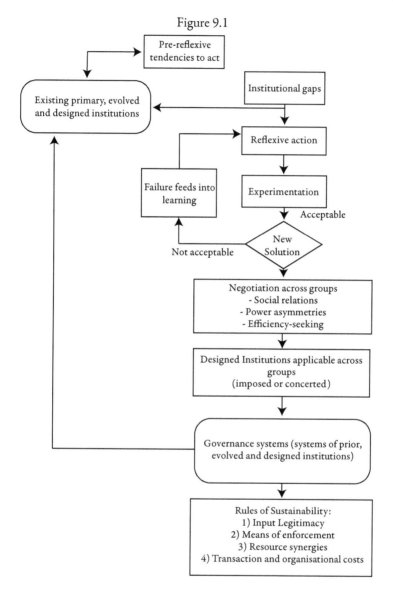

Three categories of institutions (rules of action) are distinguished. The highest by ontological level and resilience are prior institutions, which constitute the arena in which socioeconomic action takes place. The second type is evolved out of practice or regularity. The third is designed institutions, formulated in response to institutional gaps.

New solutions and the designed institutions that follow are only partially new; they refer to already operating institutions. Once a social network has found an acceptable solution, it still needs to be scrutinized by other groups before it becomes a designed rule of action across groups in society. This stage may not happen at all; the economic action of the poor, for example, is guided by different institutions than those applicable to the wealthier sections of the population. The rules of action of the poor have no bearing on the economic life of others less pressed by the need to survive.

Power asymmetries, efficiency-seeking and social relations across groups need to be reconciled. In the end, new designed institutions can be concerted or imposed, the latter being possible only if one group has the means to enforce others' compliance. New designed institutions also depend on previous and current choices (path dependency and imitation). Whether they are efficient in reducing uncertainty can only be evaluated ex-post, since efficiency is not decisive enough as an argument to persuade others to accept a solution above their own intentions and interests. Part of the reason for this is that different agents have divergent understandings of what is 'efficient'.

The process that leads to building a new institution, termed reconstitutive upward causation, is now complete. It describes the path from economic action to new institutions, which stick and continue operating once the designers are gone and the circumstances that originated them are forgotten. That is, at least, until the process starts again, triggered by a new change in the institutional structure, another wave of structural reform policies or a new crisis.

NOTES

1 Economic Life as an Institutional Process

1. J. L. Borges (1941) 'The Lottery in Babylon', in D. Yates and J. Irby (eds), *Labyrinths: Selected Stories and Other Writings by Jorge Luis Borges* (New York: New Directions Publishing Corporation 1964).
2. K. Polanyi, *The Great Transformation: The Political and Economic Origin of Our Times* (New York and Boston, MA: Beacon Press, 1957).
3. I. Fisher, *Stamp Scrip* (New York: Adelphi Co., 1933).
4. S. Gesell, *The Natural Economic Order* (London: Peter Owen, 1958).
5. C. De Sanzo, H. Covas and H. Primavera, *Reinventando El Mercado* (Buenos Aires: Programa de Autosuficiencia Regional, 1998). H. Primavera, 'Política social, imaginación y coraje: Reflexiones sobre la moneda social, reforma y democracia', Revista del CLAD (Caracas), 17 (1999), pp. 161–88.
6. P. North, *Alternative Currency Movements as a Challenge to Globalisation? A Case Study of Manchester's Local Currency Networks* (Aldershot: Ashgate, 2006).
7. G. Ingham, 'Money is a Social Relation', *Review of Social Economy*, 54:5 (1996), pp. 507–29; G. Ingham, 'On the Underdevelopment of the Sociology of Money', *Acta Sociologica*, 41:1 (1998), pp. 1–17.
8. S. Hintze (ed.), *Trueque y Economía Solidaria* (Universidad Nacional de General Sarmiento and Programa de Naciones Unidas para el Desarrollo, Buenos Aires: Prometeo Libros 2003), pp.111–116.
9. De Sanzo et al., *Reinventando El Mercado*. H. Primavera, *Cómo formar un primer club de trueque pensando en la economía global* (Medellín (Bogotá): Redlases, 1999). H. Primavera, 'Editorial', *Revista Trueque*, 2:3 (1999), p. 3.
10. A. Toffler, *The Third Wave* (London: Collins, 1980).
11. E. Ovalles, 'Argentina es el país del mundo en el cual el fenómeno del trueque tiene mayor dimensión social', *Carta Económica*, Centro de Estudios Nueva Mayoría (Buenos Aires): May (2002), pp. 42–5.
12. I. Gonzalez Bombal, 'Sociabilidad en las clases medias en descenso: Experiencias en el trueque', in *Sociedad y sociabilidad en la Argentina de los 90*; L. Beccaria, et al. (eds) (Buenos Aires: Universidad Nacional de General Sarmiento and Editorial Biblos, 2002), 97–136; I. González Bombal, F. Leoni and M. Luzzi, 'Nuevas Redes Sociales: Los Clubes De Trueque', in I. González Bombal (ed.) *Respuestas de la Sociedad Civil a la Emergencia Social: Brasil y Argentina Comparten Experiencias* (Buenos Aires: CEDES – UNGS, 2002).

13. P. Lecaro and B. Altschuler, 'Políticas Sociales y Desarrollo Local, Dos Experiencias Diversas: Club del Trueque y Unión de Trabajadores Desocupados (UTD) de Mosconi', in *Congreso Nacional de Políticas Sociales 'Estrategias de articulación de políticas, programas y proyectos sociales en Argentina'* (Buenos Aires: Universidad de Quilmes, 2002); Parysow and Bogani, 'Perspectivas de Desarrollo Económico y Social para las Mujeres Pobres y Empobrecidas en los Clubes del Trueque. Estudio De Caso: La Bernalesa' (Paper presented at the Seminario Las Caras de la Pobreza, Buenos Aires 2002).

14. M. A. Barreto, M. A. Benitez and A. M. Attias, 'Política Social, Pobreza, Identidad y Fragmentación Social' (Paper presented at the Seminario Las Caras de la Pobreza (Buenos Aires: Universidad Catolica, 2002). M. Murmis and S. Feldman, 'La Heterogeneidad Social De Las Pobrezas', in A. Minujin (ed.), *Cuesta Abajo: Los Nuevos Pobres: Efectos De La Crisis En La Sociedad Argentina* (Buenos Aires: Losada and UNICEF, 1993), pp. 45–92.

15. C. Morisio, '¿Complementan los Clubes de Trueque al Empleo en el Mercado Formal?', *MA Thesis* (Buenos Aires: Instituto Superior Economistas de Gobierno, 1998).

16. M. Ford and M. Picasso, 'Representaciones Sociales Acerca de la Pobreza, el Trabajo y la Identidad' (Paper presented at the Seminario Las Caras de la Pobreza, Buenos Aires, 2002).

17. Parysow and Bogani, 'Perspectivas de Desarrollo Económico y Social para las Mujeres Pobres y Empobrecidas en los Clubes del Trueque.

18. The word used for such work in Argentina is *changas*, denoting informal irregular work.

19. Parysow and Bogani, 'Perspectivas de Desarrollo Económico y Social para las Mujeres Pobres y Empobrecidas en los Clubes del Trueque'.

20. H. Primavera, 'Riqueza, Dinero y Poder: El Efímero "Milagro Argentino" de las Redes de Trueque'; Hintze (ed.), *Trueque y Economía Solidaria*; H. Primavera and F. Wautiez, 'Social Money: Lever of the New Economy Paradigm' (Paper presented at the Conference on Social money (Findhorn, Finland, June 2002).

21. F. Leoni, 'Ilusión para Muchos, Alternativa para Pocos. La Práctica del Trueque en los Sectores Populares' (MA Thesis: Universidad Nacional de General Sarmiento, 2003).

22. R. Pearson, 'Argentina's Barter Network: New Currency for New Times', *Bulletin of Latin American Research*, 22:2 (2003), pp. 214–30.

23. Primavera, 'Política Social, Imaginación y Coraje', 17 (1999), pp. 161–88; North, *Alternative Currency Movements as a Challenge to Globalisation?*; P. North, *Money and Liberation: The Micropolitics of Alternative Currency Movements* (Minneapolis, MN and London: University of Minnesota Press, 2007).

24. P. North, *Money and Liberation*; Powell, 'The Mouse That Roared'.

25. J. Powell, 'Petty Capitalism, Perfecting Capitalism or Post-Capitalism?: Lessons from the Argentine Barter Network', *Working Paper* (The Hague: Institute of Social Studies, 2002). P. North and U. Huber, 'Alternative Spaces of The "Argentinazo"', *Antipode*, 36:5 (2004), pp. 963–84

26. Ford and Picasso, 'Representaciones Sociales Acerca de la Pobreza, el Trabajo y la Identidad'; Gonzalez Bombal, 'Sociabilidad en las clases medias en descenso'; I. González Bombal et al., 'Nuevas Redes Sociales'.

27. Powell, 'Petty Capitalism, Perfecting Capitalism or Post-Capitalism?'.

28. A. L. Abramovich and G. Vazquez, 'La Experiencia Del Trueque En La Argentina: Otro Mercado Es Posible' (Paper presented at the Seminario de Economía Social, Buenos Aires (4 July 2003); Hintze (ed.), *Trueque y Economía Solidaria*; S. Hintze, 'Desarrollo y

Crisis del Trueque en la Argentina. Condiciones Para la Recuperación de la Experiencia' (mimeo, 2005).

29. J. L. Coraggio, 'Las Redes Del Trueque Como Institución De La Economía Popular, Reedited', in Hintze (ed.), *Trueque y Economía Solidaria*.

30. L. Barreiro and L. Leite, '*La Confianza En La Economía Popular: Caso Red De Trueque Nodo Astral*' (*IDICSO - Universidad del Salvador*, 2003), www.salvador.edu.ar/csoc/idicso/docs/aongpp003.pdf, accessed 1 April 2006. González Bombal et al., 'Nuevas Redes Sociales'; F. Leoni and M. Luzzi, 'Nuevas Redes Sociales: Los Clubes De Trueque', in I. Gonzalez Bombal (ed.), *Respuestas De La Sociedad Civil a La Emergencia Social* (Buenos Aires: Cedes, 2003), pp. 13–42.

31. Ford and Picasso, 'Representaciones Sociales Acerca de la Pobreza, el Trabajo y la Identidad'; I. González Bombal, et al., 'Nuevas Redes Sociales: Los Clubes De Trueque'.

32. Primavera, 'Riqueza, Dinero y Poder'.

33. P. North, 'Scaling Alternative Economic Practices? Some Lessons from Alternative Currencies', *Transactions of the Institute of British Geographers*, 30 (2005), pp. 221–33. Leoni, 'Ilusión para Muchos'.

34. Pearson, 'Argentina's Barter Network'.

35. Ford and Picasso, 'Representaciones Sociales Acerca de la Pobreza, el Trabajo y la Identidad', p. 224.

36. I. Gonzalez Bombal, 'Sociabilidad en las Clases Medias en Descenso', p. 106.

37. Parysow and Bogani, 'Perspectivas de Desarrollo Económico y Social para las Mujeres Pobres y Empobrecidas en los Clubes del Trueque', p. 222.

38. F. Moulaert and O. Ailenei, 'Social Economy, Third Sector and Solidarity Relations: A Conceptual Synthesis from History to Present', *Urban Studies*, 42 (2005), pp. 2037–54; A. Amin, A. Cameron and R. Hudson, *Placing the Social Economy* (London: Routledge, 2002).

39. M. Colacelli and D. Blackburn, 'Secondary Currency: An Empirical Analysis' (2005), http://www.columbia.edu/~mc2602/files/Colacelli-Currency-Dec-06.pdf, accessed 1 June 2008.

40. The unemployment rate statistics are those for the second quarter, while the population under the poverty line statistics are for the third quarter. This choice introduces a three-month lag between unemployment and the change in the poverty rate.

41. R. I. McKinnon, 'Spontaneous Order on the Road Back from Socialism: An Asian Perspective', *American Economic Review*, 82:2 (1992), pp. 31–6.

42. F. A. Hayek, *Studies in Philosophy, Politics and Economics* (Chicago, IL: University of Chicago Press, 1967), pp. 48–54.

43. W. Streeck and P. C. Schmitter, *Private Interest Government: Beyond Market and State* (London: Sage, 1985), pp.1–76.

44. A. Dixit, *Lawlessness and Economics: Alternative Modes of Governance* (Princeton, NJ: Princeton University Press, 2004), pp. 3–11

45. M. L. Djelic and K Sahlin-Andersson, *Transnational Governance: Institutional Dynamics of Regulation* (Cambridge: Cambridge University Press, 2006), pp.1–30.

46. T. Lawson, 'Institutionalism: On the Need to Firm up Notions of Social Structure and the Human Subject', *Journal of Economic Issues*, 37:1 (2003), p. 182.

47. P. Hall, *Governing the Economy: The Politics of Stated Intervention in Britain and France* (Oxford and New York: Oxford University Press, 1986), p. 19.

48. W. Powell and P. Di Maggio (eds), *The New Institutionalism in Organisational Analysis* (Chicago, IL: Chicago University Press, 1991), p. 9.

49. A. Wells, *Social Institutions* (London: Heinemann, 1970), pp. 155–61
50. G. Hodgson, 'What Are Institutions?', *Journal of Economic Issues*, 40:1 (2006), pp. 1–25, p. 2.
51. Ibid., p. 3.
52. Hodgson, 'What Are Institutions?', p. 3.
53. G. Hodgson, 'John R. Commons and the Foundations of Institutional Economics', *Journal of Economic Issues*, 37:3 (2003), pp. 547–76, p. 556.
54. Hodgson, 'What Are Institutions?', p. 6.
55. Hodgson, 'John R. Commons and the Foundations of Institutional Economics', p. 556.
56. G. Hodgson, 'The Approach of Institutional Economics', *Journal of Economic Literature*, 36 (1998), pp. 166–92, p. 172.
57. G. Hodgson, *The Evolution of Institutional Economics: Agency, Structure and Darwinism in American Institutionalism* (London: Routledge, 2004), pp. 3–77.
58. G. Hodgson, 'The Hidden Persuaders: Institutions and Individuals in Economic Theory', *Cambridge Journal of Economics*, 27 (2003), p. 164.
59. A. Giddens, *The Constitution of Society: Outline of the Theory of Structuration* (Cambridge: Polity press, 1984), pp.84–8.
60. G. Hodgson, 'The Ubiquity of Habits and Rules', *Cambridge Journal of Economics*, 21 (1997), pp. 663–84; Hodgson, 'The Hidden Persuaders', pp. 159–75.
61. S. Steinmo and K. Thelen, 'Historical Institutionalism in Comparative Politics', in S. Steinmo, K. Thelen and F. Longstreth (eds), *Structuring Politics* (Cambridge: Cambridge University Press, 1992), pp. 4–52
62. W. G. Runciman (ed.), *Maw Weber: Selections in Translations* (Cambridge: Cambridge University Press, 1978), p. 105.
63. G. Hodgson, 'Institutions and Individuals: Interaction and Evolution', *Organization Studies*, 28:1 (2007), p. 98.
64. A. Field, 'Microeconomics, Norms and Rationality', *Economic Development and Cultural Change*, 32:4 (1984), p. 709.
65. Steinmo and Thelen, 'Historical Institutionalism in Comparative Politics', pp. 4–52.
66. T. Lawson, *Economics and Reality* (London: Routledge, 1997), pp. 82–145
67. H. Joas, *The Creativity of Action* (Chicago, IL: Chicago University Press, 1996), p. 158.
68. F. A. Hayek, *Rules and Order, Book 1 of Law, Legislation and Liberty: A New Statement of the Liberal Principles of Justice and Political Economy* (London: Routledge & Kegan Paul, 1973), p. 11.
69. D. Lane et al., 'Choice and Action', *Journal of Evolutionary Economics*, 6:1 (1996), pp. 43–76.
70. Hodgson, 'The Approach of Institutional Economics', p. 173.
71. Ibid., pp. 166–92.
72. Hayek, *Rules and Order*, p. 159.

2 Perspectives on Complementary Currency Systems

1. T. Greco, *Money: Understanding and Creating Alternatives to Legal Tender* (White River Junction, VT: Chelsea Green, 2001), pp.8–86.
2. P. Ekins and M. Max-Neef (eds), *The Living Economy* (London and New York: Routledge, 1986), pp.1–167.
3. R. Lee, 'Moral Money? LETS and the Social Construction of Local Economic Geographies in Southeast England', *Environment and Planning A*, 28 (1996), pp. 1377–94.

4. J. Wheelock, 'The Household in the Total Economy', in Ekins and Max-Neef (eds), *Real Life Economics*, pp.124–36.

5. G. Seyfang, 'Community Currencies: A Small Change for a Green Economy. An Evaluation of Local Exchange Trading Schemes (LETS) as a Tool for Sustainable Local Development', *Environment and Planning A*, 33:6 (2001), pp. 975–96. G. Seyfang, 'Working for the Fenland Dollar: An Evaluation of Local Exchange Trading Schemes (LETS) as an Informal Employment Strategy to Tackle Social Exclusion', *Work, Employment and Society*, 15:3 (2001), pp. 581–93.

6. J. Blanc, 'Formes Et Rationalites Du Localisme Monetaire', *Working Paper* (Lyon: Centre Auguste et Léon Walras, 2002); J. Blanc, 'Les Monnaies Sociales: Un Outil Et Ses Limites', in J. Blanc (ed.), *Exclusions Et Liens Financiers: Monnaies Sociales* (Paris: Economica, 2006), pp. 25–42.

7. T. Cohen-Mitchell, Article, 'Community Currencies at a Crossroads: New Ways Forward.' *New Village* (2000), http://www.ratical.org/many_worlds/cc/cc@Xroads.html, accessed 23 June 2006.

8. J. Taris, Article, 'Lets Groups around the World', http://www.lets-linkup.com, accessed 1 August 2007.

9. G. Seyfang, 'Tackling Social Exclusion with Community Currencies: Learning from LETS to Time Banks', *International Journal of Community Currency Research*, 6 (2002), pp. 1–11. D. North, 'Have Confidence and Cast Your Nets into Deep Waters – Community Responses to Neo-Liberalism in Argentina' (Paper presented at the *Association of American Geographers* New Orleans, LA, 2003).

10. E. Gilbert and E. Helleiner (eds), *Nation-States and Money: The Past, Present and Future of National Currencies* (London, New York: Routledge, 1999), p.9.

11. B. J. Cohen, 'The New Geography of Money', in Gilbert and Helleiner (eds), *Nations-States and Money*, pp. 121–38.

12. J. Blanc, 'Les Monnaies Parallèles: Évaluation Et Enjeux Théoriques Du Phénomène', *Revue d'Economie Financière*, 49 (1998), pp. 81–102.

13. N. Carothers, *Fractional Money* (New York John Wiley & Sons, 1930), pp.1–90. Greco, *Money*, pp. 8–86.

14. J. Schuldt, *Dineros Alternativos: Para El Desarrollo Local* (Lima: Universidad del Pacífico, 1997), pp.19–122; Greco, *Money*, pp. 8–86.

15. I. Fisher, *Mastering the Crisis - with Additional Chapters on Stamp Script* (London: Kimble and Bradford, 1934), pp.56–99.

16. Gesell, *The Natural Economic Order*, p.6.

17. J. M. Keynes, *A Treatise on Money*, 2 vols (New York: Harcourt, Brace and Co., 1930/1976).

18. Schuldt, *Dineros Alternativos*, pp. 19–122.

19. Fisher, *Stamp Scrip*, pp.1–68.

20. Cohrssen quoted in ibid., pp.1–68.

21. W. Onken, 'Ein Vergessenes Kapitel Der Wirtschaftsgeschichte – Schwanenkirchen, Wörgl Und Andere Freigeldexperimente', *Zeitschrift für Sozialökonomie*, 57:58 (1983), pp. 60–72, p. 68 quoted in Schuldt, *Dineros Alternativos*, p.68.

22. Von Muralt, 1933 quoted in Schuldt, *Dineros Alternativos*, p. 39.

23. C. Offe and G. Heinze, *Beyond Employment: Time, Work and the Informal Economy* (Cambridge Polity Press, 1992), pp.1–124.

24. Offe and Heinze, *Beyond Employment*, pp. 1–124.

25. Schuldt, *Dineros Alternativos*, pp.19–122.

26. Greco, *Money*, p. 67.
27. Fisher, *Stamp Scrip*, pp.1–68.
28. Ibid.
29. Ibid., p.33.
30. Colacelli and Blackburn, 'Secondary Currency: An Empirical Analysis'.
31. M. Pacione, 'The Other Side of the Coin: Local Currency as a Response to the Globalisation of Capital. Debates and Reviews, Ed. by M. W. Danson', *Regional Studies*, 33:1 (1999), pp. 63–72.
32. Offe and Heinze, *Beyond Employment*, pp. 1–124.
33. P. Seabright (ed.), *The Vanishing Rouble: Barter Networks and Non-Monetary Transactions in Post-Soviet Societies* (Cambridge: Cambridge University Press, 2002), pp.67–87.
34. Cohen, 'The New Geography of Money'.
35. Pacione, 'The Other Side of the Coin'.
36. Offe and Heinze, *Beyond Employment*, pp. 1–124.
37. L. Thorne, 'Local Exchange and Trading Systems in the UK: A Case of Re-Embedding?', *Environment and Planning A*, 28:8 (1996), pp. 1361–76.
38. R. Tibbett, *Alternative Currencies: A Challenge to Globalisation?* (London: Routledge, 1997), pp.127–35.
39. G. Gibbs, 'Co-Options: Growing from Tiny Acorns', *Guardian* (25 April, 1995).
40. Pacione, 'The Other Side of the Coin'.
41. Schuldt, *Dineros Alternativos*, p. 94.
42. Schuldt, *Dineros Alternativos*, pp.19–122.
43. Pacione, 'The Other Side of the Coin'.
44. Data from www.complementarycurrency.org
45. Data from www.stro.net
46. Lee, 'Moral Money'; Pacione, 'The Other Side of the Coin'; N. Thrift and A. Leyshon, 'Moral Geographies of Money', in Gilbert and Helleiner (eds), *Nation-States and Money*, pp. 159–81.
47. T. Aldridge and A. Patterson, 'Lets Get Real: Constraints on the Development of Local Exchange Trading Schemes', *Area*, 34:4 (2002), pp. 370–81.
48. C. Williams, 'Local Exchange and Trading Systems: A New Source of Work and Credit for the Poor and Unemployed?', *Environment and Planning A*, 28 (1996), p. 1396.
49. Offe and Heinze, *Beyond Employment*, pp. 1–124.
50. Seyfang, 'Community Currencies', p. 989.
51. Pacione, 'The Other Side of the Coin'; Thrift and Leyshon, 'Moral Geographies of Money', in Gilbert and Helleiner (eds), *Nation-States and Money*, pp. 159–81. Williams, 'Local Exchange and Trading Systems'.
52. Powell, 'Petty Capitalism, Perfecting Capitalism or Post-Capitalism?'.
53. C. Williams and J. Windebank, 'The Formalisation of Work Thesis: A Critical Evaluation', *Futures*, 31 (1999), pp. 547–58. C. Williams et al., 'Bridges into Work: An Evaluation of Local Exchange Trading Schemes', *Latest Developments in LETS and Time Money* (Bristol: The Policy Press, 2001), pp.1–66.
54. M. Granovetter, 'Economic Action and Social Structure: The Problem of Embeddedness', *American Journal of Sociology*, 91:3 (1985), pp. 481–510.
55. Thorne, 'Local Exchange and Trading Systems in the UK'.
56. N. Dodd, *The Sociology of Money* (Cambridge: Polity Press, 1994), pp. 37–141; 106–28.

57. N. Thrift and A. Leyshon, 'Moral Geographies of Money', in Gilbert and Helleiner (eds), *Nation-States and Money*, p. 173
58. Seyfang, 'Working for the Fenland Dollar'.
59. Lee, 'Moral Money?', p.1393.
60. North, *Alternative Currency Movements as a Challenge to Globalisation?*, pp. 1–17; 56–119.
61. P. Lang, *Lets Work: Rebuilding the Local Community* (Bristol: Grover, 1984), pp.4–57.
62. Blanc, 'Formes Et Rationalites Du Localisme Monetaire'.
63. Gilbert and Helleiner (eds), *Nation-States and Money*, pp. 4–24.
64. Ibid., p. 3.
65. Blanc, 'Formes Et Rationalites Du Localisme Monetaire'.
66. J. Powell, 'The Mouse That Roared: State Insecurity and Thailand's First Community Currency System', *Watershed*, 6:1 (2000), pp. 48–53.
67. Greco, *Money*, pp. 8–86.
68. B. Lietaer, *The Future of Money: Creating New Wealth, Work and a Wiser World* (London: Century, 2001), pp. 3–55; 219.
69. R. Jayaraman and M. Oak., 'The Signalling Role of Municipal Currencies in Local Development', *Economica*, 72:288 (2005), pp. 597–613.
70. F.A. Hayek, *Denationalization of Money* (London: Institute of Economic Affairs, 1976), pp. 4–48.
71. L. White, *Free Banking in Britain: Theory, Experience, Debate, 1800–1845* (Cambridge: Cambridge University Press, 1984), pp.19–22. G. Selgin, *The Theory of Free Banking: Money Supply under Competitive Note Issue* (Totowa, NJ and Washington, D.C.: Rowman & Littlefield and the Cato Institute, 1988), pp.1–54. G. Selgin, 'Salvaging Gresham's Law: The Good, the Bad and the Illegal', *Journal of Money, Credit and Banking*, 28:4 (1996), pp. 637–49.
72. Coraggio, 'Las Redes Del Trueque Como Institución De La Economía Popular'.
73. P. Williams et al., 'Consumption, Exclusion and Emotion: The Social Geographies of Shopping', *Social and Cultural Geography*, 2:2 (2001), pp. 203–20. C. Williams and J. Windebank, 'Modes of Goods Acquisition in Deprived Neighbourhoods', *International Review of Retail, Distribution and Consumer Research*, 10:1 (2000), pp. 73–94.

3 The Political and Economic Context in Argentina

1. Hodgson, 'What Are Institutions?'.
2. F. Cleaver, 'Reinventing Institutions: Bricolage and the Social Embeddedness of Natural Resource Management', *European Journal of Development Research*, 12:2 (2002), pp. 11–30. D. Stark, 'Path Dependence and Privatization Strategies in East Central Europe', *East European Politics and Societies*, 1:6 (1992), pp. 17–54.
3. J. Williamson, *The Progress of Policy Reform in Latin America* (Washington, D.C.: Institute for Internacional Economics, 1990), p.4
4. J. Stiglitz, 'Más Instrumentos y Metas Más Amplias para el Desarrollo. Hacia el Consenso Post-Washington', *Desarrollo Económico (Buenos Aires)*, 38:151 (1998), pp. 691–722.
5. R. Gwynne and D. Kay, *Latin America Transformed* (London: Arnold Editors, 1999), pp.5–8.
6. Ibid., pp.5–8.
7. E. Gibson and E. Calvo., 'Electoral Coalitions and Market Reforms: Evidence from Argentina', in *XX International Congress of the Latin American Studies Association*

(Guadalajara: Mexico, 1997). A. Vacs, 'Convergence and Dissension: Democracy, Markets and Structural Reform in World Perspective', in W. Smith, C. Acuña and E. Gamarra (eds.), *Democracy, Markets, and Structural Reform in Latin America: Argentina, Bolivia, Brazil, Chile, and Mexico* (University of Miami, FL: Lynne Rienner, 1994), pp. 67–100.

8.   S. Bowles and H. Gintis, 'The Revenge of Homo Economicus: Contested Exchange and the Revival of Political Economy', *The Journal of Economic Perspectives* 7:1 (1993), pp. 83–102.

9.   A. Chandler, *The Visible Hand: The Managerial Revolution in American Business* (Cambridge, MA: Harvard University Belknap Press 1977), p. 134.

10. C. Lane, *Industry and Society in Europe* (Aldershot: Edward Elgar, 1995), pp. 2–25.

11. Dixit, *Lawlessness and Economics*, pp. 3–11.

12. Steinmo and Thelen, 'Historical Institutionalism in Comparative Politics'.

13. Stark, 'Path Dependence and Privatization Strategies in East Central Europe'; J. C. Torre, 'The Politics of Transformation in Historical Perspective', in W. Smith and R. Korzeniewics (eds), *Politics, Social Change, and Economic Restructuring in Latin America* (Coral Gables, FL: University of Miami and North-South Center Press, 1997), pp. 21–36.

14. A. Diaz, 'New Developments in Economic and Social Restructuring in Latin America', in W. Smith and R. Korzeniewics (eds.), *Politics, Social Change, and Economic Restructuring in Latin America*, pp. 37–56.

15. I. Roxborough, 'Citizenship and Social Movements under Neoliberalism', in W. Smith and R Korzeniewics (eds), *Politics, Social Change, and Economic Restructuring in Latin America*, pp. 57–78.

16. W. Smith and R. Korzeniewics (eds.), *Politics, Social Change, and Economic Restructuring in Latin America*, pp.1–44.

17. Polanyi, *The Great Transformation*, pp. 2–178.

18. P. Drake, *Labor Movements and Dictatorships: The Southern Cone in Comparative Perspectives* (Baltimore, MD: Johns Hopkins University Press, 1996), pp. 56–85.

19. A. Escobar and S. Alvarez (eds), *The Making of Social Movements in Latin America: Identity, Strategy and Democracy* (Boulder, CO: Westview Press, 1992).

20. C. Diaz Alejandro, 'No Less Than One Hundred Years of Argentine Economic History, Plus Some Comparisons', *Discussion Paper 53* (New Haven, CT: Yale University, 1982), pp. 44–57. G. Gerchunoff and L. Llach, *El Ciclo de la Ilusión y el Desencanto; Un Siglo de Políticas Económicas Argentinas*, 2nd ed (Buenos Aires: Ariel, 2005), pp.13–60; 155–242; 333–480.

21. L. Llach, 'A Depression in Perspective: The Economics and the Political Economy of Argentina's Crisis of the Millenium', in F. Fiorucci and M. Klein (eds), *The Argentine Crisis at the Turn of the Millenium: Causes, Consequences and Explanations* (Amsterdam: Aksant, 2004), pp.56–89.

22. A. Ciria, 'Argentina: An Underdeveloping Country?', pp. 195–207, in A. Ritter, M. Cameron and D. Pollock (eds), *Latin America to the Year 2000: Reactivating Growth, Improving Equity, Sustaining Democracy* (New York: Praeger, 1992).

23. Llach, 'A Depression in Perspective'.

24. L. Sawers, *The Other Argentina* (Boulder, CO: Westview Press, 1996), pp. 3–47.

25. R. Cortes Conde, *La Economía Política De La Argentina en el Siglo XX* (Buenos Aires: Edhasa, 2005), pp. 22–76.

26. The name Partido Justicialista derives from the Spanish words for justice (*justicia*) and socialist (*socialista*). For contemporary analysis of Peronsim, see S. Levitsky, *Transform-*

ing Labor-Based Parties in Latin America: Argentine Peronism in Comparative Perspective (Cambridge: Cambridge University Press, 2003), R. Munck, R. Falcón and B. Galitelli, *Argentina: From Anarchism to Peronism: Workers, Unions and Politics, 1855–1985* (ZED Books, 1987), M. Murmis and J.C. Portantiero, *Estudios Sobre Los Orígenes Del Peronismo* (Buenos Aires: Siglo Vientiuno Argentina Editores, 1972), G. Germani and S. S. de Yujnovsky, 'El Surgimiento Del Peronismo: El Rol De Los Obreros Y De Los Migrantes Internos', *Desarrollo Económico* 13:51 (1973).

27. N. Botana, *La República vacilante: entre la furia y la razón* (Buenos Aires: Taurus, 2002), pp. 67–79.

28. Gerchunoff and Llach, *El Ciclo de la Ilusión y el Desencanto*, pp. 13–60; 155–242; 333–480.

29. B. Kosacoff, *El Desafío De La Competitividad* (Buenos Aires: CEPAL-Alianza, 1993), pp. 3–93.

30. E. Tenti Fanfani, 'Cuestiones de Exclusión Social y Política', in A. Minujin and E. Cosentino (eds), *Desigualdad y Exclusión: Desafíos para la Política Social en la Argentina de Fin de Siglo* (Buenos Aires: Losada - UNICEF, 1993), pp. 27–64.

31. Botana, *La República vacilante: entre la furia y la razón*, pp.67–79.

32. Kosacoff, *El Desafío De La Competitividad*, pp. 3–93.

33. B. Kosacoff and D. Heymann, *La Argentina De Los Noventa: Desempeño Económico En Un Contexto De Reformas*, vol. 1 (Buenos Aires: EUDEBA and CEPAL Naciones Unidas, 2000), pp. 9–36.

34. Zeros were written off the currency for the first time in 1969. The banknotes of the 'Peso Moneda Nacional', in circulation between 1881 and 1969, were replaced by the 'Peso Ley' at a rate of 100 'Peso Moneda Nacional' = 1 'Peso Ley'. There was a transition period for the public to get used to the change, in which the old notes of 'Peso Moneda Nacional' continued circulating with a stamp indicating their new value. The currency was replaced again in 1983, when the 'Peso Ley' was withdrawn and the 'Peso Argentino' was issued at a rate of 1 'Peso Argentino' = 10,000 'Peso Ley'. In 1985 the 'Peso Argentino' was replaced by the 'Austral' at a rate of 1 'Austral' = 1,000 'Pesos Argentinos'. In 1992 the 'Austral' was replaced by the 'Peso Convertible' at a rate of 1 'Peso Convertible' = 10,000 'Australes'. Source: www.billetesargentinos.com.ar.

35. Cortes Conde, *La Economía Política De La Argentina en el Siglo XX.*

36. The bonds were called Bonos 9 de Julio. The Economy Minister, Alvaro Alzogaray, described their acceptance as means of payment as a 'patriotic sacrifice by public employees'.

37. The provinces were Jujuy and Tucumán, both small in terms of economy and level of development. Their bonds were perceived as a sign of backwardness.

38. J. Schvarzer and H. Finkelstein, 'Análisis - Bonos, Cuasi Monedas Y Política Económica', *Revista Realidad Económica IADE* (2003), p. 193.

39. D. Heymann, 'Políticas De Reforma Y Comportamiento Macroeconómico', in Kosacoff and Heymann (eds), *La Argentina De Los Noventa*, pp. 37–176.

40. P. Guidotti and C. Rodríguez, 'Dollarization in Latin America: Gresham's Law in Reverse?', *IMF Staff Papers*, 239 (1992), pp. 518–44, p. 526.

41. Heymann, 'Políticas De Reforma Y Comportamiento Macroeconómico', p. 162.

42. J. Streb, 'Y Si No Hay Más Remedio … Inflación, Desconfianza y la Desintegración del Sistema Financiero en la Argentina', *Desarrollo Económico (Buenos Aires)*, 38 (1998), pp. 199–215.

43. Gerchunoff and Llach, *El Ciclo de la Ilusión y el Desencanto*, pp.13–60; 155–242; 333–480.
44. J. M. Fanelli and R Frenkel, *Estabilidad y Estructura; Interacciones en el crecimiento económico* (Buenos Aires: Cedes, 1994), pp. 1–116.
45. D. Cavallo, 'The Quality of Money', Document prepared for the Award Ceremony of the Doctorate Honoris Causa University of Paris 1- Pantheon Sorbonne, published in *ASAP* (Asociación Argentina de Presupuesto y Administración Financiera Pública), (June 1999) and *Économie Internationale - La revue du CEPII, La qualité de la monnaie*, 80:4 (1999).
46. According to Cavallo ('The Quality of Money', p.3), the monetarist theory is 'based on the premise that every economy has a currency and a Central Bank that issues and manages it. Most of the attention is focused on the Central Bank's management of the national monetary policy, the quantity of money, the interest rate level and the exchange rate policy. Yet, the departing point is not exactly correct. It will be precisely in the chapter on currency as an institution, and not in the one on monetary policy, that answers will be found to most of the economic instability problems that currently beset the world.
47. It was discussed in the media and other public opinion forums, but widely dismissed as a far-fetched academic idea. It would surface again in the crisis of 2002
48. The Central Bank would no longer act as lender of last resort to the banking system. No other institution was designated for this function.
49. J.M. Fanelli and D Heymann, 'Dilemas Monetarios en Argentina', *Desarrollo Económico (Buenos Aires)*, 42:165 (2002), pp. 3–24.
50. M. I. Barbero, 'Historia Económica De La Argentina Contemporánea', mimeo (2007).
51. B. Kosacoff, *Corporate Strategy under Structural Adjustment in Argentina: Responses by Industrial Firms to a New Set of Uncertainties* (Basingstoke: Macmillan Press, 2000), pp. 57–98.
52. B. Kosacoff and G. M. Gomez, 'Industrialización en un Contexto de Estabilización y Apertura Externa. El Caso Argentino en los Noventa', in B. Kosacoff (ed.), *El Desempeño Industrial Argentino: Más Allá De La Sustitución De Importaciones* (Buenos Aires: CEPAL Naciones Unidas, 2000), pp. 275–302.
53. Kosacoff (ed.), *El Desempeño Industrial Argentino*, pp. 1–118; 275–302.
54. R. Frenkel and M. González Rozada, 'Apertura comercial, empleo y productividad en Argentina', in V. Tokman and D. Martínez (eds), *Productividad y Empleo En La Apertura Económica* (Santiago de Chile: Oficina Internacional del Trabajo, 1999), pp. 56–87.
55. Kosacoff (ed.), *El Desempeño Industrial Argentino*, pp. 1–118; 275–302.
56. Murmis and Feldman, 'La Heterogeneidad Social De Las Pobrezas', pp. 45–92.
57. D. Lvovich, 'Colgados De La Soga: La Experiencia Del Tránsito Desde La Clase Media a La Nueva Pobreza En La Ciudad De Buenos Aires', in M. Svampa (ed.), *Desde Abajo: La Transformación De Las Identidades Sociales* (Buenos Aires: UNGS and Biblos, 2000), pp. 51–80.
58. H. Palomino and J. Schvarzer, 'El Mercado de Trabajo en la Argentina: Del Pleno Empleo al Colapso', *Encrucijadas: Revista de la Universidad de Buenos Aires*, May 1996, pp. 8–17.
59. Labour statistics have been collected since 1960 in Argentina
60. V. Tokman, 'La Especificidad y Generalidad del Problema del Empleo en el Contexto de América Latina', in L. Beccaria and N. López (eds), *Sin Trabajo: Las Características del Desempleo y sus Efectos en la Sociedad Argentina* (Buenos Aires: UNICEF and Losada, 1996), pp.47–81.

61. H. Palomino and J Schvarzer, 'Entre La Informalidad y el Desempleo. Una Perspectiva de Largo Plazo sobre el Mercado de Trabajo en la Argentina', *Realidad Económica, Instituto Argentino para el Desarrollo Económico, Buenos Aires* (10 April–15 May 1996) pp. 17–43.
62. L. Beccaria and N. López (eds), *Sin Trabajo*, pp. 9–46.
63. Palomino and J. Schvarzer, 'El Mercado de Trabajo en la Argentina'.
64. P. Lloyd-Sherlock, 'Policy, Distribution and Poverty in Argentina since Redemocratisation', *Latin American Perspectives*, 24:6 (1997), pp. 22–55.
65. R. Cortes and A. Marshall, 'Estrategia Económica, Instituciones Y Negociación Política En La Reforma Social De Los Noventa', *Desarrollo Económico,* 39:154 (1999), pp. 195–212.
66. L. Beccaria, 'Empleo, Remuneraciones y Diferenciación Social en el Último cuarto de Siglo XX', in L. Beccaria et al. (eds), *Sociedad y Sociabilidad en la Argentina de los Noventa* (Buenos Aires: Universidad Nacional de General Sarmiento and Editorial Biblos, 2002), pp. 27–54. Beccaria and López, *Sin Trabajo*, pp.35–45.
67. Statistics cover the Buenos Aires conglomeration, which covers 55 per cent of the total sample for the Household and Employment Survey at www.indec.gov.ar
68. Beccaria and López (eds), *Sin Trabajo*; R. Frenkel and J. Ros, 'Desempleo, Políticas Macroeconómicas y Flexibilidad del Mercado Laboral. Argentina y México en los Noventa', *Desarrollo Económico*, 44:173 (2004), pp. 33–56.
69. Palomino and Schvarzer, 'Entre La Informalidad y el Desempleo'.
70. M. Novick, 'Reconversión Segmentada en la Argentina, Empresas, Mercado de Trabajo de Relaciones Laborales a Fines de los 90', in *Reestructuracion Productiva, Mercado de Trabajo y Sindicatos en América Latina* (Buenos Aires: Consejo Latinoamericano de Ciencias Sociales (CLACSO), 2000), pp. 49–72.
71. C. Graham, *Safety Nets, Politics and the Poor: Transitions to Market Economies* (Washington, D.C.: The Brookings Institution, 1994), pp. 44–51.
72. M. Pastor Jr and C. Wise, 'Stabilization and Its Discontents: Argentina's Economic Restructuring in the 1990s', *World Development*, 27:3 (1999), pp. 477–503.
73. Cortes and Marshall, 'Estrategia Económica, Instituciones Y Negociación Política En La Reforma Social De Los Noventa'.
74. Barreto et al., 'Política Social, Pobreza, Identidad y Fragmentación Social'.
75. P. Gerchunoff and J.C. Torre, 'La Política De Liberalización Económica en la Administración de Menem', *Desarrollo Económico*, 36:143 (1994), pp. 37–58.
76. Lloyd-Sherlock, 'Policy, Distribution and Poverty in Argentina'.
77. Cortes and Marshall, 'Estrategia Económica, Instituciones Y Negociación Política En La Reforma Social De Los Noventa'.
78. Pastor and Wise, 'Stabilization and Its Discontents: Argentina's Economic Restructuring in the 1990s', *World Development*, 27:3 (1999), pp. 477–503.
79. Gibson and Calvo, 'Electoral Coalitions and Market Reforms.
80. P. Lloyd-Sherlock, *Old Age and Urban Poverty in the Developing World: The Shanty Towns of Buenos Aires* (London: Macmillan, 1997), pp. 37–65
81. D. Campione, 'El Estado en la Argentina. Cambio de paradigmas y abandono del tema social', in Hintze (ed.), *Estado y Sociedad*, pp. 93–115; Cortes and Marshall, 'Estrategia Económica, Instituciones Y Negociación Política En La Reforma Social De Los Noventa'.

82. S. Saiegh and M. Tommasi, 'Why Is Argentina's Fiscal Federalism So Inefficient? Entering the Labyrinth' (Paper presented at the Conference *Modernization and Institutional Development in Argentina* Buenos Aires: PNUD, 1999).

83. In case of default, payments to creditors would be deducted from future federal transfers.

84. O. Cetrangolo and J. P. Jiménez, 'Algunas Reflexiones Sobre El Federalismo Fiscal en la Argentina', *Desarrollo Económico*, 38: Special Issue (1998), pp. 293–326.

85. A. Minujin (ed.), *Cuesta Abajo: Los Nuevos Pobres: Efectos De La Crisis En La Sociedad Argentina*, 2nd edn (Buenos Aires: Losada and Unicef, 1993), pp. 9–44.

86. D. Lvovich, 'Colgados De La Soga'. A. Minujin, 'Estrujados. La Clase Media En América Latina', in E. Villanueva (eds.), *Empleo y Globalización: La Nueva Cuestión Social en la Argentina* (Buenos Aires: Universidad Nacional de Quilmes, 1997), pp. 85–106. Murmis and Feldman, 'La Heterogeneidad Social De Las Pobrezas'.

87. P. Pozzi, 'Popular Upheaval and Capitalist Transformation in Argentina', *Latin American Perspectives*, 27:5 (2000), pp. 63–87.

88. J. Grugel and M.P. Riggirozzi, 'The Return of the State in Argentina', *International Affairs,* 83:1 (2007), pp. 87–107.

89. C. Harman, 'Argentina: Rebellion at the Sharp End of the World Crisis', *International Socialism*, 94 (2002), pp. 3–48.

90. Gerchunoff and Llach, *El Ciclo de la Ilusión y el Desencanto*, pp.13–60; 155–242; 333–480.

91. Pastor and Wise, 'Stabilization and Its Discontents: Argentina's Economic Restructuring in the 1990s', *World Development*, 27:3 (1999), pp. 477–503.

92. Schvarzer and Finkelstein, 'Análisis - Bonos, Cuasi Monedas Y Política Económica', p. 193.

93. S. Chelala, 'Las Terceras Monedas.', mimeo, Buenos Aires (2002).

94. S. Chelala, 'Las Terceras Monedas.', mimeo, Buenos Aires (2002).

95. Pozzi, 'Popular Upheaval and Capitalist Transformation in Argentina'.

96. A. Dinerstein, 'Que Se Vayan Todos! Popular Insurrection and the Asambleas Barriales in Argentina', *Bulletin of Latin American Research*, 22:2 (2003), pp. 187–200.

97. C. Harman, 'Argentina: Rebellion at the Sharp End of the World Crisis', *International Socialism*, 94 (2002), pp. 3–48.

98. A. Bryer, 'Beyond Bureaucracies? The Struggle for Self-Determination and Social Responsibility in the Argentine Worker-Run Companies' (Paper presented at the conference *Rethinking Economic Anthropology: a Human Centred Approach* School of Oriental and Asian Studies: London, 2008), 11-12 January 2008, available online: http://rethinkingeconomies.org.uk/web/d/doc_71.pdf, last accessed 20 January 2009; Gonzalez Bombal (ed.), *Respuestas De La Sociedad Civil a La Emergencia Social*, pp.3–34.

99. Grugel and Riggirozzi. 'The Return of the State in Argentina'.

100. Ibid.

101. H. Schaumberg, 'In Search of Alternatives: The Making of Grassroots Politics and Power in Argentina', *Bulletin of Latin American Research*, 27:3 (2008), pp. 368–87.

102. Data for Asian countries from the Asian Development Bank, Key Indicators 2006 (www.adb.org/statistics), GDP growth, annual change at constant prices. Data for African countries from the African Development Bank, www.afdb.org, country tables, GDP growth, annual change at constant prices. Data for Latin America from the Interamerican Development Bank, country statistics, www.iadb.org/countries

103. A. Minujin and E. Anguita, *La Clase Media - Seducida y Abandonada* (Buenos Aires: Edhasa, 2004), pp.3–50.

104. N. Giarraca (ed.), *La Protesta Social En La Argentina: Transformaciones Econónicas Y Crisis Social En El Interior Del País* (Buenos Aires: Alianza, 2001), pp. 12–44.

4 Launching the Club de Trueque

1. D. Slater and F. Tonkiss, *Market Society: Markets and Modern Social Theory* (Cambridge and Malden, MA: Polity Press and Blackwell Publishers, 2001), pp.6–189.

2. G. Thompson et al. (eds), *Markets, Hierarchies and Networks: The Coordination of Social Life* (London and Milton Keynes: Sage and Open University Press, 1991), pp. 9–189.

3. J. G. Carrier, *Meanings of the Market: The Free Market in Western Culture* (Oxford: Berg, 1997), pp. 5–96.

4. O. Giarini, 'Some Considerations on the Future of Work: Redefining Productive Work', in M. Simai (ed.), *Global Employment: An International Investigation into the Future of Work* (London and Tokyo: Zed Books for UNU/WIDER and UN University Press, 1995), pp. 89–108.

5. A. Smith, *The Wealth of Nations* (London: Everyman's Library, 1776/1991), pp. 67–298.

6. Polanyi, *The Great Transformation*, pp. 2–178.

7. R. Boyer and J. R. Hollingsworth, 'The Variety of Institutional Arrangements and Their Complementarity in Modern Economies', in R. Boyer and J. R. Hollingsworth (eds), *Contemporary Capitalism: The Embeddedness of Institutions* (Cambridge and New York: Cambridge University Press, 1997), pp. 49–54.

8. J. Davis, *Exchange* (Buckingham: Open University Press, 1992), pp.20–44.

9. F.A. Hayek, *The Road to Serfdom*, pp.16–76; F. A. Hayek and W. W. Bartley, *The Fatal Conceit: The Errors of Socialism* (London: Routledge, 1988), pp. 5–67. L. Von Mises, *The Free and Prosperous Commonwealth: An Exposition of the Ideas of Classical Liberalism* (Princeton: Van Nostrand, 1962), pp.84–89.

10. Boyer and Hollingsworth, 'The Variety of Institutional Arrangements and Their Complementarity in Modern Economies'; A. Schotter, *Free Market Economics: A Critical Appraisal* (New York: St Martin's Press, 1985), pp.15–22.

11. J. Beckert, *Beyond the Market: The Social Foundations of Economic Efficiency* (Princeton, NJ: Princeton University Press, 2002), pp. 5–133.

12. F. Braudel, *The Wheels of Commerce* (New York: Harper and Row, 1982), pp. 130–42.

13. Ibid.

14. Ibid., p. 136.

15. Slater and Tonkiss, *Market Society*, pp. 6–189.

16. O. Williamson, 'The Lens of Contract: Private Ordering', *American Economic Review*, 92:2 (2002), pp. 438–43.

17. Streeck and Schmitter, *Private Interest Government*, pp.1–76.

18. R. Cornes and T. Sandler, *The Theory of Externalities, Public Goods, and Club Goods*, 2nd edn (Cambridge: Cambridge University Press, 1996), p. 9.

19. Ibid., p. 347.

20. Ibid., pp. 1–22.

21. O. Williamson, *Market and Hierarchies* (Cambridge, MA: Harvard University Press, 1975), pp.2–144.

22. F. Braudel, *The Structures of Everyday Life: The Limits of the Possible* (London: Fontana, 1981), pp. 167–89; Braudel, *The Wheels of Commerce*, pp. 130–42.

23. A. Greif, P. Milgrom and B. Weingast, 'Coordination, Commitment and Enforcement: The Case of the Merchant Guild', *Journal of Political Economy*, 102:4 (1994), pp. 745–6.

24. M. F. Garcia, 'La Construction Sociale D'un Marche Au Cadran De Fontaine-En-Sologne', *Actes de la Recherche en Sciences Sociales*, 65 (1986), pp. 1–13.

25. C. Hay, 'Globalisation and the Institutional Re-Embedding of Markets: The Political Economy of Price Formation in the Bordeaux En Primeur Market', *New Political Economy*, 12:2 (2007), pp. 185–209.

26. P. Kollock, Article, 'Managing the Virtual Commons: Cooperation and Conflict in Computer Communities' (1994), http://www.sscnet.ucla.edu/soc/csoc/papers/virt-comm/Virtcomm.htm#Virtual_Commons_1, accessed 1 September 2008.

27. A. Sbragia, 'Governance, the State and the Market: What Is Going On?' *Governance: An International Journal of Policy and Administration*, 13:2 (2000), pp. 243–450.

28. J. Beckert, 'Economic Sociology and Embeddedness: How Shall We Conceptualize Economic Action?', *Journal of Economic Issues*, 37:3 (2003), p. 769.

29. Hodgson, 'The Approach of Institutional Economics'.

30. Joas, *The Creativity of Action*, pp.33–158. T. Veblen, 'The Vested Interests and the Common Man' (Kessinger Publishings, 1919/ 2004), http://books.google.com/books, accessed 9 January 2009.

31. Beckert, *Beyond the Market*, pp. 5–133.

32. Ibid.

33. Hodgson, 'The Hidden Persuaders'.

34. Joas, *The Creativity of Action*, p. 128.

35. M. Bunge, *Emergence and Convergence: Qualitative Novelty and the Unity of Knowledge*, Toronto Studies in Philosophy (Toronto: University of Toronto Press, 2003), p. 11.

36. G. Hodgson, 'Reconstitutive Downward Causation: Social Structure and the Development of Institutional Agency', in E. Fullbrook (eds), *Intersubjectivity in Economics: Agents and Structures* (London: Routledge, 2002), pp. 159–80.

37. Giddens, *The Constitution of Society*, pp. 84–8.

38. Hodgson, 'Reconstitutive Downward Causation, pp. 159–80.

39. De Sanzo et al., *Reinventando El Mercado*, pp.1–84.

40. H. Covas, *Un nuevo Modelo de Organización Comunitaria (*Buenos Aires: Red Global de Trueque, 2000), pp.1–67.

41. I. Gonzalez Bombal, 'Sociabilidad en las Clases Medias en Descenso', pp. 97–136. I. González Bombal et al., 'Nuevas Redes Sociales: Los Clubes De Trueque'; Parysow and Bogani, 'Perspectivas de Desarrollo Económico y Social para las Mujeres Pobres y Empobrecidas en los Clubes del Trueque'.

42. Dodd, *The Sociology of Money*, p. 141.

43. Ingham, 'Money Is a Social Relation'.

44. A. Dow and S. Dow, 'Endogenous Money Creation and Idle Balances', in J. Pheby (eds), *New Directions in Post-Keynesian Economics* (Aldershot and Brookfield, VT: Edward Elgar, 1989), pp. 94–123; Ingham, 'On the Underdevelopment of the Sociology of Money'; R. Wray, *Understanding Modern Money: The Key to Full Employment and Price Stability* (Cheltenham: Edward Elgar, 1998), pp.3–74.

45. The fact that means of payment are non-inflationary only means that there is no causal link between issuance and level of prices. It does not preclude other types or sources of inflation (for example, demand outstripping supply) that may be present.

46. D. Lvovich, 'Colgados De La Soga'.

47. G. Kessler, 'Algunas Implicancias de la Experiencia de Desocupación para el Individuo y su Familia', in Beccaria and López (eds), *Sin Trabajo*, pp. 111–60.

5 From Club de Trueque to Network

1. D. North, 'Institutions and Economic Growth: An Historical Introduction', *World Development*, 17:9 (1989), pp. 1319–32. North, *Institutions, Institutional Change and Economic Performance*, pp.1–144.

2. O. Williamson, *The Economic Institutions of Capitalism: Firms, Markets and Relational Contracting* (New York and London: The Free Press and Macmillan, 1985), pp. 9–136.

3. Williamson, *Market and Hierarchies*, pp. 2–144.

4. O. Williamson, 'The Economics of Organisation: The Transaction Cost Approach', *American Journal of Sociology*, 87:3 (1981), p. 551.

5. R. Coase, 'The Nature of the Firm', *Economica* (1937), pp. 386–405.

6. Williamson, *Market and Hierarchies*, pp. 2–144.

7. Williamson, 'The Economics of Organisation', p. 551.

8. R. Swedberg, 'Socioeconomics and the New Battle of the Methods - Towards a Paradigm Shift?', *Journal of Behavioural Economics*, 19:2 (1990), pp. 141–54.

9. K. Arrow, 'The Organisation of Economic Activity', in *The Analysis and Evaluation of Public Expenditure: The Ppb System* (Joint Economic Committee: 91st Congress, 1969), pp. 59–73.

10. Neoclassical economics refers to a world of perfect competition in which agents are all-knowing all the time. Agents seek their self-interest but there is no specific mention of guile in doing so. Under the welfare theorem, trade always results in win-win situations.

11. [Blank in original text]

12. Williamson, *The Economic Institutions of Capitalism*, pp. 9–136.

13. P. Bardhan, 'The New Institutional Economics and Development Theory: A Brief Critical Assessment', *World Development*, 17:9 (1989), pp. 1389–95.

14. D. North, 'Institutions and Economic Growth: An Historical Introduction', *World Development*, 17:9 (1989), pp. 1319–32. North, *Institutions, Institutional Change and Economic Performance*, pp.1–144. D. North, 'The New Institutional Economics and Development', in *Economics Working Paper Archive*, 1–8 (St. Louis, MO: Washington University at St Louis, 1995), pp.1–8, available online at http://www.nju.edu.cn/cps/site/NJU/njuc/dep/shangyuan/2.doc.

15. North, *Institutions, Institutional Change and Economic Performance*, pp.1–144.

16. Bardhan, 'The New Institutional Economics and Development Theory: A Brief Critical Assessment'.

17. S. M. Shafaeddin, 'Who Is the Master? Who Is the Servant? Market or Government? An Alternative Approach: Towards a Coordination System', *Discussion papers* (Geneva: UNCTAD, 2004), http://www.unctad.org/en/docs/osgdp20049_en.pdf H. A. Simon, *Models of Thought* (New Haven: Yale University Press, 1979), last accessed December 2007.

18. Williamson, 'The Economics of Organisation', p. 551.

19. North, *Institutions, Institutional Change and Economic Performance*, pp.1–144.

20. Boyer and J. R. Hollingsworth, 'From National Embeddedness to Spatial and Institutional Nestedness', in R. Boyer and J. R. Hollingsworth (eds), *Contemporary Capitalism* (Cambridge: Cambridge University Press, 1997), pp. 449–52.
21. Boyer and Hollingsworth, 'The Variety of Institutional Arrangements and Their Complementarity in Modern Economies'.
22. Hodgson, *Evolution and Institutions*, pp. 28–87.
23. G. Hodgson, 'What Is the Essence of Institutional Economics?', *Journal of Economic Issues*, 34:2 (2000), pp. 317–29.
24. Bowles and Gintis, 'The Revenge of Homo Economicus'.
25. A. Etzioni, *The Moral Dimension: Towards a New Economics* (New York: Free Press, 1988), pp.67–9. V. Zelizer, 'The Social Meaning of Money: "Special Monies"', *American Journal of Sociology*, 95 (1989), pp. 342–77.
26. N. Luhman, *Trust and Power* (Chichester: Wiley, 1979), pp. 3–77.
27. S. Helper, 'Comparative Supplier Relations in the US and Japanese Auto Industries: An Exit – Voice Approach', *Business Economic History*, 19 (1990), pp. 153–62. A. Larson, 'Network Dyads in Entrepreneurial Settings: A Study of Governance of Exchange Processes', *Administrative Science Quarterly*, 37 (1992), pp. 76–104.
28. M. Granovetter, 'Economic Action and Social Structure: The Problem of Embeddedness', *American Journal of Sociology*, 91:3 (1985), pp. 481–510.
29. B. Uzzi, 'The Sources and Consequences of Embeddedness for the Economic Performance of Organizations: The Network Effect', *American Sociological Review*, 61 (1996), pp. 674–98.
30. R. Dore, *Flexible Rigidities: Industrial Policy and Structural Adjustment in the Japanese Economy, 1970–1980* (Stanford, CA: Stanford University Press, 1986), pp.1–26.
31. Boyer and Hollingsworth, 'From National Embeddedness to Spatial and Institutional Nestedness', p. 450.
32. S. Marglin, 'Understanding Capitalism: Control Versus Efficiency', in B. Gustafsson (ed.), *Power and Economic Institutions* (Aldershot (England): Edward Elgar, 1991), pp. 225–52.
33. J. Stiglitz, 'Dependence of Quality on Price', *Journal of Economic Literature*, 25 (1987), pp. 1–48.
34. J. Campbell and L. Lindberg, 'Property Rights and the Organization of Economic Activity by the State', *American Sociological Review*, 55 (1990), pp. 3–14. W. Streeck, *Social Institutions and Economic Performance* (Newbury Park, CA: and London: Sage, 1992), pp.12–66.
35. Boyer and Hollingsworth, 'From National Embeddedness to Spatial and Institutional Nestedness', p. 452.
36. P. Bardhan, 'The New Institutional Economics and Development Theory: A Brief Critical Assessment', *World Development*, 17:9 (1989), pp. 1389–95.
37. P. DiMaggio and W. Powell, 'The Iron Cage Revisited: Institutional Isomorphism and Collective Rationality in Organizational Fields', *American Sociological Review*, 48 (1983), pp. 147–60. J. Meyer and B. Rowan, 'Institutionalised Organisations: Formal Structure as Myth and Ceremony', *American Journal of Sociology*, 83 (1977), pp. 340–63.
38. Barreiro and Leite, '*La Confianza En La Economía Popular: Caso Red De Trueque Nodo Astral*'.
39. Toffler, *The Third Wave*, pp. 5–13.
40. Leoni, 'Ilusión para Muchos'. Parysow and Bogani, 'Perspectivas de Desarrollo Económico y Social para las Mujeres Pobres y Empobrecidas en los Clubes del Trueque'.

41. The state was hardly involved in conflict resolution or regulation. There were several attempts to regulate the activity but none was successful. Around the year 2000, representatives in both chambers of Congress expressed concern over the unregulated nature of the *Trueque*. See Hintze, *Trueque y Economía Solidaria*.
42. *La Nación*, 10 November 1996
43. DiMaggio and Powell, 'The Iron Cage Revisited'.
44. Translated as Network of Knowledge Exchange and Social Cybernetics.
45. There was some regional travel but none over longer distances. So the question arises as to whether people travelled per se or because a national voucher encouraged them to do so.
46. San Pedro is located 160 km north of the city of Buenos Aires and has a population of 50,000. The suspicion that the forgery was politically induced was voiced by *PAR* leaders.
47. Primavera, 'Editorial'.
48. Uzzi, 'The Sources and Consequences of Embeddedness for the Economic Performance of Organizations'.
49. Minutes at <http://ar.groups.yahoo.com/group/rgt/message/671>. The organisational structure described here is based on interviews.
50. Minutes at <http:// ar.groups.yahoo.com/group/rgt> and in interviews.
51. Primavera, 'Política Social, Imaginación y Coraje'.
52. H. Primavera, 'Los Clubes De Trueque Deben Preservar El Sentido Solidario', *Clarín* (24 April 2002).
53. Powell, 'Petty Capitalism, Perfecting Capitalism or Post-Capitalism?'.
54. Primavera, *Cómo Formar Un Primer Club De Trueque*; H. Primavera, '¿Red? ¿Global? ¿De Trueque? ¿Solidario? O Cómo Desarmar la que Pudo Haber Sido una Hermosa Revolución Pacífica', mimeo (2002).
55. If one kilo of flour cost 3 pesos in official money, it would cost 3 *créditos* in the *Trueque*. When participants chose flour as the equivalent, they determined that their product should be exchanged, for example, for 2 kilos of flour. Therefore, the price of their product would be 2 * 3 = 6 *créditos*.
56. M. Dobb, *Studies in the Development of Capitalism*, 2nd edn (New York: International Publishers, 1970), pp. 11–64.
57. With some exceptions, there were no consolidated lists of members. Therefore, it was not possible to check whether new entrants received their 50 *créditos* only once; that is, that they did not register as members in two nodes.
58. Available at <http://ar.groups.yahoo.com/group/rgt/message/691.
59. The publications included the principles of the *Trueque*, organizational stages of a *CT*, instructions to train assistants and negotiate the cooperation of social partners (for example, municipalities and firms), and the fundamentals of social money. Franchised nodes were committed to accepting these rules and undertaking a weekend's training. They had to keep in touch with the *PAR* at least once a week to provide information on the members' list and details about their distribution of *créditos*.
60. An anti-*PAR* leader said, 'There was no return from this move. The *PAR* actually privatised the *Trueque* and declared they were the owners.
61. Some nodes asked for a voluntary contribution from members, but the collection of a fee in formal money was never allowed.
62. All quotations from Primavera, unless specified otherwise, are from interviews with the author.

63. Posted on <http://ar.groups.yahoo.com/group/rgt/message/691>
64. *PAR* justified the social franchise, denouncing 'the formation of internal interest groups that conspire against common understandings and the self-help purpose' of the scheme'. <http://ar.groups.yahoo.com/group/rgt/ message/691>.
65. Partly in messages 705 and 712 on <http://ar.groups.yahoo.com/group/ rgt>.
66. Message 701 on < http://ar.groups.yahoo.com/group/rgt>.
67. These figures were provided by the *PAR* leaders.
68. Partly in message 814 on <http://ar.groups.yahoo.com/group/ rgt>.
69. These accounts are partially given in messages 813 and 815 on <http://ar.groups.yahoo.com/group/ rgt>.
70. Sampayo was the owner and manager of one of the 500 largest firms in Argentina before going bankrupt during the structural reforms of the 1990s. A man of action, he is more experienced in implementing and commanding than in militancy and discussion of ideas in meetings
71. North, *Alternative Currency Movements as a Challenge to Globalisation*, pp. 1–17; 56–119.

6 Governance of the Networks

1. S. Strange, *States and Markets* (London: Pinter, 1988), pp. 1–7.
2. J. N. Rosenau and E. O. Czempiel (eds), *Governance without Government: Order and Change in World Politics* (Cambridge: Cambridge University Press, 1992), pp.12–29. H. J. Chang, 'Breaking the Mould: An Institutionalist Political Economy Alternative to the Neo-Liberal Theory of the Market and the State', *Cambridge Journal of Economics*, 26 (2002), pp. 539–59; Streeck and Schmitter, *Private Interest Government*, pp.1–76.
3. P. Hirst, 'Democracy and Governance', in J. Pierre (ed.), *Debating Governance: Authority, Steering and Democracy* (Oxford: Oxford University Press, 2000), pp. 13–35.
4. J. Pierre and B.G. Peters (eds), *Governance, Politics and the State* (Houndmills: MacMillan, 2000), p. 3.
5. K. Van Kersbergen and F. Van Waarden, '"Governance" as a Bridge between Disciplines: Cross-Disciplinary Inspiration Regarding Shifts in Governance and Problems of Governability, Accountability and Legitimacy', *European Journal of Political Research*, 43 (2004), pp. 143–71.
6. G. Hollingsworth, P. Schmitter and W. Streeck, *Governing Capitalist Economies: Performance and Control of Economic Sectors* (Oxford and New York: Oxford University Press, 1994), p. 5.
7. G. Underhill, 'States, Markets and Governance for Emerging Market Economies: Private Interests, the Public Good and the Legitimacy of the Development Process', *International Affairs*, 79:4 (2003), pp. 755–81.
8. Jessop locates the Regulation School as part of the 'revival of institutional and evolutionary economics'. For a discussion, see B. Jessop, 'Survey Article: The Regulation Approach', *Journal of Political Philosophy*, 5:3 (1997), pp. 287–326, in particular, p. 287.
9. Jessop, 'Survey Article'; B. Jessop, *The Parisian Regulation School* (Aldershot: Edward Elgar, 2001), pp.1–78.
10. Streeck and Schmitter, *Private Interest Government*, pp.1–76. J. Campbell, J. R. Hollingsworth and L. Lindberg, *Governance of the American Economy* (Cambridge, New York and Melbourne: Cambridge University Press, 1991), pp. 2–37.

11. G. Hollingsworth and R. Boyer (eds), *Contemporary Capitalism* (Cambridge University Press: Cambridge, 1997), pp. 1–93; 189–219; 431–84. C. Crouch and W. Streeck, *Political Economy of Modern Capitalism: Mapping Convergence and Diversity* (London: Sage, 1997), pp. 9–36. F. Van Waarden, 'Persistence of National Policy Styles: A Study of Their Institutional Foundations', in B. Unger and F. Van Waarden (eds.), *Convergence or Diversity? Internationalization and Economic Policy Response* (Avebury: Aldershot, 1995), pp.56–76.

12. Hodgson, 'The Approach of Institutional Economics'; Hodgson, *The Evolution of Institutional Economics: Agency, Structure and Darwinism in American Institutionalism* (London: Routledge, 2004), pp. 3–77.

13. Jessop, 'Survey Article'; Jessop, *The Parisian Regulation School*, pp.1–78.

14. Streeck and Schmitter, *Private Interest Government*, pp.1–76.

15. Ibid., pp. 11–15.

16. Ibid., p.11

17. G. Hollingsworth and R. Boyer, 'Coordination of Economic Actors and Social Systems of Production', in J. R. Hollingsworth and R. Boyer (eds), *Contemporary Capitalism* (Cambridge: Cambridge University Press, 1997), pp. 9–11.

18. Streeck and Schmitter, *Private Interest Government*, pp.1–76.

19. Hollingsworth and Boyer (eds), *Contemporary Capitalism*, pp. 1–93; 189–219; 431–84.

20. Jessop, 'Survey Article', p. 291.

21. Hollingsworth and Boyer (eds), *Contemporary Capitalism*, p. 50.

22. Van Kersbergen and Van Waarden, '"Governance" as a Bridge between Disciplines', p. 154.

23. J. Thomassen and H. Schmitt, 'In Conclusion: Political Representation and Legitimacy in the European Union', in H. Schmitt and J. Thomassen (eds), *Political Representation and Legitimacy in the European Union* (Oxford: Oxford University Press, 1999), pp.255–68. F.W. Scharpf, *Games Real Actors Play: Actor-Centered Institutionalism in Policy Research* (Boulder, CO : Westview Press, 1997), pp.32–86.

24. B. Jessop, 'The Rise of Governance and the Risks of Failure: The Case of Economic Development', *International Social Science Journal*, 155 (1998), p. 36.

25. B. Cashore, 'Legitimacy and the Privatization of Environmental Governance: How Non-State Market-Driven (Nsmd) Governance Systems Gain Rule-Making Authority', *Governance: An international Journal of Policy, Administration and Institutions*, 15:4 (2002), pp. 503–29.

26. Williamson, *The Economic Institutions of Capitalism*, pp. 2–144.

27. K. Ronit and V. Schneider, 'Global Governance through Private Organizations', *Governance: An international Journal of Policy, Administration and Institutions*, 12:3 (1999), p. 258.

28. He declared: 'We believe the *Red de Trueque* so far has had a great development but very low profile. Now we want to enhance its organisation at the national level as a tool for development. We are lucky it exists. Otherwise, all those people would be protesting out in the streets'.

29. Details of the assistance provided by the government are posted on <www. geocities. com/music*Trueque*/acuerdo/acuerdo2.htm> and www.appropriate-economics-org/ latin/argentina/agreementRGT.html>.

30. Many applications were received but never processed, so they do not count in the 1.2 million. There was no check for duplications either (by applying twice, members could get another 50 *créditos* for 2 pesos). So the exact membership is unknown.
31. Ovalles, 'Argentina Es el País del Mundo en el cual el Fenómeno del Trueque Tiene Mayor Dimensión Social', pp. 42–5.
32. 'Te Cambio', *La Nación* (5 May 2002).
33. S. Hintze, 'La Construccion Mediatica Del Trueque En La Argentina', in Blanc (ed.), *Exclusion Et Liens Financiers*, pp. 443–58.
34. According to an interview in *La Nación* (18 June 2002).
35. The Social Economy section of the Instituto del Conurbano in the Universidad Nacional de General Sarmiento compiled a database of articles that had appeared in the main newspapers.
36. Hintze, in *Trueque y Economía Solidaria*, compiled several proposed laws.
37. Leoni, 'Ilusión para Muchos'.
38. The main *CT*, La Bernalesa, had 3,000 visitors a day. The second-largest, *Club* Los Andes, held its Sunday markets in a football field with 1,500 people participating.
39. Training in hygienic handling of food was then required of participants. The courses were given by local governments or qualified participants. Other rules, like compulsory product labelling, followed.
40. North, *Money and Liberation*, pp.1–40; 149–75.
41. Respondents in the villages of Pergamino, Cañuelas and Campana told the author they went to La Bernalesa to sell at higher prices and enjoy the wider variety of goods. They returned the same day, travelling a maximum of 239 km twice. Trips were paid for in a mix of pesos and *créditos*.
42. [Blank in original]
43. Inequality did not have a clear gender component: an hour of cleaning by a woman was rewarded at the same rate as an hour of cleaning by a man. This was tested during fieldwork, using a kilo of regular flour as the equivalent (1 peso in the formal economy). Rates vary across *CT*, so prices were compared within a single *CT* on the same day. An hour of childcare was offered for the equivalent of 2 kg of flour (2 pesos). An hour of cleaning by either a man or a woman was offered for 1.5 k of flour (1.50 pesos). A woman altering clothes charged 4 kg of flour an hour, the same as a plumber (4 pesos), both using comparable machinery and skills. In the formal economy, an hour of childcare costs 7 pesos, an hour of cleaning 5 pesos, an hour of sewing 15 pesos and an hour of plumbing 25 pesos.
44. North, *Money and Liberation*, pp.1–40; 149–75.
45. *Clarín* (17 October 2002).
46. *La Nación* (16 December 2002) and interview with Horacio Covas (4 November 2006).
47. *La Nación* (26 July 2003).
48. Although participants had made a commitment to return the 50 *créditos* they had been given as starting capital, most never did so.
49. Unless specified otherwise, all the quotations are from interviews conducted by the author in the second quarter of 2004.
50. By December 2004, the limit was set at 100 *créditos* per participant per market day on Saturdays and 300 *créditos* per participant per market day on Sundays.
51. Demurrage is a reverse interest rate, stimulating spending instead of saving.
52. Estimation by Pablo Perez, owner of a newspaper that circulated in the nodes
53. Primavera, '¿Red? ¿Global? ¿De Trueque? ¿Solidario?'.

54. Hintze, 'Desarrollo y Crisis del Trueque en la Argentina'.
55. P. North, 'Scaling Alternative Economic Practices?'.
56. M. Meyer, 'The Growth of Public and Private Bureaucracies', in S. Zukin and P. DiMaggio (eds), *Structures of Capital: The Social Organization of the Economy* (Cambridge: Cambridge University Press, 1990), pp. 153–72; J. Mitchell, 'Hierarchies: Introduction', in G. Thompson et al. (eds), *Markets, Hierarchies and Networks: The Coordination of Social Life* (London and Milton Keynes: Sage and Open University, 1991), pp.168–72.
57. G. Sartori, 'Market, Capitalism, Planning and Technocracy', in G. Thompson et al. (eds), *Markets, Hierarchies and Networks: The Coordination of Social Life* (London and Milton Keynes: Sage and Open University Press, 1991), p.156.
58. Hayek, *The Road to Serfdom*, pp. 16–76.

7 Smaller Scale Trueque

1. *Clarín* (19 February 2003).
2. Blanc, 'Formes Et Rationalites Du Localisme Monetaire'.
3. R. Lee and J. Wills (eds), *Geographies of Economies* (London: Arnold, 1997), pp.1–87; Seyfang, 'Community Currencies'; Seyfang, 'The Euro, the Pound and the Shell in Our Pockets: Rationales for Complementary Currencies in a Global Economy', *New Political Economy*, 5:2 (2001), pp. 227–46.
4. Gilbert and Helleiner (eds), *Nation-States and Money*, pp. 4–24. F. Van Dun, 'National Sovereignty and International Monetary Regimes', in K. Dowd and R. H. Timberlake (eds.), *Money and the Nation State: The Financial Revolution, Government and the World Monetary System* (New Brunswick, NJ and London: Transaction Publishers, 1998), pp. 47–76.
5. M. Jones and G MacLeod, 'Towards a Regional Renaissance? Reconfiguring and Rescaling England's Economic Governance', *Transactions of the Institute of British Geographers*, 24 (1999), pp. 295–313.
6. Blanc, 'Formes Et Rationalites Du Localisme Monetaire'.
7. Blanc, 'Les Monnaies Sociales'.
8. S. DeMeulenaere, 'An Overview of Parallel, Local and Community Currencies', mimeo (1997). North, *Money and Liberation*, pp.1–40; 149–75. North, 'Scaling Alternative Economic Practices'.
9. Blanc, 'Formes Et Rationalites Du Localisme Monetaire'.
10. R. A. Mundell, 'A Theory of Optimum Currency Areas', *American Economic Review*, 51 (1961), pp. 657–65.
11. S. Fisher, 'Seignoriage and the Case for a National Money', *Journal of Political Economy*, 90:2 (1982), pp. 295–313.
12. Blanc, 'Formes Et Rationalites Du Localisme Monetaire'; Blanc, 'Les Monnaies Sociales'.
13. Fisher, 'Seignoriage and the Case for a National Money'.
14. Polanyi, *The Great Transformation*, p. 199.
15. Thorne, 'Local Exchange and Trading Systems in the UK'.
16. Blanc, 'Formes Et Rationalites Du Localisme Monetaire', p. 34.
17. Hintze, in *Trueque y Economía Solidaria*, compiled several proposed laws.
18. Gonzalez Bombal, 'Sociabilidad en las Clases Medias en Descenso', pp. 97–136. I. González Bombal et al., 'Nuevas Redes Sociales: Los Clubes De Trueque'; Leoni and Luzzi, 'Nuevas Redes Sociales', pp. 13–42.

19. Lecaro and Altschuler, 'Políticas Sociales y Desarrollo Local; North, *Money and Liberation*, pp.1–40; 149–75.
20. M. Pacione, 'Local Exchange Trading Systems as a Response to the Globalisation of Capitalism', *Urban Studies*, 34:8 (1997), pp. 1179–99.
21. S. Dow and C. Rodríguez Fuentes, 'Regional Finance: A Survey', *Regional Studies*, 31:9 (1997), p. 904.
22. M. Pacione, 'Local Exchange Trading Systems'; Pacione, 'The Other Side of the Coin'. Seyfang, 'The Euro, the Pound and the Shell in Our Pockets'.
23. UNCED, *Agenda 21: The United Nations Program of Action from Rio* (New York: UN Publications, 1992).
24. Blanc, 'Formes Et Rationalites Du Localisme Monetaire'; Blanc, 'Les Monnaies Sociales'.
25. North, *Alternative Currency Movements as a Challenge to Globalisation?*, pp. 1–17; 56–119. Seyfang, 'Community Currencies'.
26. C. Moser, 'The Asset Vulnerability Framework: Reassessing Urban Poverty Reduction Strategies', *World Development*, 26:1 (1998), pp. 1–19. DFID, Guidence Sheet, *Sustainable Livelihoods Guidance Sheets, Section 2: Framework* (2000), http://www.livelihoods.org/info/info_guidancesheets.html#1, accessed 1 October 2008.
27. A. Plasencia, 'La Oxidación Monetaria y la Moneda Social. Aportes Teóricos y Análisis de un Caso: La Moneda Social Oxidable de Venado Tuerto, Pcia. De Santa Fe' (MA Thesis, Universidad Nacional de General Sarmiento, 2008).
28. Holidays were defined as a period spent out of the city of residence for recreational purposes other than visiting relatives.
29. Blanc, 'Les Monnaies Sociales'.
30. M. Granovetter and R. Swedberg (eds), *The Sociology of Economic Life.* (Boulder, CO: Westview Press, 1992), pp. 11–67.
31. Thorne, 'Local Exchange and Trading Systems in the UK'.
32. Thorne, 'Local Exchange and Trading Systems in the UK'.
33. D. Burns and M. Taylor, *Mutual Aid and Self-Help: Coping Strategies for Excluded Communities* (Bristol: University of Bristol and The Policy Press, 1998), pp. 3–27. M. González de la Rocha, 'Are Poor Households Coping? Assets, Vulnerability and Decreasing Opportunities', *Development and Society*, 30:2 (2001), pp. 1–40.
34. M. Pacione, 'The Ecclesiastical Community of Interest as a Response to Urban Poverty and Deprivation', *Transactions of the Institute of British Geographers*, 15:2 (1990), pp. 193–204. J. C. Scott, *The Moral Economy of the Peasant: Rebellion and Subsistence in Southeast Asia* (New Haven, CT: Yale University Press, 1976), pp. 1–166.
35. Pearson, 'Argentina's Barter Network'; Powell, 'Petty Capitalism, Perfecting Capitalism or Post-Capitalism?'.
36. The figure includes goods bought from nearby sources as inputs, adding secondary demand.
37. Hintze (ed.), *Trueque y Economía Solidaria*; Abramovich and Vazquez, 'La Experiencia Del Trueque En La Argentina'.
38. J. Blanc, 'Formes Et Rationalites Du Localisme Monetaire'.
39. Pacione, 'Local Exchange Trading Systems'.
40. For example, if the household had no pesos they walked instead of taking a bus.
41. What respondents considered to be 'basic needs' of their household was left up to them to define. Their perception was also interesting to capture.

42. For example, the state gave the poor above the age of seventy a box of foods with a high carbohydrate and fat content, which many could not eat for health reasons. Similarly, an Italian donor distributed kilos maize flour suitable for polenta, a food not popular in Argentina.

43. This sometimes operated almost as a barter circle. For example, participants who made bread asked their regular clients with an income in pesos to buy flour, yeast, and so on in the supermarkets, which they then traded for bread.

44. North, *Alternative Currency Movements as a Challenge to Globalisation?*, pp. 1–17; 56–119. P. North, *Money and Liberation: The Micropolitics of Alternative Currency Movements* (Minneapolis & London: University of Minnesota Press, 2007), pp.1–40; 149–75. E. Collom, 'The Motivations, Engagement, Satisfaction, Outcomes, and Demographics of Time Bank Participants: Survey Findings from a U.S. System', *International Journal of Community Currency Research*, 11 (2007), pp. 36–83. Seyfang, 'The Euro, the Pound and the Shell in Our Pockets'.

45. Thorne, 'Local Exchange and Trading Systems in the UK'.

46. C. Williams and J. Windebank, 'Helping Each Other Out? Community Exchange in Deprived Neighbourhoods', *Community Development Journal*, 35:2 (2000), pp. 146–56.

47. J. Oviedo, 'Las Implacables Reglas del Mercado', *La Nación* (17 August 2003). M. Krause, 'Las Limitaciones Del Trueque', in Hintze (ed.), *Trueque y Economía Solidaria*, pp. 107–20.

48. R. Pearson, 'Income Generation Strategies in a Globalising World: Learning from International Experience' (Paper presented at the *Seminario Internacional hacia una sociedad más igualitaria* Buenos Aires: Ministry of Social Development and Environment, 2000).

49. Lecaro and Altschuler, 'Políticas Sociales y Desarrollo Local'; F. Leoni and M. Luzzi, *Rasguñando la Lona: La Experiencia de un Club de Trueque en el Conurbano Bonaerense* (Buenos Aires: CLASPO, 2003), pp.1–35.

50. Leoni and Luzzi, *Rasguñando la Lona*, pp.1–35.

51. Gonzalez Bombal, 'Sociabilidad en las Clases Medias en Descenso', pp. 97–136.

52. Leoni, 'Ilusión para Muchos'.

8 Replacing Money for Economic Development

1. A. Amin, 'An Institutionalist Perspective on Regional Economic Development', *International Journal of Urban and Regional Research*, 23 (1999), pp. 365–78. G. MacLeod, 'The Learning Region in an Age of Austerity: Capitalizing on Knowledge, Entrepreneurialism and Reflexive Capitalism', *Geoforum*, 31 (2000), pp. 219–32; R. Scott, *Institutions and Organizations*, 2nd edn (Thousand Oaks, CA: Sage, 2001), pp. 24–33.

2. A. Amin, 'Regions Unbound: Towards a New Politics of Place', *Geografiska Annaler: Series B, Human Geography*, 86:1 (2004), pp. 33–44. G. MacLeod and M. Goodwin, 'Reconstructing an Urban and Regional Political Economy: On the State, Politics, Scale and Explanation', *Political Geography*, 18 (1999), pp. 697–730. G. MacLeod, 'Beyond Soft Institutionalism: Accumulation, Regulation and Their Geographical Fixes', *Environment and Planning*, A33 (2001), pp. 1145–67.

3. D. Gibbs, A. Jonas, S. Reimer and D. Spooner, 'Governance, Institutional Capacity and Partnerships in Local Economic Development: Theoretical Issues and Empirical Evidence from the Humber Sub-Region', *Transactions of the Institute of British Geographers*,

26 (2001), pp. 103–19. M. Raco, 'Competition, Collaboration and the New Industrial Districts: Examining the Institutional Turn in Local Economic Development', *Urban Studies*, 36 (1999), pp. 951–68.

4.   MacLeod and Goodwin, 'Reconstructing an Urban and Regional Political Economy', p. 704.

5.   M. Storper, 'The Resurgence of Regional Economies, Ten Years Later: The Region as a Nexus of Untraded Interdependencies', *European Urban and Regional Studies*, 2:3 (1995), pp. 191–221.

6.   P. Hirst, *Associative Democracy: New Forms of Economic and Social Governance* (Cambridge and Oxford: Polity Press Disent and Blackwell, 1994), pp. 11–65.

7.   M. Raco, 'Competition, Collaboration and the New Industrial Districts'.

8.   A. Amin and N. Thrift, 'Globalisation, Institutional Thickness and the Local Economy', in P. Healey et al. (eds), *Managing Cities: The New Urban Context* (Chichester: John Wiley & Sons, 1995), pp. 91–108.

9.   MacLeod, 'Beyond Soft Institutionalism'; Raco, 'Competition, Collaboration and the New Industrial Districts'.

10. Gibbs et al., 'Governance, Institutional Capacity and Partnerships in Local Economic Development'.

11. R. Hudson, 'The Learning Economy, the Learning Firm and the Learning Region: A Sympathetic Critique of the Limits to Learning', *European Urban and Regional Studies*, 6 (1999), pp. 59–72.

12. A. E. Jonas, 'In Search of Order: Traditional Business Reformism and the Crisis of Neo-Liberalism in Massachussets', *Transactions of the Institute of British Geographers*, 21 (1996), pp. 617–34.

13. R. O'Doherty, J. Dürrschmidt and D. Purdue, 'Cultural Innovation in Alternative Milieux: LETS as CED' (Paper presented at the *Regional Studies Association 'Community Economic Development: Linking the Grassroots to Regional Economic Development'* South Africa, November 1997).

14. R. Martin, 'Institutional Approaches in Economic Geography', in T. Barnes and E. Sheppard (eds), *Companion to Economic Geography* (Oxford: Blackwell, 2001).

15. A. H. J. Helmsing, 'Partnerships, Meso-Institutions and Learning: New Local and Regional Economic Development Initiatives in Latin America', in I. Baud and J. Post (eds), *Re-Aligning Actors in an Urbanized World: Governance and Institutions from a Development Perspective* (Ashgate: Aldershot, 2002), p. 81.

16. A. H. J. Helmsing, 'Local Economic Development. New Generations of Actors, Policies and Instruments for Africa', *Public Administration and Development*, 23:1 (2003), pp. 67–76.

17. Seyfang, 'Working for the Fenland Dollar'.

18. Plasencia, 'La Oxidación Monetaria y la Moneda Social. Aportes Teóricos y Análisis de un Caso: La Moneda Social Oxidable de Venado Tuerto, Pcia. De Santa Fe' (MA Thesis, Universidad Nacional de General Sarmiento, 2008).

19. While Ilari is away in the countryside doing his work as an agrarian engineer, his personnel have little to do, so their time is used to update the information on participants, implement the change in vouchers, prepare the balance sheets of *puntos* earned by each participant, and so on.

20. The bakery is a small family enterprise and in November 2004 it received an average of 420 *puntos* a month, in comparison with 13,400 pesos.

21. Y. Hirota, 'The RGT in Argentina' (MA Thesis, University of Tokyo, 2002).

22. Seyfang, 'Community Currencies'. G. Seyfang, 'Money That Makes a Change: Community Currencies, North and South', *Gender and Development*, 9:1 (2001), pp. 60–9.
23. D. Reisman, *Theories of Collective Action: Downs, Olson and Hirsch* (Basingstoke: Macmillan, 1990), pp. 45–54.
24. North, 'Scaling Alternative Economic Practices?'.
25. J. P. Platteau, 'Behind the Market Stage Where Real Societies Exist - Published in Two Issues: Part 1: The Role of Public and Private Order Institutions', *Journal of Development Studies*, 30:3 (1994), pp. 533–77. J. P. Platteau, 'Behind the Market Stage Where Real Societies Exist - Published in Two Issues: Part 2: 'The Role of Moral Norms', *Journal of Development Studies*, 30:3 (1994), pp. 753–817.
26. Pearson, 'Argentina's Barter Network'.
27. Gonzalez Bombal, 'Sociabilidad en las Clases Medias en Descenso', pp. 97–136. González Bombal et al., 'Nuevas Redes Sociales'.
28. K. Norman, 'Barter Nation', *Buenos Aires Herald* (2002).
29. Primavera, 'Política Social, Imaginación y Coraje'; Primavera, 'Riqueza, Dinero y Poder'.
30. Ford and Picasso, 'Representaciones Sociales Acerca de la Pobreza, el Trabajo y la Identidad', p. 224; Primavera and Wautiez, 'Social Money'.
31. C. De la Torre, 'The Ambiguous Meanings of Latin American Populism', *Social Research*, 59:2 (1992), pp. 385–414.
32. J. Auyero, *Favores Por Votos, Estudios Sobre Clientelismo Político Contemporáneo* (Buenos Aires: Losada, 1997), pp. 1–53; J. Auyero, 'The Logic of Clientelism in Argentina: An Ethnographic Account', *Latin American Research Review*, 35:5 (2002), pp. 55–81; J. Auyero, *Poor People's Politics: Peronist Survival Networks and the Legacy of Evita* (London: Duke University Press, 2002), pp.1–84; G. Lodola, 'Protesta Popular Y Redes Clientelares En La Argentina: El Reparto Federal Del Plan Trabajar (1996–2001)', *Desarrollo Económico*, 44:176 (2005), pp. 515–35.
33. North, *Money and Liberation*, pp.1–40; 149–75.
34. J. Daito, 'Sustainability Innovations and Local Currency Systems: Bridging the Green and the Brown Agendas' (Paper presented at the *Oikos Phd Summer Academy 2005 'Sustainability Management and Innovation'* Switzerland: University of St. Gallen, 2005).
35. I. Baud, J. Post and C. Furedy, *Solid Waste Management and Recycling: Actors, Partnerships, and Policies in Hyderabad, India and Nairobi, Kenya* (New York: Kluwer Academic Publishers, 2004), pp. 1–54; 130–95.
36. G. Gomez, 'Le Réseau De Trueque Zone Ouest, Partenaire De L'économie Locale', in J. Blanc (ed.), *Rapport Exclusion Et Liens Financiers 2005–06, Monnaies Sociales* (Paris: Economica, 2006), pp. 497–513.

9 Conclusions

1. Greco, *Money*, pp. 8–86. M. Kennedy, *Interest and Inflation Free Money* (Philadelphia, PA: New Society, 1995), pp.45–122; Lietaer, *The Future of Money*, pp. 3–55; 125–235.
2. A. Dow and S. Dow, 'Endogenous Money Creation and Idle Balances', pp. 94–123. G. Ingham, 'Capitalism, Money and Banking: A Critique of Recent Historical Sociology', *British Journal of Sociology*, 50:1 (1999), pp. 76–96; L.P. Rochon and S. Rossi, *Modern Theories of Money: The Nature and Role of Money in Capitalist Economies* (Cheltenham: Edward Elgar, 2003), pp.187–96. R. Wray, *Understanding Modern Money: The Key to Full Employment and Price Stability* (Cheltenham: Edward Elgar, 1998), pp. 3–74.

3. Keynes, *A Treatise on Money*.
4. Ingham, 'Capitalism, Money and Banking'; R. Wray, *Understanding Modern Money: The Key to Full Employment and Price Stability* (Cheltenham: Edward Elgar, 1998), pp. 3–74.
5. H. Ganssman, 'Money – a Symbolically Generalised Médium of Communication? On the Concept of Money in Recent Sociology', *Economy and Society*, 17:4 (1988), pp. 285–315.
6. Cavallo, 'The Quality of Money'.
7. M. Kennedy, *Interest and Inflation Free Money* (Philadelphia, PA: New Society, 1995), pp. 45–122; Lietaer, *The Future of Money*, pp. 3–55; 125–235.
8. J. Schumpeter, *History of Economic Analysis* (London: Allen & Unwin, 1994), pp. 2–155.
9. Ingham, 'Money Is a Social Relation'; A. Leyshon and N. Thrift, *Money / Space* (London: Routledge 1996), pp. 1–80.
10. North, *Money and Liberation*, pp.1–40; 149–75.
11. Hodgson, 'Reconstitutive Downward Causation'; Hodgson, 'The Hidden Persuaders'.
12. Hodgson, 'What Are Institutions?'.
13. Hodgson, 'Reconstitutive Downward Causation'; Hodgson, 'The Hidden Persuaders'.
14. Giddens, *The Constitution of Society*, pp. 84–8.
15. Lawson, *Economics and Reality*, pp. 82–145.
16. Granovetter and Swedberg (eds), *The Sociology of Economic Life*, pp.11–67; Hodgson, 'The Hidden Persuaders'.
17. Beckert, 'Economic Sociology and Embeddedness.
18. E. Fullbrook (ed.), *Intersubjectivity in Economics: Agents and Structures* (London: Routledge, 2002), pp. 1–8.
19. P. David, 'Path Dependence, Its Critics and the Quest for 'Historical Economics', pp.120–44, in G. Hodgson (ed.) in Association with the European Association for Evolutionary Political Economy, *The Evolution of Economic Institutions: A Critical Reader* (Cheltenham: Edward Elgar, 2007), pp. 120–44.
20. R. Nelson, 'Recent Evolutionary Theorizing About Economic Change', *Journal of Economic Literature*, 33:1 (1995), p. 48.
21. R. Nelson and S. Winter, *An Evolutionary Theory of Economic Change* (Cambridge, MA: The Belknap Press of Harvard University Press, 1982), pp. 1–87.
22. B. Nooteboom (ed.), *Learning and Innovation in Organizations and Economies* (Oxford: University Press, 2000), pp. 7–17.
23. S. Wuyts, M. Colombo, S. Dutta and B. Nooteboom, 'Empirical Tests of Optimal Cognitive Distance', *Journal of Economic Behavior & Organization*, 58 (2003), p. 278.
24. W. Jackson, 'Social Structure in Economic Theory', *Journal of Economic Issues*, 37:3 (2003), p. 732.
25. S. Bowles, R. Edwards and F. Roosevelt, *Understanding Capitalism: Competition, Command, and Change*, 3rd edn (New York: Oxford University Press, 2005), p.62.
26. Hollingsworth and Boyer (eds), *Contemporary Capitalism*, pp. 1–93; 189–219; 431–84.
27. Ibid., pp. 1–93; 189–219; 431–84; G. Hollingsworth, P. Schmitter and W. Streeck, *Governing Capitalist Economies: Performance and Control of Economic Sectors* (Oxford and New York: Oxford University Press, 1994), pp. 1–84.
28. Jessop, 'Survey Article'.

29. Hollingsworth and Boyer (eds), *Contemporary Capitalism*, pp. 1–93; 189–219; 431–84.

30. J. L. Laville, B. Eme and J. P. Maréchal, 'Economía Solidaria: 'Ilusión O Vía De Futuro?' (Paper presented at the Mesa redonda sobre la economía Solidaria, Universidad de verano Arles, France, August 2001). L. Razeto, *Los Caminos De La Economía Solidaria* (Buenos Aires: Luhmen-Humanitas, 1997).

31. J. L. Coraggio, 'La Propuesta De La Economía Solidaria Frente a La Economía Neoliberal' Paper presented at the *Social Economic Forum* Porto Alegre, Brazil, 2002); Platteau, 'Behind the Market Stage Where Real Societies Exist - Published in Two Issues: Part 1'; Platteau, 'Behind the Market Stage Where Real Societies Exist - Published in Two Issues: Part 2'.

32. F. A. Hayek, 'Individualism and Economic Order' (London and Chicago, IL: Routledge and University of Chicago Press, 1948), pp. 8–178; Beckert, *Beyond the Market*, pp. 5–133; Hodgson, *The Evolution of Institutional Economics: Agency, Structure and Darwinism in American Institutionalism* (London: Routledge, 2004), pp. 3–77.

WORKS CITED

Abramovich, A. L. and G. Vazquez, 'La Experiencia Del Trueque En La Argentina: Otro Mercado Es Posible' (Paper presented at the Seminario de Economía Social, Buenos Aires 4 July 2003).

Aldridge, T. and A. Patterson, 'Lets Get Real: Constraints on the Development of Local Exchange Trading Schemes', *Area*, 34:4 (2002), pp. 370–81.

Amin, A., 'An Institutionalist Perspective on Regional Economic Development', *International Journal of Urban and Regional Research*, 23 (1999), pp. 365–78.

—, 'Regions Unbound: Towards a New Politics of Place', *Geografiska Annaler: Series B, Human Geography*, 86:1 (2004), pp. 33–44.

—, A. Cameron and R. Hudson, *Placing the Social Economy* (London: Routledge, 2002).

—, and N. Thrift, 'Globalisation, Institutional Thickness and the Local Economy', in P. Healey, S. Cameron and S. Davoudi et al. (eds), *Managing Cities: The New Urban Context* (Chichester: John Wiley & Sons, 1995), pp. 91–108.

Arrow, K. 'The Organisation of Economic Activity', in *The Analysis and Evaluation of Public Expenditure: The Ppb System* (Joint Economic Committee: 91st Congress, 1969), pp. 59–73.

Auyero, J. *Favores Por Votos, Estudios Sobre Clientelismo Político Contemporáneo* (Buenos Aires: Losada, 1997).

—, 'The Logic of Clientelism in Argentina: An Ethnographic Account', *Latin American Research Review*, 35:5 (2002), pp. 55–81.

—, *Poor People's Politics: Peronist Survival Networks and the Legacy of Evita* (London: Duke University Press, 2002).

Barbero, M. I., 'Historia Económica De La Argentina Contemporánea', mimeo (2007).

Bardhan, P. 'The New Institutional Economics and Development Theory: A Brief Critical Assessment', *World Development*, 17:9 (1989), pp. 1389–95.

Barreiro, L., and L. Leite, 'La Confianza En La Economía Popular: Caso Red De Trueque Nodo Astral' (*IDICSO – Universidad del Salvador*, 2003), www.salvador.edu.ar/csoc/idicso/docs/aongpp003.pdf, accessed 1 April 2006.

Barreto, M. A., M. A. Benitez and A. M. Attias, 'Política Social, Pobreza, Identidad y Fragmentación Social' (Paper presented at the Seminario Las Caras de la Pobreza Buenos Aires: Universidad Catolica, 2002).

Baud, I., J. Post and C. Furedy, *Solid Waste Management and Recycling: Actors, Partnerships, and Policies in Hyderabad, India and Nairobi, Kenya* (New York: Kluwer Academic Publishers, 2004).

Beccaria, L., 'Empleo, Remuneraciones y Diferenciación Social en el Último cuarto de Siglo XX', in L. Beccaria, S. Feldman, I. González Bombal, G. Kessler, M. Murmis and M. Svampa (eds), *Sociedad y Sociabilidad en la Argentina de los Noventa*, (Buenos Aires: Universidad Nacional de General Sarmiento and Editorial Biblos, 2002), pp. 27–54.

—, and N. López, *Sin Trabajo: Las Características del Desempleo y sus Efectos en la Sociedad Argentina, Edited by UNICEF* (Buenos Aires: Losada, 1996).

Beckert, J., *Beyond the Market: The Social Foundations of Economic Efficiency* (Princeton, NJ: Princeton University Press, 2002).

—, 'Economic Sociology and Embeddedness: How Shall We Conceptualize Economic Action?', *Journal of Economic Issues*, 37:3 (2003), pp. 769–87.

Blanc, J., 'Formes Et Rationalites Du Localisme Monetaire', *Working paper* (Lyon: Centre Auguste et Léon Walras, 2002).

—, 'Les Monnaies Parallèles: Évaluation Et Enjeux Théoriques Du Phénomène', *Revue d'Economie Financière*, 49 (1998), pp. 81–102.

—, 'Les Monnaies Sociales: Un Outil Et Ses Limites', in J. Blanc (ed.), *Exclusions Et Liens Financiers: Monnaies Sociales* (Paris: Economica, 2006), pp. 25–42.

Botana, N., *La República vacilante: entre la furia y la razón* (Buenos Aires: Taurus, 2002).

Borges, J., 'The Lottery in Babylon' (1941), in D. Yates and J. Irby (eds), *Labyrinths: Selected Stories and Other Writings by Jorge Luis Borges* (New York: New Directions Publishing Corporation 1964).

Bowles, S., R. Edwards and F. Roosevelt, *Understanding Capitalism: Competition, Command, and Change*, 3rd. ed (New York: Oxford University Press, 2005).

Bowles, S. and H. Gintis, 'The Revenge of Homo Economicus: Contested Exchange and the Revival of Political Economy', *The Journal of Economic Perspectives*, 7:1 (1993), pp. 83–102.

Boyer, R. and J. R. Hollingsworth, 'From National Embeddedness to Spatial and Institutional Nestedness', in R. Boyer and J. R. Hollingsworth (eds), *Contemporary Capitalism* (Cambridge: Cambridge University Press, 1997), pp. 433–84.

Boyer, R., and J. R. Hollingsworth, 'The Variety of Institutional Arrangements and Their Complementarity in Modern Economies', in R. Boyer and J. R. Hollingsworth (eds), *Contemporary Capitalism: The Embeddedness of Institutions*, (Cambridge (UK) and New York: Cambridge University Press, 1997), pp. 49–54.

Braudel, F., *The Structures of Everyday Life: The Limits of the Possible* (London: Fontana, 1981).

—, *The Wheels of Commerce* (New York: Harper and Row, 1982).

Bryer, A., 'Beyond Bureaucracies? The Struggle for Self-Determination and Social Responsibility in the Argentine Worker-Run Companies' (Paper presented at the conference *Rethinking Economic Anthropology: a Human Centred Approach* School of Oriental and Asian Studies: London, 2008), 11-12 January 2008, available online: http://rethinkingeconomies.org.uk/web/d/doc_71.pdf, last accessed 20 January 2009.

Bunge, M., *Emergence and Convergence: Qualitative Novelty and the Unity of Knowledge*, Toronto Studies in Philosophy (Toronto: University of Toronto Press, 2003).

Burns, D., and M. Taylor, *Mutual Aid and Self-Help: Coping Strategies for Excluded Communities* (Bristol: University of Bristol and The Policy Press, 1998).

Campbell, J., J. R. Hollingsworth and L. Lindberg, *Governance of the American Economy* (Cambridge, New York and Melbourne: Cambridge University Press, 1991).

Campbell, J., and L. Lindberg, 'Property Rights and the Organization of Economic Activity by the State', *American Sociological Review*, 55 (1990), pp. 3–14.

Campione, D.,'El Estado en la Argentina. Cambio de paradigmas y abandono del tema social', in S. Hintze (ed.), *Estado y Sociedad: Las Políticas Sociales en los Umbrales del Siglo XXI*, (Buenos Aires: EUDEBA, 2000), pp. 93–115.

Carothers, N., *Fractional Money* (New York John Wiley & Sons, 1930).

Carrier, J. G., *Meanings of the Market: The Free Market in Western Culture* (Oxford: Berg, 1997).

Cashore, B., 'Legitimacy and the Privatization of Environmental Governance: How Non-State Market-Driven (Nsmd) Governance Systems Gain Rule-Making Authority', *Governance: An international Journal of Policy, Administration and Institutions*, 15:4 (2002), pp. 503–29.

Cavallo, D., 'The Quality of Money', Document prepared for the Award Ceremony of the Doctorate Honoris Causa University of Paris 1- Pantheon Sorbonne, published in *ASAP* (Asociación Argentina de Presupuesto y Administración Financiera Pública), 33 (June 1999) and *Économie Internationale - La revue du CEPII, La qualité de la monnaie*, 80:4 (1999).

Cetrangolo, O., and J. P. Jiménez, 'Algunas Reflexiones Sobre El Federalismo Fiscal en la Argentina', *Desarrollo Económico*, 38: Special Issue (1998), pp. 293–326.

Chandler, A., *The Visible Hand: The Managerial Revolution in American Business* (Cambridge, MA: Harvard University Belknap Press 1977).

Chang, H. J., 'Breaking the Mould: An Institutionalist Political Economy Alternative to the Neo-Liberal Theory of the Market and the State', *Cambridge Journal of Economics*, 26 (2002), pp. 539–59.

Chelala, S., 'Las Terceras Monedas', mimeo, Buenos Aires, (2002).

Ciria, A., 'Argentina: An Underdeveloping Country?', in A. Ritter, M. Cameron and D. Pollock (eds), *Latin America to the Year 2000: Reactivating Growth, Improving Equity, Sustaining Democracy*, (New York: Praeger, 1992), pp. 195–207.

Cleaver, F., 'Reinventing Institutions: Bricolage and the Social Embeddedness of Natural Resource Management', *European Journal of Development Research*, 12:2 (2002), pp. 11–30.

Coase, R., 'The Nature of the Firm', *Economica* (1937), pp. 386–405.

Cohen-Mitchell, T., 'Community Currencies at a Crossroads: New Ways Forward' *New Village* (2000), http://www.ratical.org/many_worlds/cc/cc@Xroads.html, accessed 23 June 2006.

Cohen, B., J., 'The New Geography of Money', in E. Gilbert and E. Helleiner (eds), *Nations-States and Money: The Past, Present and Future of National Currencies* (New York and London: Routledge, 1999), pp. 121–38.

Cohrssen, H., 'Wära', *The New Republic* (10 August 1932).

Colacelli, M., and D. Blackburn, 'Secondary Currency: An Empirical Analysis' (2005), http://www.columbia.edu/~mc2602/files/Colacelli-Currency-Dec-06.pdf, accessed 1 June 2008.

Collom, E., 'The Motivations, Engagement, Satisfaction, Outcomes, and Demographics of Time Bank Participants: Survey Findings from a U.S. System', *International Journal of Community Currency Research*, 11 (2007), pp. 36–83.

Coraggio, J. L., 'Las Redes Del Trueque Como Institución De La Economía Popular, Reedited', in S. Hintze (ed.), *Trueque y Economía Solidaria* (Buenos Aires: Prometeo Libros, 1998), pp. 233–50.

—, 'La Propuesta De La Economía Solidaria Frente a La Economía Neoliberal' (Paper presented at the *Social Economic Forum* Porto Alegre, 2002).

Cornes, R., and T. Sandler, *The Theory of Externalities, Public Goods, and Club Goods*, 2nd edn (Cambridge: Cambridge University Press, 1996).

Cortes Conde, R., *La Economía Política De La Argentina en el Siglo XX* (Buenos Aires: Edhasa, 2005).

Cortes, R., and A Marshall, 'Estrategia Económica, Instituciones Y Negociación Política En La Reforma Social De Los Noventa', *Desarrollo Económico*, 39:154 (1999), pp. 195–212.

Covas, H., *Un nuevo Modelo de Organización Comunitaria*, (Buenos Aires: Red Global de Trueque, 2000).

Crouch, C., and W. Streeck, *Political Economy of Modern Capitalism: Mapping Convergence and Diversity* (London: Sage, 1997).

Daito, J., 'Sustainability Innovations and Local Currency Systems: Bridging the Green and the Brown Agendas' (Paper presented at the *Oikos Phd Summer Academy 2005 'Sustainability Management and Innovation'* Switzerland: University of St. Gallen, 2005).

David, P., 'Path Dependence, Its Critics and the Quest for 'Historical Economics' in G. Hodgson, (eds) in Association with the European Association for Evolutionary Political Economy, *The evolution of economic institutions: A critical reader*, (Cheltenham: Edward Elgar, 2007), pp. 120–44.

Davis, J., *Exchange* (Buckingham: Open University Press, 1992).

De la Torre, C., 'The Ambiguous Meanings of Latin American Populism', *Social Research*, 59:2 (1992), pp. 385–414.

De Sanzo, C., H. Covas and H. Primavera, *Reinventando El Mercado* (Buenos Aires: Programa de Autosuficiencia Regional, 1998).

DeMeulenaere, S., 'An Overview of Parallel, Local and Community Currencies', mimeo (1997).

DFID, Guidence Sheet, *Sustainable Livelihoods Guidance Sheets, Section 2: Framework* (2000), http://www.livelihoods.org/info/info_guidancesheets.html#1, accessed 1 October 2008.

Diaz, A., 'New Developments in Economic and Social Restructuring in Latin America', in W. Smith and R. Korzeniewics (eds.), *Politics, Social Change, and Economic Restructuring in Latin America* (Coral Gables, FL: North-South Center Press, 1997), pp. 37–56.

Diaz Alejandro, C., 'No Less Than One Hundred Years of Argentine Economic History, Plus Some Comparisons', *Discussion Paper 53* (New Haven, CT: Yale University, 1982), pp. 44–57.

DiMaggio, P., and W. Powell, 'The Iron Cage Revisited: Institutional Isomorphism and Collective Rationality in Organizational Fields', *American Sociological Review*, 48 (1983), pp. 147–60.

Dinerstein, A., 'Que Se Vayan Todos! Popular Insurrection and the Asambleas Barriales in Argentina', *Bulletin of Latin American Research*, 22:2 (2003), pp. 187–200.

Dixit, A., *Lawlessness and Economics: Alternative Modes of Governance* (Princeton, NJ: Princeton University Press, 2004).

Djelic, M. L., and K Sahlin-Andersson, *Transnational Governance: Institutional Dynamics of Regulation* (Cambridge: Cambridge University Press, 2006).

Dobb, M., *Studies in the Development of Capitalism*, 2nd ed (New York: International Publishers, 1970).

Dodd, N., *The Sociology of Money* (Cambridge: Polity Press, 1994).

Dollar, D., and A. Kraay, 'Spreading the Wealth', *Foreign Affairs*, January/February (2002), pp. 120–33.

Dore, R., *Flexible Rigidities: Industrial Policy and Structural Adjustment in the Japanese Economy, 1970–1980* (Stanford , CA: Stanford University Press, 1986).

Dow, A., and S. Dow, 'Endogenous Money Creation and Idle Balances', in J. Pheby (eds), *New Directions in Post-Keynesian Economics* (Aldershot and Brookfield, VT: Edward Elgar, 1989), pp. 94–123.

Dow, S., and C. Rodríguez Fuentes, 'Regional Finance: A Survey', *Regional Studies*, 31:9 (1997), pp. 903–20.

Drake, P., *Labor Movements and Dictatorships: The Southern Cone in Comparative Perspectives* (Baltimore, MD: Johns Hopkins University Press, 1996).

Ekins, P., and M. Max-Neef (eds.), *The Living Economy* (London and New York: Routledge, 1986).

Escobar, A., and S. Alvarez (eds), *The Making of Social Movements in Latin America: Identity, Strategy and Democracy* (Boulder, CO: Westview Press, 1992).

Etzioni, A., *The Moral Dimension: Towards a New Economics* (New York: Free Press, 1988).

Fanelli, J. M., and R Frenkel, *Estabilidad y Estructura; Interacciones en el crecimiento económico* (Buenos Aires: Cedes, 1994).

—, and D Heymann, 'Dilemas Monetarios en Argentina', *Desarrollo Económico (Buenos Aires)*, 42:165 (2002), pp. 3–24.

FIEL, 'Las Pequeñas y Medianas Empresas en la Argentina' (Buenos Aires: Fundación de Investigaciones Latinoamericanas, 1996), pp. 1–135.

Field, A., 'Microeconomics, Norms, and Rationality', *Economic Development and Cultural Change*, 32:4 (1984), pp. 683–711.

Fisher, I., *Mastering the Crisis - with Additional Chapters on Stamp Script* (London: Kimble and Bradford, 1934).

—, *Stamp Scrip* (New York: Adelphi Co., 1933).

Fisher, S., 'Seignoriage and the Case for a National Money', *Journal of Political Economy*, 90:2 (1982), pp. 295–313.

Ford, M., and M. Picasso, 'Representaciones Sociales Acerca de la Pobreza, el Trabajo y la Identidad' (Paper presented at the Seminario Las Caras de la Pobreza, Buenos Aires 2002).

Frenkel, R., and M. González Rozada, 'Apertura comercial, empleo y productividad en Argentina', in V. Tokman and D. Martínez (eds), *Productividad y Empleo En La Apertura Económica* (Santiago de Chile: Oficina Internacional del Trabajo, 1999), pp. 56–87.

—, and J. Ros, 'Desempleo, Políticas Macroeconómicas y Flexibilidad del Mercado Laboral. Argentina y México en los Noventa', *Desarrollo Económico*, 44:173 (2004), pp. 33–56.

Fullbrook, E. (ed.), *Intersubjectivity in Economics: Agents and Structures* (London: Routledge, 2002).

Ganssman, H., 'Money – a Symbolically Generalised Médium of Communication? On the Concept of Money in Recent Sociology', *Economy and Society*, 17:4 (1988), pp. 285–315.

Garcia, M. F. 'La Construction Sociale D'un Marche Au Cadran De Fontaine-En-Sologne', *Actes de la Recherche en Sciences Sociales*, 65 (1986), pp. 1–13.

Gerchunoff, G., and L. Llach, *El Ciclo de la Ilusión y el Desencanto; Un Siglo de Políticas Económicas Argentinas*, 2nd edn (Buenos Aires: Ariel, 2005).

Gerchunoff, P., and J. C. Torre, 'La Política De Liberalización Económica en la Administración de Menem', *Desarrollo Económico*, 36:143 (1994), pp. 37–58.

Germani, G., and S. S. de Yujnovsky, 'El Surgimiento Del Peronismo: El Rol De Los Obreros Y De Los Migrantes Internos', *Desarrollo Económico*, 13:51 (1973), pp. 435–88.

Gesell, S., *The Natural Economic Order* (London: Peter Owen, 1958).

Giarini, O., 'Some Considerations on the Future of Work: Redefining Productive Work', in M. Simai (ed.), *Global Employment: An International Investigation into the Future of Work* (London and Tokyo: Zed Books for UNU/WIDER and UN University Press, 1995), pp. 89–108.

Giarraca, N. (ed.), *La Protesta Social En La Argentina: Transformaciones Econónicas Y Crisis Social En El Interior Del País* (Buenos Aires: Alianza, 2001)

Gibbs, D., A. Jonas, S. Reimer and D. Spooner, 'Governance, Institutional Capacity and Partnerships in Local Economic Development: Theoretical Issues and Empirical Evidence from the Humber Sub-Region', *Transactions of the Institute of British Geographers*, 26 (2001), pp. 103–9.

Gibbs, G., 'Co-Options: Growing from Tiny Acorns', *Guardian* (25 April, 1995).

Gibson, E. and E. Calvo, 'Electoral Coalitions and Market Reforms: Evidence from Argentina', in *XX International Congress of the Latin American Studies Association* (Guadalajara: Mexico, 1997).

Giddens, A., *The Constitution of Society: Outline of the Theory of Structuration* (Cambridge: Polity Press, 1984).

Gilbert, E., and E. Helleiner (eds), *Nation-States and Money: The Past, Present and Future of National Currencies* (London, New York: Routledge, 1999).

Gomez, G., 'Le Réseau De Trueque Zone Ouest, Partenaire De L'économie Locale', in J. Blanc (eds), *Rapport Exclusion Et Liens Financiers 2005–06, Monnaies Sociales* (Paris: Economica, 2006), pp. 497–513.

Gonzalez Bombal, I. (ed), *Respuestas De La Sociedad Civil a La Emergencia Social* (Buenos Aires: Cedes, 2003).

—, 'Sociabilidad en las Clases Medias en Descenso: Experiencias en el Trueque', in L. Beccaria, S. Feldman, I. González Bombal, G. Kessler, M. Murmis and M. Svampa (eds.), *Sociedad y Sociabilidad en la Argentina de los 90* (Buenos Aires: Universidad Nacional de General Sarmiento and Editorial Biblos, 2002), pp. 97–136.

—, F. Leoni and M. Luzzi, 'Nuevas Redes Sociales: Los Clubes De Trueque', in *Respuestas de la Sociedad Civil a la Emergencia Social: Brasil y Argentina Comparten Experiencias* (Buenos Aires: CEDES - UNGS, 2002).

González de la Rocha, M., 'Are Poor Households Coping? Assets, Vulnerability and Decreasing Opportunities', *Development and Society*, 30:2 (2001), pp. 1–40.

Graham, C., *Safety Nets, Politics and the Poor: Transitions to Market Economies* (Washington, DC: The Brookings Institution, 1994).

Granovetter, M., 'Economic Action and Social Structure: The Problem of Embeddedness', *American Journal of Sociology*, 91:3 (1985), pp. 481–510.

Granovetter, M., and R. Swedberg (eds), *The Sociology of Economic Life* (Boulder, CO: Westview Press, 1992).

Greco, T., *Money: Understanding and Creating Alternatives to Legal Tender* (White River Junction, VT: Chelsea Green, 2001).

Greif, A., P. Milgrom and B. Weingast, 'Coordination, Commitment and Enforcement: The Case of the Merchant Guild', *Journal of Political Economy*, 102:4 (1994), pp. 74–6.

Grugel, J., and M. P. Riggirozzi. 'The Return of the State in Argentina', *International Affairs*, 83:1 (2007), pp. 87–107.

Guidotti, P., and C. Rodríguez, 'Dollarization in Latin America: Gresham's Law in Reverse?', *IMF Staff Papers*, 239 (1992), pp. 518–44.

Gwynne, R., and D. Kay, *Latin America Transformed* (London: Arnold Editors, 1999).

Hall, P., *Governing the Economy: The Politics of Stated Intervention in Britain and France* (Oxford and New York: Oxford University Press, 1986).

Harman, C., 'Argentina: Rebellion at the Sharp End of the World Crisis', *International Social-ism*, 94 (2002), pp. 3–48.

Hay, C., 'Globalisation and the Institutional Re-Embedding of Markets: The Political Economy of Price Formation in the Bordeaux En Primeur Market', *New Political Economy*, 12:2 (2007), pp. 185–209.

Hayek, F. A. *The Road to Serfdom* (London: Routledge, 1946).

—, *Individualism and Economic Order* (London and Chicago, IL: Routledge and University of Chicago Press, 1948).

—, *Rules and Order, Book 1 of Law, Legislation and Liberty: A New Statement of the Liberal Principles of Justice and Political Economy* (London: Routledge and Kegan Paul, 1973).

—, *Studies in Philosophy, Politics and Economics* (Chicago, IL: University of Chicago Press, 1967).

—, *Denationalization of Money* (London: Institute of Economic Affairs, 1976).

—, and W.W. Bartley, *The Fatal Conceit: The Errors of Socialism* (London: Routledge, 1988).

Helmsing, A. H. J., 'Local Economic Development. New Generations of Actors, Policies, and Instruments for Africa', *Public Administration and Development*, 23:1 (2003), pp. 67–76.

—, 'Partnerships, Meso-Institutions and Learning: New Local and Regional Economic Development Initiatives in Latin America', in I. Baud and J. Post (eds), *Re-Aligning Actors in an Urbanized World: Governance and Institutions from a Development Perspective* (Ashgate: Aldershot, 2002), pp. 79–101.

Helper, S., 'Comparative Supplier Relations in the US and Japanese Auto Industries: An Exit - Voice Approach', *Business Economic History*, 19 (1990), pp. 153–62.

Heymann, D., 'Políticas De Reforma Y Comportamiento Macroeconómico', in B. Kosacoff and D. Heymann (eds), *La Argentina De Los Noventa: Desempeño Económico En Un Contexto De Reformas* (Buenos Aires: EUDEBA and CEPAL Naciones Unidas, 2000), pp. 37–176.

Hintze, S. (ed.), *Trueque y Economía Solidaria* (Universidad Nacional de General Sarmiento and Programa de Naciones Unidas para el Desarrollo, Buenos Aires: Prometeo Libros 2003).

—, 'Desarrollo y Crisis del Trueque en la Argentina. Condiciones Para la Recuperación de la Experiencia' (mimeo, 2005).

—, 'La Construccion Mediatica Del Trueque En La Argentina', in J. Blanc (eds), *Exclusion Et Liens Financiers - Rapport Du Centre Walras 2005- Monnaies Sociales* (Paris: Economica, 2006), pp. 443–58.

Hirota, Y., 'The RGT in Argentina' (MA Thesis, University of Tokyo, 2002).

Hirst, P., *Associative Democracy: New Forms of Economic and Social Governance* (Cambridge and Oxford: Polity Press Disent and Blackwell, 1994).

—, 'Democracy and Governance', in J. Pierre (ed.), *Debating Governance: Authority, Steering and Democracy* (Oxford: Oxford University Press, 2000), pp.13–35.

Hodgson, G., 'The Ubiquity of Habits and Rules', *Cambridge Journal of Economics*, 21 (1997), pp. 663–84.

—, 'The Approach of Institutional Economics', *Journal of Economic Literature*, 36 (1998), pp. 166–92.

—, *Evolution and Institutions: On Evolutionary Economics and the Evolution of Economics* (Cheltenham: Edward Elgar, 1999).

—, 'What Is the Essence of Institutional Economics?', *Journal of Economic Issues*, 34:2 (2000), pp. 317–29.

—, 'Reconstitutive Downward Causation: Social Structure and the Development of Institutional Agency', in E. Fullbrook (eds), *Intersubjectivity in Economics: Agents and Structures* (London: Routledge, 2002), pp. 159–80.

—, 'The Hidden Persuaders: Institutions and Individuals in Economic Theory', *Cambridge Journal of Economics*, 27 (2003), pp. 159–75.

—, 'John R. Commons and the Foundations of Institutional Economics', *Journal of Economic Issues*, 37:3 (2003), pp. 547–76.

—, *The Evolution of Institutional Economics: Agency, Structure and Darwinism in American Institutionalism* (London: Routledge, 2004).

—, 'What Are Institutions?', *Journal of Economic Issues*, 40:1 (2006), pp. 1–25.

—, 'Institutions and Individuals: Interaction and Evolution', *Organization Studies*, 28:1 (2007), pp. 95–111.

Hodgson, G., 'On the Institutional Foundations of Law: The Insufficiency of Custom and Private Ordering', in *IX Workshop on Institutional Economics* (Hatfield (UK): University of Hertfordshire, 2007).

Hollingsworth, G., and R. Boyer, 'Coordination of Economic Actors and Social Systems of Production', in J. R. Hollingsworth and R. Boyer (eds), *Contemporary Capitalism* (Cambridge: Cambridge University Press, 1997), pp. 1–48.

— (eds), *Contemporary Capitalism* (Cambridge University Press: Cambridge, 1997).

—, P. Schmitter and W. Streeck, *Governing Capitalist Economies: Performance and Control of Economic Sectors* (Oxford and New York: Oxford University Press, 1994).

Hudson, R., 'The Learning Economy, the Learning Firm and the Learning Region: A Sympathetic Critique of the Limits to Learning', *European Urban and Regional Studies*, 6 (1999), pp. 59–72.

Ingham, G., 'Money Is a Social Relation', *Review of Social Economy*, 54:5 (1996), pp. 507–29.

—, 'On the Underdevelopment of the Sociology of Money', *Acta Sociologica*, 41:1 (1998), pp. 1–17.

—, 'Capitalism, Money and Banking: A Critique of Recent Historical Sociology', *British Journal of Sociology*, 50:1 (1999), pp. 76–96.

Ingham, G., 'Fundamentals of a Theory of Money: Untangling Fine, Lapavitsas and Zelizer', *Economy and Society*, 30:3 (2001), pp. 304–23.

Jackson, W., 'Social Structure in Economic Theory', *Journal of Economic Issues*, 37:3 (2003), pp. 727–46.

Jayaraman, R., and M. Oak., 'The Signalling Role of Municipal Currencies in Local Development', *Economica*, 72:288 (2005), pp. 597–613.

Jessop, B., 'Survey Article: The Regulation Approach', *Journal of Political Philosophy*, 5:3 (1997), pp. 287–326.

—, 'The Rise of Governance and the Risks of Failure: The Case of Economic Development', *International Social Science Journal*, 155 (1998), pp. 29–45.

—, *The Parisian Regulation School* (Aldershot: Edward Elgar, 2001).

Joas, H., *The Creativity of Action* (Chicago, IL: Chicago University Press, 1996).

Jonas, A. E., 'In Search of Order: Traditional Business Reformism and the Crisis of Neo-Liberalism in Massachussets', *Transactions of the Institute of British Geographers*, 21 (1996), pp. 617–34.

Jones, M., and G MacLeod, 'Towards a Regional Renaissance? Reconfiguring and Rescaling England's Economic Governance', *Transactions of the Institute of British Geographers*, 24 (1999), pp. 295–313.

Kennedy, M., *Interest and Inflation Free Money* (Philadelphia, PA: New Society, 1995).

Kessler, G. 'Algunas Implicancias de la Experiencia de Desocupación para el Individuo y su Familia', in L. Beccaria and N. López (eds.), *Sin Trabajo: Las Características del Desempleo y sus Efectos en la Sociedad Argentina* (Buenos Aires: UNICEF and Losada, 1996), pp. 111–60.

Keynes, J. M., *A Treatise on Money*, 2 vols (New York: Harcourt, Brace and Co., 1930/1976).

Kollock, P. Article, 'Managing the Virtual Commons: Cooperation and Conflict in Computer Communities' (1994), http://www.sscnet.ucla.edu/soc/csoc/papers/virtcomm/Virtcomm.htm#Virtual_Commons_1, accessed 1 September 2008.

Kosacoff, B., *El Desafío De La Competitividad* (Buenos Aires: CEPAL-Alianza, 1993).

—,*Corporate Strategy under Structural Adjustment in Argentina: Responses by Industrial Firms to a New Set of Uncertainties* (Basingstoke: Macmillan Press, 2000).

— (ed.), *El Desempeño Industrial Argentino: Más Allá De La Sustitución De Importaciones* (Buenos Aires: CEPAL Naciones Unidas, 2000).

—, and G. M. Gomez, 'Industrialización en un Contexto de Estabilización y Apertura Externa. El Caso Argentino en los Noventa', in B. Kosacoff (ed.), *El Desempeño Industrial Argentino: Más Allá De La Sustitución De Importaciones* (Buenos Aires: CEPAL Naciones Unidas, 2000), pp. 275–302.

—, and D. Heymann (eds), *La Argentina De Los Noventa: Desempeño Económico En Un Contexto De Reformas* (Buenos Aires: EUDEBA and CEPAL Naciones Unidas, 2000), vol. 1.

Krause, M. 'Las Limitaciones Del Trueque', in S. Hintze (ed.), *Trueque y Economía Solidaria* (Universidad Nacional de General Sarmiento and Programa de Naciones Unidas para el Desarrollo, Buenos Aires: Prometeo Libros, 2003), pp.107–20.

Lane, C., *Industry and Society in Europe* (Aldershot: Edward Elgar, 1995).

Lane, D. F., Malerba, R. Maxfield and L. Orsenigo, 'Choice and Action', *Journal of Evolutionary Economics*, 6:1 (1996), pp. 43–76.

Lang, P.,*Lets Work: Rebuilding the Local Community* (Bristol: Grover, 1984).

Larson, A., 'Network Dyads in Entrepreneurial Settings: A Study of Governance of Exchange Processes', *Administrative Science Quarterly*, 37 (1992), pp. 76–104.

Laville, J. L., B. Eme and J. P. Maréchal, 'Economía Solidaria: 'Ilusión O Vía De Futuro?' (Paper presented at the Mesa redonda sobre la economía Solidaria, Universidad de verano, Arles, France, August 2001).

Lawson, T. *Economics and Reality* (London: Routledge, 1997).

—, 'Institutionalism: On the Need to Firm up Notions of Social Structure and the Human Subject', *Journal of Economic Issues*, 37:1 (2003), pp. 175–207.

Lecaro, P. and B. Altschuler, 'Políticas Sociales y Desarrollo Local, Dos Experiencias Diversas: Club del Trueque y Unión de Trabajadores Desocupados (UTD) de Mosconi' (Paper presented at the Conference in *Congreso Nacional de Políticas Sociales 'Estrategias de articulación de políticas, programas y proyectos sociales en Argentina'* (Buenos Aires: Universidad de Quilmes, 2002).

Lee, R. 'Moral Money? LETS and the Social Construction of Local Economic Geographies in Southeast England', *Environment and Planning A*, 28 (1996), pp. 1377–94.

—, and J. Wills (eds.), *Geographies of Economies* (London: Arnold, 1997).

Leoni, F. 'Ilusión para Muchos, Alternativa para Pocos. La Práctica del Trueque en los Sectores Populares', (MA Thesis: Universidad Nacional de General Sarmiento, 2003).

—, and M. Luzzi, 'Nuevas Redes Sociales: Los Clubes De Trueque', in I. Gonzalez Bombal (eds.), *Respuestas De La Sociedad Civil a La Emergencia Social* (Buenos Aires: Cedes, 2003), pp. 13–42.

—, and M. Luzzi, *Rasguñando la Lona: La Experiencia de un Club de Trueque en el Conurbano Bonaerense* (Buenos Aires: CLASPO, 2003).

LETSLinkUK, 'What Are Councils Doing for Lets? Lets-Link!', *LETS Magazine*, 3 (1997), pp. 14–15.

Levitsky, S., *Transforming Labor-Based Parties in Latin America: Argentine Peronism in Comparative Perspective* (Cambridge: Cambridge University Press, 2003).

Leyshon, A. and N. Thrift, *Money / Space* (London: Routledge 1996).

Lietaer, B.,*The Future of Money: Creating New Wealth, Work and a Wiser World* (London: Century, 2001).

Llach, L., 'A Depression in Perspective: The Economics and the Political Economy of Argentina's Crisis of the Millenium', in F. Fiorucci and M. Klein (eds), *The Argentine Crisis at the Turn of the Millenium: Causes, Consequences and Explanations* (Amsterdam: Aksant, 2004), pp. 56–89.

Lloyd-Sherlock, P., *Old Age and Urban Poverty in the Developing World: The Shanty Towns of Buenos Aires* (London: Macmillan, 1997).

—, 'Policy, Distribution and Poverty in Argentina since Redemocratisation', *Latin American Perspectives*, 24:6 (1997), pp. 22–55.

Lodola, G. 'Protesta Popular Y Redes Clientelares En La Argentina: El Reparto Federal Del Plan Trabajar (1996-2001)', *Desarrollo Económico*, 44:176 (2005), pp. 515–35.

Luhman, N., *Trust and Power* (Chichester: Wiley, 1979).

Lvovich, D., 'Colgados De La Soga: La Experiencia Del Tránsito Desde La Clase Media a La Nueva Pobreza En La Ciudad De Buenos Aires', in M. Svampa (ed.), *Desde Abajo: La Transformación De Las Identidades Sociales* (Buenos Aires: UNGS and Biblos, 2000), pp. 51–80.

MacLeod, G., 'The Learning Region in an Age of Austerity: Capitalizing on Knowledge, Entrepreneurialism and Reflexive Capitalism', *Geoforum*, 31 (2000), pp. 219–32.

—, 'Beyond Soft Institutionalism: Accumulation, Regulation and Their Geographical Fixes', *Environment and Planning*, A33 (2001), pp. 1145–67.

—, and M. Goodwin, 'Reconstructing an Urban and Regional Political Economy: On the State, Politics, Scale and Explanation', *Political Geography*, 18 (1999), pp. 697–730.

Marglin, S., 'Understanding Capitalism: Control Versus Efficiency', in B. Gustafsson (ed.), *Power and Economic Institutions* (Aldershot: Edward Elgar, 1991), pp. 225–52.

Martin, R., 'Institutional Approaches in Economic Geography', in T. Barnes and E. Sheppard (eds), *Companion to Economic Geography* (Oxford: Blackwell, 2001).

McKinnon, R. I., 'Spontaneous Order on the Road Back from Socialism: An Asian Perspective', *The American Economic Review*, 82:2 (1992), pp. 31–6.

Meyer, M., 'The Growth of Public and Private Bureaucracies', in S. Zukin and P. DiMaggio (eds), *Structures of Capital: The Social Organization of the Economy* (Cambridge: Cambridge University Press, 1990), pp. 153–72.

Meyer, J., and B. Rowan, 'Institutionalised Organisations: Formal Structure as Myth and Ceremony', *American Journal of Sociology*, 83 (1977), pp. 340–63.

Minujin, A. (ed.), *Cuesta Abajo: Los Nuevos Pobres: Efectos De La Crisis En La Sociedad Argentina*, 2nd edn (Buenos Aires: Losada and Unicef, 1993).

—, 'Estrujados. La Clase Media En América Latina', in E. Villanueva (eds.), *Empleo y Globalización: La Nueva Cuestión Social en la Argentina* (Buenos Aires: Universidad Nacional de Quilmes, 1997), pp. 85–106.

—, and E. Anguita, *La Clase Media - Seducida y Abandonada* (Buenos Aires: Edhasa, 2004).

Mitchell, J., 'Hierarchies: Introduction', in G. Thompson, J. Frances, J. Mitchell and R. Levacic (eds), *Markets, Hierarchies and Networks: The Coordination of Social Life* (London and Milton Keynes: Sage and Open University, 1991), pp.168–72.

Morisio, C. '¿Complementan los Clubes de Trueque al Empleo en el Mercado Formal?', *MA Thesis* (Buenos Aires: Instituto Superior Economistas de Gobierno, 1998).

Moser, C. 'The Asset Vulnerability Framework: Reassessing Urban Poverty Reduction Strategies', *World Development*, 26:1 (1998), pp. 1–19.

Moulaert, F., and O. Ailenei, 'Social Economy, Third Sector and Solidarity Relations: A Conceptual Synthesis from History to Present', *Urban Studies*, 42 (2005), pp. 2037–54.

Munck, R., R. Falcón and B. Galitelli, *Argentina: From Anarchism to Peronism: Workers, Unions and Politics, 1855-1985* (London and New York: ZED Books, 1987).

Mundell, R. A., 'A Theory of Optimum Currency Areas', *American Economic Review*, 51 (1961), pp. 657–65.

Murmis, M. and S. Feldman, 'La Heterogeneidad Social De Las Pobrezas', in A. Minujin (eds.), *Cuesta Abajo: Los Nuevos Pobres: Efectos De La Crisis En La Sociedad Argentina* (Buenos Aires: Losada and UNICEF, 1993), pp. 45–92.

Murmis, M. and J.C. Portantiero, *Estudios Sobre Los Orígenes Del Peronismo* (Buenos Aires: Siglo Vientiuno Argentina Editores, 1972).

Nelson, R., 'Recent Evolutionary Theorizing About Economic Change', *Journal of Economic Literature*, 33:1 (1995), pp. 48–90.

Nelson, R., and S. Winter, *An Evolutionary Theory of Economic Change* (Cambridge, MA: The Balknap Press of Harvard University Press, 1982).

Nooteboom, B. (ed.), *Learning and Innovation in Organizations and Economies* (Oxford: University Press, 2000).

Norman, K., 'Barter Nation', *Buenos Aires Herald* (2002).

North, D. 'Institutions and Economic Growth: An Historical Introduction', *World Development*, 17:9 (1989), pp. 1319–32.

—, *Institutions, Institutional Change and Economic Performance* (Cambridge: Cambridge University Press, 1990).

—, 'The New Institutional Economics and Development', in *Economics Working Paper Archive*, 1-8 (St Louis, MO: Washington University at St Louis, 1995), pp.1–8, available online at http://www.nju.edu.cn/cps/site/NJU/njuc/dep/shangyuan/2.doc.

—, 'Have Confidence and Cast Your Nets into Deep Waters – Community Responses to Neo-Liberalism in Argentina' (Paper presented at the *Association of American Geographers* New Orleans, LO, 2003).

North, P. 'Scaling Alternative Economic Practices? Some Lessons from Alternative Currencies', *Transactions of the Institute of British Geographers*, 30 (2005), pp. 221–33.

—, *Alternative Currency Movements as a Challenge to Globalisation? A Case Study of Manchester's Local Currency Networks* (Aldershot: Ashgate, 2006).

—, *Money and Liberation: The Micropolitics of Alternative Currency Movements* (Minneapolis & London: University of Minnesota Press, 2007).

North, P. 'Voices from the Trueque: Argentina's Barter Networks Resisting Neoliberalisation', in A. Smith, A. Stenning and K. Willis (eds.), *Social Justice and Neoliberalism: Global Perspectives* (London: Zed, 2008), pp. 30–54.

— and U. Huber, 'Alternative Spaces of The "Argentinazo"', *Antipode*, 36:5 (2004), pp. 963–84.

Novick, M., 'Reconversión Segmentada en la Argentina, Empresas, Mercado de Trabajo de Relaciones Laborales a Fines de los 90', in *Reestructuracion Productiva, Mercado de Trabajo y Sindicatos en América Latina* (Buenos Aires: Consejo Latinoamericano de Ciencias Sociales (CLACSO), 2000), pp. 49–72.

O'Doherty, R., J. Dürrschmidt and D. Purdue, 'Cultural Innovation in Alternative Milieux: LETS as CED' (Paper presented at the *Regional Studies Association 'Community Economic Development: Linking the Grassroots to Regional Economic Development'*, South Africa, November 1997).

Offe, C., and G. Heinze, *Beyond Employment: Time, Work and the Informal Economy* (Cambridge Polity Press, 1992).

Onken, W. 'Ein Vergessenes Kapitel Der Wirtschaftsgeschichte – Schwanenkirchen, Wörgl Und Andere Freigeldexperimente', *Zeitschrift für Sozialökonomie*, 57:58 (1983), pp. 60–72.

Ovalles, E., 'Argentina Es el País del Mundo en el cual el Fenómeno del Trueque Tiene Mayor Dimensión Social', *Carta Económica* (Centro de Estudios Nueva Mayoría Buenos Aires: May 2002), pp. 42–5.

Oviedo, J., 'Las Implacables Reglas del Mercado', *La Nación* (17 August 2003).

Pacione, M. 'The Ecclesiastical Community of Interest as a Response to Urban Poverty and Deprivation', *Transactions of the Institute of British Geographers*, 15:2 (1990), pp. 193–204.

—, 'Local Exchange Trading Systems as a Response to the Globalisation of Capitalism', *Urban Studies*, 34:8 (1997), pp. 1179–99.

—, M. 'The Other Side of the Coin: Local Currency as a Response to the Globalisation of Capital. Debates and Reviews, Ed. by M. W. Danson', *Regional Studies*, 33:1 (1999), pp. 63–72.

Palomino, H. and J. Schvarzer, 'El Mercado de Trabajo en la Argentina: Del Pleno Empleo al Colapso', *Encrucijadas: Revista de la Universidad de Buenos Aires* (May 1996), pp. 8–17.

Palomino, H. and J Schvarzer, 'Entre La Informalidad y el Desempleo. Una Perspectiva de Largo Plazo sobre el Mercado de Trabajo en la Argentina', *Realidad Económica, Instituto Argentino para el Desarrollo Económico, Buenos Aires* (10 April–15 May 1996), pp. 17–43.

Parysow, J., and E Bogani, 'Perspectivas de Desarrollo Económico y Social para las Mujeres Pobres y Empobrecidas en los Clubes del Trueque. Estudio De Caso: La Bernalesa' (Paper presented at the *Seminario Las Caras de la Pobreza*, Buenos Aires, 2002).

Pastor Jr, M., and C. Wise, 'Stabilization and Its Discontents: Argentina's Economic Restructuring in the 1990s', *World Development*, 27:3 (1999), pp. 477–503.

Pearson, R. 'Income Generation Strategies in a Globalising World: Learning from International Experience' (Paper presented at the *Seminario Internacional hacia una sociedad más igualitaria* Buenos Aires: Ministry of Social Development and Environment, 2000).

—, 'Argentina's Barter Network: New Currency for New Times', *Bulletin of Latin American Research*, 22:2 (2003), pp. 214–30.

Pierre, J., and B.G. Peters (eds), *Governance, Politics and the State* (Houndmills: MacMillan, 2000).

Plasencia, A., 'La Oxidación Monetaria y la Moneda Social. Aportes Teóricos y Análisis de un Caso: La Moneda Social Oxidable de Venado Tuerto, Pcia. De Santa Fe', (MA Thesis, Universidad Nacional de General Sarmiento, 2008).

Platteau, J. P., 'Behind the Market Stage Where Real Societies Exist - Published in Two Issues: Part 1: The Role of Public and Private Order Institutions', *Journal of Development Studies*, 30:3 (1994), pp. 533–77.

—, 'Behind the Market Stage Where Real Societies Exist - Published in Two Issues: Part 2: 'The Role of Moral Norms', *Journal of Development Studies*, 30:3 (1994), pp. 753–817.

Platteau, J. P. *Institutions, Social Norms and Economic Development* (Amsterdam: Harwood Academic Publishers & Routledge, 2000).

Polanyi, K., 'The Economy as Instituted Process', in M. Granovetter and R. Swedberg (eds.), *The Sociology of Economic Life* (Boulder: Westview Press, 1992), pp. 29–52.

Polanyi, K. *The Great Transformation: The Political and Economic Origin of Our Times* (New York and Boston, MA: Beacon Press, 1957).

Powell, J., 'Petty Capitalism, Perfecting Capitalism or Post-Capitalism?: Lessons from the Argentine Barter Network', *Working Paper* (The Hague: Institute of Social Studies, 2002).

Powell, J., 'The Mouse That Roared: State Insecurity and Thailand's First Community Currency System', *Watershed*, 6:1 (2000), pp. 48–53.

Powell, J. and M. Salverda, Article, 'A Snapshot of Community Currencies in Europe and North America' (1998), http://www.ccdev.lets.net, accessed 1 January 2006.

Powell, W. and P. Di Maggio (eds), *The New Institutionalism in Organisational Analysis* (Chicago, IL: Chicago University Press, 1991).

Pozzi, P., 'Popular Upheaval and Capitalist Transformation in Argentina', *Latin American Perspectives*, 27:5 (2000), pp. 63–87.

Primavera, H., *Cómo Formar Un Primer Club De Trueque Pensando En La Economía Global* (Medellín (Bogotá): Redlases, 1999).

—, 'Editorial', *Revista Trueque* 2:3 (Buenos Aires: December 1999), p. 3.

—, 'Política Social, Imaginación y Coraje: Reflexiones sobre la Moneda Social, Reforma y Democracia', *Revista del CLAD (Caracas)*, 17 (1999), pp. 161–88.

—, Article, 'Moneda Social: Gattopardismo O Ruptura De Paradigma?' (2001), http://money.socioeco.org, accessed 1 November 2007.

—, 'Los Clubes De Trueque Deben Preservar El Sentido Solidario', *Clarín*, 24-04-2002 (2002).

—, '¿Red? ¿Global? ¿De Trueque? ¿Solidario? O Cómo Desarmar la que Pudo Haber Sido una Hermosa Revolución Pacífica', mimeo (2002).

—, 'Riqueza, Dinero y Poder: El Efímero "Milagro Argentino" de las Redes de Trueque', in, S. Hintze (eds.), *Trueque y Economía Solidaria* (Universidad Nacional de General Sarmiento and Programa de Naciones Unidas para el Desarrollo, Buenos Aires: Prometeo Libros, 2003), pp.121–44

— and F. Wautiez, 'Social Money: Lever of the New Economy Paradigm' (Paper presented at the *Conference on Social Money* (Findhorn, Finland, June 2002).

Raco, M., 'Competition, Collaboration and the New Industrial Districts: Examining the Institutional Turn in Local Economic Development', *Urban Studies*, 36 (1999), pp. 951–68.

Razeto, L. *Los Caminos De La Economía Solidaria* (Buenos Aires: Luhmen-Humanitas, 1997).

Reisman, D., *Theories of Collective Action: Downs, Olson and Hirsch* (Basingstoke: Macmillan, 1990).

Rochon, L. P. and S. Rossi, *Modern Theories of Money: The Nature and Role of Money in Capitalist Economies* (Cheltenham: Edward Elgar, 2003).

Ronit, K., and V. Schneider, 'Global Governance through Private Organizations', *Governance: An international Journal of Policy, Administration and Institutions*, 12:3 (1999), pp. 243–66.

Rosenau, J. N., and E. O. Czempiel (eds.), *Governance without Government: Order and Change in World Politics* (Cambridge: Cambridge University Press, 1992).

Roxborough, I., 'Citizenship and Social Movements under Neoliberalism', in W. Smith and R Korzeniewics (eds), *Politics, Social Change, and Economic Restructuring in Latin America* (Coral Gables, FL: University of Miami and North-South Center Press, 1997), pp. 57–78.

Saiegh, S., and M. Tommasi, 'Why Is Argentina's Fiscal Federalism So Inefficient? Entering the Labyrinth' (Paper presented at the Conference *Modernization and Institutional Development in Argentina* (Buenos Aires: PNUD, 1999).

Sartori, G., 'Market, Capitalism, Planning and Technocracy', in G. Thompson, J. Frances, J. Mitchell and R. Levacic (eds), *Markets, Hierarchies and Networks: The Coordination of Social Life* (London and Milton Keynes: Sage and Open University Press, 1991), pp.156–203.

Sawers, L., *The Other Argentina* (Boulder, CO: Westview Press, 1996).

Sbragia, A. 'Governance, the State and the Market: What Is Going On?' *Governance: An International Journal of Policy and Administration*, 13:2 (2000), pp. 243–450.

Schacter, M. *Public Sector Reform in Developing Countries: Issues, Lessons and Future Directions*, (Ottawa: Policy Branch, Canadian International Development Agency, 2000).

Scharpf, F. W. *Games Real Actors Play: Actor-Centered Institutionalism in Policy Research* (Boulder, CO : Westview Press, 1997).

Schaumberg, H., 'In Search of Alternatives: The Making of Grassroots Politics and Power in Argentina', *Bulletin of Latin American Research*, 27:3 (2008), pp. 368–87.

Schotter, A. *Free Market Economics: A Critical Appraisal* (New York: St. Martin's Press, 1985).

Schuldt, J., *Dineros Alternativos: Para El Desarrollo Local* (Lima: Universidad del Pacífico, 1997).

Schumpeter, J., *History of Economic Analysis* (London: Allen & Unwin, 1994).

Schvarzer, J., and H. Finkelstein, 'Análisis - Bonos, Cuasi Monedas Y Política Económica', *Revista Realidad Económica IADE,* (2003).

Scott, J. C. *The Moral Economy of the Peasant: Rebellion and Subsistence in Southeast Asia* (New Haven, CT: Yale University Press, 1976).

Scott, R., *Institutions and Organizations*, 2nd. ed (Thousand Oaks, CA: Sage, 2001).

Seabright, P. (ed.), *The Vanishing Rouble: Barter Networks and Non-Monetary Transactions in Post-Soviet Societies* (Cambridge: Cambridge University Press, 2002).

Selgin, G., *The Theory of Free Banking: Money Supply under Competitive Note Issue* (Totowa, NJ and Washington, D.C: Rowman & Littlefield and the Cato Institute, 1988).

—, 'Salvaging Gresham's Law: The Good, the Bad and the Illegal', *Journal of Money, Credit and Banking*, 28:4 (1996), pp. 637–49.

Seyfang, G. 'Community Currencies: A Small Change for a Green Economy. An Evaluation of Local Exchange Trading Schemes (LETS) as a Tool for Sustainable Local Development', *Environment and Planning A*, 33:6 (2001), pp. 975–96.

—, 'The Euro, the Pound and the Shell in Our Pockets: Rationales for Complementary Currencies in a Global Economy', *New Political Economy*, 5:2 (2001), pp. 227–46.

—, 'Money That Makes a Change: Community Currencies, North and South', *Gender and Development*, 9:1 (2001), pp. 60–9.

—, 'Working for the Fenland Dollar: An Evaluation of Local Exchange Trading Schemes (LETS) as an Informal Employment Strategy to Tackle Social Exclusion', *Work, Employment and Society*, 15:3 (2001), pp. 581–93.

—, 'Tackling Social Exclusion with Community Currencies: Learning from LETS to Time Banks', *International Journal of Community Currency Research*, 6 (2002), pp. 1–11.

Shafaeddin, S. M. 'Who Is the Master? Who Is the Servant? Market or Government? An Alternative Approach: Towards a Coordination System', *Discussion papers*, (Geneva: UNCTAD, 2004), http://www.unctad.org/en/docs/osgdp20049_en.pdf H. A. Simon, *Models of Thought* (New Haven: Yale University Press, 1979), last accessed December 2007.

Slater, D., and F. Tonkiss, *Market Society: Markets and Modern Social Theory* (Cambridge and Malden, MA: Polity Press and Blackwell Publishers, 2001).

Smith, A., *The Wealth of Nations* (London: Everyman's Library, 1776/1991).

Smith, W. and R. Korzeniewics (eds.), *Politics, Social Change, and Economic Restructuring in Latin America,* (Coral Gables, FL: University of Miami and North-South Center Press, 1997).

Stark, D. 'Path Dependence and Privatization Strategies in East Central Europe', *East European Politics and Societies*, 1:6 (1992), pp. 17–54.

Steinmo, S., and K. Thelen, 'Historical Institutionalism in Comparative Politics', in S. Steinmo, K. Thelen and F. Longstreth (eds), *Structuring Politics* (Cambridge: Cambridge University Press, 1992).

Stiglitz, J. 'Dependence of Quality on Price', *Journal of Economic Literature*, 25 (1987), pp. 1–48.

—, 'Más Instrumentos y Metas Más Amplias para el Desarrollo. Hacia el Consenso Post-Washington', *Desarrollo Económico (Buenos Aires)*, 38:151 (1998), pp. 691–722.

Storper, M., 'The Resurgence of Regional Economies, Ten Years Later: The Region as a Nexus of Untraded Interdependencies', *European Urban and Regional Studies*, 2:3 (1995), pp. 191–221.

Strange, S., *States and Markets* (London: Pinter, 1988).

Streb, J., 'Y Si No Hay Más Remedio... Inflación, Desconfianza y la Desintegración del Sistema Financiero en la Argentina', *Desarrollo Económico (Buenos Aires)*, 38 (1998), pp. 199–215.

Streeck, W., *Social Institutions and Economic Performance* (Newbury Park, CA and London: Sage, 1992).

—, and P. C. Schmitter, *Private Interest Government: Beyond Market and State* (London: Sage, 1985).

Swedberg, R. 'Socioeconomics and the New Battle of the Methods - Towards a Paradigm Shift?', *Journal of Behavioural Economics*, 19:2 (1990), pp. 141–54.

Taris, J., Article, 'Lets Groups around the World.' http://www.lets-linkup.com, accessed 1 August 2007.

Tenti Fanfani, E., 'Cuestiones de Exclusión Social y Política', in A. Minujin and E. Cosentino (eds), *Desigualdad y Exclusión: Desafíos para la Política Social en la Argentina de Fin de Siglo* (Buenos Aires: Losada - UNICEF, 1993), pp. 27–64.

Thomassen, J., and H. Schmitt, 'In Conclusion: Political Representation and Legitimacy in the European Union', in H. Schmitt and J. Thomassen (eds), *Political Representation and Legitimacy in the European Union* (Oxford: Oxford University Press, 1999), pp. 255–68.

Thompson, G., J. Frances, R. Levacic and J. Mitchell (eds), *Markets, Hierarchies and Networks: The Coordination of Social Life* (London and Milton Keynes: Sage and Open University Press, 1991).

Thorne, L., 'Local Exchange and Trading Systems in the UK: A Case of Re-Embedding?' *Environment and Planning A*, 28:8 (1996), pp. 1361–76.

Thrift, N. and A. Leyshon, 'Moral Geographies of Money', in E. Gilbert and G. Helleiner (eds), *Nation-States and Money: The Past, Present and Future of National Currencies* (London: Routledge, 1999), pp. 159–81.

Tibbett, R., *Alternative Currencies: A Challenge to Globalisation?* (London: Routledge, 1997).

Toffler, A., *The Third Wave* (London: Collins, 1980).

Tokman, V., 'La Especificidad y Generalidad del Problema del Empleo en el Contexto de América Latina', in L. Beccaria and N. López (eds.), *Sin Trabajo: Las Características del Desempleo y sus Efectos en la Sociedad Argentina* (Buenos Aires: UNICEF and Losada, 1996), pp. 47–81.

Torre, J. C., 'The Politics of Transformation in Historical Perspective', in W. Smith and R. Korzeniewics (eds), *Politics, Social Change, and Economic Restructuring in Latin America* (Coral Gables, FL: University of Miami and North-South Center Press, 1997), pp. 21–36.

UNCED, Agenda 21: The United Nations Program of Action from Rio (New York: UN Publications, 1992).

Underhill, G., 'States, Markets and Governance for Emerging Market Economies: Private Interests, the Public Good and the Legitimacy of the Development Process', *International Affairs*, 79:4 (2003), pp. 755–81.

Uzzi, B., 'The Sources and Consequences of Embeddedness for the Economic Performance of Organizations: The Network Effect', *American Sociological Review*, 61 (1996), pp. 674–98.

Vacs, A. 'Convergence and Dissension: Democracy, Markets and Structural Reform in World Perspective', in W. Smith, C. Acuña and E. Gamarra (eds.), *Democracy, Markets, and Structural Reform in Latin America: Argentina, Bolivia, Brazil, Chile, and Mexico* (Miami, FL: Lynne Rienner, 1994), pp. 67–100.

Van Dun, F. 'National Sovereignty and International Monetary Regimes', in K. Dowd and R. H. Timberlake (eds.), *Money and the Nation State: The Financial Revolution, Government and the World Monetary System* (New Brunswick and London: Transaction Publishers, 1998), pp. 47–76.

Van Kersbergen, K., and F. Van Waarden, '"Governance" as a Bridge between Disciplines: Cross-Disciplinary Inspiration Regarding Shifts in Governance and Problems of Governability, Accountability and Legitimacy', *European Journal of Political Research*, 43 (2004), pp. 143–71.

Van Waarden, F. 'Persistence of National Policy Styles: A Study of Their Institutional Foundations', in B. Unger and F. Van Waarden (eds.), *Convergence or Diversity? Internationalization and Economic Policy Response* (Avebury: Aldershot, 1995), pp. 56–76.

Veblen, T. 'The Vested Interests and the Common Man' (Kessinger Publishings, 1919/ 2004), http://books.google.com/books, accessed 9 January 2009.

Von Mises, L. *The Free and Prosperous Commonwealth: An Exposition of the Ideas of Classical Liberalism* (Princeton: Van Nostrand, 1962).

Von Muralt, A. 'Der Wörgl Versuch Mit Schwundgeld', in K. Schmitt (eds.), *Silvio Gesell- 'Marx' Del Anarchisten?* (Berlin: Karin Kramer Verlag, 1933), pp. 265–89.

Runciman. W. G. (ed.), *Maw Weber: Selections in Translations* (Cambridge: Cambridge University Press, 1978).

Wells, A. *Social Institutions* (London: Heinemann, 1970).

Wheelock, J. 'The Household in the Total Economy', in P. Ekins and M. Max-Neef (eds.), *Real Life Economics* (London and New York: Routledge, 1992), pp.124–36.

White, L., *Free Banking in Britain: Theory, Experience, Debate, 1800–1845* (Cambridge: Cambridge University Press, 1984).

Williams, C., 'Local Exchange and Trading Systems: A New Source of Work and Credit for the Poor and Unemployed?' *Environment and Planning A*, 28 (1996), pp. 1395–415.

Williams, C. 'An Appraisal of Local Exchange and Trading Systems (LETS) in the United Kingdom', *Local Economy*, 11:3 (1996), pp. 275–82.

Williams, C., and J. Windebank, 'The Formalisation of Work Thesis: A Critical Evaluation', *Futures*, 31 (1999), pp. 547–58.

Williams, C. and J. Windebank, 'Helping Each Other Out? Community Exchange in Deprived Neighbourhoods', *Community Development Journal*, 35:2 (2000), pp. 146–56.

Williams, C., and J. Windebank, 'Modes of Goods Acquisition in Deprived Neighbourhoods', *International Review of Retail, Distribution and Consumer Research*, 10:1 (2000), pp. 73–94.

Williams, C., T. Aldridge, R. Lee, A. Leyshon, N. Thrift and J. Tooke, 'Bridges into Work: An Evaluation of Local Exchange Trading Schemes', *Latest Developments in LETS and Time Money* (South Bank University, Bristol: The Policy Press, 2001), pp. 1–66.

Williams, P., P. Hubbard, D. Clark and N. Berkeley, 'Consumption, Exclusion and Emotion: The Social Geographies of Shopping', *Social and Cultural Geography*, 2:2 (2001), pp. 203–20.

Williamson, J., *The Progress of Policy Reform in Latin America* (Washington, D.C.: Institute for Internacional Economics, 1990).

Williamson, O. *Market and Hierarchies* (Cambridge, MA: Harvard University Press, 1975).

—, 'The Economics of Organisation: The Transaction Cost Approach', *American Journal of Sociology*, 87:3 (1981), pp. 548–77.

—, *The Economic Institutions of Capitalism: Firms, Markets and Relational Contracting* (New York and London: The Free Press and Macmillan, 1985).

—, O. 'The Lens of Contract: Private Ordering', *American Economic Review*, 92:2 (2002), pp. 438–43.

Wray, R. *Understanding Modern Money: The Key to Full Employment and Price Stability* (Cheltenham: Edward Elgar, 1998).

Wuyts, S., M. Colombo, S. Dutta and B. Nooteboom, 'Empirical Tests of Optimal Cognitive Distance', *Journal of Economic Behavior & Organization*, 58 (2003), pp. 277–302.

Zelizer, V. 'The Social Meaning of Money: "Special Monies"', *American Journal of Sociology*, 95 (1989), pp. 342–77.

INDEX

acceptance, 77, 97, 108, 111–12, 114, 123–4, 128–9, 132, 164, 186, 188, 190
accountability, 51, 100, 107, 113
accountancy system, 21–2, 27–9, 75, 78
action motive, 110, 121
adaptation, 35, 37, 79, 192
Agenda 21, 136
alternative, 2, 9, 26–7, 29, 30–1, 55, 71, 78, 94–5, 101, 104, 117, 125, 130, 136, 146–7, 162, 172, 178–9, 189, 191
Amin, Ash, 156
Angola, 57
anti-cyclical, 10, 59, 152, 181, 184
anti-PAR, 93, 95, 97–9, 100–2, 113–17, 119–20, 124
Asian crisis, 53
associational model, 110, 121–2, 128–9, 131–32, 138, 175, 187
Austria, 2, 24
autarchy, 95
authority, 37, 66, 76, 83, 103, 110, 132, 134, 176, 182, 187

Barrio Belgrano, 121, 125, 132, 139
barter, 2–5, 25–6, 29, 62, 70, 72, 74, 127, 169, 182
basic needs, 52, 89, 115, 149, 154, 183
Beckert, Jens, 68
Bernal, 5, 18, 70, 87, 95, 97
bimonetarism, 43, 45, 58, 78
Blanc, Jerome, 21, 134, 136, 147
bounded rationality, 82
Bowles, Samuel, 37
Boyer, Robert, 84, 110–11, 195
Braudel, Fernand, 63

Buenos Aires, 5, 17–8, 44, 49, 61, 65, 70, 75, 87–8, 90–3, 115, 120–2, 134, 137–9, 162, 166, 171, 218
business, 2, 9, 23, 25, 28–9, 31, 44, 48, 65–6, 75, 108, 115, 120, 138, 145, 146, 151, 157, 158, 161–3, 165–6, 169, 172, 175–6, 179, 181, 188

cacerolazos, 55–6
Cahn, Edward, 29
Capitán Bermúdez, 17, 121
Catholic Church, 62, 121, 132, 162, 168, 176
Cavallo, Domingo, 45, 183
CCS, 2, 3, 9, 21–2, 24–30, 103, 107, 133–4, 141, 184, 186
    in the world, 3, 4, 8, 9, 21–2, 26–9, 35–6, 39, 40–1, 50–2, 57–8, 65, 69, 78–9, 83–4, 91, 130–3, 136, 151, 171–2, 186–7, 189
central bank, 23–4, 32, 41, 45, 54, 66, 103, 134–5, 141,182–3
Centro Poriahyu, 139
Chandler, Alfred, 37
civil society, 2, 12, 21, 37, 42, 53, 55–6, 59, 66, 75, 107–9, 111, 156–7, 171
clientelistic networks, 50, 178, 188
Club de Trueque, 3, 4, 5, 16, 61, 65, 69, 73, 76, 78–9, 81, 87, 89, 91, 94, 98, 182, 186
club market, 64–7, 69, 71–3, 76–80, 84, 86–9, 92–3, 95, 121, 157, 174, 179, 181, 186, 191
Coase, Ronald, 82, 84
Cohen, Benjamin, 26

collective enterprises, 137, 168, 169, 170, 171, 174, 189, 196
Commons, John, 13, 82
community, 4, 8, 21–2, 26, 28–9, 30–1, 55, 91, 109, 110, 115, 121–2, 125, 128, 130, 132–3, 152, 157, 161, 170, 175–6, 181, 184, 187, 188
community currency systems *see* CCS
competition, 33, 46, 65, 85, 95, 97, 110, 164, 172
complementary currency systems *see* CCS
compliance, 13, 37, 83, 108, 110, 112, 119, 124–5, 137–9, 187, 191, 195–6, 198
Comunidades Solidarias, 121, 126, 139
conflicts, 8, 10, 37, 82–3, 95, 100, 108–9, 112, 127, 175, 187
Congress, 45, 114
consumption, 3, 5, 7, 8, 21, 26, 55, 58, 62, 64, 66, 71, 78, 79, 115, 145, 163, 165, 185
continuity, 61, 68, 70, 72, 80, 186, 191–3
Convertibility Plan, 41, 45, 50, 53, 55, 58
coordination, 27, 36–7, 61–3, 77, 84, 98, 109, 110, 120, 126, 128, 157, 181, 187
coordinator, 17, 89, 90–5, 97–8, 115–19, 121–9, 131–3, 137–9, 140, 143, 150, 174, 187–8
Coraggio, José Luis, 9
Córdoba, 91
Cornes, Richard, 64
corralito, 54
counter-cyclical *see* anti-cyclical
counterfeit *see* forgery
Covas, Horacio, 17, 71–7, 88–92, 98, 100, 124
credit, 21–2, 27–9, 53, 76–7, 135–6, 143–4, 166, 171, 175, 182
créditos, 2, 4, 25–6, 76–8, 89, 90, 92–9, 100–1, 112–19, 122, 124, 126–7, 129, 136–41, 143–4, 146–8, 155, 158, 160–1, 166, 168–9, 174, 176–9, 182–4, 188

De la Rua, Fernando, 55
De Sanzo, Carlos 17, 70–5, 78, 87, 90–2, 118, 124–6, 140
Del Valle, Carlos, 17, 91, 138
demurrage, 26, 119, 137, 163

denationalising money, 33
designed institutions, 15–6, 36, 45, 61–3, 66–7, 84, 90, 103, 186, 189–94, 197–8
developed countries, 83
developing countries, 36–7, 48, 59, 83, 136, 147, 150, 185, 191
development model, 53, 57
development strategy, 40–1, 50, 164, 171
Diaz Alejandro, Carlos, 38
disenfranchised, 2, 5, 6, 59, 65, 75, 79, 116, 120, 139, 151–3, 158, 166, 178, 181
    disenfranchised middle class, 7, 116, 151, 178
diversification, 102, 136, 150, 157, 176, 179
division of labour, 8, 40, 81, 83–4, 92, 173, 177, 186, 187
Dodd, Nigel, 76
dollar, 24, 29, 41–5, 53, 55, 75–6, 100, 103, 113, 185
dollarisation, 45
Duhalde, Eduardo, 55

economic action, 4, 12, 67, 69, 81, 83, 104, 109, 111, 130, 195, 198
economic activity, 2, 12, 37–8, 42, 45, 81, 85, 133, 144–5, 147, 151, 156–8, 170, 173, 179, 181, 188
economic crisis, 3, 23–4, 27, 42, 53, 56, 58, 73, 107, 115, 131, 136, 168, 183
economic demise, 2, 3, 4, 54–7
economic development, 136, 155–7, 159, 161, 171, 179, 188
economic recovery, 3, 4, 6, 10, 23–6, 45, 53–6, 107, 151, 158, 179
economic reforms, 3
Economic Sociology, 85
education, 7, 50–1, 58–9, 115, 139
efficiency, 33, 35–6, 81, 83–4, 86–8, 93, 96, 98, 101–3, 109, 134, 146, 154, 163, 165, 179, 186, 194, 198
El Comedero, 18, 140
Elias, Norbert, 193
embeddedness, 14, 31, 66, 79, 81–5, 87, 96, 98, 102–3, 111, 133, 141, 144, 151, 156, 186
employment, 7, 8, 9, 13, 25, 27, 31, 47–9, 51–4, 56, 59, 79, 118, 141, 144, 147,

149, 152–3, 159, 161, 165, 170, 177, 179

Emprendedores Anónimos, 70

endogenous development, 157

endogenous monetary system, 79, 182

enforcement, 104, 112, 119, 124–5, 128–9, 177, 188, 191, 194–6

entrance fees, 137

environment, 71, 135

Estonia, 134

Europe, 3, 22, 26, 28, 39, 40, 65, 182

Evolutionary, 13, 109, 193

evolved institutions, 16

exchange, 2, 5, 7, 8, 13, 16, 21–9, 30–5, 41, 51, 55, 59, 61–6, 72–7, 80–9, 96, 98, 107–8, 125, 130, 133, 136, 141, 144, 151–5, 163, 169, 172–9, 181–7, 194

experiment, 22–5, 73, 76–7, 161, 189, 193

experimentation, 15, 16, 68, 72, 76, 189, 191–5

fake créditos *see* forged créditos

fiat money, 25, 75, 182, 183

Field, Alexander, 14

financial crisis, 2, 48, 56

Fisher, Irving, 2, 22–5

Fisher, Stanley, 135

forgery, 28, 30, 92, 98, 117, 119, 122, 127, 136–7, 188

    forged créditos, 28, 92, 117–8, 127, 137–9, 182, 184

formal economy, 8, 31, 76, 116, 138, 168

France, 21–2, 39, 65–6, 134

franchisers, 122, 124

Freire, Paulo, 121

Garcia, Marie-France, 65

GDP, 10, 11, 36, 39, 40, 41, 42, 44, 45, 50, 54, 56, 107, 118

gender, 8, 31–2, 63, 74, 89, 141, 152, 159, 176–7, 195

Gente Linda 155, 162–6, 169, 170–1

Germany, 2, 22, 39

Gesell, Sylvio, 2, 22–6, 163

Giddens, Anthony, 14, 69, 190

Gintis, Herbert, 37

global financial system, 9

Glover, Paul, 28

González Bombal, Ines, 6

Goodwin, Mark, 155

governance, 12, 16, 40, 55, 82–3, 107–13, 119, 122–32, 137–8, 157, 172–4, 187–8, 195–6

    governance systems, 16, 107–13, 119–28, 131–2, 187–8, 195–6

    private interest governance, 12, 64

    rules of governance, 16, 107, 174, 195

government, 4, 8, 24–5, 35–6, 41–9, 51–5, 58–9, 65, 79, 92, 95, 113–14, 118, 121, 126, 132, 145, 148, 156–7, 165, 168, 171, 176, 178

    failure, 83

Great Depression, 2, 4, 10, 24–6, 40

Gresham's Law, 44

Gross Domestic Product *see* GDP

Grupo Poriahju, 121

habit *see* institutions

Hawarden scrip, 24–5

Hayek, Friedrich, 15–6, 33, 132

Helmsing, Albert (Bert), 157

hierarchy, 83, 84, 89, 100, 110–11, 120, 122, 125–6, 128–9, 130–2, 174, 187

hoarding, 2

Hodgson, Geoffrey, 13–5, 35, 67–9, 189

Hollingsworth, J. Rogers, 84, 110–11, 195

hyper-inflation, 41, 50, 57, 70

idle resources, 5, 9, 77, 79, 171, 189

Ilari, Daniel, 162–5, 170–3

impersonal exchange, 81–6, 90–6, 101–2, 175, 184

impoverishment, 57

income generation, 2, 7, 30–1, 53–6, 80, 95, 98, 112, 133, 152, 174, 185

income sources 133, 147

income, 2, 7, 8, 9, 21, 28, 30–1, 36–8, 47–8, 52–6, 59, 61, 66, 70–1, 77, 80, 95, 98, 114–17, 120–1, 130–41, 144–9, 151–2, 157–61, 165, 169, 173–79, 181, 185–8

independent nodes, 122, 124, 132, 187

Industrial Revolution, 62

inequality, 116

inflation, 22, 36, 41–8, 50–3, 56, 58, 69, 78, 116–17, 129, 131, 135, 139, 183, 188

informal, 9, 13, 29, 43, 47–8, 55, 59, 71, 78, 101, 148, 157, 161, 177, 196
information asymmetries, 112, 195
Ingham, Geoffrey, 4, 78, 218
innovation, 16, 47, 68–9, 70–5, 80, 186, 191–3
Institutions
    habit, 7, 13–5, 45
    institutional change, 35
    institutional construction, 4, 16, 43, 87, 94, 157, 184, 189, 191, 193–5
    institutional design, 4, 16, 80, 84, 86, 95–6, 101–2, 131, 157, 193–4
    Institutional Economics, 13, 36, 37, 84, 194
    institutional gap, 35–8, 52, 57–9, 65, 68, 74, 79, 152, 181, 185, 186, 189, 190, 197
    institutional process, 2, 12, 92
    Institutional Regionalism, 155
    institutional thickness, 156–7, 160–5, 169–73
    isomorphism, 91, 97
    path-dependency, 86
    prior institutions, 14–6, 38, 66–9, 72, 80, 189, 195–7
    routines, 14, 16, 35, 39, 43, 46, 66, 67, 69, 80, 189, 191
International Monetary Fund, 53, 58
Internet, 22, 61, 65–6, 89, 140
Inter-zone Coordinators' Committee *see* IZ
Italy, 21–2, 39, 101, 134, 167
Ithaca Hours, 22, 28, 30
IZ, 94–9, 100–2, 113, 119, 123–6, 138, 187

Jayaraman, Rajshri, 33
Jessop, Bob, 109, 111, 195
Jornada de la Economía del No Dinero, 93

Keynes, John Maynard, 23, 182
Kirchner, Néstor, 56

La Bernalesa, 91, 99, 100, 218
La Estación, 115, 120, 139
La Fábrica, 91
La Nación, 88
La Plata, 17, 91, 138
labour market, 10, 30, 47, 48, 50, 74, 152

Larkin scrip, 25
Latin America, 39, 40–1, 47, 56, 134
leaders, 4, 6, 8, 9, 17, 28, 30, 49, 70–6, 81, 88–9, 90–9, 100–2, 107, 113–19, 122–9, 131–3, 137, 141–2, 162, 171–6, 187–8
learning, 14, 18, 68–9, 70, 74, 79, 80, 85, 155, 159, 163, 170, 177, 192
legitimacy, 55–6, 98, 107–8, 111–13, 125, 128–9, 131–2, 188, 195–6
    input legitimacy, 111–12, 122, 123, 129, 195
    output legitimacy, 111–2, 127, 130, 195
Leoni, Fabiana, 115, 153, 218
LETS, 21–2, 27–9, 31–2, 134, 141
Linton, Michael, 27
livelihood, 131, 136, 147, 179, 185, 192
local
    economy, 21, 27, 32, 114, 133–6, 144–5, 155–6, 158, 160–6, 169, 172–6, 188
    economic development, 17, 29, 30, 136, 151, 155, 157, 161–8, 170–5, 179, 188
    economic rehabilitation, 25, 27
    exchange, 27, 30, 71, 134, 184
    government, 8, 24–5, 114, 122, 126, 130–32, 156–7, 164, 169–77
    market, 2, 3, 95
    monetary networks, 134–5
    money, 8, 32, 136, 165, 170
    taxes, 8, 24, 163–4, 166, 176
local nodes, 122, 124, 126, 127, 128, 132
locality, 27–8, 32, 87, 90, 96, 122, 135, 147, 155–62, 170–71, 175
Luzzi, Mariana, 153, 218

MacLeod, Gordon, 155
macroeconomic variables, 10, 42, 152
Mar del Plata, 17–8, 91, 118–19, 134, 138
Mar y Sierras, 119, 138
market exchange, 62, 72, 78, 80, 84, 154
market failure, 82–3
market institutions, 5, 7, 9, 10, 18, 29, 30–9, 46–8, 59, 61–9, 71–9, 81–3, 90–5, 101–2, 109–10, 115–17, 121, 125, 132, 137, 141, 146–54, 160–69, 170–74, 178, 186–89
market prices, 62, 72, 78

market society, 61, 80, 108
market-makers, 66, 69, 73–77, 87–9, 90, 94, 102–4, 186, 192
market-making, 66, 67, 69
Martinez, Enrique, 113
means of payment, 2, 10, 21–9, 32, 43–5, 58, 69, 75–8, 90, 108, 112, 117, 127, 135–39, 144, 155, 176, 182–5
media, 42, 90, 91, 114, 115
membership, 5, 6, 64–6, 74, 87, 97, 113, 118–24, 131, 153, 162, 168, 176, 182
Menem, Carlos, 41, 53
Mexico, 48, 50
micro-enterprises, 70, 77–9, 95, 101, 113, 157–60, 166–67, 170
middle-class, 5, 6, 7, 8, 9, 36, 42, 47–8, 52–9, 65, 69, 71–5, 79, 95, 116, 120, 135, 139, 151–3, 158, 162–7, 176–78, 181, 185
modes of regulation, 109
moneda sociale, 134
Monetarist School, 36
monetary networks, 96, 133–4, 156, 167, 171, 188
monetary reserves, 26, 45, 54, 135
monetary sovereignty, 134, 183
monetary system, 13, 21–7, 32–6, 45, 58, 78, 91, 103, 134, 157, 162, 166, 170–2, 181–3
money
  money, concepts of 43
  regular money, 7, 10, 21–7, 43, 76–7, 97, 101, 103, 116–7, 123, 140–4, 151–2, 158–9, 160–1, 167, 171–2, 177–8, 181–4, 188
  promises to pay, 76–8, 182–84
  reserve of value, 43, 45, 77, 118, 127, 182–3
  surrogates, 43, 76–78
  unit of account, 43–5, 74–6, 182–3
  unofficial currency, 89
monnaies de nécessité, 134
monnaies parallèles, 134
morality, 9, 31, 86, 143–4, 151
Moreno Municipality, 169
Morisio, Carlos, 7
motivations, 4, 33, 86, 133, 141
Mundell, Robert, 134

municipal taxes *see* local taxes
municipality, 26, 33, 51, 114–16, 126, 134, 162–4, 166, 169, 176

national currency, 21, 32, 45, 69
Nelson, Richard, 192–3
New Political Economy, 12, 84–5
new poor, 52, 58–9, 79, 95, 178–79, 181, 186
newcomers, 73, 85, 90–3, 140, 178
NGO, 88
nodes, 89, 92–9, 100–2, 112–19, 124–43, 150–5, 158–9, 166, 170, 174–9, 187–8
non-members, 64–5, 77, 79, 110
Nooteboom, Bart, 193
North, Douglas, 83–4
North, Peter, 32, 130, 186

O'Doherty, Richard, 156
official economy *see* regular economy
official money *see* regular money
Old Institutional Economics, 13, 82–4
opportunism, 25, 82–5, 95, 119, 122, 138, 187–8
organisational costs, 67, 104, 112, 127–9, 140, 174–6, 188, 192–6
organisers, 2, 8, 9, 26, 31, 81, 90, 95, 129, 172, 186, 189
outlet market, 90, 145

Pacione, Michael, 28, 135
PAR, 69, 70–1, 75–7, 80, 88, 90–9, 100–19, 122–9, 131–9, 141, 155, 187–8
parallel economy, 3
Parliament *see* Congress
participants, 2, 3, 4, 5, 6, 8, 9, 10, 17–8, 21, 27–9, 31–3, 59, 70–9, 81, 87–9, 91–2, 95–9, 100–2, 107, 114–19, 122–9, 130–49, 151–69, 170–9, 182–8
participation, 7, 37, 51–5, 63–6, 96–7, 101–3, 110, 121, 125, 130–31, 135, 140–6, 152, 171, 174–8, 181, 196
Patacón, 134
Perez Llora, Carlos, 119
Perón, Juan Domingo, 40–1
Peronist, 40, 47–9, 51, 55, 59, 117
personal exchange, 81–7, 90–2, 102, 175, 184, 187

personal relations, 81, 102

pesos, 3, 8, 26, 41–4, 53–5, 66, 74–6, 93–8,
    101, 114–19, 122–6, 137–9, 140,
    146–9, 158–9, 160–3, 167–9, 171,
    178, 185

piqueteros, 55

Polanyi, Karl, 2, 39, 57, 62, 85, 135, 141, 218

policies, 35–6, 41–6, 50–2, 55, 59, 60, 157,
    171, 183, 198

poor, 29, 32–3, 41, 50–2, 58, 80, 88, 101,
    121, 124, 136, 144, 147, 152–4, 157,
    160–5, 171–6, 179, 188, 192, 198

Post-Keynesian theory *see* Keynes

poverty, 2, 7, 10–2, 30–1, 41–2, 50–9,
    71–4, 79, 80, 115, 120, 125, 130–9,
    147–9, 150–8, 178, 192–4

Powell, Jeff, 9, 95

power, 16, 30–2, 37–8, 40, 44–9, 52, 57,
    62–6, 78, 81–7, 92–9, 102, 110, 120,
    141, 144, 156–7, 184, 187–8, 191, 194

primary institutions *see* institutions, prior

Primavera, 17, 91–9, 101, 113, 119, 123,
    129, 138

private markets, 63

production, 5, 13, 21, 32–5, 47, 50, 62–6,
    71–5, 78, 81, 90, 96, 113–19, 121–6,
    131, 145–9, 151–6, 165–9, 175–6,
    181–8, 196

profile, 6, 18, 152

Programa de Autosuficiencia Regional *see*
    PAR

prosumers, 5, 78, 89, 94, 95, 97, 124, 129,
    132

province, 3, 17, 43, 51–54, 134, 162

provincial currencies, 54, 75, 185

public markets, 63, 93

quasi-money *see* money surrogates

rationality, 14, 62, 63, 84–5, 93, 195

Ravera, Anibal, 17, 70–5

reciprocity, 72, 91, 97, 101, 121, 127, 144,
    151, 181, 184

reconstitutive downward causation, 69

reconstitutive upward causation, 69, 189,
    198

Red de Intercambio de Saberes y Cibernética
    Social, 91

Red de Trueque Solidario *see* RTS

Red de Trueque Zona Oeste *see* ZO

Red Global de Trueque *see* RGT

Red Global de Trueque Solidario, 91

Red Profesional, 69, 71

regional economy, 136, 155, 159

regular economy, 2, 3, 4, 6, 7, 10, 32, 36,
    57, 78–9, 95, 99, 118, 131–2, 142–7,
    151–2, 158, 160–7, 170–2, 177–8,
    181–9

regular market economy, 78, 143–6, 179,
    181

regulated market, 119, 122, 128–9, 187

regulation, 16, 35–8, 64, 74, 81, 86, 88,
    90–6, 108–9, 111, 127, 132, 150, 163,
    187, 195–6

replication, 75, 87, 90, 97–9, 102, 112, 124,
    177, 186

resistance, 2, 15, 32, 35–7, 49, 58, 107, 112,
    124, 191, 195

resource synergy, 112, 125, 128–9

RGT, 90, 100, 113, 117–19, 122–9, 131,
    136–41, 166, 187, 129

risk, 15, 24, 27, 30–1, 33, 37, 70, 77–9, 80,
    85, 90–2, 98, 102, 109, 110–12, 117,
    127, 129, 143, 163, 167, 170, 173–5,
    178–9, 185, 192, 195

Roosevelt, Franklin D., 25

Rosario, 17, 18, 121, 134

RTS, 113, 119, 121–2, 125–9, 131, 138,
    142, 174, 187

rules of action, 35–8, 42, 46, 50, 53–8, 64,
    67, 87, 93, 108, 173, 183, 189, 190–8

rural, 126, 165–6, 175–9

Russian crisis, 53

Sampayo, Fernando, 100–1, 119, 123–7,
    130–2, 137–8, 146, 166–71

San Pedro, 91–2

Sandler, Todd, 64

Satori, Giovanni, 131

Sbragia, Alberta, 66

scale, 4, 6, 7, 8, 9, 10–2, 16, 26–9, 31, 40,
    47, 57, 64–6, 78–9, 81–4, 90–1, 99,
    100–2, 107, 113–19, 123–8, 130–3,
    137–8, 147, 150, 162, 165, 168, 170–4,
    177, 182–9

Schmitter, Philippe, 109, 111

schwundgeld, 2
scope, 4, 7, 8, 9, 19, 27–8, 81, 88, 113–15, 123, 131, 150, 172–6, 184, 189, 192
scrip, 2, 3, 4, 10, 22–9, 30, 61, 77–8, 88–9, 90–2, 99, 103, 135, 140, 166, 182, 185–6
   stamp scrip, 2, 25
Second National Workshop on Multi-reciprocal Exchange, 94
second-hand goods, 18, 116, 146, 149, 153, 179
seigniorage, 133, 135, 140, 141, 151, 188
self-employed, 47, 59, 71
self-organized market, 132
Seyfang, Gill, 31, 161
SHARE, 28
size *see* scale
skills, 5, 7, 8, 30–2, 47, 59, 66, 75, 79, 80, 88, 115, 123, 130–2, 136, 148, 151–3, 165–7, 171, 185
Smith, Adam, 62
sociability, 7, 9, 72, 135, 153, 178
social capital, 7
social cohesion, 9, 28, 30, 174, 181, 184
social economy, 9, 16, 18, 73, 174, 184, 196
social franchise, 97–9, 100–3, 120, 122, 125, 129, 177, 187
social welfare *see* welfare system
Socialist, 71
solidarity, 91–5, 101, 104, 107, 110, 113, 125, 142, 162–3, 168, 196
specialisation, 62, 83, 84, 88, 102, 157, 173
spontaneous private ordering, 132
standardised, 90, 97
state, 4, 8, 9, 12, 16, 21–8, 31–8, 40–8, 50–9, 63–6, 76, 79, 83–5, 92, 95, 98, 101, 108–9, 112, 126–8, 130–2, 137, 140, 149–50, 163, 177–9, 181–9, 196
Streeck, Wolfgang, 109, 111
street-markets, 18, 158, 160
Strohalm Foundation, 29
structural poor, 7, 52, 59, 79, 115–16, 120, 132, 139, 149, 150, 153–4, 158, 174–9, 181, 185
structural reform, 35–8, 42, 47, 57–9, 104, 185, 190, 198
structuration, 14, 69, 190
supply chain, 120, 168, 175

survival strategies, 7, 59
sustainability, 16–8, 27, 30, 70, 95, 107–8, 111–13, 122–9, 131–2, 170–4, 188, 195–6

Tecnohuerta, 70
Thailand, 33
Thorne, Lorraine, 31, 141–2
Thrift, Nigel, 156
Time Banks system, 29
Toffler, Alvin, 5
traditional poor *see* structural poor
transaction costs, 64, 78, 81–6, 89, 91–8, 102–4, 112, 127–9, 174, 186, 193
trust, 3, 27–8, 30–1, 45, 63–5, 76, 81–5, 88, 90–1, 102–3, 111, 135, 141–4, 151, 182–6, 196

umbrella organisation, 3, 5, 113, 186
uncertainty, 15, 37–8, 43, 46, 68, 79, 80–6, 102–4, 110–2, 127, 185, 194, 198
unemployed, 2, 5, 7, 8, 10, 29, 30, 50, 55, 58–9, 80, 88–9, 96, 101, 113, 118, 142, 147–8, 151–2, 156–7, 160–9, 172–3, 178–9, 181, 186–8
unemployment, 3, 10, 11, 24, 31, 41–2, 47–9, 51–9, 79, 80, 114, 138, 144, 147–8, 158, 162, 181, 185
United Kingdom, 3, 21–2, 27, 29, 39, 59, 142, 151, 156, 161
Universidad Nacional de General Sarmiento, 4, 18, 114
unpaid work, 8, 74, 97, 147, 151–2, 158, 160, 170, 174, 177
urban, 12, 47, 48, 50, 70, 175
USA, 2, 3, 10, 21, 24, 28, 39, 151

Valot, Eduardo, 91
Veblen, Thorstein, 13
Venado Tuerto, 17, 162–6, 170–1, 176
   proveedurías, 164–6
   puntos, 162–6
Venezuela, 56
voluntary compliance, 12

Wära Exchange Society, 23
Washington Consensus, 36, 41, 57
waste, 70, 81, 145–6, 151–4, 179, 188, 194
Weber, Max, 14

welfare system, 45, 118, 145, 165, 166, 178
  bolsón, 178
Williams, Colin, 152
Williamson, Oliver, 65, 82, 84
Windebank, Jan, 152
Winter, Sidney, 193
women, 8, 10, 48, 74, 89, 95, 102, 114, 120, 139, 147–8, 152, 158–9, 170, 177–8, 195

Wörgl, 24–5, 33
Workshop of Multi-reciprocal Exchange, 92
Workshop on the Non-money Economy, 93
World Bank, 50, 51

Zimbabwe, 57
ZO, 100–1, 113, 119–31, 137–40, 146, 155, 158, 162, 166–74, 177, 187–189
Zona Oeste *see* ZO

For Product Safety Concerns and Information please contact our EU
representative GPSR@taylorandfrancis.com
Taylor & Francis Verlag GmbH, Kaufingerstraße 24, 80331 München, Germany

www.ingramcontent.com/pod-product-compliance
Ingram Content Group UK Ltd.
Pitfield, Milton Keynes, MK11 3LW, UK
UKHW021617240425
457818UK00018B/605